# The
# NATURAL FOODS
## Cookbook

**BEATRICE TRUM HUNTER**

SIMON AND SCHUSTER • NEW YORK

*To Mildred Hatch*

# Acknowledgments

*The author wishes to thank the following for recipes and suggestions:*

Dori Billing, June Burn, Mrs. Thomas Cooper, Mrs. Frank Crumback, Ethel De Loach, Mrs. Frank Finnegan, Doris Grant, Mrs. Peter Gregg, Mrs. Austin Griffin, Helen Hadley, Mrs. Roderick Hall, Rosemary Harris, Marian Hatch, Mildred Hatch, Dr. D. C. Jarvis, Isobel Karl, Mrs. Joshua Loring, Jr., Etta Lublintz, Helen Marer, Celia Massie, Mrs. Alfred Mausolff, Jean Mitchell, Niles Newton, Violet Perkins, Betty Pettit, Helen Philbrick, Jane Preston, Ruth Robinson, Mrs. R. Ronning, Mrs. Anthony Roothbert, Maija Salo, Verne Thomas, Francesca Van der Kley, and Adele Wehmeyer.

# Contents

# Introduction

*In spite of the deluge of TV dinners, mixes, instant puddings, precooked cereals, cut-up vegetables, tenderized meats, tempting sweets and foodless foods, there is a movement for food that is honest, natural and healthful—a movement that is steadily gaining strength and momentum. Beatrice Trum Hunter has thrown her efforts into that movement.*

*This is a great cookbook—a nutritionist's delight. From beginning to end, you will find no white flour or white sugar, no baking powder or soda; and the unhydrogenated oils have replaced the fats. Honey is the chief sweetener. Soy flour and "nutritional yeast" are frequently included. The grain sections are especially appealing, with homemade crackers and many interesting breads calling for sesame and wheat germ, sunflower seeds, millet and rye. In fact, we counted nine different recipes for rye bread in contrast to none in most general cookbooks.*

*Mrs. Hunter does not try to cover all of the standard recipes usually dealt with, but she is liberal with suggestions for preparing the high-quality foods often neglected such as liver, kidney, heart, tripe and lungs. Detailed methods for sprouting beans and grains are included, as well as how to make yoghurt and how to make yeast. She often calls out that invaluable kitchen aid, the blender.*

*So you see that we have found this not just another cookbook to grow dusty on the shelf, but a book to study, to find stimulation in and to follow daily. May we wish you good cooking, good eating and good health!*

CLIVE M. McCAY AND JEANETTE B. McCAY

ITHACA, N. Y.

# Foreword

Over thirty years ago *The New Yorker* magazine published a cartoon by Carl Rose showing a small boy scowling at his mother over a plate of food. The caption read: "I say it's spinach and I say the hell with it." The American language was thereby enriched with another trenchant idiom for calling a spade a spade. It also became a handy slogan for all those people who subscribe to the notion that healthful food is necessarily dull and unpalatable. Needless to say, I am not one of them. I believe that if cooking is approached as a creative art as well as a science, healthful food can be prepared in a variety of attractive, tasteful forms and still retain its nutritional values.

Today many thoughtful people are turning back the pages of modern food-processing history, seeking out the good old flavors, textures and nutrients of the natural foods their grandparents enjoyed. This is no longer just a passing whim of a small minority, but an earnest search by doctors, dentists, nutritionists and health-minded people everywhere. Many physicians are convinced that improper eating habits and devitalized foods are among the most serious contributing factors to the soaring incidence of cancer, heart disease and other degenerative conditions. Modern processing methods remove or destroy the vital nutrients of many foods. Artificial colors, chemical preservatives and a host of other additives further alter their natural qualities. From the consumer's viewpoint, most of these additives are unnecessary. They have no nutritive value. They are used by the food industry for economic advantage in a highly competitive market. Foods treated in this manner may appear brighter and may last longer, but the people who eat them don't.

The recipes in this book stress the use of whole, natural foods. They call for whole grains rather than refined flours and cereals; honey and other natural sweetening agents rather than refined sugar; herbs rather than salt and spices; vegetable oils rather than animal fats. Vitamin-rich yeast and sour dough replace vitamin-destroying leavening agents such as baking powder and baking soda. Seeds, sprouts, wheat germ, yoghurt, dulse, soybean products and nutritional yeast (nonleavening or "primary" yeast) are also used. Some of the recipes are original; others are adaptations of traditional ones. All are as simple to prepare as ordinary recipes. Certain foods which are cursorily covered in the average cookbook are given extensive attention here: for instance, a wide variety of recipes is included in Chapter 9, Organ Meats. By the same token, other foods are given limited treatment because they are covered sufficiently in other books.

The proof of the pudding is, of course, in the eating. For those who have never savored the goodness of whole foods, there is a pleasant discovery in store. Whole foods, well prepared, can delight even the most jaded palate. As one of my skeptical gourmet friends said, after sampling some of these dishes, "They are definitely not hair shirt." Coming from him, it was a high compliment.

*The Natural Foods Cookbook* will, I believe, open up new horizons for both novice and experienced cook.

*Beatrice Trum Hunter*

HILLSBORO, NEW HAMPSHIRE 03244

# The
# **NATURAL FOODS**
# Cookbook

# 1

# How to Use This Book

## A Word from the Author

To make using this book as simple as possible, keep in mind the following:

1. *When an item in the list of ingredients is capitalized*—"1 teaspoon Essence of Sweet Herbs" as in the recipe for Egg-Celery Spread on page 14—this means that a recipe for making Essence of Sweet Herbs is also included in the book and listed in the Index. (Ingredients which are obviously treated elsewhere are not capitalized.)

2. When items which are normally bought ready made (cottage cheese, yoghurt, vinegar, etc.) appear in the list of ingredients *followed by an asterisk,* this indicates that recipes for making them in the home are also included. These recipes will be listed in the Index under "Homemade" as well as in other categories.

### ABOUT THE BLENDER

To avoid tiresome repetition in the many recipes made with an electric blender—and also because various brands may differ slightly in their operation—detailed directions on speed, timing, etc. are not given with each recipe. I would suggest that you carefully review the instructions that came with your own appliance and adjust the recipes accordingly.

Here are a few more general hints:

Before using the blender, make sure that the container is resting firmly on its base.

In blending soft foods or liquids, place all ingredients in the container together. Do not fill more than three-quarters full. Before switching on the current, hold the cover firmly in place. This will avoid splashing and brace the machine against the first impact of the blades against the food.

To blend solids, work with small amounts cut or broken up into small pieces (1-inch cubes or smaller); fill container up to the one-third mark or, at most, one-half. When blending solids, operate blender by quick on-and-off switches. While the current is off, scrape the food from the sides of the container with a rubber or plastic spatula.

When combining solids with liquid, pour liquid into container first and add solids gradually.

## Check List of Basic Natural Foods

The following items are recommended for use, wherever possible, in these recipes. Many of them can be bought in health-food stores, the health-food sections of department stores, and the special-purpose sections of large supermarkets. For information on health-food stores in your vicinity, consult the yellow pages of your telephone directory. If you cannot locate any, write to the Executive Secretary of the National Dietary Foods Association, 1542 Knowlton St., Cincinnati, Ohio 45200. Also consult the classified advertisers in *Natural Food & Farming*, published by Natural Food Associates, Atlanta, Texas 75551; and the annual Organic Foods Directory, published by Organic Gardening & Farming, Emmaus, Pennsylvania 18409 (enclose 10¢ and a large self-addressed stamped envelope). For the benefit of people who live in areas where some of these foods may not be available, there are mail-order suppliers who will ship.

Agar-agar—vegetable gelatin
Apple cider—unsweetened, no preservatives
Baking yeast—cakes or dried; more economical when bought
     in bulk

Barley—whole grain, hulled; not pearled

Barley flour

Barley grits

Bran siftings—residue after sifting wholewheat flour

Buckwheat—whole grain, hulled

Buckwheat flour—freshly ground, unfumigated

Bulgur or Bulghur or Borghul—parched wheat from Near East

Butter—freshly churned from sweet cream, natural coloring, no preservative except salt

Buttermilk

Carob powder or flour—ground from St. John's Bread (carob pods)

Cheeses—natural (unprocessed), from raw whole milk or skim milk

Corn grits—freshly cracked, unfumigated, from yellow, un-degerminated corn

Cornmeal—freshly ground, unfumigated, from yellow, un-degerminated corn

Cottage cheese—made from raw, fresh whole milk or skim milk

Cottonseed flour—freshly ground, unfumigated

Cream, sour—made from sweet, raw cream

Cream, sweet—raw, fresh

Cream cheese—made from raw, fresh cream

Dried legumes—untreated, unfumigated

Dulse—seaweed

Eggs—fresh, fertilized

Flavorings—pure almond extract, pure vanilla extract or pod, etc.

Flours—freshly ground; preferably stone ground (from un-fumigated whole grains)

Fruit juices—unsweetened, freshly squeezed, unstrained

Fruit rinds—from unsprayed fruit, without artificial coloring or wax

Fruits, dried—sun-dried, unsulphured, raw, unfumigated. (Dried fruit may be softened by soaking overnight in cold water, or for a few hours in hot water. This eliminates extra cooking.)

Fruits, fresh—unsprayed

Gelatin—plain, unflavored, unsweetened

Gluten flour—freshly ground, unfumigated

Gruenkern—unripened grain

Herbs—preferably fresh

Honey—raw, unfiltered, 100 per cent pure

Irish Moss (Carrageen)—seaweed

Kefir—cultured milk beverage made with kefir grains

Maple syrup—100 per cent pure

Meat—fresh, from animals raised without hormones or tranquilizers,

Milk—fresh, raw certified, if possible; whole or skim

Milk powder—low-heat spray process

Millet—whole grain

Molasses—unsulphured, dark, 100 per cent pure

Nutritional yeast, also called Primary yeast, formerly called Brewer's yeast, when it was a by-product of the brewery industry—a nonleavening yeast grown especially for human consumption. Basamin yeast extract is a yeast extract derived from primary grown yeast and may be used where nutritional yeast is recommended. All nutritional yeast should be kept in tightly covered jars, away from light. Under these conditions it keeps many months and does not require refrigeration.

Nuts—fresh, raw, unsalted, unoiled

Oatmeal—steel cut or stone ground, freshly ground, unfumigated

Oats—whole grain

Oil—of vegetable origin, unhydrogenated, crude (unrefined), 100 per cent pure, fresh, cold-pressed: corn, cottonseed, olive, peanut, safflower, sesame, soybean, or sunflower.

Generally, safflower, sunflower and sesame oils are preferable for their mild flavor. Crude soy oil has a strong flavor.

Peanut butter—from whole peanuts with skins, no additives except salt and unhydrogenated oil

Potato flour

Potato water—water in which potatoes have been cooked

Rice—brown, whole grain

Rice flour

Rice grits

Rice polishings—outer coating of rice, rich in minerals; may be added to cooked cereal or flour for breads and cakes.

Rose hips—fruit of the rose

Rye—whole grain

Rye flour or Rye meal—freshly ground, unfumigated, whole grain

Salt—trace element sea salt

Sea foods—fresh, without antibiotic treatment

Seeds—whole, untreated, not fumigated; use mortar and pestle or seed mill to grind.

Sesame seeds—raw, unhulled

Sorghum—100 per cent pure

Soy flour—freshly ground, unfumigated; soy flour is available as: full-fat soy flour (produced from the whole soybean); minimum-fat soy flour (good for making soy milk); and low-fat soy flour (good for baking)

Soy grits or Soy flakes—defatted soy flour; grits absorb more liquid than flakes.

Soybeans

Soy-lecithin spread—unsaturated spread; a substitute for animal fat

Sprouts—from whole, untreated seeds, beans or peas

Sugar—raw

Sunflower seeds—freshly hulled, unoiled, unsalted

Vegetables—fresh, unsprayed; to steam, use SteaMarvel (see under Appliances), to purée, use Foley Mill.

Vinegar—made from whole, unsprayed apples, 100 per cent pure

Wheat germ—raw, fresh

Whole grains—unfumigated

Wholewheat flour—freshly ground, unfumigated, preferably stone ground; hard spring wheat from the West, Midwest and Southwest is preferable for bread; soft winter wheat from the East is good for pastries and porridge. Grind in home grinder, or order small amounts freshly ground and keep in a cool place in tightly covered jars. Use as soon as possible.

Wild rice—whole grain

Yoghurt or Yogurt—made from Bulgarian yoghurt culture

# 2
# SPREADS

Many spreads can be prepared in a blender. Dice solids coarsely and add gradually, about a half-cup at a time.
Small amounts of leftovers may provide the base for tasty spreads.

## Meat Spreads

### LIVER SPREAD

1 onion, chopped
1 clove garlic, minced
1 tablespoon oil
½ pound liver, trimmed and diced
½ teaspoon salt
1 tablespoon soy flour
2 tablespoons nutritional yeast
1 sprig parsley
½ teaspoon rosemary
stock

Sauté onion and garlic in oil. Remove. Sauté liver. Cool. Combine all ingredients in blender or grinder, adding only enough stock to blend into smooth paste. Chill. *Makes about 1 cup.*

VARIATION:
Add 2 hard-cooked eggs when blending.

### LIVER PÂTÉ

1 green pepper, minced
1 onion, minced
2 stalks celery and tops, minced
1 tablespoon oil
1 pound liver, trimmed and diced
boiling stock, to cover liver
1 bay leaf
1 scallion, minced
½ teaspoon salt
dash of clove, ground
dash of nutmeg, ground
3 tablespoons nutritional yeast
¼ cup soy grits, soaked in
¼ cup stock

Sauté pepper, onion and celery in oil. Remove. Arrange liver in same pan. Cover with boiling stock, bay leaf, scallion, salt, clove, nutmeg and yeast. Cover pan. Simmer gently 5 minutes. Remove bay leaf. Cool. Combine sautéed vegetables with liver mixture in blender or grinder. Blend into smooth paste. Add soaked soy grits. Blend. *Makes about 2 cups.*

VARIATIONS:
Add 1 grated carrot to sautéed vegetables. Blend into pâté.
Add 3 slices broiled bacon, minced. Blend into pâté.

[Continued on next page]

[Continued from previous page]

Add leftover cooked oatmeal in proportion of 1 part oatmeal to 2 parts liver. Blend into pâté.

## LIVER-CARROT SPREAD

½ pound liver, cooked and ground
½ cup raw carrot, grated
2 tablespoons nutritional yeast
yoghurt*

Blend all ingredients, adding only enough yoghurt to make it spread. *Makes about 1½ cups.*

## KIDNEY-CHEESE SPREAD

½ pound kidney, cooked and ground
4 tablespoons cream cheese*
¼ teaspoon each: thyme, sage, marjoram and basil
2 tablespoons nutritional yeast
½ onion, grated
¼ cup wheat germ
yoghurt*

Blend all ingredients, adding only enough yoghurt to make it spread. *Makes about ¾ cup.*

VARIATION:
Use cooked liver instead of kidney.

## MEAT SPREAD (in blender)

½ pound meat, cooked, cut up (leftovers)
1 onion, coarsely diced
2 tablespoons nutritional yeast
¼ cup wheat germ
2 tablespoons soy flour
sprig of parsley

Blend all ingredients. Moisten with favorite salad dressing. *Makes about 1¼ cups.*

VARIATION:
Use leftover fish or fowl instead of meat.

# Sea Food Spreads

## CLAM DIP

1 cup clams, minced
1 cup cottage cheese*
3 tablespoons yoghurt*
2 tablespoons nutritional yeast
¼ teaspoon thyme
1 onion, grated

Blend all ingredients together. *Makes about 2 cups.*

## CRAB MEAT SPREAD

1 cup crab meat, shredded fine
1 stalk celery and top, chopped
1 onion, grated
½ green pepper, minced fine
1 cup Sprouts
1 cup cottage cheese*
1 sprig of parsley, minced
favorite salad dressing

Blend all ingredients together, adding only enough dressing to moisten the spread. *Makes about 3 cups.*

VARIATIONS:
Lobster, shrimp, tuna, etc., may be substituted for the crab meat.

## FISH SPREAD

1 cup haddock, cooked and flaked
1 carrot, grated fine
1 onion, grated fine
¼ cup chives, chopped fine
1 teaspoon dill seeds, crushed
favorite salad dressing

Blend all ingredients together, adding only enough dressing to moisten the spread. *Makes about 1½ cups.*

VARIATIONS:
Any mild-flavored leftover fish may be substituted for the haddock.

# Vegetable Spreads

## TOMATO SPREAD

1 cup tomato purée
¼ cup nutritional yeast
¼ cup soy grits
1 tablespoon sesame seeds
¼ cup cheddar or other natural cheese, grated
¼ teaspoon basil

Blend all ingredients. *Makes about* 1¾ *cups.*

## AVOCADO SPREAD (in blender)

2 avocados, well ripened
1 clove garlic
juice and rind of 2 lemons
⅛ teaspoon salt
1 tablespoon nutritional yeast
3 tablespoons chives

Blend all ingredients. *Makes about* 1 *cup.*

## GUACAMOLE (in blender)

1 avocado, well ripened
1 green pepper
1 tomato
1 sprig parsley
1 tablespoon oil
½ tablespoon lemon juice
⅛ teaspoon salt
1 tablespoon nutritional yeast

Blend all ingredients. *Makes about* 1 *cup.*

## CRESS SPREAD (in blender)

¼ cup cress
¼ cup radishes
1 cup cucumbers, cut up
¼ cup Sprouts

Blend all ingredients. Moisten with favorite dressing. *Makes about* 1¾ *cups.*

## CUCUMBER SPREAD (in blender)

1 cup cucumbers, cut up
1 cup almonds
½ cup bran
½ cup whole-grain bread crumbs

Blend all ingredients. Moisten with favorite dressing. *Makes about* 3 *cups.*

## CARROT-NUT SPREAD (in blender)

1 cup carrots, cut up
1 cup pecans
1 tablespoon oil
1 teaspoon lemon juice
1 tablespoon nutritional yeast
1 sprig dill

Blend all ingredients. Moisten with favorite dressing. *Makes about* 2 *cups.*

## SPRING SPREAD (in blender)

1 onion
3 stalks celery and tops
1 cucumber, cut up
1 head lettuce, cut up
1 green pepper
1 egg, hard-cooked

Blend all ingredients. Moisten with favorite dressing. *Makes about* 3 *cups.*

## AUTUMN SPREAD (in blender)

¼ head cabbage
1 tart apple with skin
3 stalks celery with tops
6 walnuts
3 carrots
½ green pepper
½ onion
3 tablespoons Soybeans, Roasted, ground

[Recipe continued on next page]

[Recipe continued from previous page]
Blend all ingredients. Moisten with favorite dressing. *Makes about 3 cups.*

## CARROT-HONEY SPREAD

3 carrots, grated
3 tablespoons rice polishings
1 tablespoon honey
1 tablespoon nutritional yeast

Blend all ingredients together. *Makes about 1½ cups.*

## SWEET POTATO SPREAD

1 cup sweet potatoes, cooked, puréed
1 tablespoon oil
½ cup Coconut Shreds
½ cup milk powder

Blend all ingredients together. *Makes about 2 cups.*

## DANDELION SPREAD (in blender)

1 cup young dandelion leaves, raw
½ cup cottage cheese*
¼ cup nuts
favorite dressing

Blend all ingredients, adding enough dressing for mixture to spread. *Makes about 1¾ cups.*

## COMBINATION VEGETABLE SPREADS (in blender)

Young spring onions, yoghurt, dash of ground clove
Cucumbers, yoghurt, poppy seeds, soy flour
Radishes, cottage cheese, dill seeds
Watercress, sour cream, fennel seeds
Raw spinach, broiled bacon bits, dash of ground mace
Green pepper, celery, onion, celery seeds

Carrot, parsley, caraway seeds, yoghurt
Mung Bean Sprouts, green pepper, fennel, sour cream

# Egg Spreads

## EGG-CELERY SPREAD (in blender)

2 eggs, hard-cooked
1 stalk celery with top, cut up
¼ cup soy flour
1 tablespoon nutritional yeast
3 tablespoons chives, chopped
1 teaspoon Essence of Sweet Herbs

Blend all ingredients together. Moisten with favorite dressing. *Makes about 1 cup.*

## EGG-LENTIL SPREAD (in blender)

2 eggs, hard-cooked
1 cup lentils, cooked
3 tablespoons cottage cheese*
pinch of nutmeg, ground
pinch of sage, ground
1 tablespoon nutritional yeast

Blend all ingredients together. Moisten with favorite dressing. *Makes about 1½ cups.*

# Soy Spreads
## SOY FLOUR SPREAD

½ cup soy flour
½ cup peanut butter*
1 tablespoon nutritional yeast
3 tablespoons chives, chopped
3 tablespoons parsley, minced
½ cup favorite dressing

Blend all ingredients together until smooth. *Makes about 1½ cups.*

## SOYBEAN SPREAD (in blender)

1 cup Soybean Pulp
¼ cup green pepper
1 tablespoon nutritional yeast
½ onion
1 tablespoon Essence of Sweet Herbs
2 tablespoons favorite dressing

Blend all ingredients together until smooth. *Makes about 1½ cups.*

## SOY CHEESE SPREAD

1 cup soy cheese *
3 tablespoons chives, minced
3 tablespoons yoghurt *
1 tablespoon nutritional yeast
1 tablespoon parsley, minced
¼ teaspoon basil

Blend all ingredients together until smooth. *Makes about 1½ cups.*

## SOY BUTTER

soy flour
oil

Beat oil into flour until mixture is consistency of nut butter. Salt, honey and/or nutritional yeast may be added, if desired. This butter may be thinned to use as salad dressing.

VARIATION:
Soy flour may first be roasted in shallow pan in 200° F. oven, until browned.

# Cheese Spreads

## COTTAGE CHEESE SPREAD

½ pound cottage cheese *
¼ teaspoon celery seeds, crushed
¼ teaspoon dill seeds, crushed
¼ teaspoon caraway seeds, crushed

⅛ teaspoon salt
3 tablespoons nutritional yeast
1 tablespoon parsley, minced
1 tablespoon onion, grated
3 tablespoons soy flour
¼ cup wheat germ

Blend all ingredients together. This spread is also good molded into balls and served on bed of salad greens. *Makes about 1½ cups.*

## CREAM CHEESE SPREAD

½ pound cream cheese *
½ cup soy flour
1 tablespoon nutritional yeast
2 tablespoons Soybeans, Roasted, ground
1 tablespoon parsley, minced
yoghurt *

Blend all ingredients, adding enough yoghurt to make spread. *Makes about 1¾ cups.*

# Fruit Spreads

## RAISIN-COCONUT SPREAD

½ cup raisins
½ cup Coconut Shreds

Blend ingredients. Moisten with yoghurt. *Makes about 1 cup.*

## SPICED DATE SPREAD
## (in blender)

1 cup dates, pitted
½ teaspoon cinnamon, ground
¼ cup yoghurt *
½ cup milk powder (about)

Blend all ingredients. If too thin to spread, add more milk powder. *Makes about 1¾ cups.*

## DATE-ORANGE SPREAD
(in blender)

2 cups dates, pitted
1 teaspoon Powdered Fruit Rind
juice of 1 orange
1/4 cup wheat germ (about)

Blend all ingredients. If too thin to spread, add more wheat germ. *Makes about 2 1/2 cups.*

## DATE-APPLE SPREAD (in blender)

1 cup dates, pitted
2 tart apples, with skins

Blend ingredients. Moisten with yoghurt. *Makes about 1 3/4 cups.*

## DATE-NUT SPREAD (in blender)

1 cup dates, pitted
1/2 cup nuts
1/4 cup yoghurt *
1/2 cup milk powder (about)

Blend ingredients. If too thin to spread, add more milk powder. *Makes about 2 1/4 cups.*

NOTE:
Figs may be substituted for dates in any of the above date recipes.

## ORIENTAL SPREAD (in blender)

1/4 cup dates, pitted
1/4 cup figs
1/4 cup raisins
1/4 cup nuts
1/4 cup Coconut Shreds
unsweetened orange juice

Blend all ingredients, adding enough orange juice to moisten. *Makes about 1 1/4 cups.*

## MIXED FRUIT SPREAD
(in blender)

1/2 cup prunes, pitted
1/2 cup dried apricots, soaked
1/2 cup raisins
1/4 cup Soybeans, Roasted, ground
1/2 cup cream cheese *

Blend all fruits. Turn into bowl. Mix with soybeans and cream cheese until smooth. *Makes about 2 1/4 cups.*

## APPLE BUTTER SPREAD

1 cup apple butter
1/2 cup soy flour
1 tablespoon nutritional yeast
1/4 cup sesame seeds

Blend all ingredients together. *Makes about 1 3/4 cups.*

# Butters

HINTS:
Many butters can be prepared in a blender. Solids combined with butters should be cut coarsely and added to blender gradually.
Use butters as: spreads for sandwiches, open-faced sandwiches, crackers to accompany salad or soup; garnishes for vegetables, meat, fowl or fish; toppings for starch dishes, quick breads of all kinds.

## LEMON BUTTER

1/2 cup butter, softened
2 tablespoons lemon juice
rind of 1 lemon, grated

Blend all ingredients. Use with fowl or fish. *Makes about 3/4 cup.*

## TARRAGON BUTTER

½ cup butter, softened
1 sprig fresh tarragon, minced
1 teaspoon nutritional yeast
1 teaspoon lemon juice
1 tablespoon parsley, minced

Blend all ingredients. Use over broiled fish, broccoli, asparagus. *Makes about ½ cup.*

## DILL BUTTER

½ cup butter, softened
1 sprig fresh dill, minced
½ teaspoon dill seeds, crushed
1 teaspoon nutritional yeast
1 teaspoon lemon juice
1 tablespoon parsley, minced

Blend ingredients. Use with fish or baked potato. *Makes about ¾ cup.*

## LEMON-HERB BUTTER

½ cup butter, softened
1 tablespoon lemon rind, grated
½ teaspoon basil, minced
½ teaspoon chervil, minced
1 tablespoon parsley, minced
1 teaspoon chives, minced

Blend ingredients. Use with fish or vegetables. *Makes about ¾ cup.*

## CRESS BUTTER

½ cup butter, softened
½ cup cress, minced
1 teaspoon nutritional yeast
1 tablespoon parsley, minced

Blend ingredients. Use as spread with salad or soup. *Makes about 1 cup.*

VARIATION:
Nasturtium buds and leaves may be substituted for cress.

## GREEN PEPPER BUTTER

½ cup butter, softened
½ cup green pepper, chopped fine
1 teaspoon nutritional yeast
1 teaspoon onion, grated

Blend ingredients. Use as spread with salad or soup, or serve over potatoes and other starch foods. *Makes about 1 cup.*

## CHEESE BUTTER

½ cup butter, softened
¼ cup cream cheese *
¼ cup Roquefort cheese
1 tablespoon chives, minced
1 teaspoon celery seeds, crushed
1 tablespoon soy flour

Blend ingredients. Use as spread with crackers or bread. *Makes about 1 cup.*

## ORANGE BUTTER

½ cup butter, softened
juice and grated rind of 1 orange
1 teaspoon Powdered Fruit Rind
pinch of cinnamon, ground
pinch of nutmeg, ground
1 tablespoon soy flour

Blend ingredients. Use on toast, waffles, pancakes or muffins. *Makes about ¾ cup.*

## BERRY BUTTER

½ cup butter, softened
3 tablespoons fresh berries, crushed
1 teaspoon lemon juice
1 sprig mint, minced

Blend ingredients. Use on toast or quick breads. *Makes about ¾ cup.*

## Nut Butters

HINTS:
Nut butters may be made in a grinder (food mill). Use the "worm feed" crusher, which is especially designed for oily substances.
Homemade nut butters should be made in small amounts, refrigerated in closed containers and used within a reasonable time.
Homemade nut butters should be made of fresh, raw, unsalted nuts.
Use as spreads, toppings for vegetables or desserts.
Nut butters may be thinned with water or milk and used as toppings over cereal or dessert.

## HOMEMADE PEANUT BUTTER

raw peanuts, unsalted
oil

Grind a cupful of peanuts at a time. They should be the consistency of flour. Turn them into bowl. After grinding all peanuts, add only enough oil to blend mixture into thick paste. Salt and/or nutritional yeast may be added, if desired. Pack into container. Cover. Refrigerate.

VARIATIONS:
Homemade nut butter may be made from raw almonds, filberts, pignolias, walnuts (English and black), cashews, Brazil nuts, etc. Most of these nuts have enough oil so that no extra oil need be added.

## HOMEMADE PEANUT-SUNFLOWER SEED BUTTER

1½ pounds raw peanuts
½ pound sunflower seeds, hulled
½ pound nutritional yeast
1 pint oil
1 tablespoon salt

Grind nuts and seeds. Blend in remaining ingredients. Pack into container. Cover. Refrigerate. *Makes about 4½ cups.*

## NUT BUTTER SPREAD

2 cups nuts
1 cup sunflower seeds, hulled
1 cup sesame seeds
oil
honey

Grind nuts and seeds. Blend in enough oil to make mixture into thick paste. Add honey to taste. Blend thoroughly. Pack into container. Cover. Refrigerate. Use as spread or roll into small balls and serve as dessert.

## COMBINATION NUT-BUTTER SPREADS

Nut butter, lemon juice, grated carrot, raisins, nutritional yeast, soy flour
Nut butter, chopped green peppers, celery
Nut butter, Sprouts

OTHER RECIPES USING NUT BUTTERS:
See under *Peanut Butter:* Frosting; Cookies; Dandies; Squares; Balls.

## Snacks and Pickups

HINTS:
Use celery or thin chips of crisp carrot or turnip, as a change from

bread or crackers, as a base for spreads or dips.

## STUFFED CELERY

*Fill cavity of celery stalk with mixture of:*

cream cheese, minced green peppers, onion juice

cottage cheese, soybean pulp, minced chives

cottage cheese, sprouts, caraway seeds

cream cheese, minced fresh pineapple, mint

## ADDITIONAL SNACK SUGGESTIONS

STICKS: carrots, celery, turnip, fresh pineapple, rutabaga

RINGS: cucumbers, green peppers, pimentos, apples

WEDGES: cabbage, lettuce, tomatoes, oranges, tangerines, pears

FLOWERETTES: cauliflower

ROSES: radishes

CURLS: carrots, celery

HALVES: apricots, plums, peaches

TOOTHPICK PICKUPS: cubes of cheese or meat, deviled eggs

For more snack and pickup suggestions, see Crackers; Eggs.

# 3

# CRACKERS

## WHOLEWHEAT WAFERS
(uncooked)

4 pounds wholewheat berries, raw
water to cover
1 pint oil
cold water

Soak wheat berries overnight in water. In morning, drain. Reserve liquid as stock for soup. Grind wheat. Add oil. Mix thoroughly. Add enough cold water to thin dough sufficiently to roll out. Toss onto floured pastry board. Roll thin. Cut into wafers. Expose to sunshine and dry thoroughly.

## WHOLEWHEAT WAFERS

1½ cups wholewheat flour, sifted
1 teaspoon salt
½ cup heavy sweet cream, sour cream, yoghurt,* milk or soy milk *

Blend flour and salt. Gradually work in liquid to make dough. Toss onto lightly floured pastry board. Knead 15-20 minutes. Dough should be stiff. Roll until tissue thin. Cut into small strips, squares or diamonds. Arrange on oiled cooky sheet. Prick with fork. Bake for

8-10 minutes, until light brown, at 350° F.

VARIATIONS:
Use part wholewheat, part whole-rye flour.
Add celery seeds, cumin seeds, caraway seeds, dill seeds or sesame seeds to dough to vary flavor. With addition of seeds, however, dough cannot be rolled as thin. If home grinding mill is available, grind seeds along with flour. If slightly sweetened wafer is desired, add 2 tablespoons honey.
Tops of wafers may be brushed with egg yolk diluted with a little milk or water before baking.

## WHOLEWHEAT CRACKERS

Save some dough from wholewheat bread batter. Work in additional flour. Roll out thin. Cut into small strips, squares or diamonds. Arrange on oiled cooky sheet. Prick with fork. Bake for 8-10 minutes, until light brown, at 325° F.

VARIATIONS:
Add grated cheese, seeds, ground nuts or ground, Roasted Soybeans to batter.

## WHOLEWHEAT STICKS

3 cups wholewheat flour
pinch of salt
⅔ cup milk
3 tablespoons honey
3 tablespoons oil
1 teaspoon pure vanilla extract

Sift flour and salt. Add rest of ingredients. Knead until smooth. Toss onto floured pastry board. Roll to ¼-inch thickness. Cut into strips 1 inch by 4 inches. Arrange on oiled cooky sheet. Bake at 350° F. for 8-10 minutes, until golden brown.

VARIATION:
Add ½ cup Coconut Shreds to dough.

## WHOLEWHEAT-PEANUT BUTTER CRISPS

1 cup milk
½ cup peanut butter *
4 cups wholewheat flour
2 tablespoons nutritional yeast
2 tablespoons soy flour
¼ teaspoon salt

Blend milk and peanut butter. Add remaining ingredients. Blend until smooth. Toss onto floured pastry board. Roll thin. Cut into strips, squares or diamonds. Arrange on oiled cooky sheet. Prick with fork. Bake at 350° F. for 8-10 minutes, until golden brown.

## WHOLEWHEAT-SOY CRACKERS

1 cup honey
1 cup oil
½ cup hot water, potato
   water, or milk
3¼ cups wholewheat flour
¾ cup soy flour
3 tablespoons nutritional yeast
½ teaspoon salt

Blend honey, oil and water or milk. Sift together remaining ingredients and stir with liquid. Blend well. Toss onto floured pastry board. Roll thin. Cut into strips, squares or diamonds. Arrange on oiled cooky sheet. Bake at 375° F. for 15-20 minutes.

## WHOLEWHEAT-OATMEAL CRACKERS

2 tablespoons honey
⅓ cup oil
⅔ cup cold water, potato
   water, or milk
2 cups wholewheat flour
1½ cups oatmeal
2 tablespoons soy flour
2 tablespoons nutritional yeast
½ teaspoon salt

Blend honey, oil and water or milk. Stir in remaining ingredients. Blend well. Dough should be stiff. Knead 5 minutes. Toss onto floured pastry board. Roll to piecrust thinness. Brush with oil. Cut into strips, squares or diamonds. Arrange on oiled cooky sheet. Bake at 350° F. for 10-15 minutes, until golden brown.

VARIATION:
After brushing tops of crackers with oil, sprinkle with sesame seeds, sunflower seeds, ground nuts or ground, Roasted Soybeans.

## LEAVENED ZWIEBACK

2 cakes or 2 tablespoons dried
   yeast
1 cup lukewarm milk
4 tablespoons honey
¾ cup oil
4 cups wholewheat flour
3 tablespoons nutritional yeast
4 tablespoons soy flour
¼ teaspoon salt

[Recipe continued on next page]

[Recipe continued from previous page]

Soften yeast in ¼ cup of milk. Blend remainder of milk with honey and oil. Sift together remainder of ingredients and stir into liquid. Add yeast mixture. Knead. Turn into oiled bowl. Cover. Set in warm place to rise until double in bulk. Punch down. Roll into little balls the size of walnuts. Arrange on oiled cooky sheet. Allow to rise. Bake at 350° F. about 10 minutes. Allow to cool. Cut into halves with sharp knife. Return to oven. Bake thoroughly at 200° F. until dry, brown and crisp.

## QUICKIE ZWIEBACK

8 slices whole-grain bread
¾ cup milk
½ cup milk powder
1 egg, beaten
3 tablespoons soy flour
1 tablespoon nutritional yeast

Cut bread (very stale, dry bread, or fresh bread which has been toasted or dried out in the oven) into half slices or strips. Mix remaining ingredients together as batter. Soak each piece of bread into mixture until it has absorbed as much liquid as possible. Drain off excess liquid. Arrange bread in shallow, well-oiled baking dish. Bake at 200° F., turning with spatula when top is brown. Continue baking slowly until dried to desired state of hardness.
See also Teething Cookies.

## WHEAT GERM STICKS

1 tablespoon honey
½ cup oil
1¼ cups milk
2 cups wholewheat flour
2 cups wheat germ
1 teaspoon salt

Blend honey, oil and milk. Stir in remaining ingredients. Knead lightly. Roll out on floured pastry board. Cut into sticks 1 inch by 3 inches. Bake at 325° F. for about 20 minutes or until light brown. *Makes 4-5 dozen sticks.*

## HERBED WHOLEWHEAT STRAWS

2⅔ cups wholewheat flour
⅔ cup oil
1 cup cold water or potato water (about)
3 tablespoons mixed herbs (rosemary, basil, marjoram, oregano, tarragon, etc.)

Blend all ingredients, adding enough liquid to make stiff dough. Chill. Roll out on floured pastry board. Cut into strips 1 inch by 3 inches. Bake at 400° F. for about 10 minutes. *Makes 4-5 dozen straws.*

## SWEDISH HARDTACK

2 cups yoghurt *
½ cup honey
½ cup oil
6 cups rye flour, or half rye and half wholewheat
3 tablespoons nutritional yeast
1 teaspoon salt

Blend yoghurt, honey and oil. Stir in remaining ingredients. Dough should be stiff. Knead. Roll out very thin on floured pastry board. Cut into desired shapes. Bake at 425° F. about 15 minutes, until brown. Wafers should be crisp and tender. Keep in tightly covered container.

## 100% OATMEAL CRACKERS
(wheatless)

1 tablespoon honey
½ cup oil

1 cup water or potato water
4 cups oatmeal
1 teaspoon salt

Blend honey, oil and water. Stir in remaining ingredients. Mix well. Dough should be stiff. Chill. Roll out, cut into squares. Bake at 350° F. about 20 minutes. *Makes 2 dozen crackers.*

## MILLET CRACKERS

1 cake or 1 tablespoon dried yeast
½ cup lukewarm potato water
½ cup boiling potato water
1 cup dried fruits, cut fine
1 cup oil
3 cups millet flour
1 cup wholewheat flour, about
3 tablespoons soy flour

Soften yeast in lukewarm liquid. Pour boiling water over fruit. Let stand 15 minutes. Combine yeast and fruit mixtures. Stir in oil and flours. If necessary, add more wholewheat flour to make dough stiff. Roll out thin on floured pastry board. Cut into squares. Arrange on oiled cooky sheet. Let stand for 15 minutes, then bake at 250° F. for about 30 minutes. *Makes 4 dozen crackers.*

## UNSWEETENED CORN CRISPS
(wheatless)

½ cup cornmeal
1⅓ cups water or potato water
½ teaspoon salt
2 tablespoons oil

Mix cornmeal with about ½ of liquid to make paste. Pour remainder of liquid into top of double boiler, set over direct heat and bring to boil. Blend in cornmeal paste. Stir until smooth. Add salt and oil and stir again. Cover. Place over hot water. Simmer 30 minutes. Turn mixture into 2 oiled 9-inch by 9-inch pans and spread out ¼ inch thick. Bake at 425° F. about 50 minutes, until light brown and crisp. Cut into 1-inch squares.

## GRAIN-SEED WAFERS
(in blender)

1 cup millet
½ cup cracked wheat
½ cup sunflower seeds, hulled
water or potato water to cover

Cover millet, wheat and seeds with liquid. Soak overnight. In morning, drain off liquid. Reserve it as soup stock. Blend grains and seeds. Batter will be coarse. Drop onto hot, unoiled soapstone griddle or into heated, oiled pan. Brown lightly on each side; inside should be raw.

VARIATION:
Add chopped dried fruits to batter.

## CHEESE CRACKERS

½ pound sharp cheddar, grated
½ cup oil
1½ cups wholewheat or rye flour
milk powder

Blend cheese and oil. To bind, add flour and as much milk powder as mixture will hold. Mix well. Shape into two long rolls. Wrap in wax paper. Chill. Slice thin. Bake at 375° F. for about 6 minutes.

VARIATIONS:
Add to dough 2 tablespoons soy flour or ¼ cup wheat germ.
Add to dough caraway, sesame, dill, celery or cumin seeds.
Substitute bleu cheese for cheddar.

## SESAME SEED NIBBLES

1 cup wholewheat flour
¼ cup oil
½ teaspoon salt
2 tablespoons ice water, (about)
½ cup sesame seeds

Blend flour and oil. Add salt and only enough water to make dough of piecrust consistency. Chill. Roll to ⅛-inch thickness. Cut into desired shapes. Arrange on oiled cooky sheet. Sprinkle with sesame seeds, pressing seeds lightly into dough. Bake at 350° F. for about 10 minutes, until light brown.

LEFTOVER CRACKER CRUMBS:
Use in making crumb pie shells; as topping for soup, salads, casseroles; as binding in meat, fish, cheese, egg or fowl loaves.
Add to porridge, bread dough, quick breads or cookies.

# 4

# BEVERAGES

Beverages incorporating solid foods are conveniently prepared in electric appliances. A blender grinds to pulp and purée; a juicer extracts only the liquid, separating the pulp from it.

Most of the recipes in this chapter are suitable for the blender. Cut solid foods coarsely before blending. Beverages containing only liquids and fine solids may, of course, be blended in an ordinary shaker.

## Appetizers

### CARROT-PINEAPPLE APPETIZER

2 cups unsweetened pineapple juice
½ cup raw carrots, coarsely diced
1 tablespoon lemon juice
1 tablespoon nutritional yeast
⅛ teaspoon basil

Blend all ingredients. *Serves 4-6.*

### WATER CRESS-PINEAPPLE APPETIZER

2 cups unsweetened pineapple juice
1 bunch water cress

1 tablespoon lemon juice
1 tablespoon nutritional yeast
⅛ teaspoon tarragon

Blend all ingredients. *Serves 4-6.*

### CRANBERRY-PINEAPPLE APPETIZER

2 cups unsweetened pineapple juice
½ cup cranberries, raw
sprig of mint
pinch of clove, ground

Blend all ingredients. *Serves 4-6.*

### APRICOT APPETIZER

2 cups apricot nectar, unsweetened
½ cup nutritional yeast
pinch of mace, ground
sprig of mint

Blend all ingredients. *Serves 4-6.*

### GREEN PEA APPETIZER

2 cups green peas, cooked, cold
stock in which peas were cooked
2 tablespoons cheese, grated
sprig of mint
2 tablespoons nutritional yeast
1 tablespoon wheat germ
1 tablespoon soy flour
2 cups milk

Blend all ingredients. *Serves 4-6.*

## SAUERKRAUT-TOMATO JUICE APPETIZER

2 cups raw sauerkraut * juice
2 cups tomato juice
pinch of mace, ground
3 tablespoons nutritional yeast
1 sprig parsley

Blend all ingredients. *Serves 6.*

## SAUERKRAUT JUICE APPETIZER

2 cups raw sauerkraut * juice
2 tablespoons lemon juice
½ cup diced apple, with skin
½ teaspoon caraway seeds

Blend all ingredients. *Serves 4-6.*

## MIXED VEGETABLE APPETIZER

3 cups tomato juice
1 stalk celery and leaves, diced
2 sprigs parsley
½ lemon and rind
½ green pepper
½ onion
3 tablespoons nutritional yeast

Blend all ingredients. *Serves 6.*

## TOMATO JUICE APPETIZER

4 cups tomato juice
1 scallion
½ cup nutritional yeast
sprig of parsley
pinch of marjoram
dash of Essence of Sweet Herbs

Blend all ingredients. *Serves 6.*

## TOMATO JUICE-LIVER APPETIZER

4 cups tomato juice
4 tablespoons liver, raw, diced
2 teaspoons lemon juice
pinch of mace, ground
3 tablespoons nutritional yeast

Blend all ingredients. *Serves 6.*

## TOMATO JUICE-ROSE HIP APPETIZER

3 cups tomato juice
3 cups rose-hip juice
1 tablespoon lemon juice
sprig of mint

Blend all ingredients.
    To prepare rose-hip juice: Place
½ cup of rose hips in saucepan.
Cover with 3 cups of water. Simmer
for 15 minutes. Strain and reserve
juice, discarding rose hips. Cool and
use immediately, or process while
hot in sterilized jars for later use.

## SEED DRINK (blender)

3 cups squash, pumpkin or
    cucumber seeds, with mem-
    branes, scooped out of
    vegetable
3 cups water, stock or milk
¼ teaspoon basil
sprig of parsley

Blend until hulls are ground.
Strain. *Serves 6.*

# Smoothies

## HOMEMADE SOYBEAN MILK

1 cup soybeans
3 cups cold water

Place soybeans in large jar. Cover
with water. Refrigerate 24 to 48
hours, changing water 4 times.
Drain. Place soaked soybeans in
saucepan. Cover with 4 cups fresh
warm water. Bring to slow boil.
Simmer gently for 15 minutes. Remove from heat. Cool. Pour into
blender. Blend until ground. Strain.
This milk may be used like cow's
milk in beverages and in cooking.
For beverages, a small amount of

honey or a dash of salt may be added. The leftover pulp may be added to batters, casseroles, porridge, etc.

## HOMEMADE SOY MILK

1 cup soy flour
4 cups water

Blend ingredients together in top of double boiler. Let mixture stand two hours. Place over hot water. Cook for 20 minutes. Cool. Strain. Use milk as soybean milk. Leftover flour residue may be added to batters, casseroles, porridge, etc.

## SPICED SOY MILK

4 cups soybean or soy milk
  (see above)
½ teaspoon ginger, ground
½ teaspoon nutmeg, ground
3 tablespoons honey
¼ teaspoon salt

Blend ingredients. *Serves 4-6.*

## SOY-FIG SHAKE

4 cups soybean or soy milk
  (see above)
1 cup unsweetened fig juice

Blend all ingredients. *Serves 4-6.*

## MILK-SOY SMOOTHIE

4 cups milk
½ cup soy flour
4 tablespoons molasses
2 eggs, raw
½ teaspoon pure vanilla extract
3 tablespoons nutritional yeast

Blend all ingredients. *Serves 4-6.*

## ALMOND MILK

4 cups water
1 cup almonds, blanched
2 tablespoons honey

Blend all ingredients. *Serves 4-6.*

## PEANUT MILK

4 cups water
1 cup peanuts, raw
2 tablespoons molasses
2 tablespoons nutritional yeast

Blend all ingredients. *Serves 4-6.*

## CASHEW MILK

4 cups water
1 cup cashews, raw
5 dates, pitted

Blend all ingredients. *Serves 4-6.*

VARIATION:
Use less water for mixture of creamy consistency. This can also be used as garnish over cereal.

## MILK-WHOLEWHEAT SHAKE

4 cups milk
2 tablespoons wholewheat flour
2 tablespoons molasses
2 tablespoons nutritional yeast
¼ cup almonds, blanched

Blend all ingredients. *Serves 4-6.*

## ORANGE-COCONUT MILK

2 cups unsweetened orange juice
2 cups milk
½ cup Coconut Shreds
1 teaspoon Powdered Fruit Rind

Blend all ingredients. *Serves 4-6.*

## COCONUT MILK

4 cups warm water
pinch of salt
4 cups Coconut Shreds
2 tablespoons honey

Blend all ingredients. Strain. The leftover coconut pulp may be added to puddings, etc. *Serves 4-6.*

## MILK-FRUIT SHRUB

1 cup fresh berries
1 tablespoon honey
1 tablespoon lemon juice
2 cups milk
pinch of salt
sprig of mint

Blend all ingredients. If thinner drink is preferred, add more milk. *Serves 4-6.*

## STRAWBERRY SMOOTHIE

2 cups fresh strawberries
3 tablespoons honey
2 cups milk
1 teaspoon Powdered Fruit Rind

Blend all ingredients. If thinner drink is preferred, add more milk. *Serves 4-6.*

## APRICOT SHAKE

1 pound apricots, soaked
2 cups water in which apricots
    were soaked
2 cups milk
3 drops pure almond extract

Blend all ingredients. *Serves 4-6.*

## ANISE MILK

4 cups milk
2 tablespoons honey
1 tablespoon anise seeds
1 cup milk powder

Blend all ingredients. *Serves 4-6.*

## MILK SMOOTHIE

4 cups milk
½ cup milk powder
2 tablespoons nutritional yeast
2 tablespoons wheat germ
1 tablespoon molasses
1 tablespoon honey

Blend all ingredients. *Serves 4-6.*

## FRUIT MILK SHAKE

2 cups milk
2 cups unsweetened fruit juice
½ cup milk powder
1 ripe banana

Blend all ingredients. *Serves 4-6.*

## BANANA SMOOTHIE

4 cups milk
1 cup milk powder
3 bananas
¼ teaspoon nutmeg, ground

Blend all ingredients. *Serves 4-6.*

## LEMON EGG NOG

4 tablespoons lemon juice
2 eggs, separated
2 tablespoons honey
3 cups milk
⅔ cup milk powder
pinch of cinnamon, ground

Beat lemon juice, egg yolks and 1 tablespoon of honey. Add milk, milk powder, and beat until smooth. Beat egg whites stiff. Add remaining tablespoon of honey to egg whites. Beat again. Fold egg whites into lemon mixture. Dust with cinnamon and serve. *Serves 4-6.*

## HONEY EGG NOG

3 cups milk
4 eggs
4 tablespoons honey
⅔ cup milk powder
pinch of nutmeg, ground

Blend all ingredients except nutmeg. Pour into glasses. Dust lightly with nutmeg. *Serves 4-6.*

## CAROB MILK

4 cups milk
1 tablespoon honey
6 tablespoons carob powder
½ teaspoon pure vanilla extract

Blend all ingredients. *Serves 4-6.*

## CAROB SMOOTHIE

4 cups milk
3 tablespoons molasses
½ cup milk powder
⅓ cup carob powder
1 ripe banana
¼ cup peanuts, raw
3 tablespoons nutritional yeast

Blend all ingredients. *Serves 4-6.*

# Summer Coolers

## HOMEMADE CLABBERED MILK

Add 3 tablespoons of sour milk to 1 quart of fresh raw milk. Stir. Leave at room temperature 12 to 24 hours, or until it clabbers. Use immediately, or refrigerate. Honey or fruits may be added. Keep enough clabber as "starter" for new supply.
See also Clabbered Milk Dessert.

## HOMEMADE YOGHURT DRINK

Heat 1 quart of milk until lukewarm. Milk may be raw or pasteurized, whole or skim, or even reconstituted powdered milk (dissolved in water or liquid milk), for this drink. Add 2 tablespoons of yoghurt to milk. (To get yoghurt for "starter" see Yoghurt, Homemade.) Let stand at room temperature until mixture thickens. Use immediately or refrigerate. This will be of a thinner consistency than dessert yoghurt and thus suitable as a drink. (For thick, Bulgarian-style yoghurt, see Yoghurt, Homemade.)
Reserve 2 tablespoons of Yoghurt Drink as "starter" for new supply.

## ORANGE YOGHURT

3 cups homemade yoghurt drink
  (see above)
1 cup unsweetened orange juice
1 teaspoon Powdered Fruit Rind
pinch of mace, ground

Blend all ingredients. *Serves 4-6.*

OTHER RECIPES USING YOGHURT:
See: Yoghurt Dessert (directions for making yoghurt); Cabbage with Yoghurt; Chicken with Yoghurt; Yoghurt Sherbet; Date-Yoghurt Sherbet; Cottage Cheese Yoghurt Cake; Raisin-Yoghurt Frosting; Yoghurt Pie Filling; Yoghurt Cream Cheese Pie Filling.

## HOMEMADE SOUR CREAM

*Method No. 1*
Add 2 teaspoons of sour milk to 1 cup of heavy sweet cream. Stir. Leave at room temperature until mixture sours. Use immediately or refrigerate. Keep few teaspoons of sour cream as "starter" for new supply.

*Method No. 2*
Add 1 teaspoon of lemon juice or

[Recipe continued on next page]

[Recipe continued from previous page]
cider vinegar to 1 cup of heavy sweet cream. Stir. Proceed as above.

## HOMEMADE KEFIR

Kefir is a cultured-milk beverage made with kefir grains. The grains are colonies of milk-fermenting yeasts and bacteria. No special conditions or equipment are required to culture kefir. Once the grains are obtained, the culture can be kept active for years without replacement, or the grains can be dried and stored for future use.

To obtain kefir grains, see Sources of Supply for Natural Foods.

*Method*
Place 1 order of kefir grains in 1 quart fresh whole or skim milk. Allow the mixture to stand at room temperature at least 12 hours. It may stand for several days, depending on the degree of sourness desired. Strain. Use as a beverage or in cooking. The kefir grains that have been strained out are ready to be transferred to a fresh batch of milk. Kefir may be substituted in recipes calling for buttermilk or sour milk.

For Kefir Cheese, see p. 206.

## HOMEMADE BUTTERMILK

½ cup buttermilk
4 cups milk

Stir buttermilk into milk. Milk may be raw or pasteurized, whole or skim, or reconstituted powdered milk (dissolved in water or milk). Cover. Let stand at room temperature until mixture thickens. If not used immediately, refrigerate. Always keep last ½ cup as "starter" for new supply.

## BUTTERMILK COOLER

4 cups homemade buttermilk
(see above)
juice of 1 lemon
juice of 2 oranges
2 tablespoons honey

Blend all ingredients. *Serves 4-6.*

## BUTTERMILK SHAKE

4 cups homemade buttermilk
(see above)
½ cup wheat germ
3 tablespoons nutritional yeast
1 teaspoon fennel seeds

Blend all ingredients. *Serves 4-6.*

OTHER RECIPES USING BUTTERMILK: See: Buttermilk Soup, Cold; Buttermilk Sherbet.

NOTE: Yoghurt, sour cream and buttermilk may be used interchangeably in many recipes.

# Teas

Mineral-rich herb teas may be made by steeping in boiling water any of the following ingredients, alone or in any desired combination.

FRESH OR DRIED LEAVES OF: alfalfa, oat straw, shavegrass, rue, blueberry, raspberry, blackberry, parsley, celery, mint, sage, costmary, bee balm, comfrey, hyssop.
FRESH OR DRIED BLOSSOMS OF: clover, elderberry, linden, camomile.
FRESH OR DRIED BERRIES OF: rose hips.
SEEDS OF: fenugreek, alfalfa, anise, fennel, dill, caraway, celery, coriander.
ROOT OF: licorice.

Use amounts depending upon strength desired. Serve hot or cold. Serve plain or flavor with Powdered Fruit Rind, honey or lemon juice. Herb teas may also be combined with fresh fruit juices.

# Punch

## PARTY PUNCH

1 quart currants
1 quart sweet cider
½ cup honey
juice of 5 oranges
juice of 3 lemons
1 stick cinnamon bark

Extract juice of currants in juicer. Blend with cider. Dissolve honey in mixture. Add remaining ingredients. Garnish bowl with additional currants or orange and lemon slices. Use remaining currant pulp in fruit compotes. *Serves 10-12.*

VARIATION:
Substitute unsweetened pineapple or cranberry juice for citrus juice.

## THANKSGIVING PUNCH

3 cups sweet cider
3 cups cranberries, raw
6 tablespoons honey
12 pecans, raw
1 banana
1 sprig mint

Blend all ingredients. If thinner drink is desired, add more cider. *Serves 6-8.*

## CHRISTMAS PUNCH

1 quart sweet cider
2 cups unsweetened pineapple juice
1 cup unsweetened cranberry juice
1 cup unsweetened orange juice
¼ cup lemon juice
pinch of clove, ground
1 banana, sliced
1 large slice fresh pineapple, cut into small chunks

Blend all liquids. Chill. Place in punch bowl. Dust with cloves. Float pineapple and banana slices in punch. *Serves 12-16.*

# Mead

## APPLE MEAD

Mix equal parts raw (not pasteurized) sweet cider and raw (not pasteurized) honey. Stir until honey is entirely dissolved. Turn into clean stone crock. Cover. Let stand in warm place several weeks. Skim, if necessary. Bottle and seal with corks.

## CURRANT MEAD

1 gallon water, boiling
4½ pounds honey
3 quarts red currant juice
1 pound seedless raisins, chopped
1 tablespoon or 1 cake dried yeast
1 slice toast

Pour water over honey. Stir to dissolve. Cool. Add currant juice and raisins. Turn into clean stone crock. Make paste of yeast in small amount of water. Spread yeast mixture on top of toast. Float toast on top of liquid in crock. Cover. Let stand in warm place 16 days. Skim, if necessary. Strain. Let stand another 10 days. Bottle and seal with corks.

For homemade Mead Vinegar, see Vinegar, Homemade.

# 5
# SALADS

## Greens

lettuce, all types
celery and tops
spinach
dandelion
kale
chicory
water cress
endive
romaine
fennel
Chinese cabbage
green cabbage
red cabbage
savoy cabbage
escarole
collards
pepper grass
swiss chard
arugula
comfrey
sorrel
mustard greens
beet tops
turnip tops
carrot tops
green onions
scallions
shallots
kohlrabi leaves
broccoli leaves
cauliflower leaves

nasturtium leaves and buds
young green peas and pods
young milkweed
young fern
young salsify and tops
young yarrow
sour clover
shepherd's purse
lamb's quarters
purslane

## Herbs (fresh or dried)

tarragon
basil
dill
chervil
chive
thyme
savory
marjoram
rosemary
parsley
mint
oregano
sage

## Seeds (whole or crushed)

sunflower (hulled)
pumpkin (hulled)

squash (hulled)
celery
dill
caraway
poppy
ginger
sesame
cumin
coriander
mustard
anise
fennel
flax

## Additional Suggestions:

avocado
garlic
onions, all types
raw kohlrabi, grated
raw celeriac, diced
raw beets, grated
raw broccoli
raw cauliflower
raw peas
raw young asparagus tips
tomatoes, all types
leeks
Sprouts
cucumber
hard-cooked eggs
soy cheese*
cottage cheese*
raw eggplant
raw turnip, grated
raw rutabaga, grated
raw parsnip
sweet red peppers
sweet green peppers
radishes
kelp and dulse
nuts, whole, slivered, ground
Roasted Soybeans, whole or ground
ripe olives
cold cooked vegetables, diced
grated cheese
Coconut Shreds

fresh fruit and berries
dried fruits

## Tossed Salads

### SPRING SALAD

½ cup asparagus tips, steamed
½ cup string beans, steamed
½ cup young peas, raw
½ cup radishes, sliced
2 artichoke hearts, cooked and
    sliced
2 eggs, hard-cooked and quartered

Toss all vegetables lightly. Moisten
with favorite dressing. Garnish with
eggs. *Serves 6.*

### SUMMER SALAD

4 tomatoes, sliced
2 green peppers, diced
2 cups cucumbers, diced
1 Bermuda onion, chopped
2 hearts of celery and tops, diced
3 tablespoons mixed fresh herbs,
    minced

Toss all ingredients lightly. Moisten
with yoghurt. *Serves 6.*

### AUTUMN SALAD

1 cup beets, cooked and diced
½ cup potatoes, cooked and diced
¼ cup carrots, raw and grated
½ cup apple with skin, diced
1 green pepper, diced
1 onion, grated
¼ cup cabbage, grated
1 stalk celery and top, diced

Toss all ingredients lightly. To tint
mixture, moisten with juice in
which beets were cooked. Add favorite dressing. *Serves 6.*

## WINTER SALAD

3 cups cooked beans (soybeans,
  limas, lentils, etc.)
3 tablespoons oil
1 lemon, juice and rind
3 tablespoons parsley, minced
1 tablespoon dill, minced
4 scallions, sliced
1 tablespoon mint, minced
1 hard-cooked egg, sliced
1 tomato, sliced
1 green pepper, minced

Toss all ingredients lightly. Serve
cold. *Serves 6.*

## CABBAGE SLAW

4 cups cabbage, shredded fine
½ onion, grated
½ cup mung bean Sprouts
1 tablespoon dulse, minced
1 raw kohlrabi, grated
⅓ cup radishes, sliced thin
⅔ cup green peppers, diced
1 teaspoon dill seeds, crushed

Toss all ingredients lightly. Moisten
with favorite dressing. *Serves 6.*

## GOLDEN SLAW

1 cup raw rutabaga, shredded
1 cup raw carrot, shredded
1 cup raw cabbage, shredded
½ cup raw kohlrabi, grated
1 raw parsnip, grated
½ cup radish Sprouts
1 onion, grated
1 teaspoon tarragon, minced

Toss all ingredients lightly. Moisten
with favorite dressing. *Serves 6.*

## EGGPLANT SALAD

1 raw eggplant, diced
cider vinegar *
½ teaspoon basil
½ teaspoon parsley, minced
1 onion, sliced
1 bunch water cress
2 hard-cooked eggs, quartered
ripe olives

Marinate eggplant in vinegar with
herbs and onion for 2 hours. Toss
with water cress. Garnish with eggs
and olives. Serve with favorite dressing. *Serves 4-6.*

## SPINACH SALAD

1 pound raw, crisp spinach
pinch of salt
clove of garlic, minced
1 onion, grated
2 tablespoons lemon juice
7 tablespoons oil
tomato wedges
3 hard-cooked eggs, quartered

Wash spinach. Drain. Cut into bite-
size pieces. Blend salt, garlic, onion,
lemon juice and oil together. Pour
over spinach. Toss until well mixed.
Garnish with tomatoes and eggs.
*Serves 4-6.*

## STUFFED TOMATO SALAD

6 large tomatoes
1½ cups beans, cooked (soybeans,
  limas, lentils, etc.)
2 tablespoons celery, minced fine
2 tablespoons Sprouts
1 tablespoon dulse, minced
1 tablespoon parsley, minced
1 teaspoon onion juice
½ cup nuts, ground
1 teaspoon soy flour
1 tablespoon nutritional yeast

Scoop out insides of tomatoes. Re-
serve for soup, stew or casseroles.
Mix remaining ingredients together.
Stuff mixture into tomato cavities.
Serve on bed of crisp greens. *Serves
6.*

## FARMER'S CHOP SUEY SALAD

4 radishes, sliced thin
2 green onions, sliced thin
¼ small cucumber, sliced thin
1 cup Sprouts
½ cup cottage cheese *
½ cup yoghurt*

Mix Sprouts and other vegetables. Combine cheese with mixture. Moisten with yoghurt. *Serves 4.*

## GREEN SALAD WITH JULIENNE CHEESE

greens to *serve 6*
1 cup hard cheese, cut into julienne strips
favorite French Dressing

Marinate cheese in dressing several hours and add to greens.

## SOYBEAN-CHEESE SALAD

2 cups cooked soybeans
2 cups cooked vegetables, diced
½ cup cheese, grated
yoghurt *

Toss all ingredients and add enough yoghurt to moisten. *Serves 6.*

## SOYBEAN-VEGETABLE SALAD

2 cups cooked soybeans
1 cup celery and tops, diced
1 cup raw carrots, shredded
1 cup asparagus tips
½ teaspoon basil
1 tablespoon chives, minced

Combine and toss all ingredients. Moisten with favorite dressing. *Serves 6.*

VARIATIONS:
Use cabbage, cucumber, green pepper, chopped apple, or any other raw, crisp vegetables or fruits instead of, or in addition to, celery and carrots.

## SWEETBREAD SALAD

1 cup sweetbreads, cooked, cold, diced
1 cup veal or ham, cooked, cold, diced
½ cup peas, cooked, cold
½ cup celery and tops, diced
1 cup mung bean Sprouts
2 tablespoons sweet red pepper, minced
½ teaspoon rosemary
½ teaspoon salt

Combine and toss all ingredients. Moisten with favorite dressing. Serve on bed of crisp greens. *Serves 6.*

## SWEETBREAD-CHICKEN SALAD

5 sweetbreads, cooked, cold, diced
2 cups chicken, cooked, cold, diced
2 hard-cooked eggs, diced
2 tablespoons green peppers, diced
1 cup celery and tops, diced
1 onion, grated
½ teaspoon salt
½ teaspoon tarragon

Combine and toss all ingredients. Moisten with favorite dressing. Serve on bed of crisp greens. *Serves 6.*

SUGGESTED COMBINATION SALADS:
Carrots, raisins, wheat germ
Celery, carrots, cashew nuts, coconut shreds
Diced raw apple, nuts, sprouts, carrots
Shredded green and red cabbage, garlic, green peppers
Mung and alfalfa sprouts, nuts, dried fruits
Soybean sprouts, water cress, carrots

[Continued on next page]

[Continued from previous page]

Wholewheat sprouts, walnuts, raisins, celery, apple

Fenugreek, sprouts, carrots, celery, radishes, cucumbers, green peppers

## YAM-FRUIT SALAD

5 yams, cooked and diced
4 bananas, sliced
3 apples with skins, diced
1 cup seedless grapes

Lightly toss all ingredients. Moisten with favorite dressing. *Serves 6.*

## SALAD OF INDIA

6 bananas, sliced
3 tablespoons mint, minced
½ cup dates, pitted and chopped
½ cup nuts, ground

Arrange banana slices on bed of greens. Garnish with other ingredients. *Serves 6.*

SUGGESTED COMBINATION FRUIT SALADS:

Pineapple, grapefruit, bananas, alfalfa sprouts

Apple, celery, pear, fenugreek sprouts

Banana, apple, raisins, coconut shreds

# Molded Salads

## SPRING MOLDED SALAD

1 envelope or 1 tablespoon unflavored gelatin
1½ cups unsweetened orange juice
2 cups fresh strawberries
1 cucumber, diced
1 cup celery and tops, diced
1 tablespoon mint, minced
1 teaspoon Powdered Fruit Rind

Soften gelatin in ½ cup orange juice. Heat remainder of juice. Dissolve gelatin mixture in it. Cool. Add remainder of ingredients. Turn into mold or individual molds. Chill until firm. Unmold on bed of salad greens. *Serves 6.*

VARIATIONS:

Substitute green pepper and sprouts for cucumber and celery.

Substitute any fresh berries in season for strawberries.

For further suggestions on cooking with gelatin and agar-agar, see Chapter 20, Desserts.

## SUMMER MOLDED SALAD

1 envelope or 1 tablespoon unflavored gelatin
1½ cups unsweetened pineapple juice
2 cups fresh pineapple, diced
1 cup mung bean Sprouts
½ cup Coconut Shreds
1 tablespoon mint, minced
2 peaches with skins, sliced
1 teaspoon Powdered Fruit Rind

Soften gelatin in ½ cup pineapple juice. Heat remainder of juice. Dissolve gelatin mixture in it. Cool. Add remaining ingredients. Turn into mold or individual molds. Chill until firm. Unmold on bed of salad greens. *Serves 6.*

NOTE:

If fresh pineapple juice is used in this salad, bring juice to boil and cool before softening gelatin in it. Fresh pineapple contains an enzyme which makes gelatin liquefy. This presents no problem once the pineapple juice is boiled.

## AUTUMN MOLDED SALAD
### (in blender)

1 envelope or 1 tablespoon
 unflavored gelatin
1 cup sweet cider
1 orange with peel, quartered
 and pitted
1½ cups raw cranberries
1 apple with skin, cored and
 quartered
4 tablespoons honey
pinch of mace, ground
1 sprig mint

Soften gelatin in ¼ cup cider. Heat
remaining cider and in it dissolve
gelatin mixture. Cool to lukewarm.
Place all ingredients in blender.
Blend until smooth. Turn into
mold or small molds. Chill until
firm and unmold. *Serves 6.*

## WINTER MOLDED SALAD

1 envelope or 1 tablespoon
 unflavored gelatin
1 cup unsweetened grape juice
1 cup alfalfa Sprouts
½ cup celery and tops, chopped
½ cup cabbage, shredded
¼ cup green pepper, chopped
1 apple with skin, diced

Soften gelatin in ¼ cup grape juice.
Heat remaining grape juice and dissolve gelatin mixture in it. Cool to
lukewarm. Add remaining ingredients. Turn into mold or small
molds. Chill until firm and unmold.
*Serves 6.*

## CUCUMBER-YOGHURT MOLDED
### SALAD (In blender)

2 cucumbers, cut in pieces
2 envelopes or 2 tablespoons
 unflavored gelatin
2 cups yoghurt *
½ clove garlic
¼ teaspoon salt

2 tablespoons nutritional yeast
1 tablespoon lemon juice and rind
¼ teaspoon salt
1 sprig mint

Blend cucumber until liquefied.
Turn into bowl. Add gelatin. Place
remaining ingredients in blender.
Blend until smooth. Heat gelatin
mixture in top of double boiler over
hot water until gelatin dissolves.
Blend gelatin mixture with yoghurt
mixture. Mold. Chill until firm and
unmold. *Serves 6.*

VARIATION:
Before turning mixture into mold,
add ½ cup cooked soybeans.

## CUCUMBER-LEMON MOLDED
## SALAD

1 envelope or 1 tablespoon
 unflavored gelatin
juice of 2 lemons
1 cup hot, unsweetened fruit juice
1 cup cucumbers, cubed
½ cup cashews

Soften gelatin in lemon juice. Dissolve in hot fruit juice. Cool to lukewarm. Add remaining ingredients.
Mold and chill. Unmold on salad
greens. *Serves 4-6.*

## CARROT MOLDED SALAD

1 envelope or 1 tablespoon
 unflavored gelatin
juice of 2 lemons
1½ cups hot sweet cider
1½ cups carrots, shredded
½ cup raisins
¼ cup sunflower seeds, hulled

Soften gelatin in lemon juice. Dissolve in hot cider and cool mixture
to lukewarm. Add remaining ingredients. Mold and chill. Unmold on
salad greens. *Serves 4-6.*

## BEET MOLDED SALAD
(in blender)

1 envelope or 1 tablespoon
   unflavored gelatin
juice of 2 lemons
1 cup hot beet juice
2 cups beets, cooked and diced,
   or raw and grated fine
2 carrots, raw
1 stalk celery and top
1 teaspoon tarragon
1 sprig parsley
½ cup stock

Soften gelatin in lemon juice. Dissolve in beet juice. Combine remaining ingredients in blender and blend until smooth. Add to gelatin mixture. Mold and chill. Unmold on salad greens. *Serves 4-6.*

## AVOCADO MOLDED SALAD
(in blender)

1 envelope or 1 tablespoon
   unflavored gelatin
juice of 2 lemons
1½ cups hot, unsweetened fruit
   juice
2 avocados
½ onion
2 tablespoons nutritional yeast
¼ teaspoon basil
1 sprig dill

Soften gelatin in lemon juice. Dissolve in hot fruit juice. Cool to lukewarm. Combine gelatin mixture and remaining ingredients in blender. Blend until smooth. Mold and chill. Unmold on salad greens. *Serves 4-6.*

## SOYBEAN MOLDED SALAD

1 envelope or 1 tablespoon
   unflavored gelatin
1 cup tomato juice
1 cup hot stock
1 tablespoon lemon juice

1 cup green soybeans, cooked
1 green pepper, diced
½ cup celery and tops, diced
2 tablespoons nutritional yeast
¼ teaspoon sage, ground

Soften gelatin in tomato juice. Dissolve in stock. Cool to lukewarm. Add remaining ingredients. Mold and chill. Unmold on salad greens. *Serves 4-6.*

## MOLDED SALAD LOAF

1 envelope or 1 tablespoon
   unflavored gelatin
juice of 2 lemons
1½ cups hot stock
½ cup Sprouts
2 cups cooked meat, fish or fowl
   (leftovers)
½ cup celery and tops, diced
½ green pepper, diced
1 onion, grated
2 tablespoons nutritional yeast

Soften gelatin in lemon juice. Dissolve in stock. Cool. Add remaining ingredients. Turn into loaf pan. Chill. Unmold and slice. *Serves 6.*

## SEA FOOD MOLD

1 envelope or 1 tablespoon
   unflavored gelatin
½ cup cold milk
½ cup fish stock
2 egg yolks
1 teaspoon dulse, minced
2 teaspoons soy flour
1 teaspoon marjoram
1 tablespoon nutritional yeast
2 tablespoons parsley, minced
2 tablespoons lemon juice
2 cups fish, cooked and flaked

Soften gelatin in milk. Heat fish stock in top of double boiler, directly over heat. Dissolve gelatin mixture in stock. Set over bottom of double boiler, to which hot water has been added, and continue to cook. Blend together egg yolks, dulse, flour, marjoram, yeast and parsley, and gradually add to mixture in double boiler. Cook, stirring occasionally, until mixture thickens. Remove from heat. When cool, add lemon juice and fish. Mold and chill. Unmold on salad greens. *Serves 6.*

LEFTOVER SALADS

Tossed vegetable salads (without dressing) may be puréed in blender and added to stock or soup. They may also be minced fine and added to casseroles and loaves of meat, fish or fowl.

Cut molded salads into cubes and use as garnish over salad greens.

OTHER SALAD RECIPES

See: Cottage Cheese with Herbs; Roquefort Mousse.

# Vegetable Salad Dressings

Many of the following salad dressings may be prepared in blender. Solid ingredients should be cut or diced coarsely and added to blender about a half-cup at a time.

## TOMATO JUICE DRESSING

¼ cup tomato juice
¼ cup cider vinegar *
2 tablespoons honey
2 tablespoons nutritional yeast
1 egg yolk
2 tablespoons chives
1 sprig parsley
½ cup oil

Blend all ingredients, except oil, until well blended. Gradually add oil. Blend until smooth. *Makes 1 cup.*

## YOGHURT DRESSING

1 cup yoghurt *
1 onion, chopped
½ clove garlic
¼ cup celery leaves
¼ cup parsley
½ teaspoon salt
1 teaspoon honey
3 tablespoons nutritional yeast

Blend all ingredients. *Makes 1⅓ cups.*

## BEET DRESSING

¼ cup cider vinegar *
2 beets, cooked and cubed
1 hard-cooked egg
1 teaspoon honey
1 tablespoon nutritional yeast
1 onion, sliced
1 teaspoon tarragon
⅛ teaspoon salt
1 teaspoon Powdered Fruit Rind
¾ cup oil

Blend thoroughly all ingredients except oil. Gradually add oil. Blend until smooth. *Makes 1¼ cups.*

## BLEU CHEESE DRESSING

1 cup yoghurt *
1 cup bleu cheese
1 tablespoon chives
1 sprig parsley

Blend all ingredients. *Makes 2 cups.*

## CHEDDAR CHEESE DRESSING

1 cup yoghurt *
1 cup cheddar cheese, grated
¼ cup cider vinegar *
1 teaspoon caraway seeds

[Recipe continued on next page]

[Recipe continued from previous page]
Blend all ingredients. *Makes 2¼ cups.*

## CUCUMBER DRESSING

1 cup cucumber, cubed
1 cup yoghurt *
1 tablespoon cider vinegar *
pinch of salt
1 sprig dill
½ teaspoon dill seeds

Blend all ingredients. *Makes 2 cups.*

## AVOCADO DRESSING

1 avocado (in chunks)
½ onion
1 tomato, sliced
¼ teaspoon salt
2 tablespoons cider vinegar *
1 tablespoon nutritional yeast
1 teaspoon soy flour
3 tablespoons oil

Blend all ingredients. *Makes 1 cup.*

## CARROT DRESSING

½ cup raw carrots, diced
3 tablespoons cider vinegar *
2 raw eggs
1 cup oil

Blend all ingredients. *Makes 1¾ cups.*

## COTTAGE CHEESE DRESSING

½ cup yoghurt *
½ cup cottage cheese *
¼ cup cider vinegar *
2 tablespoons nutritional yeast
¼ teaspoon salt
3 hard-cooked egg yolks
½ green pepper
4 radishes
2 tablespoons chives
1 tablespoon poppy seeds

Blend all ingredients. *Makes 1¾ cups.*

## BASIC FRENCH DRESSING

¼ cup cider vinegar *
2 tablespoons honey
⅛ teaspoon salt
⅓ cup oil

Blend all ingredients. Shake well before using. *Makes ½ cup.*

**VARIATIONS:**
Instead of cider vinegar use homemade mead vinegar, mint, tarragon or dill vinegars (see under Vinegars); or fruit juices such as lemon, lime, grapefruit or orange.

## HAWAIIAN DRESSING (cooked)

½ cup oil
3 egg yolks
1½ tablespoons lemon juice
1 teaspoon salt
½ cup unsweetened pineapple
juice

Blend all ingredients thoroughly in top of double boiler. Cook over hot water, stirring constantly, until sauce is consistency of boiled custard. *Makes 1½ cups.*

## COLE SLAW DRESSING (cooked)

2 eggs, beaten
3 tablespoons honey
1 teaspoon salt
1 cup yoghurt *
½ cup tarragon vinegar *
1 teaspoon celery seeds

Blend all ingredients thoroughly in top of double boiler. Cook over hot water until mixture is the texture of smooth custard. *Makes 2 cups.*

## GREEN SUMMER DRESSING

2 tablespoons cider vinegar *
1/4 cup chopped greens (water cress, parsley, spinach, scallion, etc.)
1 egg
1/4 teaspoon salt
1 sprig parsley
1 sprig dill
1 sprig savory
1 teaspoon honey
1/4 cup oil

Blend all ingredients in blender. *Makes 3/4 cup.*

## SOY BUTTER DRESSING

1/2 cup soy butter*
juice of 1 lemon
1/2 teaspoon salt
1/4 cup tomato juice
1 stalk celery and top
3 tablespoons water cress

Blend all ingredients in blender. *Makes 1 cup.*

## SOY CHEESE DRESSING

Blend soy cheese* with favorite dressing in proportions to achieve desired consistency. If consistency is very stiff, this mixture can be molded into balls, rolled in ground nuts or wheat germ and used as garnish for vegetables or fruit salads.

## UNCOOKED MAYONNAISE (in blender)

1 raw egg
1 teaspoon salt
1 teaspoon honey
1/2 cup cider vinegar *
1 1/4 cups oil

Blend all ingredients except oil until well blended. Add oil gradually.

Blend until smooth and thick. *Makes 2 cups.*

## EGGLESS MAYONNAISE

2 tablespoons soy flour
3 tablespoons water
1 cup oil
1/2 teaspoon salt
juice of 1/2 lemon
3 tablespoons parsley, minced
1/4 teaspoon basil

Blend flour and water into smooth paste in top of double boiler. Heat over hot water. Gradually beat in oil with rotary beater. When thick, remove from heat. Add remaining ingredients. Continue beating until smooth and thick. *Makes 1 cup.*

## OILLESS DRESSING (in blender)

2 eggs, hard-cooked
1/2 clove garlic
3 tablespoons cider vinegar *
1/4 cup yoghurt *
1 sprig basil
1 teaspoon tarragon

Blend all ingredients until smooth. *Makes 1/2 cup.*

# Fruit Salad Dressings

## CRANBERRY DRESSING (in blender)

2/3 cup raw cranberries
2 tablespoons sweet cider
3 tablespoons honey
1 tablespoon lemon juice
1/3 cup yoghurt *
3 tablespoons oil

Blend all ingredients until smooth. *Makes 1 1/4 cups.*

## FRUIT JUICE DRESSING

1 cup yoghurt *
1 tablespoon honey
2 tablespoons unsweetened orange
   juice
2 tablespoons unsweetened
   pineapple juice

Blend all ingredients. *Makes* 1½ *cups.*

## FRUIT SALAD DRESSING (cooked)

½ cup unsweetened fruit juice
⅛ teaspoon salt
4 tablespoons honey
2 egg yolks, beaten
1 cup yoghurt *
pinch of cinnamon, ground

Blend fruit juice, salt and honey in top of double boiler. Cook over hot water. Add egg yolks gradually. Beat well. Continue to cook, stirring constantly, until slightly thickened. Remove from heat. Cool. Fold in yoghurt and add cinnamon. *Makes* 1¾ *cups.*

## HONEY DRESSING

½ cup honey
½ cup oil
juice of 1 lemon
1 teaspoon Powdered Fruit Rind

Blend all ingredients. *Makes* 1¼ *cups.*

## HONEY-YOGHURT DRESSING

⅓ cup honey
½ cup yoghurt *
1 teaspoon lemon juice
pinch of mace, ground

Blend all ingredients. *Makes* ¾ *cup.*

## HONEY-CELERY SEED DRESSING

½ cup honey
⅓ cup mint vinegar *
1 tablespoon onion juice

1 tablespoon celery seeds
1 cup oil

Blend all ingredients. *Makes* 1¾ *cups.*

## FRUIT DRESSING (in blender)

¼ cup yoghurt *
2 tablespoons raisins
1 tablespoon nuts
1 tablespoon Coconut Shreds
2 tablespoons honey
1 tablespoon lemon juice

Blend all ingredients until smooth. *Makes* ¾ *cup.*

GARNISHES FOR SALADS:
Circles of thin strips of red and
   green peppers
Celery stuffed with savory cheese
   mix, celery curls, celery hearts
Radishes (slices or radish roses)
Endive  stuffed  with  Roquefort
   cheese
Carrots, grated fine or cut into thin
   strips
Thin  onion  rings,  marinated  or
   tinted in beet juice
Wedges of  tomatoes,  hard-cooked
   eggs or avocados
Scored cucumbers, sliced thin
Sieved hard-cooked egg yolks
Finely  chopped  hard-cooked  egg
   whites
Cheese (cubes, strips or grated)
Soy cheese
Cottage cheese
Nuts, whole, ground or slivered
Wheat germ
Sprouts
Raw beets, grated
Chives, minced
Ripe olives
Roasted Soybeans, whole or ground
Seeds
Coconut Shreds
Yoghurt

# 6
# SOUPS

## Stock

HINTS:

To enrich stocks or soups, save all liquids rich in food values, such as water in which potatoes or other vegetables have been cooked; fish juices (for chowders or fish soups); liquids in which grains, seeds, beans or peas have been soaked prior to sprouting; fruit juices from salads, stewed fruit, or soaked dried fruit (for making fruit soups); meat juices from which the fat has been skimmed; liquid in which organ meats have been scalded.

Pour a small amount of water or stock into pan in which meat has been roasted or broiled and allow to soak or simmer.

Add to stock or soup trimmed outer leaves of cabbage, lettuce, kale, etc.; tops of celery, carrots, green onions, beets, chard; less tender parts of asparagus stalk.

### STRAINED VEGETABLE STOCK

4 cups vegetables, chopped (carrots, celery, fennel, spinach, turnip, knob celery or any preferred combination)
1 onion, sliced
1 sprig parsley
½ teaspoon thyme
½ teaspoon savory
1 tablespoon salt
1 quart water

Put all ingredients in a large pot. Cover tightly. Simmer gently for 30 minutes. Cool. Strain.

### MEAT STOCK

1 pound soup bones, cracked
4 pounds shin beef, cubed
½ cup celery with tops, chopped
½ cup carrots, diced
2 onions, sliced
4 sprigs parsley
2 cloves, whole
2 sprigs thyme
1 sprig marjoram
1 tablespoon salt
3 tablespoons cider vinegar *
3 quarts water

Put all ingredients in a large pot and cover tightly. Simmer for 3 hours. Occasionally remove scum from top. Cool. Skim off fat. Strain.

## FISH STOCK

Use whole fish, heads or trimmings. Wash with cold water. For each cup of fish, add the following:

½ cup celery with tops, chopped, *or*
½ cup fennel, chopped, *or*
½ cup celeriac, chopped
½ cup onions, carrots, turnips or parsnips, chopped
1 tablespoon soy flour
1 bay leaf
¼ teaspoon fennel seeds
1 sprig parsley
1 sprig dill
¼ teaspoon dulse, chopped fine
1 tablespoon nutritional yeast

Put all ingredients in a large pot and add water to cover. Cover pot tightly. Simmer gently for 30 minutes. Strain.

## HOMEMADE DRY SOUP MIX

1 cup dry milk powder
1 cup nutritional yeast
1 cup soy flour
¼ cup dried herbs, mixed

Blend all ingredients. Store in tightly covered jar. In making soup, use 3 tablespoons of this mix to each cup of liquid.

If a home grinder is available, dried peas and beans, barley, lentils or other dried legumes and cereals may also be ground to add to this soup mix.

# Flavorings for Soups and Stews

## FINES HERBES

Blend together in desired proportions freshly dried thyme, sweet marjoram, oregano, parsley and basil.

Mix thoroughly. Place one tablespoon of the mixture in the center of two thicknesses of cheesecloth (large enough for a sachet), or one thickness of Miracloth (a lintless cloth obtainable at hardware stores). Fold edges of cloth and bind with white carpet thread. Leave 12 inches of thread hanging on each sachet so that it may be suspended into a pot. Store sachets in tightly covered jars. Put into soup or stew pot for last 10 minutes of cooking. Similar sachets may be made with fresh herbs, adding chives if desired. One teaspoonful of fresh herbs in a sachet is sufficient.

For *Kitchen Bouquet:* 2 teaspoons dried parsley leaves, 2 teaspoons dried celery leaves or a grated root of knob celery, 1 teaspoon thyme, 1 teaspoon sweet marjoram, ¼ teaspoon sage, ½ teaspoon savory, 2 bay leaves, 1 clove to each sachet.

For *Bouquet for Fish Stock:* 2 tablespoons celery leaves, 2 tablespoons parsley leaves, ½ teaspoon sage, ½ teaspoon savory, 1 teaspoon basil, ½ teaspoon fennel seeds, 2 bay leaves, 3 cloves to each sachet.

For *Bouquet Garni:* 2 sprigs of parsley, 1 sprig of marjoram, 2 sprigs of thyme, ½ bay leaf.

VARIATIONS:
Combinations of parsley, chervil and chive; burnet, thyme and parsley.

## ESSENCE OF SWEET HERBS

1 carrot, grated
1 onion, grated
1 sweet potato, peeled and grated
1 parsnip, grated
1 shallot, chopped
1 clove garlic, minced

3 tablespoons honey
½ cup cold water
¼ teaspoon cloves, ground
¼ teaspoon allspice, ground
¼ teaspoon cinnamon, ground
¼ teaspoon mace, ground
3 bay leaves
1 tablespoon salt

Mix vegetables. Spread one third at bottom of unoiled baking pan. Drizzle one tablespoon of honey over layer. Repeat with vegetables and honey twice again. Bake in 450° F. oven until mixture becomes dark brown. Transfer to top of stove. Add water, spices and salt. Cover. Simmer, stirring occasionally, until mixture forms brown, thick, rich syrup. Strain. This concentrated mixture may be kept in a tightly covered jar in the refrigerator for several weeks, or reheated and sealed in hot sterilized jars. Use sparingly. The solids removed in straining may be made into mock chutney by removing bay leaves and adding raw, diced apples, raisins and walnut meats.

## Soups

HINTS FOR MAKING SOUP:
Soups should be heated only long enough for ingredients to become tender. If vegetables are shredded fine beforehand, soups may be cooked briefly, thus retaining food values.
Shredded cabbage is best added to soup shortly before serving. Simmer soup only a few minutes after cabbage has been put in.
For variety, vegetables may be sliced, cubed, grated or puréed. A cream soup is enriched by the addition of milk powder, sour cream or yoghurt. Beat a raw egg into a clear soup just before serving, or drizzle the white of an egg into it—this will form noodle-like strands. Soups welcome leftover bits of cooked vegetables, meats, fish, fowl, grains, porridge, sauce. When stock is used as a base for soup, use less salt than when starting with water.

## Hearty Cold Weather Soups

### NEW ENGLAND CHEESE SOUP

3 tablespoons oil
¼ cup celery and tops, chopped
¼ cup carrots, chopped
¼ cup onions, chopped
¼ cup green pepper, chopped
1 tablespoon wholewheat flour
½ cup milk powder
3 tablespoons nutritional yeast
1 cup hot stock
1 pint milk
1 cup cheddar cheese, grated
3 tablespoons almonds, blanched, slivered

Heat oil in pot and in it sauté lightly all vegetables. Mix flour, milk powder and yeast. Sprinkle over vegetables. Add stock and blend. Gradually add milk and cheese. Stir until blended. Serve hot, garnished with almonds. *Serves 6.*

### NORTH EUROPEAN LIVER SOUP

3 tablespoons oil
1 onion, sliced
½ pound mushrooms, sliced
½ pound liver, cubed
3 cups stock
3 egg yolks
2 tablespoons nutritional yeast
2 tablespoons parsley, minced

Heat oil in pot. Lightly sauté onion, mushrooms and liver. Add stock.

[Recipe continued on next page]

[Recipe continued from previous page]

Cover. Simmer gently for 15 minutes. Remove from heat. Mix yolks and yeast in small bowl. Add a small quantity of hot stock. Blend thoroughly. Gradually stir egg-yeast mixture into soup. Serve at once. *Serves 6.*

## CARROT-CHEESE SOUP
(in blender)

2 cups milk
2 cups stock
1 onion, sliced
4 carrots, cut in chunks
1/4 cup parsley
3 tablespoons wholewheat flour
1/4 cup soy flour
1 teaspoon salt
3 tablespoons oil
3 tablespoons nutritional yeast
1/4 teaspoon summer savory
1 cup cheddar cheese, grated

Add all ingredients to blender gradually and blend until smooth. Heat thoroughly. *Serves 6.*

## HEARTY BEEF SOUP

1 shin bone
1 marrow bone
stock to cover
3 tablespoons cider vinegar *
1 onion, chopped
3 tablespoons parsley, minced
2 carrots, diced
1 bay leaf
2 stalks of celery and tops, chopped
1 raw potato, diced
1 cup tomatoes, stewed
1/2 cup savoy cabbage, diced, and, if desired, zucchini, escarole, etc. cut into small pieces
3 tablespoons nutritional yeast

Cover bones with stock and vinegar. Simmer for 2 hours. Remove bones and skim soup. Add remaining in-

gredients, cover and simmer for 20 minutes more. *Serves 6.*

## TURKISH YOGHURT-BEEF SOUP
(in blender)

1 1/2 quarts beef stock
1/2 teaspoon salt
3 tablespoons nutritional yeast
3 tablespoons oil
1/4 cup wholewheat flour
2 tablespoons soy flour
1 tablespoon dried mint leaves
2 cups yoghurt *

Blend all ingredients together until smooth. Heat thoroughly. *Serves 6.*

## CHICKEN LIVER-CELERY SOUP
(in blender)

1 quart milk
1/2 pound chicken liver, broiled
1/2 cup celery, diced
1/4 cup oil
1 teaspoon salt
3 tablespoons nutritional yeast
1/2 cup wholewheat flour
3 tablespoons soy flour
1/4 teaspoon savory
slices of lemon

Gradually blend all ingredients except lemon slices until smooth. Heat thoroughly. Garnish with lemon slices. *Serves 6.*

## SPANISH LIVER SOUP

1 calf's liver, whole
1 pork liver, whole
stock to cover
4 tablespoons oil
1 onion, minced
1 green pepper, minced
2 cloves, whole
1/4 teaspoon cinnamon, ground
1/4 teaspoon caraway seeds, ground
1/2 teaspoon saffron

1 teaspoon salt
3 tablespoons nutritional yeast

Arrange livers at bottom of pot.
Cover with cold stock. Cover pot.
Simmer gently about 30 minutes, or
until tender. Remove livers. Cut
into small cubes. Arrange them at
bottom of casserole. Pour oil over
liver. Add onions and green peppers. Mix remaining ingredients
with stock. Pour into casserole.
Cover. Bake at 350° F. for 30 minutes. *Serves 6.*

## GERMAN KIDNEY SOUP

3 tablespoons oil
2 calf's kidneys, sliced
1 onion, chopped
3 tablespoons wholewheat flour
3 tablespoons nutritional yeast
1 teaspoon salt
1 bay leaf
1 sprig thyme
2 quarts stock
¼ cup celery leaves, chopped
2 egg yolks
3 tablespoons milk, warm

Heat oil in pot. Sauté kidneys and
onion. Blend flour, yeast, salt, bay
leaf and thyme in stock. Add kidneys and cover pot. Gradually bring
to boil. Add celery leaves. Simmer
gently 20 minutes. Remove from
stove. Beat egg yolks into milk.
Gradually add egg mixture to soup.
Serve. *Serves 6.*

## RUSSIAN KIDNEY SOUP

2 calf's kidneys, sliced
1 cup turnips, diced
2 carrots, diced
1 onion, minced
4 potatoes, diced
1 stalk celery and tops, diced
2 quarts stock
¼ cup cider vinegar*

3 tablespoons wholewheat flour
1 teaspoon salt
3 tablespoons nutritional yeast
1 tablespoon oil
¼ cup dill
1 cup sour cream* or yoghurt*

Arrange kidneys and vegetables in
pot. Cover with stock. Cover pot.
Simmer gently until kidneys and
vegetables are tender. Remove one
cup of stock. Mix with vinegar,
flour, salt, yeast, oil and dill. Blend
thoroughly and return mixture to
the pot. Blend. Cover. Cook until
soup is slightly thickened. Serve
garnished with sour cream or yoghurt. *Serves 6.*

## PHILADELPHIA TRIPE SOUP

1 onion, chopped
1 stalk celery and top, chopped
2 potatoes, diced
1 bay leaf
¼ teaspoon savory
½ teaspoon salt
3 tablespoons nutritional yeast
2 quarts meat stock (beef or veal
    bones)
¼ pound tripe, cooked, diced fine
3 tablespoons parsley, minced

Combine all vegetables and seasonings together with meat stock. Simmer gently in covered pot until
vegetables are tender. Add tripe.
Heat thoroughly. Serve garnished
with parsley. *Serves 6.*

## TURKISH TRIPE SOUP (in blender)

2 pounds tripe, cooked, coarsely
    diced
1 quart stock
½ clove garlic
1 teaspoon salt
3 tablespoons nutritional yeast
½ teaspoon rosemary
1 egg
juice and rind of 1 lemon

[Recipe continued on next page]

[Recipe continued from previous page]
Gradually blend tripe in stock with garlic, salt, yeast and rosemary. Heat gently in pot. Remove from heat. Beat egg with lemon juice and rind in small bowl. Gradually add egg mixture to soup. Blend. *Serves 6.*

## FISH BISQUE

Save fish trimmings. Cook in stock with onion, mace or nutmeg. Strain. Add equal amount of milk to liquid. Thicken with wholewheat flour. Add small amount of oil, herbs, nutritional yeast and dulse. Serve.

## ITALIAN FISH CHOWDER

3 tablespoons oil
1 onion, chopped
1 clove garlic, minced
1/4 cup celery and tops, chopped
2 cups tomatoes, stewed
1 sprig parsley, minced
1/2 teaspoon marjoram
1 teaspoon celery seeds, ground
1/4 teaspoon sage, ground
2 tablespoons dulse, minced
1 teaspoon salt
3 tablespoons nutritional yeast
1 quart fish stock
1 pound rock cod or striped bass, cut into chunks, cooked
1/4 pound shrimp, cooked
1 large crab, cooked

Combine all ingredients in pot, except fish. Cover. Simmer until onion and celery are tender. Add fish. Heat thoroughly. *Serves 6.*

## BOUILLABAISSE

1/4 cup oil
1 carrot, diced
2 onions, chopped
1 stalk celery and tops, diced
1 stalk leek, chopped
1/4 cup fennel, chopped
1 clove garlic, minced
1 cup tomatoes, stewed
1 bay leaf
1/2 teaspoon thyme
1/8 teaspoon saffron
2 tablespoons parsley, minced
1 tablespoon soy flour
3 tablespoons nutritional yeast
2 cups fish stock
1 teaspoon salt
1 teaspoon dulse, minced
1 dozen oysters, clams or scallops
2 tablespoons lemon juice
1 cup sweet cider

Heat oil in bottom of pot and in it lightly sauté all raw vegetables and garlic. Add tomatoes, herbs, flour, yeast, fish stock, salt and dulse. Cover. Simmer for 15 minutes. Remove bay leaf. Add shellfish, lemon juice and cider. Cook for 5 minutes longer. *Serves 6-8.*

## ITALIAN EGG SOUP

1 quart beef stock
1 cup tomato juice
4 eggs
1 1/2 tablespoons wholewheat flour
3 tablespoons nutritional yeast
3 tablespoons parsley, minced

Heat stock and tomato juice. Beat eggs. Blend flour and yeast into eggs. Gradually drizzle egg mixture into stock so that egg coagulates like fine strands of noodle. Serve garnished with parsley. *Serves 6.*

## NUT SOUP (in blender)

1 quart stock
1 cup milk
2 cups nuts
2 onions
3 tablespoons oil
1 teaspoon marjoram
1 teaspoon oregano
1 teaspoon salt

3 tablespoons nutritional yeast
1 tablespoon chives, minced

Gradually blend all ingredients, except chives, until smooth. Heat thoroughly. Garnish with chives. *Serves 6.*

## SOYBEAN SOUP

1 cup soybeans, cooked and sieved
1 cup stock
1 stalk celery and top, chopped
2 onions, chopped
1 cup tomatoes, stewed
½ cup turnip, grated
1 carrot, grated
½ green pepper, chopped
1 cup milk
1 tablespoon wholewheat flour
1 teaspoon salt
3 tablespoons nutritional yeast
1 teaspoon summer savory
1 teaspoon chervil

Combine all ingredients in pot. Cover. Simmer until vegetables are tender. *Serves 6.*

## CREAM OF SOY SOUP
(in blender)

3 cups soybeans, cooked, puréed
1½ cups milk
½ cup milk powder
1½ cups stock
½ teaspoon chervil
3 tablespoons nutritional yeast

Blend all ingredients together. Heat thoroughly. *Serves 6.*

## LENTIL SOUP

1½ cups lentils, washed
1½ quarts stock
½ teaspoon salt
3 tablespoons nutritional yeast
2 stalks celery and tops, chopped

1 tablespoon celery seeds, ground
1 onion, sliced
2 carrots, diced
1½ cups tomatoes, stewed
2 tablespoons oil
1 tablespoon lemon juice
½ teaspoon tarragon

Place lentils in pot. Add stock, salt and yeast. Cover. Simmer until almost tender. Add rest of ingredients. Cover. Simmer until carrots are done, about 15 minutes longer. *Serves 6.*

VARIATION:
For a thicker soup, purée cooked lentils and return to soup.

## LIMA BEAN SOUP

1 cup dried lima beans, washed
    and soaked overnight in
    1 quart stock
½ cup celery and tops, diced
½ cup carrots, diced
2 onions, quartered
3 tablespoons parsley, minced
1 cup greens (leek, escarole, etc.),
    chopped
¼ cup oil
1 cup tomatoes, stewed
¼ cup millet
½ teaspoon sage, ground
1 teaspoon caraway seeds, ground
3 tablespoons nutritional yeast
pinch of nutmeg, ground
grated cheese

Combine in pot all ingredients except cheese. Cover. Simmer until tender. Garnish with cheese. *Serves 6.*

VARIATIONS:
Substitute lentils or other dried beans for lima beans.
Substitute brown rice for millet. Cook 10 minutes longer.

## BLACK BEAN SOUP

3 tablespoons oil
1 onion, chopped
1 stalk celery and top, chopped
1½ cups black beans, soaked
    overnight in 1½ quarts
    stock
¼ teaspoon salt
3 tablespoons nutritional yeast
1 teaspoon celery seeds, ground
3 tablespoons wholewheat flour
1 teaspoon soy flour
juice of 2 lemons
1 or 2 hard-cooked eggs, sliced

Heat oil in bottom of pot and in it lightly sauté onion and celery. Add beans and stock. Cover. Simmer for 3 hours, or until beans are tender. Purée. Add salt, yeast, celery seeds, flours to purée and blend well. If too thick, add more stock. Cook until thoroughly heated. Add lemon juice. Blend. Garnish with egg slices. *Serves 6.*

## BEAN SPROUT SOUP

1½ quarts stock, seasoned
2 cups bean Sprouts
3 eggs, beaten
3 tablespoons parsley, minced

Heat stock. Add bean sprouts. Simmer for 3 minutes. Remove from heat. Stir in beaten eggs. Garnish with parsley. *Serves 6.*

## WHOLEWHEAT BERRY CHOWDER

3 tablespoons oil
1 tablespoon wholewheat flour
1 teaspoon soy flour
½ cup milk powder
3 tablespoons nutritional yeast
1 pint milk, warm
1 pint stock, warm
1 teaspoon Essence of Sweet Herbs
2 cups carrots, diced and cooked
2 cups wholewheat berries, cooked

1 onion, chopped, sautéed in oil
2 slices bacon, broiled, minced

Heat oil in bottom of soup pot. Mix flours, milk powder and yeast. Blend into paste with oil. Add milk and stir until smooth. Add stock and stir again. Add remaining ingredients, except bacon. Heat thoroughly. Garnish with bacon. *Serves 6.*

## HERBED RICE SOUP

3 cups stock
2 tablespoons wholewheat flour
½ teaspoon salt
3 tablespoons nutritional yeast
¼ cup milk powder
½ cup brown rice, raw
3 sprigs dill, chopped
1 teaspoon basil
½ cup milk
1 cup peas, raw
2 teaspoons oil
1 tablespoon lemon juice

Place stock in top of double boiler over direct heat. Mix flour, salt, yeast and milk powder together. When stock boils, add dry mixture. Blend thoroughly. Stir in rice. Place top over bottom of double boiler, to which hot water has been added. Simmer gently for 30 minutes. Add remaining ingredients. Heat thoroughly and serve. *Serves 6.*

## CEREAL SOUP

3 tablespoons oil
½ pound onions, sliced
¼ pound mushrooms, sliced
2 bay leaves
1 sprig parsley, minced
1 teaspoon chervil
3 tablespoons nutritional yeast
1 teaspoon soy flour
1 tablespoon each of barley, brown

rice, oats, millet, wholewheat,
whole rye and buckwheat,
soaked in
1½ quarts of stock for ½ hour

Heat oil in bottom of pot and in it
lightly sauté onions and mushrooms. Add bay leaves, parsley,
chervil, yeast and soy flour. Blend.
Cover pot. Steam gently for 5 minutes. In another pot, simmer grains
in stock ½ hour or until tender.
Combine with steamed onions and
mushrooms. Heat thoroughly. *Serves
6.*

## BUCKWHEAT AND POTATO SOUP

1½ quarts stock
4 potatoes, raw, cubed
2 large onions, sliced
¼ cup buckwheat groats
3 tablespoons nutritional yeast
1 cup milk
1 sprig parsley, minced
1 teaspoon oregano

Bring stock to boil. Add potatoes,
onions, buckwheat and yeast. Blend.
Cover. Simmer until potatoes are
tender. Stir in milk and herbs. Simmer 5 minutes longer. *Serves 6.*

## GERMAN GRUENKERN SOUP

1½ quarts stock
1½ cups gruenkern
3 tablespoons nutritional yeast
1 teaspoon soy flour
1 sprig dill, minced
½ cup onions, sliced and sautéed
in oil

Bring stock to boil. Slowly add
gruenkern, yeast and soy flour.
Blend. Cover. Simmer gently for 40
minutes. Add dill and onions and
serve. *Serves 6.*

## BASIC CREAM OF VEGETABLE SOUP (in blender)

1 quart milk
2 cups vegetable purée (celery, corn,
asparagus, tomatoes, cauliflower,
carrots, etc.)
¼ cup soy flour
3 tablespoons nutritional yeast
1 teaspoon salt
1 sachet Fines Herbes

Blend all ingredients together in
blender, except sachet. When
smooth, turn mixture into pot with
sachet. Heat thoroughly. Remove
sachet. Serve soup garnished with
toasted soybeans. *Serves 6.*

## WINTER BORSCHT

2 tablespoons oil
3 large onions, chopped
5 beets, grated
1 carrot, chopped
1 potato, cubed
1 head cabbage, shredded
stock to cover
2 cups tomatoes, stewed
1 sprig dill
1 tablespoon soy flour
3 tablespoons nutritional yeast
1 teaspoon salt

Heat oil in pot. Lightly sauté vegetables in oil. Pour in stock and
cover pot. Simmer until vegetables
are tender. Add remaining ingredients. Heat thoroughly. Garnish
with sour cream or yoghurt. *Serves
6.*

## POTATO SOUP

2 cups stock
4 potatoes, raw, cubed
1 teaspoon dill seeds, ground
1 cup onions or leek, chopped
2 cups milk
1 tablespoon soy flour
3 tablespoons nutritional yeast
½ teaspoon salt

[Recipe continued on next page]

[Recipe continued from previous page]

Bring stock to boil. Add potatoes, seeds and onions. Cover. Simmer until potatoes are tender. Purée. Mix milk with flour, yeast and salt. Add to purée. Blend thoroughly. Heat. Garnish with chopped chives if desired. *Serves 6.*

### DILLED VEGETABLE SOUP

2 tablespoons oil
2 onions, chopped
1 green pepper, chopped
2 cups cabbage, shredded
1 cup beans, cut
2 sprigs dill
1 leaf costmary or bay
2 cups tomatoes, stewed
2 cups milk
1 tablespoon wholewheat flour
1 teaspoon soy flour
3 tablespoons nutritional yeast

Heat oil in pot and sauté vegetables lightly in oil. Add herbs and tomatoes. Mix milk with flours and yeast. Blend into soup. Heat thoroughly. *Serves 6.*

### ONION SOUP

3 tablespoons oil
4 large Spanish onions, chopped
1 clove garlic, minced
3 cups stock
½ teaspoon tarragon
4 sprigs parsley, minced
1 cup tomato juice
1 tablespoon soy flour
3 tablespoons nutritional yeast
1 teaspoon salt
6 slices wholewheat bread, toasted
Parmesan cheese, grated

Heat oil in pot and in it lightly sauté onions and garlic. Add stock and herbs. Mix tomato juice with flour, yeast and salt. Blend and add to soup mixture. Cover pot. Sim-

mer 15 minutes. Serve topped with toast and cheese. *Serves 6.*

### PUMPKIN (or squash) SOUP

2 cups pumpkin, raw, cubed
2 cups stock
3 cups milk
1 tablespoon soy flour
½ cup milk powder
2 tablespoons oil
3 tablespoons nutritional yeast
1 tablespoon parsley, minced

Cook pumpkin or squash in stock until soft. Purée. Add remaining ingredients. Heat thoroughly. *Serves 6.*

### SQUASH-CHESTNUT SOUP

1 quart stock
1 cup squash, cubed
1 onion, chopped
¼ cup celery and tops, chopped
¼ cup carrots, cubed
½ pound chestnuts, shelled and boiled
1 bay leaf
1 cup milk
½ cup milk powder
1 teaspoon soy flour
3 tablespoons nutritional yeast
1 sprig parsley, minced

Heat stock. Add vegetables, chestnuts and bay leaf. Cover. Simmer until vegetables are tender. Remove bay leaf. Blend milk, milk powder, flour and yeast. Add to soup mixture. Heat thoroughly. Serve garnished with parsley. *Serves 6.*

### QUICK CARROT SOUP

3 tablespoons oil
3 onions, chopped
3 tablespoons wholewheat flour
1 teaspoon soy flour

½ cup milk powder
½ teaspoon salt
3 tablespoons nutritional yeast
1 bay leaf
1 quart milk, hot
1 cup carrots, grated fine
¼ teaspoon thyme
½ teaspoon cumin seeds, crushed

Heat oil and in it lightly sauté onions. Blend flours, milk powder, salt, yeast and bay leaf in milk. Stir into onions. Add carrots, thyme and cumin seeds. Cover. Simmer gently for 10 minutes. *Serves 6.*

## EGGPLANT SOUP

2 cups eggplant, raw, cubed
stock to cover
1 cup milk
3 tablespoons nutritional yeast
1 teaspoon basil
¼ cup parsley, minced

Combine eggplant and stock in pot and cover. Simmer for 8 minutes. Blend milk with remaining ingredients. Gradually blend with soup mixture. Heat thoroughly. *Serves 6.*

## CREAM OF SPINACH SOUP
(in blender)

1 quart stock
2 pounds spinach, washed, stemmed
2 tablespoons wheat germ
2 tablespoons oil
1 onion, cut
1 teaspoon salt
3 tablespoons nutritional yeast
1 tablespoon soy flour
½ cup milk powder
pinch of nutmeg, ground

Gradually blend all ingredients together in blender. Turn mixture into pot. Cover. Heat thoroughly. Garnish with sesame seeds. *Serves 6.*

VARIATIONS:
Lettuce or parsley may be substituted for the spinach.

## TOMATO SOUP (in blender)

2 cups tomatoes, stewed
1 quart milk
3 tablespoons wholewheat flour
1 teaspoon soy flour
3 tablespoons nutritional yeast
1 onion, cut
1 teaspoon salt
½ cup sunflower seeds, hulled

Gradually blend all ingredients together. Turn mixture into pot. Cover. Heat thoroughly. Garnish with fresh mint. *Serves 6.*

## GREEK LEMON SOUP

1½ quarts stock
½ cup brown rice, raw
¼ teaspoon savory
3 tablespoons nutritional yeast
4 eggs, beaten
juice and rind of 1 lemon

Heat stock in pot. When stock boils, stir in rice. Cover pot. Simmer 30 minutes. Mix savory and yeast with eggs. Add lemon juice and rind and mix again. Gradually add ½ cup of hot stock to egg-lemon mixture, stirring constantly. Remove pot from heat. Add egg mixture to soup. Garnish with minced chives, if desired, and serve. *Serves 6.*

## Summer Soups (Chilled)

### AVOCADO SOUP
(in blender: uncooked)

2 avocados, peeled and pitted
1 quart stock
2 cups yoghurt *
3 tablespoons nutritional yeast

[Recipe continued on next page]

[Recipe continued from previous page]
Blend all ingredients until smooth. Chill. Garnish with nasturtium blossoms. *Serves 6.*

## SOY-VEGETABLE SOUP
### (in blender: uncooked)

½ cup onions, cut
1 green pepper, cut
1 avocado, peeled and pitted
1 sprig parsley
1 quart soy milk
1 teaspoon salt
3 tablespoons nutritional yeast
¼ cup wheat germ

Put all ingredients in blender and blend until smooth. Chill. *Serves 6.*

## MADRILÈNE

3 cups stock, seasoned
3 cups tomatoes, stewed
½ cup onion, chopped
1 cup carrots, chopped
½ cup turnip, chopped
½ cup celery, chopped
1 sprig parsley
1 sprig thyme

Cook all ingredients together slowly until vegetables and their juices have thoroughly flavored stock. Strain. Chill. Garnish with Sprouts. *Serves 6.*

## VICHYSSOISE

3 tablespoons oil
3 leeks, chopped
1 onion, chopped
3 potatoes, cubed
1 quart chicken stock
1 teaspoon salt
2 cups milk
½ cup milk powder
1 tablespoon soy flour
3 tablespoons nutritional yeast
1 cup yoghurt *
¼ cup chives, minced

Heat oil in pot and in it sauté leeks and onions. Add potatoes, stock and salt and cover. Simmer for 30 minutes. Purée mixture. Return to pot. Add mixture of milk, milk powder, soy flour and yeast. Cover and heat just until soup comes to a boil. Remove from heat. Chill. Blend in yoghurt. Serve garnished with chives. *Serves 6.*

## GAZPACHO
### (in blender: uncooked)

1 clove garlic
1 green pepper, cut
1 Spanish onion, cut
½ cup mixture of chives, parsley, basil, thyme, tarragon, chervil
1 pint chicken stock
1 pint meat stock
1 pint tomato juice
juice of 2 lemons
3 tablespoons oil
1 cucumber, peeled and diced
1 tomato, chopped

Blend garlic, pepper, onion, herbs and stock in blender until smooth. Add rest of ingredients. Blend thoroughly. Chill at least 8 hours before serving. *Serves 6.*

## HERB SOUP
### (in blender: uncooked)

1½ quarts stock
1 small head lettuce, cut into pieces
1 bunch water cress
1 bunch sorrel
1 sprig parsley
3 tablespoons chives
1 teaspoon chervil
3 tablespoons nutritional yeast
1 egg yolk
1 teaspoon Essence of Sweet Herbs

Blend all ingredients until smooth.

Chill. Garnish with yoghurt. *Serves 6.*

## WATER CRESS SOUP
### (in blender: uncooked)

1 quart stock
2 bunches water cress
1 teaspoon salt
3 tablespoons nutritional yeast
1 teaspoon soy flour
1 cup yoghurt *

Blend all ingredients until smooth. Chill. Garnish with nasturtium blossoms. *Serves 6.*

## RUSSIAN BEET BORSCHT
### (in blender)

1 quart stock
1 cup beet juice
1 cup beets, cooked and cubed
juice and rind of 1 lemon
1 cup yoghurt *
1 teaspoon soy flour
3 tablespoons nutritional yeast
½ teaspoon salt
1 sprig parsley
½ teaspoon tarragon

Blend all ingredients until smooth. Chill. Serve garnished with minced chives. *Serves 6.*

## SPINACH SOUP (in blender)

1½ quarts stock
2 pounds spinach, raw, stemmed
½ teaspoon salt
1 teaspoon soy flour
½ cup milk powder
3 tablespoons nutritional yeast
3 tablespoons parsley
pinch of nutmeg, ground

Bring stock to boil in large pot. Remove from heat. Add spinach and cover. When cool, pour into blender with remaining ingredients. Gradually blend until smooth. Chill. Gar-

nish each serving with dab of yoghurt. *Serves 6.*

## TOMATO SOUP
### (in blender: uncooked)

6 tomatoes, raw, cubed
1 onion, cut
1 cup stock
1 cup Nut Cream
3 tablespoons nutritional yeast
1 tablespoon chives

Blend all ingredients until smooth. Chill. Garnish with toasted soybeans. *Serves 6.*

## EAST INDIAN COCONUT SOUP
### (in blender: uncooked)

1 quart stock
1 cup milk
1 coconut (meat cut in chunks, and juice)
¼ cup milk powder
1 teaspoon soy flour
3 tablespoons nutritional yeast
juice and rind of 1 lemon
1 sprig parsley

Blend all ingredients together until smooth. Chill. Garnish with Sprouts. *Serves 6.*

## TURKISH YOGHURT SOUP
### (in blender: uncooked)

1 pint yoghurt *
3 cucumbers, chopped
juice and rind of 1 lemon
1 teaspoon dill
1 clove garlic
3 tablespoons nutritional yeast
1 teaspoon soy flour
3 tablespoons oil
1 teaspoon dill seeds
1 tablespoon mint leaves

Blend all ingredients together until smooth. Chill. *Serves 6.*

## BUTTERMILK SOUP
### (in blender: uncooked)

1 quart buttermilk *
3 eggs
3 tablespoons honey
1 teaspoon vanilla extract
juice and rind of 1 lemon
pinch of mace, ground

Blend all ingredients together until smooth. Chill. Garnish with thin slices of cucumber. *Serves 6.*

## FRUIT SOUP
### (in blender: uncooked)

1 pint Nut Milk
1 pint fresh fruit or berries
1 tablespoon honey
1 sprig mint

Blend all ingredients together until smooth. Chill. *Serves 6.*

# Soup Garnishes

These garnishes will add nourishment, variety and eye appeal to soups:
grated cheese
soy cheese
sesame seeds, sunflower seeds, etc.
dab of yoghurt
dab of sour cream
wheat germ
wholewheat croutons
homemade cracker crumbs
Sprouts
leftover bacon, crumbled
Toasted Soybeans
hard-cooked egg whites
hard-cooked egg yolks
grated or slivered nuts
thin slices of lemon
leftover unsweetened pancakes, cut into strips
minced parsley
minced celery leaves
minced chives
minced mint leaves
nasturtium blossoms
grated raw carrot
grated raw turnip
grated raw beet
paper-thin slices of radishes
paper-thin slices of cucumbers
grated coconut

*The recipes that follow are for garnishes of a heartier variety. They are especially good in clear soups and broths, and some also go well with stews. Quantities are to serve 6.*

## CZECH LIVER DUMPLINGS

¼ cup oil
3 eggs, slightly beaten
1 clove garlic, minced
rind of 1 lemon, grated
pinch of allspice, ground
1 pound calf's liver, sliced, cooked, ground
3 tablespoons nutritional yeast
3 tablespoons parsley, minced
¼ teaspoon salt
wholewheat bread crumbs

Blend all ingredients, adding enough breadcrumbs to make stiff batter. Let batter stand for 30 minutes. Then form into small balls. Drop into simmering soup. Cover pot. Simmer, without lifting cover, for 20 minutes.

## LITHUANIAN LIVER DUMPLINGS

½ pound liver, cooked and ground
¼ pound bacon, broiled and crumbled
2 eggs, slightly beaten
3 tablespoons oil
¼ teaspoon salt
2 tablespoons nutritional yeast
1 tablespoon parsley, minced

¼ teaspoon thyme
½ teaspoon savory
¼ teaspoon marjoram
1 cup wholewheat bread crumbs
½ cup wheat germ

Combine all ingredients and blend thoroughly. If mixture is too loose, bind with milk powder. Form into small balls. Drop into pot of simmering soup. Cover tightly. Simmer, without lifting cover, for 20 minutes.

VARIATION:
Chopped celery leaves or spinach leaves may be added to batter.

## NUT DUMPLINGS

½ cup nuts, ground
½ cup wholewheat bread crumbs
2 eggs, beaten
1 tablespoon soy flour
3 tablespoons wheat germ
2 tablespoons nutritional yeast
2 tablespoons milk
2 tablespoons oil
½ cup milk powder
pinch of nutmeg, ground

Combine all ingredients. Blend thoroughly. If mixture is too loose, bind with more milk powder. Form into balls the size of walnuts. Drop into pot of simmering soup or stew. Cover tightly. Simmer for 5 minutes.

## WHOLEWHEAT DUMPLINGS

1 pint stock
¼ teaspoon savory
½ teaspoon salt
2 tablespoons nutritional yeast
2 cups wholewheat flour
4 eggs

Heat stock. Combine savory, salt, yeast and flour. Blend with stock and keep over heat, stirring until

mixture forms ball and leaves sides of pan. Remove from stove. Cool slightly. Add whole eggs, one at a time. Beat until smooth. Drop from teaspoon into simmering soup. Cover. Simmer for 5 minutes.

## WHOLEWHEAT SPONGE DUMPLINGS

6 eggs, separated
1 pint stock
½ teaspoon salt
1 tablespoon parsley, minced
2 tablespoons nutritional yeast
2 cups wholewheat flour

Beat egg yolks. Add to stock and blend. Add remaining ingredients, except egg whites. Blend again. Fold in stiffly beaten egg whites. Turn mixture into oiled custard cups, and set in pan of hot water. Steam in oven at 350° F. until firm. Cool. Remove dumplings from cups. Cut into small pieces and serve in hot, clear soup.

## FISH-CORNMEAL BALLS

1 cup fish, cooked, flaked
2 cups cornmeal mush, cooked
1 egg
1 tablespoon oil
1 tablespoon soy flour
1 tablespoon dulse, minced
2 tablespoons nutritional yeast
½ teaspoon fennel seeds, ground
3 tablespoons chives, minced
wheat germ

Combine all ingredients and mold into balls. Roll in wheat germ. Drop into simmering fish stock or soup. Cover. Simmer for 10 minutes.

VARIATION:
Shape mixture into patties. Broil until brown on each side.

## CORNMEAL DUMPLINGS

2 cups cornmeal
1 teaspoon salt
2 tablespoons nutritional yeast
1 egg, beaten
boiling stock
rice flour, for dredging

Mix cornmeal, salt and yeast. Blend in egg. Pour enough stock over mixture to make a thick paste. Stir thoroughly. Form small balls. Dredge in flour. Drop dumplings into simmering soup or stew. Cover. Simmer 10 to 15 minutes.

## MASHED POTATO DUMPLINGS

1 cup potatoes, mashed
½ cup wholewheat bread crumbs
½ cup wheat germ
2 tablespoons oil
2 eggs, beaten
2 tablespoons milk
½ cup milk powder
2 tablespoons nutritional yeast
¼ teaspoon thyme
¼ teaspoon salt

Blend all ingredients. Dough should be firm. If it is too loose, add more wheat germ; if too stiff, add more liquid milk. Shape into balls the size of walnuts. Roll in wheat germ. Drop into simmering soup or stew. Cover pot. Simmer for 3 minutes.

## FISH BALLS

2 pounds fresh fish in any desired combination
1 egg
2 tablespoons wheat germ
1 tablespoon soy flour
1 tablespoon dulse, minced
2 tablespoons nutritional yeast
pinch of mace, ground
2 tablespoons parsley, minced
1 sprig mint, minced

Grind raw fish. Combine with remaining ingredients. Shape into balls. Drop into simmering fish stock or soup. Cover. Simmer for 10 minutes.

## CHEESE CUBES

2 eggs, beaten
3 tablespoons oil
6 slices wholewheat toast, cubed
1 cup cheddar or Swiss cheese, grated

Mix eggs and oil. Dip bread cubes in batter. Roll in cheese. Place on oiled cooky sheet and bake in 375° F. oven for 6 or 7 minutes. Use as garnish for soup or tossed salads.

## RICE SQUARES

1 cup brown rice, cooked
1 small onion, grated
2 tablespoons nutritional yeast
1 egg, beaten
¼ teaspoon salt
pinch of nutmeg, ground

Blend all ingredients. Pat mixture into oiled pan, to depth of ½ inch. Bake in 300° F. oven for 30 minutes or until dry and firm. Cool. Cut into 1-inch squares. Use as garnish for hot soups or stews.

## WHOLEWHEAT NOODLES

3 egg yolks
1 whole egg
¼ cup stock
1 teaspoon salt
1 tablespoon nutritional yeast
2 cups soft wholewheat flour (see p. 168)

Beat egg and egg yolks together until very light. Add remaining ingredients. Blend well. Divide into thirds. Roll each third, as thin as possible, on a lightly floured board or a pastry cloth. Place rolled dough between two clean towels and let remain until partly dry. Then carefully remove by rolling over, like a jelly roll. Place on a wooden board. With a very sharp knife, cut into fine strips. Shake out. Dry thoroughly. Store in a tightly closed jar until used.

## SOY NOODLES

1 cup soy flour
¼ teaspoon salt
1 egg, beaten
3 tablespoons milk

Sift soy flour and salt. Blend well with egg and milk. Knead. Chill. Roll out thin. Let dry for 15 minutes. Cut into fine noodle strips with a very sharp knife. Drop into simmering soup. Cover. Simmer for about 10 minutes or until tender. If noodles are not to be used immediately, let dry thoroughly and store in tightly closed jar.

## FLOURLESS NOODLES

1 cup milk powder
½ teaspoon salt
1 teaspoon nutritional yeast
2 eggs
½ cup milk
boiling water

In a large bowl, blend milk powder with salt and yeast. Break eggs into mixture, one at a time. Mix well. Add liquid milk gradually and mix again. Heat unoiled skillet or soapstone griddle and pour batter into pan. Brown on both sides. Place between two layers of clean towels and let remain until batter is partly dry. Carefully remove batter by rolling over like a jelly roll. Place batter on wooden board. Cut with very sharp knife into fine strips. Drop strips into boiling water. When noodles are completely coagulated and firm, lift them out of the water. Spread on towel and dry thoroughly. Store in tightly closed jar.

# 7

# VEGETABLES

Steam vegetables briefly. Place a clove of garlic or a sliced onion in steaming water to flavor vegetables. Save water for stock.

## Asparagus

HINT:
Flavorings: chives, parsley, chervil, ground nuts, tarragon vinegar, yoghurt, sour cream, grated cheese, broiled bits of bacon.

### ASPARAGUS SOUFFLÉ

3 tablespoons oil
3 tablespoons wholewheat flour
3 tablespoons nutritional yeast
½ cup milk powder
3 tablespoons parsley, minced
1 cup milk
4 eggs, separated
2½ cups asparagus, cooked, cut

Blend oil, flour, yeast, milk powder and parsley in top of double boiler. Gradually add liquid milk. Blend. Set on bottom of double boiler, to which hot water has been added, and cook, stirring, until mixture thickens slightly. Cool to lukewarm. Gradually beat in egg yolks. Add asparagus. Fold in stiffly beaten egg whites. Turn into oiled casserole or oiled individual custard cups. Bake at 325° F. for about 45 minutes, until soufflé is set. *Serves 6.*

### ASPARAGUS LOAF

3 cups asparagus, cooked, cut
2 eggs, beaten
½ teaspoon salt
⅓ cup wheat germ
⅓ cup soy grits, soaked in
⅓ cup stock
2 tablespoons oil
1 onion, grated
½ cup milk powder
3 tablespoons nutritional yeast
1 teaspoon sweet basil
1½ cups hot milk

Blend all ingredients together. Turn into oiled loaf pan. Bake at 350° F. for about 30 minutes. *Serves 6.*

## Beets

HINTS:
Bake or boil whole beets in their skins.
Steam diced or sliced beets. Cooking time may be reduced by grating beets.

Use beet tops. Cook by steaming or, if young and crisp, toss in mixed salad.

Flavorings: dill, tarragon, parsley, mint, thyme, yoghurt, sour cream, tarragon vinegar, grated nuts, Powdered Orange Rind.

### BEETS IN YOGHURT

3 cups beets, grated
beet tops, minced
pinch of salt
1 bay leaf
⅛ teaspoon basil
¼ cup stock
1 teaspoon honey
¼ cup yoghurt *

Place beets, tops, salt, bay leaf, basil and stock in steamer. Cover. Steam gently for 5 minutes. Remove bay leaf. Blend in honey and yoghurt. *Serves 6.*

### BEET SOUFFLÉ (in blender)

2 cups beets, steamed and grated
½ cup beet tops, steamed and minced
1 cup beet juice
3 tablespoons oil
3 tablespoons wholewheat flour
3 tablespoons nutritional yeast
½ cup milk powder
¼ teaspoon tarragon
1 teaspoon Essence of Sweet Herbs
4 eggs, separated

Blend all ingredients except egg whites in blender until smooth. Fold in stiffly beaten egg whites. Turn into oiled casserole or oiled individual custard cups. Bake at 375° F. for about 30 minutes, until soufflé is firm. *Serves 6.*

OTHER RECIPES USING BEETS:
See: Borscht; Autumn Salad; Beet Dressing; Beet Molded Salad.

# Broccoli, Brussels Sprouts, Cauliflower

HINTS:
Steam broccoli or cauliflower whole or in pieces. Cook briefly; they should still have a firm texture when done.
Young, tender leaves of cauliflower and broccoli are good to eat.
Garnish with one of the following: Nut Butter, poppy seeds, grated cheese, wheat germ, ground nuts, ground, Roasted Soybeans, sesame seeds, hulled sunflower seeds, lemon juice, yoghurt, pinch of ground nutmeg. Or serve with a vegetable sauce (recipes at the end of this chapter).

### BRUSSELS SPROUTS CASSEROLE

1½ pounds Brussels sprouts, steamed
1 cup tomatoes, stewed
½ cup cheddar cheese, grated
¼ teaspoon nutmeg, grated
1 cup yoghurt *
½ cup Soybeans, Roasted

Arrange Brussels sprouts in oiled casserole. Cover with tomatoes. Sprinkle with cheese and nutmeg. Cover. Bake at 350° F. for 15 minutes. Serve garnished with yoghurt and soybeans. *Serves 6.*

### BAKED BROCCOLI CASSEROLE

3 cups broccoli, steamed, cut into bite-size pieces
1 cup leftovers (meat, fish, fowl, beans), cut into bite-size pieces
1 cup seasoned stock
3 tablespoons nutritional yeast
3 tablespoons wholewheat flour
1 cup cheese, grated

Arrange layer of broccoli at bottom of oiled casserole. Top with layer

[Recipe continued on next page]

[Recipe continued from previous page]
of leftovers. Alternate layers, ending with broccoli. Blend stock with yeast and flour. Pour over casserole and sprinkle cheese on top. Bake at 350° F. for 30 minutes. Serves 6.

## BAKED CAULIFLOWER-NUT CASSEROLE (in blender)

½ cup seasoned stock
3 cups cauliflower, steamed
¼ cup oil
½ cup cheese, grated
½ cup nuts, ground
3 tablespoons nutritional yeast
3 tablespoons soy flour
½ cup wheat germ

Blend stock and cauliflower in blender until puréed, then blend with remaining ingredients. Turn into oiled casserole. Bake at 350° F. for 20 minutes. Serves 6.

# Cabbage

HINTS:
To shorten cooking time, shred cabbage or cut into wedges. Steam briefly. Cabbage should still be firm when done.
Use outer leaves for soup.
Flavorings good with cabbage: caraway, celery, dill, poppy or sesame seeds; broiled bacon bits; grated cheese or nuts; yoghurt, sour cream.

## SAUTÉED CABBAGE

4 cups cabbage, shredded
3 tablespoons oil
1 tablespoon caraway seeds
2 cups Sprouts

Sauté cabbage briefly in oil. Cabbage should be almost raw and still crisp, but slightly browned. Remove from heat. Toss with seeds and sprouts. Serves 6.

## CABBAGE WITH YOGHURT

4 cups red or green cabbage, shredded
1 onion, grated
3 tablespoons oil
¼ cup cider vinegar *
¼ cup seasoned stock
¼ cup yoghurt *

Sauté cabbage and onion briefly in oil. Add vinegar and stock. Cover. Simmer gently for 5 minutes. Remove from heat. Blend in yoghurt. Serves 6.

## CABBAGE, SWEET AND SOUR

4 cups red or green cabbage, shredded
3 onions, grated
juice of 2 lemons
4 tart apples with skins, diced
¼ cup sweet cider
3 tablespoons honey
2 tablespoons oil
1 tablespoon caraway seeds
½ cup seedless raisins
pinch of allspice, ground

Blend all ingredients in saucepan. Cover. Simmer gently for 10 minutes. Serves 6.

## STUFFED CABBAGE ROLLS

STUFFING:
Blend the following ingredients:

1 cup brown rice, cooked
¼ cup nuts, coarsely ground
¼ cup soy grits, soaked in
¼ cup stock
½ cup seedless raisins or currants
3 tablespoons nutritional yeast

1 tablespoon parsley, minced
1 stalk fennel, chopped

WRAPPER:
1 head of cabbage, parboiled
Carefully remove large outer leaves from cabbage head to use as wrappers. Cut tough ribs away from center of leaf. Steam briefly so leaves will be pliable. Place portion of stuffing in center of each leaf. Roll up and tie with white thread. Shred remaining cabbage. Place shredded cabbage at bottom of oiled casserole. Arrange stuffed cabbage rolls on top. Cover and bake for about 30 minutes at 300° F., adding small amount of stock, if dry. *Serves 6.*

VARIATIONS:
Add one or more of these to stuffing: green pepper, carrot, celery, mushroom, tomato.
Substitute other cooked grains, such as bulgur or buckwheat, for the rice.
Use grated cheese instead of raisins or currants.

OTHER RECIPES USING CABBAGE
See: Winter Borscht; Cabbage Slaw; Golden Slaw; Cole Slaw Dressing; Winter Molded Salad; Homemade Sauerkraut; Sauerkraut Appetizers.

## Carrots

HINTS:
Clean carrots by scrubbing with brush. Vitamins and minerals are close to the skin.
Steaming time may be reduced by grating.
Flavorings: tarragon, parsley, thyme, bay leaf, oregano, mint, chives, nutmeg, grated cheese, sour cream.

## CARROT LOAF

2 cups raw carrots, grated fine
1 cup whole-grain bread crumbs
⅓ cup soy flour
3 eggs, beaten
1½ cups stewed tomatoes
½ teaspoon salt
3 tablespoons nutritional yeast
½ teaspoon marjoram
1 tablespoon parsley, minced
1 teaspoon honey
1 onion, grated
½ cup leftover meat, fish or fowl, ground
¼ cup soy grits, soaked in
¼ cup stock

Blend all ingredients. Turn into oiled loaf pan. Bake at 350° F. for 1 hour. *Serves 6.*

## CARROTS POULETTE

3 tablespoons oil
3 tablespoons wholewheat flour
¼ teaspoon salt
3 tablespoons nutritional yeast
2 cups of chicken stock
½ cup yoghurt *
1 bay leaf
¼ teaspoon thyme
1 tablespoon parsley, minced
2 egg yolks
6 carrots, cubed, steamed
1 tablespoon chives, minced

Blend oil, flour, salt, yeast and stock in top of double boiler. Cook over direct heat until mixture comes to boil. Lower heat. Place over bottom of double boiler, to which hot water has been added. Gradually add yoghurt, stirring constantly. Add bay leaf, thyme and parsley. Blend small amount of hot mixture with beaten egg yolks. Gradually add egg-yolk mixture to sauce in double boiler. Continue to stir. When mixture thickens, add carrots. Heat thoroughly. Garnish with chives and serve. *Serves 6.*

## GLAZED CARROTS AND ONIONS

1 dozen small carrots
1 dozen small white onions
seasoned stock to cover
3 tablespoons oil
3 tablespoons honey
½ teaspoon tarragon

Cover carrots and onions with stock. Simmer gently until tender. Arrange vegetables in oiled casserole, reserving stock for soup. Blend remaining ingredients and pour mixture over vegetables. Bake at 350° F. for 20 minutes. *Serves 6.*

## CARROT CUSTARD
(to accompany entrée)

3 cups hot milk
½ cup milk powder
½ teaspoon salt
3 tablespoons nutritional yeast
pinch of nutmeg, ground
3 tablespoons oil
3 tablespoons soy flour
½ teaspoon marjoram
2 cups raw carrots (or turnips),
    grated fine or cooked and puréed
4 eggs

Blend milk, milk powder, salt, yeast, nutmeg, oil, soy flour, marjoram and carrots. Add eggs, one at a time. Beat well. Turn mixture into oiled casserole or oiled individual custard cups. Bake at 350° F. until custard is set in center; allow about 1 hour for large casserole, 50 minutes for cups. *Serves 6.*

## CARROT SOUFFLÉ

3 tablespoons oil
3 tablespoons wholewheat flour
2 tablespoons nutritional yeast
½ cup milk powder
pinch of nutmeg, ground

1 cup milk
4 eggs, separated
1½ cups carrots, cooked and puréed

Blend oil, flour, yeast, milk powder and nutmeg in top of double boiler. Gradually add liquid milk and blend again. Set over bottom part of double boiler, to which hot water has been added. Cook, stirring meanwhile, until mixture is slightly thickened. Cool to lukewarm. Gradually beat in egg yolks. Add carrot purée. Fold in stiffly beaten egg whites. Turn into oiled casserole or oiled individual custard cups. Bake at 375° F. for 30-40 minutes, until soufflé is slightly browned. *Serves 6.*

## BAKED CARROT RING
(in blender)

3 cups carrots, cooked
4 eggs
1 onion
3 tablespoons parsley
1 tablespoon oil
3 tablespoons nutritional yeast
½ teaspoon salt
½ teaspoon tarragon
1 tablespoon honey
½ cup wheat germ

Blend all ingredients except wheat germ. Turn into bowl. Stir in wheat germ. Turn into oiled ring mold. Set in shallow pan of water. Bake until firm, about 30 minutes at 375° F. *Serves 6.*

## CARROT-SOYBEAN RING

3 cups carrots, raw and grated
3 eggs
½ teaspoon salt
3 tablespoons nutritional yeast
3 tablespoons oil
½ cup milk
¼ cup soy grits

½ cup milk powder
1 tablespoon mint, chopped
1 cup green soybeans, cooked and hot

Mix all ingredients except soybeans. Turn into oiled ring mold. Set in shallow pan of water. Bake until firm, about 30 minutes, at 325° F. Turn mold onto hot platter. Fill center with soybeans. *Serves 6.*

OTHER RECIPES USING CARROTS
See: Quick Carrot Soup; Carrot-Cheese Soup; Rice-Carrot Casserole; Carrot Custard Dessert; Carrot-Molasses Cookies; Golden Cookies; Carrot-Chiffon Pie Filling; Carrot-Rhubarb Jam; Carrot Molded Salad; Carrot Dressing.

# Corn

HINT:
Corn can be left in the husk and steamed. If husked, steam or boil briefly.

## BAKED CORN PUDDING
(to accompany entrée)

2½ cups milk
3 tablespoons cornmeal
1 teaspoon salt
2 tablespoons nutritional yeast
1 tablespoon soy flour
1 tablespoon oil
2 cups corn, cooked
2 eggs, beaten
1 tablespoon green pepper, chopped
1 teaspoon savory

Heat 2 cups of the milk in top of double boiler over direct heat. Blend remaining ½ cup cold milk with cornmeal, salt, yeast and soy flour. Gradually add this to hot milk. Stir until well blended. Place over bottom of double boiler to which hot water has been added. Cover and continue cooking, stirring frequently, until mixture thickens. Remove from heat. Blend in remaining ingredients. Turn into oiled casserole. Set in shallow pan of hot water. Bake at 350° F. until center is firm, about 30 minutes. *Serves 4-6.*

## CORN-SOY GRITS CASSEROLE

2 cups corn, cooked
½ cup soy grits, soaked in
¼ cup milk
1¼ cups milk, scalded, cooled to lukewarm
3 eggs, beaten
2 tablespoons oil
½ teaspoon salt
3 tablespoons nutritional yeast
½ green pepper, chopped
1 onion, grated
1 teaspoon rosemary

Blend all ingredients. Turn into oiled casserole. Set in shallow pan of hot water. Bake at 350° F. for about 1 hour, until set. *Serves 6.*

## CORN-COTTAGE CHEESE CASSEROLE

2 cups corn, cooked
2 cups tomatoes, stewed
1 onion, grated
1 green pepper, chopped
½ cup wheat germ
½ cup Soybeans, Roasted, ground
1 tablespoon oil
3 tablespoons nutritional yeast
½ teaspoon chervil
2 cups cottage cheese *

Blend all ingredients except cottage cheese. Divide mixture in half. Turn one half into oiled casserole. Spread cottage cheese on top; then spread remaining vegetable mixture on top of cottage cheese. Bake for 20 minutes at 350° F. *Serves 6.*

## CORN-SOYBEAN SUCCOTASH

2 cups corn, cooked
2 cups green soybeans, cooked
¼ cup seasoned stock
1 tablespoon oil
1 tablespoon parsley, minced
pinch of nutmeg, ground

Combine all ingredients. Heat thoroughly. *Serves 6.*

## CORN-CHEESE PIE (in blender)

Cheddar Cheese Pie Dough to line
    1 9-inch pie plate
1 cup yoghurt *
½ teaspoon salt
½ green pepper
1 onion
¼ cup parsley
2 eggs
2 cups corn, cooked
½ cup wheat germ
3 tablespoons nutritional yeast
1 teaspoon basil
2 tablespoons soy flour
½ cup cheese, grated

Blend all ingredients except cheese in blender. Turn into pie plate lined with dough. Sprinkle with cheese. Bake until center is firm, 10 minutes at 450° F., then about 25 minutes at 350° F. *Serves 6.*

# Eggplant

## BAKED STUFFED EGGPLANT

2 eggplants, parboiled, whole
stuffing (see below)

Cut eggplant in half. Scoop out pulp to within ¾ inch of skin. Dice pulp and blend with filling. Pack into eggplant shell. Place in shallow pan. Bake at 350° F. for about 30 minutes. *Serves 6.*

STUFFINGS:

*No. 1*
eggplant pulp, diced
¼ cup parsley, minced
1 onion, minced
2 raw eggs
¼ teaspoon salt
1 green pepper, minced
1 stalk celery and top, chopped
3 tablespoons nutritional yeast
pinch of sage
¼ teaspoon marjoram
¼ cup nuts, ground
¼ cup Soybeans, Roasted, ground
1 cup whole-grain bread crumbs
½ cup wheat germ

Blend all ingredients together. If mixture is dry, moisten with small amount of stock.

*No. 2*
eggplant pulp, diced
3 onions, chopped
2 tomatoes, diced
1 cup brown rice, cooked
¼ cup soy grits, soaked in
¼ cup stock
1 clove garlic, minced
¼ cup cheese, grated
2 tablespoons oil
3 tablespoons nutritional yeast
½ teaspoon salt
1 teaspoon oregano

Blend all ingredients together.

## EGGPLANT CASSEROLE

3 small eggplants
3 tablespoons oil
½ clove garlic, minced
½ teaspoon mint, minced
1 cup cheese, grated
2 cups stewed tomatoes
1 onion, sliced
1 stalk celery and top, chopped

Leave skins on eggplants. Wash. Slice into rounds about ¼-inch thick. Sauté in oil with garlic and mint. Arrange a layer of eggplant slices in bottom of oiled casserole. Add layer of cheese, tomatoes, onion and celery. Alternate layers until all ingredients are used, topping with cheese. Bake at 350° F. for about 30 minutes. *Serves 6.*

## BAKED EGGPLANT SLICES

3 small eggplants
3 tablespoons oil
¼ teaspoon basil
1 cup cheese, grated

Leave skins on eggplants. Wash. Slice into rounds about ¼-inch thick. Brush both sides with oil. Arrange on cooky sheets. Sprinkle with basil. Bake at 350° F., 10 minutes on each side. Sprinkle cheese on top. Put under broiler till cheese bubbles. *Serves 6.*

## EGGPLANT SOUFFLÉ

1½ cups milk
3 tablespoons cornmeal
1½ cups eggplant, cooked and puréed
½ cup milk powder
½ teaspoon salt
2 tablespoons nutritional yeast
½ teaspoon oregano
½ teaspoon basil
4 eggs, separated

Heat milk over hot water in double boiler. Sprinkle cornmeal over milk and stir until smooth, continuing to cook. Cover. Let cook gently for 1 hour, stirring occasionally until thickened. Remove from heat. Add remaining ingredients, except eggs. When cool, add egg yolks and blend well. Fold in stiffly beaten egg whites. Turn into oiled casserole or

oiled custard cups. Bake at 400° F. for 15 minutes, then lower oven temperature to 325° F. and bake for 30-40 minutes longer, or until center is firm. *Serves 6.*

## EGGPLANT LOAF

3 cups eggplant, cooked and puréed
⅓ cup oil
1 onion, grated
½ cup nuts, ground
¼ cup Soybeans, Roasted, ground
dash of allspice, ground
¼ cup celery and tops, chopped
1 egg
3 tablespoons nutritional yeast
1½ cups whole-grain bread crumbs
¼ cup soy grits, soaked in
¼ cup stock

Blend all ingredients together. Turn into oiled loaf pan. Bake at 350° F. for 25-30 minutes. *Serves 6.*

# Onions, Parsnips

SUGGESTED FLAVORINGS FOR ONIONS:
yoghurt, sour cream, grated nuts, cloves, parsley, mint, nutmeg, caraway seeds.

## BAKED ONION RING
## (in blender)

1 cup onions, steamed
½ cup milk
2 tablespoons oil
2 tablespoons wholewheat flour
¼ cup milk powder
2 tablespoons nutritional yeast
1 teaspoon celery seeds
½ teaspoon salt
1 teaspoon savory
½ cup cheese
3 eggs, separated

Blend all ingredients except egg whites. Turn mixture into top of

[Recipe continued on next page]

[Recipe continued from previous page]

double boiler. Set on bottom of double boiler, to which hot water has been added. Cook until mixture thickens, stirring occasionally. Remove from heat. Fold in stiffly beaten egg whites. Turn into oiled ring mold. Set in shallow pan of hot water. Bake at 350° F., about 1 hour, until set. *Serves 6.*

## ONION PIE

PIE SHELL:

2 cups rye or wholewheat flour or 1 cup of each
½ teaspoon salt
¼ cup oil
1 tablespoon poppy seeds
ice-cold water

Blend all ingredients, adding only enough water to make firm dough. Pat into two oiled 9-inch pie pans. Chill.

FILLING:

3 cups onions, sliced and sautéed
1 cup sharp cheese, grated
1 cup milk, scalded, cooled to lukewarm
¼ cup milk powder
3 eggs, beaten
½ teaspoon salt
¼ teaspoon thyme
3 tablespoons nutritional yeast
2 tablespoons oil

Spoon onions over pie shells. Cover with cheese. Blend remaining ingredients and pour mixture over cheese. Bake at 350° F. for 20-25 minutes, until knife inserted in center of pie comes out clean.

This pie is good served hot or cold. It can be cut into small wedges for appetizers or snacks. *Makes 2 pies.*

VARIATIONS:
Sprinkle broiled bacon bits over top of pie.
Add leftover bits of vegetables, meat, fish or fowl to mixture before baking.

## STEAMED PARSNIPS

6 parsnips, scrubbed, sliced thin
¼ cup seasoned stock
pinch of cinnamon, ground
3 tablespoons parsley, minced

Steam parsnips in stock over gentle heat. Parsnips should be firm, not overdone. Serve with cinnamon and parsley as garnish. *Serves 6.*

# Potatoes

HINTS:
Potatoes retain most of their food value when baked. For baking, select potatoes of similar size. Set oven at moderate temperature (350° F.). Allow adequate baking time (about 1 hour for large potatoes) but don't overcook. After potatoes are baked, prick skins to allow steam to escape. Eat potato skin as well as the inside.
Reserve water in which potatoes are boiled for use in soups, bread doughs, quick bread batters, cake and cooky batters, and in cooking grains.
Mashed potatoes may be enriched with milk powder, soy milk, raw egg and nutritional yeast.
Suggested flavorings: parsley, dill, rosemary, mint, chives, basil, celery, caraway, cumin, poppy seeds,

sesame seeds, grated cheese, yoghurt, sour cream.

## BAKED POTATO PANCAKES

2 cups potatoes, raw and grated
¼ cup hot milk
½ teaspoon salt
1 tablespoon nutritional yeast
2 eggs, separated
2 tablespoons soy flour
¼ cup soy grits, soaked in
¼ cup milk

Blend potatoes, hot milk, salt and yeast. Cool to lukewarm. Add egg yolks, soy flour and soaked soy grits. Fold in stiffly beaten egg whites. Pour small amounts of batter onto hot, unoiled soapstone griddle over moderately high direct heat. If baked in oven, pour into heated, oiled pan and allow 15 minutes at 400° F. *Serves 4-6.*

## POTATO LOAF

2 cups potatoes, cooked and puréed
1 onion, grated
½ green pepper, minced
½ cup stewed tomatoes
½ teaspoon basil
1 egg
½ teaspoon salt
3 tablespoons nutritional yeast
½ cup Soybeans, Roasted, ground
2 tablespoons soy flour

Blend all ingredients. Turn into oiled loaf pan. Bake in medium oven about 25 minutes. Brown top under broiler during last few minutes. *Serves 6.*

## POTATO CASSEROLE (in blender)

6 raw potatoes, quartered
4 tablespoons parsley
1 onion

1 green pepper
1½ cups milk
2 tablespoons soy flour
4 eggs
1 teaspoon salt
3 tablespoons nutritional yeast
1½ cups cheese, grated
4 tablespoons oil
1 sprig dill

Blend all ingredients. Turn into oiled casserole or 6 oiled custard cups. Bake at 350° F., 1 hour for large casserole, 45 minutes for individual cups. *Serves 6.*

## POTATO-NUT CASSEROLE (in blender)

6 raw potatoes, quartered
1 onion
1 cup nuts
2 eggs
2 tablespoons soy flour
3 tablespoons nutritional yeast
3 tablespoons oil
½ teaspoon salt
¼ teaspoon thyme
½ cup wheat germ

Blend all ingredients except wheat germ. Turn into oiled casserole or 6 oiled custard cups. Sprinkle wheat germ on top. Bake at 350° F. about 45 minutes for large casserole, 35 minutes for individual cups. *Serves 6.*

## POTATO PATTIES

3 cups potatoes, cooked and puréed
½ cup nuts, ground
½ cup cottage cheese*
1 egg
1 onion, grated
3 teaspoons soy flour
1 teaspoon salt
½ cup milk powder
3 tablespoons nutritional yeast
pinch of nutmeg, ground
¼ teaspoon rosemary
1 cup wheat germ

[Recipe continued on next page]

[Recipe continued from previous page]

Blend all ingredients except wheat germ. Mixture should be stiff. Shape into patties. Coat with wheat germ. Arrange on oiled cooky sheet. Broil until golden brown on each side. *Serves 6.*

### LEFTOVER POTATOES

Slice or dice leftover baked or boiled potatoes and use for hash.

Dice leftover baked or boiled potatoes. Add to tossed vegetable salads, soups or casseroles.

Use leftover mashed potatoes in bread dough; in soup, meat, fish or fowl loaves; to bind patties; to thicken sauces.

### OTHER POTATO RECIPES

See: Rye Bread Torte; Autumn Salad; Milwaukee Rye Bread; Mashed Potato Dumplings; Potato Soup; Buckwheat and Potato Soup; Potato Stuffing; Potato Bread; Potato Rolls; Yeast Piecrust with Potatoes.

# Soybeans and Limas (Green)

### GREEN SOYBEANS IN PODS

Wash pods thoroughly. Drop into boiling water or stock. Cover. Cook gently until beans are tender. Slip beans from pods by pressing pod between thumb and index finger. Serve with desired sauce.

### STEAMED GREEN SOYBEANS

Steam beans until tender. Remember that they will not soften as peas do. They will retain firm, nutty texture. Serve with desired sauce.

## BAKED LIMA BEANS

5 cups green lima beans
¼ pound bacon, cut small
1 cup tomato juice
⅓ cup molasses
1 onion, grated
½ teaspoon salt
3 tablespoons nutritional yeast
¼ teaspoon sage

Mix all ingredients and turn into oiled casserole or bean pot. Cover and bake at 250° F. for 2 to 3 hours. Uncover during last hour of baking. *Serves 6.*

### OTHER RECIPES USING SOYBEANS AND LIMAS

See: Dried Beans and Peas; Lima Bean Soup.

# Spinach

### HINT:

Flavorings: nutmeg, cinnamon, grated cheese, grated nuts, sesame seeds, broiled bits of bacon, yoghurt, sour cream, tarragon vinegar.

## DEEP DISH SPINACH PIE

### FILLING:

2 pounds spinach (or beet tops), raw, washed, cut into bite-size pieces
1 cup parsley sprigs, stems removed
1 cup green onions, chopped
⅛ teaspoon salt
½ teaspoon rosemary
pinch of nutmeg, ground
2 tablespoons oil

Place all ingredients in pan. Cook briefly, stirring once or twice, over low heat, only long enough to reduce ingredients to half their original bulk. Turn into oiled casserole. Cover with rolled Cheddar Cheese Piecrust. Brush with cream. Bake at 425° F. for 15-20 minutes, only long enough to brown pastry. *Serves 6.*

## KOREAN SPINACH

2 pounds spinach (or beet tops), steamed
⅔ cup oil
juice of 1 lemon
1 onion, grated
½ cup sesame seeds

Mix all ingredients. Serve cold. *Serves 6.*

## SPINACH SOUFFLÉ (in blender)

1 pound spinach (or beet tops), steamed
1 cup stock
3 tablespoons oil
3 tablespoons wholewheat flour
pinch of mace, ground
½ cup milk powder
¼ teaspoon salt
3 tablespoons nutritional yeast
¼ cup cheese, grated
4 eggs, separated

Put all ingredients except egg whites in blender and blend until smooth. Fold in stiffly beaten egg whites. Turn into oiled casserole or oiled individual custard cups. Bake at 375° F. for 35-40 minutes. *Serves 6.*

OTHER RECIPES USING SPINACH
See: Spinach Soup; Spinach Salad; Vegetable Sukiyaki; Eggs Florentine.

# Squash and Pumpkin

HINTS:
Small squash and pumpkins can be baked whole. Cut large squash

and pumpkins into chunks and steam. Vitamins and minerals are close to the skin.
Save uncooked squash and pumpkin seeds. Remove membranes, dry and hull, and use like sunflower seeds. (See also under Seed Drink.)
Squash and pumpkin juice can be extracted for beverage and soup stock in an electric juicer.
Flavorings that combine well with squash and pumpkin: sweet fruit or fruit juices, nutmeg, mace, cinnamon, cloves, rosemary, basil, mint, grated cheese, grated onion.

## HONEYED BAKED SQUASH

3 small squash (acorn, butternut, etc.)
3 tablespoons honey
3 tablespoons oil
¼ teaspoon salt
⅛ teaspoon mace, ground
½ cup sesame seeds

Cut squash in half. Remove seeds and membranes. Arrange in shallow pan. Fill pan ¼ inch high with water. Blend remaining ingredients together. Spoon mixture into cavity of squash. Cover and bake at 350° F. for about 1 hour, uncovering during the last 10 minutes of baking time to allow to brown delicately. *Serves 6.*

## HERBED STEAMED SQUASH

4 cups raw squash or pumpkin, cubed
¼ cup stock
¼ teaspoon rosemary
¼ teaspoon basil

Place all ingredients in steamer. Steam briefly, over low heat, until squash is cooked. Squash should be firm, not overdone. *Serves 6.*

## STUFFED BAKED SQUASH

3 small squash (acorn, butternut, etc.)
1½ cups dried apricots, chopped
½ cup wheat germ
2 cups whole-grain bread crumbs
¼ cup nuts, ground
¼ cup soy grits
⅓ cup honey
½ teaspoon salt
3 tablespoons nutritional yeast
1 teaspoon Powdered Fruit Rind
pinch of nutmeg, ground
4 tablespoons oil
½ cup hot, sweet cider

Cut squash in half. Remove seeds and membranes. Arrange cut side down in shallow pan. Fill pan ¼ inch high with water. Bake at 400° F. for 30 minutes. Remove from pan. Blend remaining ingredients together. Stuff mixture into cavity of squash. Arrange again in pan and bake at 400° F. for 20 minutes, until lightly browned. *Serves 6.*

OTHER RECIPES USING SQUASH
AND PUMPKIN
See: Seed Drink; Squash-Chestnut Soup; Pumpkin Soup; Rice-Pumpkin Casserole; Squash Custard; Squash or Pumpkin Cake; Golden Cookies; Pumpkin Chiffon Pie Filling.

## String Beans

HINT:
Flavorings: yoghurt, sour cream, sautéed onions and mushrooms, grated nuts, grated cheese, mint, dill, parsley, savory, oregano, rosemary, broiled bits of bacon.

## STEAMED STRING BEANS

2 pounds string beans, cut
¼ cup stock

1 tablespoon parsley, minced
½ teaspoon salt

Place all ingredients in steamer. Steam briefly, over low heat, until beans are cooked. Beans should be firm, not overdone. *Serves 6.*

## HERBED STRING BEANS

1 onion, sliced
2 tablespoons oil
1 clove garlic, minced
1 tablespoon green pepper, minced
1 tomato, cut in pieces
1 tablespoon celery or tops, chopped
1 tablespoon parsley, minced
¼ teaspoon savory
1 whole clove
2 pounds string beans, steamed

Sauté onion in oil. Add remaining ingredients, except string beans. Cover. Simmer gently for 10 minutes. Pour over beans. *Serves 6.*

OTHER RECIPES USING STRING BEANS
See: Spring Salad; Vegetable-Soy Grits Loaf.

## Sweet Peppers

## STUFFED SWEET PEPPERS

6 large green peppers, parboiled
6 tomatoes, quartered

Stuff peppers with any one of the stuffings below. Arrange in oiled casserole. Prop peppers by surrounding with tomato wedges. Add small amount of stock to bottom of casserole. Bake at 350° F. for 30-40 minutes. *Serves 6.*

STUFFINGS:

*No. 1*

1 cup brown rice, cooked
2 mushrooms, chopped

1 onion, chopped
1 tablespoon oil
½ teaspoon thyme
¼ teaspoon salt
3 tablespoons nutritional yeast
4 tablespoons soy grits, soaked in
4 tablespoons stock

#### No. 2
1 cup lentils, cooked
½ cup cheese, grated
1 tablespoon oil
1 cup eggplant, raw and cubed
¼ teaspoon salt
pinch of nutmeg, ground
whole-grain bread crumbs to bind
stock to moisten

#### No. 3
1 cup potatoes, cooked and puréed
1 onion, chopped and sautéed
1 raw egg
¼ cup nuts, ground
¼ cup Soybeans, Roasted, ground
½ teaspoon chervil
1 tablespoon parsley, minced
1 stalk of celery and top, diced
½ teaspoon salt
2 tablespoons nutritional yeast

#### No. 4
1½ cups Soybean Pulp
½ cup celery and tops, diced and
steamed
1 tomato, cut in small pieces
1 onion, minced
2 tablespoons nutritional yeast
½ teaspoon chervil
½ cup cheese, grated

## SAUTÉED SWEET PEPPERS
6 sweet peppers, red and green
3 tablespoons oil
½ clove garlic, minced
2 tablespoons tomato juice
1 teaspoon nutritional yeast
¼ teaspoon oregano

Slice peppers into strips, removing seeds. Sauté peppers briefly in oil. Add remaining ingredients. Cover pan and simmer for a few minutes. Serve with meat, fish, eggs, cheese or sprouts. *Serves 6.*

## Sweet Potatoes and Yams

HINTS:
Bake sweet potatoes and yams in their skins to retain most of their food values. Steaming is also a good method of cooking.
Flavorings: cinnamon, clove, nutmeg, mace, sweet fruits or juices, Powdered Orange Rind.

## SWEET POTATO CASSEROLE
(in blender)
3 cups sweet potato or yam, raw and diced
½ cup milk
¼ cup milk powder
2 eggs
¼ cup oil
½ teaspoon salt
¼ teaspoon ginger, ground
¼ teaspoon cinnamon, ground
3 tablespoons nutritional yeast
⅓ cup honey

Briefly blend all ingredients. (Texture will not be smooth.) Turn into oiled casserole. Bake at 350° F. for about 45 minutes. *Serves 4-6.*

## HONEYED SWEET POTATOES
6 sweet potatoes or yams, cooked and cut in half lengthwise
½ cup honey
juice of 1 lemon
¼ cup oil
pinch of allspice, ground

[Recipe continued on next page]

[Recipe continued from previous page]

Arrange sweet potatoes in oiled casserole. Mix remaining ingredients together. Pour mixture over potatoes. Bake at 350° F. for about 30 minutes, basting occasionally with liquid. *Serves 6.*

VARIATION:
Substitute molasses for honey.

## SWEET POTATO PUFF

4 cups sweet potato or yam, cooked and puréed
¼ teaspoon salt
3 tablespoons yoghurt *
3 tablespoons nutritional yeast
¼ cup sweet cider
2 tablespoons oil
3 tablespoons honey
¼ cup milk powder
pinch of nutmeg, ground
pinch of clove, ground

Blend all ingredients and beat until fluffy. Turn into oiled casserole. Bake at 350° F. for 30-40 minutes, until puffed and delicately browned. *Serves 6.*

## SWEET POTATO-PRUNE CASSEROLE

6 sweet potatoes or yams, cut into ¼-inch slices, steamed
2 cups prunes, soaked and pitted
1 teaspoon salt
2 tablespoons water in which prunes were soaked
2 tablespoons lemon juice
3 tablespoons nutritional yeast
¼ cup unsweetened fruit juice
pinch of mace, ground
pinch of ginger, ground
1 teaspoon Powdered Fruit Rind

Arrange layer of sweet potatoes at bottom of oiled casserole. Arrange layer of prunes on top. Alternate layers of potatoes and prunes until all are used. Blend remaining ingredients together. Pour over potatoes and prunes. Bake at 350° F. for about 45 minutes, basting occasionally with liquid. *Serves 6.*

## SWEET POTATO PANCAKES

2 cups sweet potatoes or yams, raw and grated
2 eggs, beaten
1 teaspoon salt
3 tablespoons orange juice
⅓ cup milk
½ cup milk powder
⅓ cup wholewheat flour
1 teaspoon soy flour

Combine all ingredients. If mixture is too thin, add more milk powder; if too stiff, add more liquid milk. Drop by spoonfuls onto oiled pan. Bake at 350° F. for about 30 minutes, turning once to allow to brown on each side. Serve with applesauce. *Serves 6.*

OTHER RECIPES USING SWEET POTATOES AND YAMS
See: Yam Stuffing; Rice Patties; Sweet Potato Custard; Golden Cookies; Sweet Potato Pie Filling; Yam-Fruit Salad.

# Tomatoes

## TOMATO TIMBALES

2 cups tomatoes, stewed and puréed
2 eggs, beaten
1 cup soy flour, sifted
½ teaspoon salt
3 tablespoons nutritional yeast
½ teaspoon oregano

½ teaspoon marjoram
½ cup cheese, grated

Blend all ingredients except cheese. Turn into oiled custard cups. Sprinkle cheese over top. Bake at 350° F. for about 1 hour. *Serves 6.*

## STUFFED TOMATOES

6 large tomatoes
stuffing

Scoop pulp from tomatoes. Reserve for soup or casserole dishes. Fill cavities with stuffing. Arrange tomatoes in oiled baking pan. Bake at 350° F. for 30-35 minutes. *Serves 6.*

For stuffing, see recipes under Stuffed Sweet Peppers, this chapter.

## TOMATO SOUFFLÉ

1¾ cups tomatoes, stewed, puréed
3 tablespoons oil
½ teaspoon salt
3 tablespoons wholewheat flour
½ teaspoon basil
½ teaspoon dill
3 tablespoons nutritional yeast
4 eggs, separated

Blend all ingredients except egg whites. Fold in stiffly beaten egg whites. Turn mixture into oiled casserole, or oiled individual custard cups. Bake at 375° F. for 30-35 minutes. *Serves 6.*

OTHER RECIPES USING TOMATOES
See under *Tomato:* Relish; Salad; Soup; Spread; Timbales, etc.

# Zucchini, Cucumbers

## SAUTÉED ZUCCHINI
(or summer squash)

Cut into small, thin rounds. Leave skins on. Sauté briefly in oil, garlic and minced dill. Serve with lemon juice and grated cheese.

## ZUCCHINI OMELET

Arrange cooked zucchini or summer squash rounds in oiled casserole. Beat as many eggs as desired and pour over zucchini. Bake at 300° F. until eggs set. Garnish with grated cheese or minced parsley and serve at once.

## ZUCCHINI IN YOGHURT

1½ pounds young zucchini (or cucumbers)
½ cup cider vinegar*
¼ cup stock
2 cups yoghurt*
1 egg
¼ cup dill, minced

Cut zucchini or cucumber in thin slices. Leave skins on. Simmer gently in vinegar and stock for 5 minutes. Cool. Blend together yoghurt, egg and dill. Drain zucchini. Pour yoghurt over zucchini. Serve cold. *Serves 6.*

## CUCUMBERS IN SWEET AND SOUR SAUCE

4 cucumbers, sliced (or zucchini)
2 tablespoons oil
2 tablespoons onions, sliced
¼ cup yoghurt*
2 tablespoons honey
3 tablespoons cider vinegar*

Sauté cucumbers briefly in oil and remove from pan. Sauté onions in same oil. Cool. Mix yoghurt, honey, and vinegar and blend with cucumbers and onions. *Serves 6.*

# Mixed Vegetable Dishes

## VEGETABLES À LA CHINOISE

1 cup onions, sliced thin
1 cup green peppers, chopped
1 cup celery and tops, chopped
½ cup mushrooms, sliced
¼ cup oil
1 tablespoon nutritional yeast
1 teaspoon Essence of Sweet Herbs
1 cup mung bean Sprouts

Sauté onions, green peppers, celery and mushrooms briefly in oil. Remove from heat. Blend with remaining ingredients. *Serves 6.*

## VEGETABLE SUKIYAKI

1 cup vegetables, cooked and cubed
3 tablespoons oil
1 cup Chinese cabbage, shredded
1 green pepper, chopped
1 scallion, chopped
½ cup mushrooms, sliced
1 cup carrots, grated
1 cup celery and tops, chopped
1 cup raw spinach or other crisp greens
1 tablespoon honey
1 teaspoon Essence of Sweet Herbs
1 cup wholewheat Sprouts

Sauté cooked vegetables in oil. Add cabbage, pepper, scallions, mushrooms, carrots and celery. Cover with tight lid. Cook gently for 10 minutes. Add spinach, cover again and cook 2 minutes longer. Remove from heat. Add honey, sprouts and essence of sweet herbs. Toss and serve. *Serves 6.*

## CHOW MEIN

¼ cup oil
1 cup onions, sliced
2 cups celery and tops, chopped
½ cup mushrooms, sliced
2 cups leftovers (meat, fish, fowl), diced
1 cup stock
3 tablespoons wholewheat flour
1 teaspoon soy flour
1 tablespoon Essence of Sweet Herbs
2 cups alfalfa Sprouts

Heat oil in saucepan. Sauté onions, celery and mushrooms briefly. Add leftovers, stock, flours and essence of sweet herbs. Blend well. Cover and simmer gently until mixture thickens slightly. Remove from heat. Add sprouts. Serve over brown rice. *Serves 6.*

## VEGETABLE CASSEROLE

1 cup raw beets, grated
1 cup celery and tops, chopped
1 cup turnips, grated
1 cup carrots, grated
1 cup onions, sliced
½ cup stock
3 tablespoons parsley, minced
1 teaspoon chervil

Alternate layers of vegetables in oiled casserole. Blend stock and herbs. Pour over vegetables. Cover and bake at 350° F. for about 30 minutes. *Serves 6.*

## VEGETABLE STEW

2 onions, sliced
2 tablespoons oil
1 cup raw potato, cubed
1 cup zucchini, sliced
1 cup yellow squash, sliced
½ cup carrot, grated
½ cup turnip, grated
½ cup parsnip, grated
1 cup stewed tomatoes
3 tablespoons nutritional yeast
3 tablespoons parsley, minced
1 sprig dill, minced

Sauté onions in oil. Add rest of ingredients. Cover. Simmer gently until potatoes are cooked. *Serves 6.*

## HERBED MUSHROOM CASSEROLE

4 cups mushrooms, sliced
¼ cup oil
1 teaspoon marjoram
½ teaspoon rosemary
3 tablespoons nutritional yeast
¼ cup seasoned stock

Sauté mushrooms briefly in oil. Add remaining ingredients. Turn into casserole. Cover. Bake at 350° F. for 20 minutes. *Serves 6.*

## VEGETABLE-CHESTNUT STEW

1 pound chestnuts, shelled, boiled and cut in half
2 carrots, grated
1 turnip, grated
2 potatoes, grated
2 cabbage leaves, shredded
2 stalks celery and tops, chopped
¼ teaspoon salt
3 tablespoons parsley, minced
3 tablespoons nutritional yeast
1 teaspoon marjoram
stock to cover

Blend all ingredients in saucepan. Cover. Simmer until vegetables are cooked. *Serves 6.*

## VEGETABLE-SOYBEAN CASSEROLE

1 cup celery and tops, chopped
1 onion, chopped
1 green pepper, chopped
1½ cups stewed tomatoes
½ teaspoon salt
½ cup wheat germ
½ cup stock
3 tablespoons nutritional yeast
3 tablespoons oil
1 teaspoon Essence of Sweet Herbs
3 tablespoons soy flour
3 cups soybeans, cooked

Combine all ingredients except soybeans. Turn half of mixture into oiled casserole. Place soybeans on top. Spread with remaining half of mixture. Bake at 350° F. for 30 minutes. *Serves 6.*

## VEGETABLE-SOYBEAN LOAF

1 cup raw carrots, grated
1 cup soybeans, cooked
1 cup raw beets, grated
1 onion, grated
1 green pepper, minced
3 tablespoons soy flour
½ cup wheat germ (about)
⅓ cup tomato juice (about)
2 eggs
½ teaspoon salt
3 tablespoons nutritional yeast
1 teaspoon oregano

Blend all ingredients. If too dry, add more tomato juice; if too moist, more wheat germ. Turn into oiled loaf pan. Bake at 350° F. for about 1 hour. *Serves 6.*

## BAKED VEGETABLE-SOYBEAN CROQUETTES

1 cup soybeans, cooked and puréed
1 cup brown rice, cooked
1 egg
1 cup carrots, cooked and puréed
1 cup peas, cooked and puréed
1 teaspoon salt
1 teaspoon basil
3 tablespoons nutritional yeast
3 tablespoons soy flour
½ cup nuts, ground

Blend all ingredients except nuts. Shape into croquettes or patties. Roll in ground nuts. Arrange in oiled baking pan. Bake at 400° F. for about 20 minutes, turning once to allow even browning. *Serves 6.*

## COLD VEGETABLE CASSEROLE
### (for summer picnics)

1 cup mushrooms, sliced
2 onions, sliced
3 tablespoons oil
2 eggs, beaten
½ cup nuts, ground
1 cup vegetables, cooked and diced
½ teaspoon salt
1 cup brown rice, cooked
½ cup wholewheat bread crumbs
¼ cup soy grits, soaked in
¼ cup stock
3 tablespoons nutritional yeast
pinch of nutmeg, ground
1 teaspoon savory

Sauté mushrooms and onions in oil. Blend with remaining ingredients. Turn into oiled casserole. Bake at 375° F. for 30 minutes. Cool, then chill. When cold, this casserole can be sliced. *Serves 6.*

## VEGETABLE-SOY GRITS LOAF

2 cups raw carrots, grated
1 cup string beans, cooked and
    puréed
1 cup celery and tops, chopped
1 onion, grated
1 cup whole-grain bread crumbs
½ cup soy grits, soaked in
½ cup stock
½ cup sunflower-seed meal
3 tablespoons nutritional yeast
½ teaspoon sage

Blend all ingredients. Turn into oiled loaf pan. Bake at 350° F. for about 20 minutes. *Serves 6.*

## COLD STEAMED VEGETABLE
### CASSEROLE (for summer picnics)

1 cup onions, sliced and sautéed
1 cup tomatoes, chopped fine
3 eggs, beaten
¼ cup almonds, ground
¼ cup walnuts, ground
½ cup wheat germ

3 tablespoons soy flour
¼ cup soy grits, soaked in
¼ cup stock
1 tablespoon parsley, minced
½ teaspoon rosemary
pinch of nutmeg, ground
½ teaspoon salt
3 tablespoons nutritional yeast

Blend all ingredients together. Turn into oiled mold. Cover tightly. Steam for 1½ hours. Let stand 5 minutes. Unmold carefully. Chill. When cold, this casserole can be sliced. *Serves 6.*

# Sauces for Vegetables

## HOLLANDAISE SAUCE
### (in blender)

3 egg yolks
2 tablespoons lemon juice
1 sprig parsley
¼ teaspoon salt
½ cup butter, melted
½ cup hot stock

Place all ingredients, except stock, in blender. Blend thoroughly. Gradually add stock. Blend. Turn mixture into top of double boiler. Cook gently over hot water about 20 minutes, or until mixture is consistency of soft custard. Use with any vegetable. *Makes 1 pint.*

LEFTOVER HOLLANDAISE SAUCE
Serve cold as salad dressing; add to
    hot or cold soup.

## YOGHURT-CARAWAY SEED
### SAUCE (uncooked)

1 pint yoghurt *
1 tablespoon caraway seeds, crushed

Blend yoghurt and caraway seeds at

least one hour before using, to allow yoghurt to absorb caraway flavor. Buttermilk or sour cream may be substituted for yoghurt. Use with any vegetable. *Makes 1 pint.*

## WHITE SAUCE (in blender)

3 cups stock
¾ cup milk powder
½ cup wholewheat flour
¼ teaspoon salt
3 tablespoons oil
3 tablespoons nutritional yeast
1 tablespoon parsley, minced
1 tablespoon dill, minced

Blend all ingredients together. Turn into saucepan. Cook over gentle heat, stirring, until mixture is smooth and thick. For a thinner sauce, reduce quantity of flour; for a thicker sauce, add more flour. Use with any vegetable. *Makes 3½ cups.*

VARIATIONS:
Add ½ cup grated cheese to sauce while cooking.
Substitute other herbs, as desired, for dill.

## BROWNED BUTTER WITH NUTS

1½ cups butter
½ cup nuts, ground

Brown butter lightly. Mix with nuts. Serve with broccoli, asparagus, string beans, cauliflower, spinach and other vegetables. *Makes 1 pint.*

## SAVORY SAUCE

2 cups butter
1 tablespoon onion juice

½ clove garlic, minced
1 teaspoon celery seeds, crushed
pinch of mace, ground
1 tablespoon nutritional yeast

Melt butter. Add remaining ingredients. Blend well. Use with potatoes. *Makes 1 pint.*

## POPPY SEED SAUCE

2 cups butter
juice of 2 lemons
2 tablespoons poppy seeds
1 teaspoon soy flour

Melt butter. Add remaining ingredients. Blend well. Use with asparagus, broccoli, cauliflower, etc. *Makes 1 pint.*

GARNISHES FOR COOKED VEGETABLES:
Nut Butters
nuts, whole, slivered or ground
Roasted Soybeans, whole or ground
seeds
minced herbs
lemon wedges
soy cheese
whole-grain bread crumbs
wheat germ
cottage cheese
hard-cooked egg, sliced, wedged or riced
cheese, grated
Coconut Shreds
yoghurt
Sprouts
grated citrus rind
toasted croutons
ground spices

# 8

# MUSCLE MEATS

*Since many nutritious recipes using muscle meats are available in standard cookbooks, they are given only limited consideration here.*

## Broiled Beef Dishes

### KOREAN BROILED BEEF

2 pounds beef from rib roast or steak, cut into thin strips
2 tablespoons oil
3 tablespoons Essence of Sweet Herbs
2 green onions, sliced
1 clove garlic, minced
½ cup stock
½ cup sesame seeds, toasted

Marinate beef in mixture of remaining ingredients, except sesame seeds, overnight. Remove from marinade. Broil. Garnish with seeds. *Serves 6.*

### JAPANESE FLANK STEAK

2 pounds flank steak
1 cup meat stock
1 onion, chopped fine
1 clove garlic, minced
1 teaspoon salt
1 bay leaf
3 tablespoons Essence of Sweet Herbs
2 tablespoons honey

Remove membrane, gristle and fat from steak. Cut steak into diagonal strips 1 inch wide. Arrange in shallow dish. Combine remaining ingredients. Pour mixture over steak and cover. Chill 24 hours. Turn meat occasionally, so that all sides come in contact with marinade. Remove strips from marinade. Thread on skewers. Broil for 4 minutes, turning once. *Serves 6.*

## Stews and Casseroles

### PERSIAN LAMB AND PARSLEY STEW

3 tablespoons oil
3 large bunches parsley, minced
10 scallions, chopped
2 pounds lamb, lean, cubed
stock
juice of 2 lemons
3 tablespoons nutritional yeast
2 cups kidney beans, cooked

Heat oil in pot. Sauté parsley, scallions and lamb. Pour in enough stock to cover. Add lemon juice and yeast and blend. Cover. Simmer until meat is tender. Add beans and continue cooking till beans are heated thoroughly. Serve over brown rice. *Serves 6.*

## BEEF AND VEGETABLE STEW

3 tablespoons oil
2 cups carrots, cut into rounds
6 potatoes, cubed
2 pounds beef, lean, cubed
1 teaspoon thyme
1 teaspoon oregano
1 teaspoon salt
3 tablespoons nutritional yeast
6 onions, sliced
2 cups tomatoes, stewed

Heat oil in pot. Brown beef. Arrange in layers, over beef, the carrots, potatoes, seasonings, onions and tomatoes. Cover. Simmer until meat is tender. Serve over millet. *Serves 6.*

## MEAT AND VEGETABLE CASSEROLE (in blender)

2 tablespoons oil
2 onions, sliced
1/2 pound mushrooms, sliced
1 cup spinach, cooked
1 tablespoon chives
1/2 cup water cress
1/4 cup parsley
1 tablespoon lemon juice
3 tablespoons nutritional yeast
1/2 teaspoon salt
1/2 teaspoon oregano
1 1/2 cups meat (any variety), cooked, cubed
1 cup broccoli, cooked
1 cup brown rice, cooked
3 tablespoons wheat germ
wholewheat bread crumbs

Heat oil. Lightly sauté onions and mushrooms. Blend spinach, chives, water cress, parsley, lemon juice, yeast, salt and oregano together in blender until smooth. Turn out mixture over sautéed onions and mushrooms. Add meat, broccoli, brown rice and wheat germ. Mix well. Turn into oiled casserole. Sprinkle bread crumbs on top. Bake uncovered at 375° F. for 15 minutes, until top is brown. *Serves 6.*

## BEEF AND CORNMEAL CASSEROLE

1/2 cup cornmeal
1/2 cup stock, cold
1 cup stock, hot
1 tablespoon oil
1 onion, cut
2 cups ground beef, cooked
1 teaspoon salt
1 egg, beaten
3 tablespoons nutritional yeast
1 tablespoon parsley, minced
1 teaspoon summer savory
3 tomatoes, sliced

Blend cornmeal with cold stock. When smooth, add to hot stock. Blend thoroughly. Heat oil and in it sauté onion. Add cornmeal mixture, meat, salt, egg, yeast and herbs. Turn all into oiled casserole. Arrange tomatoes over top. Bake at 350° F. for 20 minutes. *Serves 6.*

## BEEF AND RYE CASSEROLE

2 pounds braising beef
1/2 cup cranberry juice
1/4 teaspoon oregano
1 bay leaf, ground
3 tablespoons oil
4 carrots, cubed, cooked
10 white onions, sliced, cooked
1 1/2 cups cracked rye
3 cups stock, hot
3 tablespoons nutritional yeast
1 teaspoon soy flour
1 teaspoon Essence of Sweet Herbs

Cut beef into cubes. Sprinkle with oregano and bay leaf. Marinate in cranberry juice for several hours. Drain. Reserve juice. Sauté beef in

[Recipe continued on next page]

[Recipe continued from previous page]
oil until brown on all sides. Arrange meat in bottom of casserole. Add reserved juice. Cover and braise until tender. Add carrots and onions. Brown cracked rye in unoiled pan. Add stock and remaining ingredients and cover pan. Simmer for 30 minutes. Add rye to casserole. Heat thoroughly and serve. *Serves 6.*

## HAM CASSEROLE

2 cups ham, cooked, ground
2 cups corn, cooked
1 teaspoon salt
3 tablespoons nutritional yeast
1 tablespoon oil
¼ teaspoon mace, ground
3 tablespoons honey
½ cup stock

Arrange half the ham in the bottom of an oiled casserole. Mix remaining ingredients, except stock, and pour over ham. Arrange rest of ham on top. Pour stock over mixture. Bake in 300° F. oven for 40 minutes. *Serves 6.*

## SURPRISE CASSEROLE

2 cups meat or chicken, cooked, diced
1 pound broccoli, cooked, cut into 1-inch strips
1 pound onions, small, white
3 tablespoons oil
4 tablespoons wholewheat flour
3 cups milk
1 cup milk powder
¼ teaspoon tarragon
3 tablespoons nutritional yeast
2 tablespoons wholewheat bread crumbs
2 tablespoons cheddar cheese, grated

Arrange a layer of meat or chicken at bottom of oiled casserole. Alternate with layer of broccoli, then layer of onions, until all ingredients are used. Prepare a white sauce as follows: Heat oil. Blend flour, milk, milk powder, tarragon and yeast together. Add to oil and blend again. Heat mixture in double boiler. Stir until smooth and thick. Pour sauce over casserole. Sprinkle top with mixture of bread crumbs and cheese. Bake at 375° F. for 20 to 25 minutes. *Serves 6.*

# Ground Meat

HINTS:
Always use meat that is freshly ground to order.
Enrich with one or more of the following: nutritional yeast, ground sesame or sunflower seeds, egg, soy flour.
Bind with one or more of the following; wheat germ, wholewheat bread crumbs, milk powder, leftover porridge (especially oatmeal), leftover cooked grains.
Flavor with one or more of the following: a pinch of ground cinnamon, nutmeg or mace.
Soy grits make a good addition to meat loaves. Use ⅓ to ½ cup of soy grits for each pound of meat. Allow the grits to soak for 5 minutes in hot stock to cover before mixing with other ingredients.

## ITALIAN POLPETTE (croquettes)

1 pound beef, ground
¼ pound each of veal and pork, ground
2 slices wholewheat bread, soaked in milk and squeezed dry
1 egg
½ cup onion, minced
2 tablespoons parsley, minced

1 tablespoon soy flour
¼ cup wheat germ
¼ cup soy grits, soaked in
½ cup stock
1 teaspoon salt
¼ teaspoon oregano
¼ teaspoon basil
3 tablespoons nutritional yeast
1 clove garlic, minced
¼ cup oil
1½ cups stock, hot
1 cup tomato purée

Blend well all ingredients except oil, stock and tomato purée. Form into 18 meat balls. Heat oil. Sauté meat balls until brown on all sides. Add stock and tomato purée. Cover. Simmer for 20 minutes. Serve over brown rice or millet. *Serves 6.*

## NORWEGIAN MEAT BALLS

1 pound beef, ground
1 pound pork, ground
1 cup milk
¼ cup milk powder
1 slice wholewheat bread
1 onion, grated
3 tablespoons nutritional yeast
1 teaspoon soy flour
3 tablespoons wheat germ
1 teaspoon salt
⅛ teaspoon mace, ground
⅛ teaspoon ginger, ground
3 tablespoons oil
stock

Blend all ingredients except oil. Form mixture into small balls (dip hands in cold water from time to time to prevent sticking). Sauté meat balls in hot oil. Cover with stock and cover pot. Simmer for 30 minutes. *Serves 6.*

## ARMENIAN MEAT BALLS

2 tablespoons oil
5 onions, chopped
1 sprig parsley, minced

2 pounds beef, ground
1 cup wholewheat berries, soaked overnight in
1 cup stock
3 tablespoons nutritional yeast
1 teaspoon soy flour
1 teaspoon salt
3 tablespoons wheat germ
2 tomatoes, sliced
stock

Heat oil in pot. Sauté onions, parsley and half the beef. Remove from heat. Cool. Combine remainder of beef with berries, yeast, flour, salt and wheat germ. Shape this mixture into flat patties. In the center of each, place 1 tablespoonful of the sautéed mixture. Press edges of patty together to enclose stuffing. Arrange patties and tomato slices in pot. Cover with stock and cover pot. Simmer for 30 minutes. *Serves 6.*

## CHINESE EGG ROLLS

FILLING:

3 tablespoons oil
1 pound beef, ground
4 cups cabbage, shredded fine
½ cup green onion, chopped fine
1½ cups celery and tops, chopped fine
2 tablespoons Essence of Sweet Herbs
1 teaspoon salt
2 tablespoons honey
3 tablespoons nutritional yeast
2 cups mung bean Sprouts

Heat oil. Lightly sauté all vegetables and seasonings. Cool. Drain off juice and save for stock. Add sprouts to mixture.

BATTER:

2 cups wholewheat flour, sifted
1 egg, beaten
2 cups water
oil

[Recipe continued on next page]

[Recipe continued from previous page]

Blend flour, egg and water into a smooth batter. Heat small amount of oil in 6-inch pan. Pour about 4 tablespoons of batter into center of pan. Tilt pan to spread batter over entire surface. Cook over low heat until edges pull away from sides. Turn gently. Cook other side. Remove. Allow to cool. Repeat with rest of batter. Place heaping tablespoonful of filling in center of each pancake. Spread to within ½ inch of edge. Roll. Tuck sides under. Arrange rolls in oiled shallow baking dish. Bake in 350° F. oven for 30 minutes, or until golden brown. *Serves 6.*

## RUSSIAN MEAT BALLS WITH BUCKWHEAT

2 pounds beef, ground
1 cup wholewheat bread crumbs
¼ cup wheat germ
3 tablespoons nutritional yeast
1 teaspoon salt
1 clove garlic, minced
1 teaspoon soy flour
3 tablespoons parsley, minced
¼ cup stock
1 cup buckwheat, cooked

Mix all ingredients together except buckwheat. Form into 12 patties. In the center of each, place small quantity of buckwheat. Bring edges of patty together to enclose stuffing. Arrange balls in oiled pan. Broil until browned. *Serves 6.*

## STEAK TARTARE (uncooked)

2 pounds round steak or tenderloin, lean, ground to order
½ cup lemon juice
1 onion, grated
1 teaspoon Essence of Sweet Herbs
3 tablespoons nutritional yeast
¼ teaspoon chervil

¼ teaspoon marjoram
6 egg yolks, raw
6 egg whites, poached, chopped

Blend all ingredients except egg whites. Form six large patties. Garnish with egg whites and serve. *Serves 6.*

## SAVORY MEAT LOAF

1½ pounds beef, freshly ground
¼ pound veal, ground
¼ pound pork, ground
1 clove garlic, minced
1 green pepper, chopped
1½ cups celery, chopped
1 cup carrots, chopped
1 tablespoon parsley, minced
¼ teaspoon sage
1 cup stewed tomatoes
1 egg
¼ cup soy grits, soaked in
½ cup stock
1 teaspoon salt
3 tablespoons nutritional yeast

Blend all ingredients well. Turn into an oiled loaf pan. Bake in 350° F. oven for 1 hour. *Serves 6.*

## MEAT LOAF WITH WHOLEWHEAT BERRIES

1½ pounds beef, ground
½ pound ham, ground
2 cups wholewheat berries, cooked
1 onion, grated
2 eggs, beaten
3 tablespoons nutritional yeast
1 teaspoon dill
1 teaspoon basil

Blend all ingredients. Turn into an oiled loaf pan. Bake in 350° F. oven for 1 hour. *Serves 6.*

## ENRICHED MEAT LOAF

1 pound beef, ground
1 cup sunflower seed meal

1 onion, grated
1 egg, beaten
¼ cup soy grits, soaked in
½ cup stock
½ cup milk powder
½ cup wheat germ
1 teaspoon salt
1 cup tomatoes, stewed
3 tablespoons nutritional yeast

Blend all ingredients. Turn into an oiled loaf pan. Bake in 350° F. oven for 1 hour. *Serves 6.*

## HAM LOAF

2 cups oatmeal, cooked
2 cups ham, cooked and ground
1 cup milk
½ cup milk powder
1 cup carrots, raw, grated
1 green pepper, minced
1 onion, grated
1 egg, beaten
3 tablespoons nutritional yeast
1 tablespoon soy flour

Blend all ingredients. Turn into an oiled loaf pan. Bake in 350° F. oven for about 45 minutes. *Serves 6.*

## BASIC CHILLED MEAT LOAF
(in blender)

1 envelope or 1 tablespoon un-
    flavored gelatin
¼ cup stock, cold
1 cup chicken stock
2 cups ham, veal, chicken, fish,
    cooked and cut into pieces
1 green pepper, cut
1 onion, cut
½ cup milk
¼ cup milk powder
3 tablespoons nutritional yeast
1 teaspoon mixed herbs

Soften gelatin in cold stock and dissolve over low heat. Place remaining ingredients in blender and blend until smooth. Add gelatin

mixture. Blend again. Turn mixture into oiled loaf pan 8 x 4 inches. Chill until firm. Turn out on chilled platter. Garnish with water cress and radish roses. *Serves 6.*

## Meat Pies

### PUERTO RICAN CORNMEAL PIE

DOUGH:

2 cups cornmeal
½ teaspoon salt
3 tablespoons nutritional yeast
1 tablespoon soy flour
2 tablespoons oil
1½ cups stock, hot

Mix all ingredients together. Dough should be stiff. Pat dough into bottom and sides of oiled 9-inch pie plate.

FILLING:

1 tablespoon oil
1 pound lean pork, cubed
1 small onion, chopped
½ green pepper, chopped
¼ cup celery and tops, chopped
2 hard-cooked eggs, chopped
½ teaspoon salt
½ cup stock, hot

Heat oil. Lightly sauté pork, onion, pepper and celery. Remove from heat. Add remaining ingredients and blend. Spread mixture over dough. Bake in 350° F. oven for 25 minutes, or until crust is crisp. *Serves 6.*

### POLISH HAM PIE

favorite pastry dough (enough to
    make top and bottom crust)
2 cups ham and potato hash, cold
1 cup prunes or apricots, pitted, cut

Divide dough in half and roll out thin. Line oiled 9-inch pie plate
[Recipe continued on next page]

[Recipe continued from previous page]

with dough. Arrange ham hash on top, and prunes or apricots over hash. Cover with remaining dough. Brush with egg yolk. Bake at 400° F., for about 30 minutes, or until crust is crisp and golden. Serve hot or cold. *Serves 6.*

For piecrust dough recipes, see under Pastries.

## Leftover Meats

### ORIENTAL CONGEE

5 cups stock
1 cup whole grain (brown rice, millet, oats, barley, cracked wheat, rye or buckwheat), uncooked
1 teaspoon salt
3 tablespoons mixed herbs
3 tablespoons nutritional yeast
½ pound spareribs, or ½ pound tenderloin, or chop, or 1 ham bone
back, neck, wingtips of 1 chicken

Bring stock to boil. Add whole grain slowly. Stir in salt, herbs and yeast. Cover. Simmer for 10 minutes. Add meat and chicken bits. Simmer gently until thick. Serve garnished with raw green onions or Sprouts. *Serves 6.*

### AMERICAN CHOP SUEY

4 tablespoons oil
1 onion, chopped
2 cups celery, diced
1 teaspoon salt
3 tablespoons nutritional yeast
1½ cups stock, hot
1 cup vegetables, cooked, cubed (carrots, string beans, peas, turnips, parsnips)
2 cups meat or chicken, cooked, cut in thin strips
bean Sprouts for garnish

Heat oil. Lightly sauté onion and celery. Add salt, yeast and stock. Cover. Simmer for 3 minutes. Add vegetables and meat. Simmer for another 3 minutes. Then add the following sauce:

2 tablespoons stock, cold
2 tablespoons wholewheat flour
1 tablespoon Essence of Sweet Herbs
1 teaspoon honey

Blend all ingredients. Cook until slightly thickened. Then pour over chop-suey mixture. Serve garnished with bean Sprouts. *Serves 6.*

### LEFTOVERS SUPREME

This dish varies according to the leftovers in the refrigerator. It is always different, always good, and a blessing to make just before defrosting the refrigerator. The base may be cubes of beef, pork, veal, ham, chicken, turkey, etc. Add to any of these raw celery, onions, green peppers, hard-cooked egg, pimento, stewed tomatoes, green peas, string beans, mushrooms or whatever else makes a flavorful combination. These, too, where necessary, should be cut into bite-size cubes. Mix all ingredients together. Add enough sauce to moisten. This may be leftover Hollandaise or cheese sauce, or a small amount of thickened soup or stock. Season to taste with herbs. Bean Sprouts, too, are an excellent addition.

Make thin Wholewheat Pancakes. Place a spoonful of the mixture in the center of each pancake, and roll up. Arrange the filled pancakes side by side in a large, shallow oiled pan. Brush tops with oil. Garnish with grated cheese. Bake in a moderate oven until contents are heated thoroughly and cheese is golden brown. This dish can be prepared in advance and heated or reheated as desired. Serve with tossed salad.

## Garnishes, Sauces, and Toppings for Meat Dishes

### BREAD CRUMB GARNISH

1 cup hot milk
1 cup wholewheat bread crumbs
1 egg, beaten
½ cup milk powder
¼ teaspoon salt
1 tablespoon parsley, minced
1 tablespoon nutritional yeast
1 teaspoon soy flour

Pour milk over bread crumbs. Let stand till crumbs absorb milk, and mixture is cool. Blend remaining ingredients together. Stir into milk-and-crumb mixture. Spread over casseroles of meat, fish, chicken or vegetables, before baking.

### CASSEROLE TOPPING

¼ cup wheat germ
½ cup cheese, grated

Combine wheat germ and cheese and sprinkle over top of meat casseroles. Heat only till cheese is melted. Also use to top creamed vegetables, scalloped tomatoes, rice.

### SAUCE FOR MEAT CASSEROLE

½ cup browned wholewheat bread
  crumbs
4 tablespoons oil

1 teaspoon lemon juice
1 teaspoon parsley, minced

Blend all ingredients. Serve over meat casseroles, or as a sauce for cauliflower, broccoli, asparagus, or Brussels sprouts. *Yields ¾ cup.*

### FLUFFY YAM TOPPING

2 cups yams, cooked and mashed
½ teaspoon salt
1 tablespoon oil
½ cup milk powder
½ cup unsweetened orange juice
1 teaspoon grated orange rind

Blend all ingredients and beat until smooth. Pile lightly around ham casserole, or use instead of pastry in meat or chicken pie. Bake at 350° F. until meat is heated through, and yam topping is lightly browned.

### HONEY-RAISIN SAUCE

1 cup seedless raisins
1 cup stock
¼ cup honey
1 tablespoon lemon juice

Simmer raisins in stock until soft. Add honey and continue simmering gently for 5 minutes. Cool. Add lemon juice. Serve with ham. *Yields 1¾ cups.*

### HONEY-MINT SAUCE

½ cup stock
1 tablespoon cider vinegar *
1 cup honey
¼ cup mint, chopped

Heat together stock and vinegar. Add honey and stir well. Add mint. Simmer for 5 minutes. This sauce can be used to baste lamb chops or lamb roasts, or served with lamb at the table. *Yields 1½ cups.*

## CHEESE PASTRY

1 cup wholewheat flour
½ teaspoon salt
1 tablespoon nutritional yeast
¼ cup cheddar cheese, grated
4 tablespoons oil
ice water

Sift flour, salt and yeast. Mix in cheese. Blend with oil. Add enough water to make dough. Roll ⅛-inch thick. Top meat or fish casseroles and bake till casserole is hot and top browned.

See also Flourless Batter Base and other recipes under Pastries.

VARIATION:
Add pinch of nutmeg to crusts for meat pies.

# 9

# ORGAN MEATS

*Since in most cookbooks a few rec-
ipes for organ meats are usually
relegated to the position of miscel-
laneous items under "variety meats"
or "unusual meats," a wide variety
of recipes using them has been included here.*

## Liver

HINTS:

1 beef liver averages 10 pounds; 1
veal liver averages 2½ pounds;
1 pork liver averages 3 pounds; 1
lamb liver averages 1 pound; 1½
pounds of liver serves 6.

Wash liver as little as possible. It
removes vitamins and minerals.
Do not soak or scald. Precook
only when liver is to be ground.
Save stock.

Cooking too long or at too high a
temperature toughens liver and
destroys its delicacy of flavor.
Liver from young animals requires only brief cooking—just
enough to heat it through and
change its color.

Flour liver. This will make it less
slippery and easier to handle.

Cut out large blood-vessel tubes
with sharp-pointed kitchen scissors. To remove membrane, insert a sharp knife just under the
membrane at one point, then pull
or scrape it from the liver.

Beef liver is not as smooth in texture as calf's liver.

Pork liver contains more connective
tissue than beef or calf's liver and
is slightly bitter and stronger in
flavor. Pork liver is good with
bacon, cheese, onion, apple, carrots or celery; it is less successful
than beef or calf's liver when
combined with tomato or lemon
juice.

Cooking in a covered pan makes
liver more tender.

## BRAISED LIVER

1½ pounds liver, sliced
wholewheat flour
3 tablespoons oil
3 tablespoons nutritional yeast
1 tablespoon parsley, minced
½ cup carrots, cubed
½ cup celery, chopped
1 onion, chopped
1 green pepper, chopped
¼ cup stock

Dredge liver in flour. Heat oil and
brown liver. Add remaining ingredients. Cover. Continue cooking on

[Recipe continued on next page]

[Recipe continued from previous page]
top of stove over gentle heat for 20 minutes, or transfer to casserole, cover and bake in 350° F. oven for 20 minutes. *Serves 6.*

## BROILED LIVER

1½ pounds liver, sliced ½-inch to
    ¾-inch thick
2 tablespoons oil
1 teaspoon lemon juice

Brush liver slices with oil and lemon juice. Broil on each side, only long enough for liver to heat through and change color. *Serves 6.*

## BROILED LIVER PATTIES (in blender)

1½ pounds liver, cubed
stock to cover
3 onions, chopped
1 egg
½ teaspoon oregano
3 tablespoons parsley
½ teaspoon salt
3 tablespoons nutritional yeast

Cook liver, stock and onions in covered pan until liver is soft. Drain and reserve stock for later use. Purée in blender with remaining ingredients. Form into 12 patties. Broil for a few minutes on each side. *Serves 6.*

## SAUTÉED LIVER (flourless)

3 tablespoons oil
1 clove garlic
1½ pounds liver, cubed
3 tablespoons nutritional yeast
¼ teaspoon salt
½ teaspoon marjoram

Heat oil. Sauté garlic, remove and discard. Dredge liver in remaining

ingredients. Sauté 3 minutes on each side. *Serves 6.*

## BROILED CORNBREAD-LIVER PATTIES (in blender)

1½ pounds liver (beef or pork)
stock to cover, hot
2 cups cornbread crumbs
¼ cup onions, grated
3 tablespoons oil
¼ teaspoon sage
1 teaspoon salt
3 tablespoons nutritional yeast

Pour stock over liver, cover and let stand for 5 minutes. Remove liver from stock. Grind in blender. Combine liver with remaining ingredients. Add enough stock to moisten mixture. Shape into patties. Broil, about 4 inches from heat, until brown on each side. *Serves 6.*

## BROILED LIVER SHASHLIK

½ cup sweet cider
juice of 1 lemon
1 teaspoon tarragon
1½ pounds liver, cut into 1-inch
    cubes
1 teaspoon salt
2 tablespoons nutritional yeast
3 onions
3 tomatoes
1 green pepper
½ pound mushrooms

Combine cider, lemon juice and tarragon, and marinate liver in mixture for 1 hour. Drain. Dust liver with salt and yeast. Cut onions, peppers and tomatoes into wedges, chunks or slices convenient for skewering, depending on their size. If mushrooms are small enough, leave these whole. Alternate liver on skewers with vegetables and mushrooms. Brush lightly with oil and broil briefly, turning skewers several times to brown liver uniformly. *Serves 6.*

## LIVER-KIDNEY KEBAB

½ pound liver, cubed
½ pound lamb kidney, cubed
½ pound lamb, cubed
3 tomatoes, cut in wedges
3 onions, sliced or in wedges
½ pound mushrooms
3 tablespoons oil
1 clove garlic, minced

Alternate liver, kidney, lamb, tomato, onion and mushrooms on skewers. Combine oil and garlic. Brush over meat and vegetables. Broil, turning frequently to cook all sides. *Serves 6.*

## BAKED BEEF LIVER

3 tablespoons oil
1 onion, chopped
½ cup mushrooms, sliced
½ green pepper, chopped
½ cup celery and tops, chopped
2 tablespoons wholewheat flour
1 cup milk
1 teaspoon salt
3 tablespoons nutritional yeast
¼ cup milk powder
½ teaspoon Essence of Sweet Herbs
1½ pound liver, sliced thin

Heat oil. Lightly sauté onion, mushrooms, green pepper and celery. Stir in flour. Gradually add milk. Blend. Cook until thickened. Add salt, yeast, milk powder and essence of sweet herbs. Arrange liver in oiled casserole and pour sauce over. Bake, covered, at 325° F. for 25 minutes. *Serves 6.*

## BAKED LIVER WITH CURRANTS

2 lamb livers, whole
2 bay leaves

9 cloves, whole
1 tablespoon oil
1½ cups currants (or gooseberries)
1 lemon, sliced

Remove membranes and tubes from livers. Arrange livers in oiled casserole. Add rest of ingredients. Cover and bake at 300° F. for one hour. *Serves 6.*

## LIVER BAKED IN SOUR CREAM

3 tablespoons oil
1½ pounds liver
1 teaspoon salt
3 tablespoons nutritional yeast
¼ cup soy grits, soaked in
½ cup stock
½ teaspoon oregano
2 tablespoons wholewheat flour
1½ cups sour cream *

Heat oil. Sauté liver lightly on both sides. Remove liver. Add remaining ingredients, except sour cream, to oil. Blend until smooth. Add sour cream to mixture. Cook over low heat, stirring constantly, for one minute. Arrange liver at bottom of oiled casserole and pour sauce over it. Cover. Bake at 300° F. for 45 minutes. *Serves 6.*

## BAKED LIVER WITH CIDER

1 slice of bacon, chopped
1½ pounds liver, in one piece
2 tablespoons wholewheat flour
2 tablespoons oil
1 clove garlic, minced
1 onion, chopped
2 stalks celery and tops, diced
1 carrot, diced
1 bay leaf
1 teaspoon thyme
2 cloves, whole
3 tablespoons nutritional yeast
½ teaspoon salt
1½ cups cider, hot

[Recipe continued on next page]

[Recipe continued from previous page]

Arrange bacon in bottom of heavy roasting pan. Dredge liver in flour. Put on top of bacon. Cover pan and place in hot oven until meat is richly browned. Meanwhile, heat oil and in it sauté garlic, onion, celery and carrot. Add all flavorings. Cover and simmer for 10 minutes. Arrange vegetable mixture around liver. Add small quantity of cider. Cover pan and return to oven. Bake at 325° F. for 1 hour, adding small quantities of cider from time to time until it is all used. *Serves 6.*

## BAKED LIVER SCALLOPED WITH POTATOES

2 tablespoons oil
1½ pounds liver, cubed
2 tablespoons wholewheat flour
6 potatoes, sliced thin
½ teaspoon salt
½ cup milk powder
3 tablespoons nutritional yeast
½ teaspoon oregano
1 tablespoon parsley, minced
1 pint milk, hot

Dredge liver in flour and heat oil. In it sauté liver. Arrange layer of potatoes at bottom of oiled casserole. Add layer of liver. Mix salt, milk powder, yeast, oregano and parsley. Sprinkle part of mixture over liver. Repeat layers of potatoes, liver and flavorings until all ingredients are used, reserving potato layer for top. Pour milk over mixture. Cover and bake at 350° F. for 1 hour, then remove cover. Continue baking till top layer of potatoes is browned. *Serves 6.*

VARIATION:
One cup of brown rice or buckwheat may be substituted for potatoes.

## FINNISH BAKED LIVER
(in blender)

1 cup stock, hot
1 pound liver, cubed
1 cup seedless raisins
1 cup milk, hot
1 cup brown rice, raw
1 onion, grated
1 egg, slightly beaten
3 tablespoons honey
1 teaspoon salt
3 tablespoons nutritional yeast
¼ teaspoon marjoram
2 tablespoons oil

Pour boiling stock over liver and raisins. Cover. Let mixture stand until cool. Drain liver and raisins. Purée in blender. Place stock, with milk, in top of double boiler over direct heat. When liquids come to boil, gradually add rice. Stir. Cover. Set top of double boiler into bottom, to which hot water has been added. Cook over low heat for 30 minutes. Thoroughly mix cooked rice and liver-and-raisin purée with remaining ingredients. Turn mixture into oiled casserole. Cover and bake at 325° F. for one hour. Serve hot or cold. *Serves 6.*

## RUSSIAN BAKED LIVER LOAF
(in blender)

1 carrot, diced
2 onions, sliced
2 sprigs celery leaves
1 sprig parsley
1 bay leaf
3 cups stock
1 pound calf's liver, cubed
½ pound pork liver, cubed
2 slices wholewheat bread, crumbled
1 teaspoon salt
3 tablespoons nutritional yeast
½ teaspoon nutmeg, ground
2 eggs, beaten
2 slices bacon, broiled, chopped

Put vegetables, parsley and bay leaf in pot with stock. Cover pot. Simmer for 20 minutes. Add liver, bring again to simmering point and cook for 10 minutes longer. Discard bay leaf. Cool. Put mixture into blender and blend until smooth. Add remaining ingredients and blend again. Turn mixture into oiled loaf pan. Bake at 350° F. for 40 minutes. May be served hot or cold. *Serves 6.*

## BAKED LIVER LOAF WITH CARROTS (in blender)

1 pound liver, cubed
2 tablespoons oil
1 onion, chopped
2 eggs, whole
½ cup pork sausage
1 cup milk
1½ cups wholewheat breadcrumbs
3 tablespoons nutritional yeast
1 tablespoon soy flour
1 teaspoon basil
1 teaspoon salt
2 carrots, cooked, cut into strips

Sauté liver and onion in oil until lightly browned. Cool. Put in blender. Add eggs and blend all until smooth. Turn into bowl. Add remaining ingredients, except carrot strips. Pack ⅓ of mixture into 5 x 9-inch loaf pan. Lay 3 strips of carrots lengthwise on top. Repeat with two more layers of liver mixture and carrots. Cover and bake at 300° F. for 1 hour. *Serves 6.*

## LIVER AND BEEF LOAF

1 pound beef, ground
½ pound liver, ground
1 cup wheat germ (or porridge made of wheat, rye, corn, rice, millet or buckwheat)
1 egg
2 onions, grated

¼ cup parsley, minced
¼ cup celery and tops, chopped
½ cup tomato juice
1 teaspoon salt
3 tablespoons nutritional yeast

Blend all ingredients together. Turn into an oiled loaf pan. Bake at 350° F. for 1 hour. *Serves 6.*

## SAVORY LIVER LOAF (in blender)

3 tablespoons oil
1 pound liver, cubed
2 onions, chopped
2 stalks celery and tops, chopped
1 egg
⅔ cup tomatoes, stewed (about)
3 tablespoons nutritional yeast
½ teaspoon rosemary
½ pound pork sausage
1 cup potatoes, cooked, mashed

Heat oil. Sauté liver, onions and celery. Cool. Place in blender, with egg and part of stewed tomatoes. Blend until smooth. Turn into bowl. Add remaining ingredients and blend again. Add only enough more stewed tomatoes to moisten. Turn into oiled loaf pan. Bake at 350° F. for 1 hour. *Serves 6.*

## GERMAN RICE RING WITH LIVER

3 tablespoons oil
1 pound calf's liver, cubed
1 onion, grated
2 cups stock
1 cup brown rice, raw
2 stalks of celery and tops, chopped
3 tablespoons parsley, minced
¼ cup Soybeans, Roasted, ground
1 teaspoon salt
3 tablespoons nutritional yeast
½ cup wholewheat bread crumbs
¼ cup milk powder

Heat oil. Sauté liver and onions 2 minutes. Remove from heat. Place

[Recipe continued on next page]

[Recipe continued from previous page]

stock in top of double boiler over direct heat. When stock boils, stir in rice. Cover pot. Set on bottom part of double boiler to which water has been added. Cook over low heat for 30 minutes. Blend liver mixture with rice. Add remaining ingredients and blend again. Turn into oiled ring mold. Bake at 400° F. for 15 minutes. Unmold on hot platter. Fill center with steamed green vegetables. *Serves 6.*

## BAKED LIVER-BACON PATTIES

1½ pounds liver, ground
2 tablespoons oil
2 onions, grated
1½ cups brown rice, cooked
2 eggs, beaten
1 teaspoon salt
¼ teaspoon thyme
¼ teaspoon marjoram
3 tablespoons nutritional yeast
6 slices bacon

Mix all ingredients except bacon. Shape into 6 large patties. Wrap a slice of bacon around each. Arrange in a shallow oiled baking pan. Bake at 350° F. for 30 minutes, or until bacon is crisp. *Serves 6.*

## LIVER STUFFED IN BAKED ONIONS (in blender)

6 large onions
¾ pound calf's liver, cubed
stock to cover liver
6 slices of bacon, broiled
3 stalks celery and tops, chopped
⅛ teaspoon celery seeds
¼ teaspoon salt
2 tablespoons nutritional yeast
2 tablespoons soy flour
⅓ cup wholewheat bread crumbs
3 tablespoons parsley, minced
3 tablespoons dill, minced

Skin onions. Remove centers, leaving firm shell. Pour boiling stock over liver. Cover and let stand for 2 minutes. Blend onion centers, liver, stock, bacon, celery until smooth. Turn into bowl. Add celery seeds, salt, yeast, flour and bread crumbs. Mix and stuff into onion cavities. Arrange in shallow baking pan. Fill pan with ⅓ cup water. Bake at 350° F. for 1 hour. Garnish with chopped parsley and dill before serving. *Serves 6.*

## LIVER-STUFFED GREEN PEPPERS

1 cup stock, hot
1 pound liver, cubed
6 green peppers
1 cup brown rice, cooked
½ cup tomatoes, stewed
1 onion, grated
½ teaspoon salt
3 tablespoons nutritional yeast
1 teaspoon oregano
¼ cup soy grits, soaked in
½ cup stock

Pour stock over liver. Cover and let stand for 5 minutes. Drain liver and grind. Cut off tops of peppers; remove seeds and membrane. Parboil peppers in hot stock for 3 minutes. Mix liver with remaining ingredients. Stuff peppers with mixture and set in baking dish. Pour stock into pan. Bake at 350° F. for 30 minutes. *Serves 6.*

## LIVER STUFFED IN CABBAGE LEAVES

12 cabbage leaves, parboiled
1 cup liver, ground
1 cup brown rice, cooked
1 egg, beaten
1 teaspoon salt
1 onion, grated
3 tablespoons nutritional yeast

1 teaspoon dill
1 cup tomato juice
2 tablespoons oil

Trim tough rib away from cabbage leaves. Blend liver, rice, egg, onion, yeast and dill. With inner side of leaf face up, place a tablespoonful of mixture on each cabbage leaf. Roll and fold under. Fasten with string or toothpick. Arrange in casserole. Combine tomato juice and oil. Pour over cabbage leaves. Cover and bake at 375° F. for 45 minutes.

VARIATIONS:
Stock may be used instead of tomato juice.
Lettuce leaves may be stuffed instead of cabbage leaves.
Rolls may be steamed instead of baked.

## LIVER ROULADES

½ pound pork sausage (bulk)
1 onion, grated
¼ cup wheat germ
¼ cup milk powder
¼ teaspoon sage
1 tablespoon soy flour
3 tablespoons nutritional yeast
1 pound beef liver, cut into 6 slices
6 strips of bacon
½ cup stock

Cook sausage meat and onions, stirring, until golden brown. Drain off excess fat. Remove from heat. Add wheat germ, milk powder, sage, flour and yeast. Blend well. Divide mixture into six portions. Place one portion on the top of each slice of liver. Roll and wrap with bacon. Fasten with string or toothpicks. Brown roulades on all sides. Arrange in casserole. Add stock. Cover and bake at 300° F. for 1 hour. *Serves 6.*

## LIVER IN SWEET-SOUR SAUCE

6 large, thin slices of liver
3 tablespoons wholewheat flour
1 egg, beaten
4 tablespoons wheat germ
3 tablespoons oil
1 tablespoon honey
juice and rind of 1 lemon
3 tablespoons parsley, minced

Dredge liver in flour, then dip in egg. Roll in wheat germ. Broil quickly on both sides in oven. Keep liver warm. In saucepan, blend oil, honey, lemon juice and rind. Heat thoroughly. Pour over liver. Garnish with parsley. *Serves 6.*

## LIVER IN MUSHROOM SAUCE

1 pound liver, cubed
3 tablespoons wholewheat flour
3 tablespoons oil
½ cup mushrooms, sliced
½ teaspoon salt
1 teaspoon Essence of Sweet Herbs
½ cup top milk
¼ cup soy grits, soaked in
¼ cup stock
3 tablespoons nutritional yeast
3 hard-cooked eggs, sliced
3 tablespoons sweet cider
3 tablespoons parsley, minced

Dredge liver in flour. Heat oil. Lightly sauté liver and mushrooms. Add salt, milk, soy grits, yeast. Cover. Simmer gently 5 minutes. Add eggs and cider. Heat thoroughly. Garnish with parsley and serve. *Serves 6.*

## CHICKEN LIVER AND BACON APPETIZERS

3 tablespoons oil
1 pound chicken livers, cut in half
1 slice bacon for each half liver

Heat oil. Sauté livers for 1 minute.

[Recipe continued on next page]

[Recipe continued from previous page]

Remove from pan. Wrap each piece of liver in strip of bacon. Fasten with toothpicks. 10 minutes before serving, place bacon-wrapped liver in shallow pan. Broil until bacon is crisp. Drain off bacon fat. Serve hot on toothpicks or on small squares of wholewheat toast. *Makes about 28 appetizers.*

## POTTED CALF'S LIVER

1½ pounds calf's liver, in 1 slice
1 onion, chopped
1 clove garlic, minced
2 tablespoons celery, chopped
2 tablespoons parsley, minced
1 teaspoon salt
1 tablespoon soy flour
3 tablespoons nutritional yeast
½ teaspoon basil
2 tablespoons wholewheat flour
3 tablespoons oil
1 cup stock

Cut 6 pockets, 1 inch wide, into liver, from top down to nearly the depth of the liver. Mix onion, garlic, celery, parsley, salt, soy flour, yeast and basil together. Fill pockets with this mixture. Tie string around liver to keep filling in place. Dredge liver in flour. Heat oil in pot. Sauté liver. Add stock and cover pot. Simmer for 20 minutes. *Serves 6.*

## PORK LIVER STEW

1 pound pork liver, cubed
¼ pound bacon, broiled, chopped
1 cup brown rice, cooked
3 carrots, cubed
2 onions, chopped
½ teaspoon salt
3 tablespoons nutritional yeast
½ teaspoon rosemary
2 cups stock, hot
3 tablespoons parsley, minced

Combine, in a pot, all ingredients except stock and parsley. Pour hot stock over mixture. Cover. Simmer for 30 minutes. Serve garnished with parsley. *Serves 6.*

## BEEF TONGUE WITH CHICKEN LIVERS

2 tablespoons oil
3 chicken livers, chopped
¼ pound mushrooms, sliced
2 tablespoons wholewheat flour
1½ cups stock, hot
¼ cup cranberry juice
½ teaspoon salt
3 tablespoons nutritional yeast
⅛ teaspoon nutmeg, ground
1 bay leaf
1 pound beef tongue, cooked, sliced
3 tablespoons parsley, minced

Heat oil. Sauté livers. Remove from pan. Sauté mushrooms in same pan and remove these, too. Blend flour with remaining oil in pan. Gradually add hot stock. Cook, stirring, until thickened. Add cranberry juice, salt, yeast, nutmeg and bay leaf. Heat until mixture comes to a boil. Add tongue, livers and mushrooms. Cover. Simmer until everything is thoroughly heated. Garnish with parsley. *Serves 6.*

## RISOTTO WITH CHICKEN LIVERS

3 tablespoons oil
3 onions, chopped
1 pound chicken livers, chopped
½ cup mushrooms, sliced
3 stalks celery and tops, chopped
1 teaspoon salt
1 teaspoon soy flour
3 tablespoons nutritional yeast
1 teaspoon basil
⅛ teaspoon nutmeg, ground
2 cups brown rice, cooked in stock
¼ cup Parmesan cheese, grated

Heat oil. Sauté onions, livers, mushrooms and celery. Remove from oil
and set aside. Stir into oil the salt,
flour, yeast, basil and nutmeg. Blend
thoroughly. Blend with rice and
sautéed mixture. Heat thoroughly.
Serve garnished with cheese. *Serves
6.*

## POLENTA WITH CHICKEN LIVERS

1 pound cornmeal
1/2 cup stock, cold
1 1/4 quarts stock, boiling
1 teaspoon salt
3 tablespoons oil
1 pound chicken livers, chopped
1/2 teaspoon sage
3 tablespoons nutritional yeast
1/4 cup tomato juice
3 slices bacon, broiled, chopped

Mix cornmeal with cold stock. Gradually add to boiling stock. Add salt.
Cook, stirring frequently for 30 minutes, or until cornmeal leaves side
of pot easily. Heat oil and sauté
chicken livers. Add sage, yeast and
tomato juice. Cover and simmer for
10 minutes. Turn polenta onto
large warm platter. Garnish with
liver mixture and top with bacon
bits. *Serves 6.*

## SMOTHERED LIVER

1 1/2 pounds beef liver, sliced
3 tablespoons wholewheat flour
3 tablespoons oil
3 onions, sliced
1/4 cup celery and tops, chopped
1 cup tomatoes, stewed
1 teaspoon salt
3 tablespoons nutritional yeast
1/4 teaspoon thyme
1/4 teaspoon celery seeds

Dredge liver in flour. Heat oil.
Sauté liver lightly on both sides. Remove liver from pan. Sauté onions.

Add remaining ingredients. Blend
thoroughly. Arrange liver slices on
top of vegetables. Cover. Simmer 30
minutes. *Serves 6.*

## CHICKEN LIVER PÂTÉ
(in blender)

2 tablespoons oil
1/2 pound chicken livers, cubed
1 onion, sliced
1 clove garlic, minced
1/4 cup stock
2 tablespoons nutritional yeast
1/2 teaspoon salt
1/4 teaspoon thyme
1/2 teaspoon sage
1/2 teaspoon marjoram
1/2 teaspoon basil
wheat germ

Heat oil. Sauté liver, onion and
garlic. Cool. Place stock in blender.
Add sautéed mixture, and remaining ingredients, except wheat germ.
Blend until smooth. Turn mixture
into bowl. Add enough wheat germ
to give pâté desired consistency.
Chill. Spread on wholewheat toast.
*Yields 1 1/4 cups.*

## DANISH LIVER PASTE

1 pound pork or beef liver, raw
2 strips bacon, broiled
1 onion
3 tablespoons oil
6 tablespoons wholewheat flour
1/2 cup milk powder
2 cups milk, hot
2 eggs, beaten
1 teaspoon salt
3 tablespoons nutritional yeast
1/4 teaspoon clove, ground
1/2 teaspoon allspice, ground

Put liver, bacon and onion through
smallest blade of food grinder at
[Recipe continued on next page]

[Recipe continued from previous page]
least twice, preferably three or four times, for fine-textured paste. Heat oil. Blend flour and milk powder with oil. Gradually add milk and cook over low heat, stirring meanwhile, until smooth and thick. Remove from heat. Cool and stir in eggs, salt and remaining ingredients. Blend thoroughly with liver mixture. If too loose, thicken with more milk powder. Pack mixture into oiled loaf pan. Bake at 350° F. for 1½ hours. Remove. Cool in pan. When cold, this paste may be unmolded. Store in refrigerator. It can be sliced or spread. *Makes 1 loaf.*

## CHICKEN LIVER SAUCE

3 tablespoons oil
1 cup onion, chopped
1 green pepper, chopped
6 chicken livers, chopped
1 cup stock
1 cup tomatoes, stewed
¼ teaspoon salt
1 tablespoon dill, chopped
3 tablespoons parsley, minced
4 strips bacon, broiled, minced

Heat oil. Sauté onions, peppers and livers. Add remaining ingredients. Cover. Simmer for 10 minutes. Serve over brown rice or mashed potatoes. *Serves 6.*

## ITALIAN LIVER BALLS
### (leftovers may be used)

1 pound liver, cooked, ground
4 slices bacon, broiled, chopped
3 slices wholewheat bread, soaked in milk, squeezed dry
1 tablespoon parsley, minced
3 tablespoons Parmesan cheese, grated
2 egg yolks
¼ teaspoon salt

3 tablespoons nutritional yeast
1 egg, beaten
wheat germ for covering

Blend liver, bacon, bread, parsley, cheese, egg yolks, salt and yeast. Shape into small meat balls. Dip balls into beaten egg, then roll in wheat germ. Brush tops with oil. Bake until golden brown. *Serves 6.*

## LIVER SOUFFLÉ
### (leftovers may be used)

1½ cups white sauce, hot (see Sauces for Vegetables)
1½ cups liver, cooked, ground
3 eggs, separated
3 tablespoons nutritional yeast

Blend together sauce, liver, egg yolks and yeast. Cool. Beat egg whites until stiff, and fold into mixture. Turn into oiled casserole or oiled individual custard cups. Bake, uncovered, at 350° F. for 1 hour for casserole; 45 minutes for custard cups. Do not open the oven door while soufflé is baking. *Serves 6.*

OTHER RECIPES USING LIVER
See under Liver: Spread; Soup (Chicken Liver-Celery, North European and Spanish); Dumplings; Chicken Liver Omelet; see also: Coratella; Tomato Juice-Liver Appetizer.

# Kidneys

HINTS:
1 beef kidney averages 1 pound and serves 4 to 6; 1 veal kidney averages ¾ pound and 2 serve 6; 1 pork kidney averages ¼ pound and 3 to 4 serve 6; 1 lamb kidney

averages ⅛ pound and 12 lamb kidneys serve 6.

Kidneys of young animals need only brief cooking, just enough to heat through.

To prepare kidneys for cooking, first remove membrane and hard parts. They may be cooked whole, split, sliced or ground.

Veal and lamb kidneys are best broiled; pork and beef kidneys, braised. Kidneys can also be baked, sautéed and stewed.

## BROILED KIDNEY

6 pairs lamb kidneys
3 tablespoons French Dressing
6 slices tomato
6 slices bacon

Marinate kidneys in French Dressing for 1 hour. Arrange tomatoes at bottom of shallow oiled baking dish. Remove kidneys from marinade. Place kidneys on top of tomato slices. Place bacon on top of kidneys. Broil until kidneys are tender and bacon is crisp. *Serves 6.*

## KIDNEY KEBAB

3 tablespoons oil
½ teaspoon salt
⅛ teaspoon thyme
⅛ teaspoon dill
12 lamb kidneys, split lengthwise
½ pound mushrooms, whole
1 tablespoon parsley, minced
1 tablespoon lemon juice

Mix oil, salt, thyme and dill together for marinade. Marinate kidneys for 3 hours. Drain. Thread kidneys on skewers, alternating with mushrooms. Brush with mixture of parsley and lemon juice. Broil, 4 inches from heat, for 5 minutes, turning skewers to brown all sides. *Serves 6.*

## VEAL KIDNEYS EN BROCHETTE

2 veal kidneys
boiling stock to cover
6 slices bacon, cut in 1-inch pieces
3 tablespoons oil
1 carrot, sliced thin
1 onion, sliced thin
12 small mushrooms
1 bay leaf
1 teaspoon thyme
1 sprig parsley, minced

Pour boiling stock over kidney and cover. Remove kidney after 5 minutes and cut into cubes. Alternate kidney, bacon strips and mushrooms on skewers. Broil on all sides. Arrange on hot platter and pour over them the following sauce:

Heat oil. Sauté carrot and onion for 5 minutes. Remove from pan. Add remaining ingredients and stock from kidney. Cover, bring to boil, then lower heat. Remove bay leaf. Add carrots and onions and cook until these are just tender. Pour over kidneys and bacon. *Serves 6.*

## KIDNEYS IN SUCCULENT SAUCE

¼ cup sweet cider
2 tablespoons Essence of Sweet Herbs
2 onions, grated
1 teaspoon salt
3 tablespoons nutritional yeast
1½ pounds beef or pork kidneys, sliced
2 tablespoons wholewheat flour
3 tablespoons oil

Blend sweet cider, Essence of Sweet Herbs, onions, salt and yeast together in bowl. Marinate kidneys in this for 15 minutes. Drain. Dredge in flour. Heat oil and sauté kidneys. Add marinade to pan and cover. Simmer until kidneys are tender. *Serves 6.*

## BROILED VEAL KIDNEYS

2 veal kidneys, cut lengthwise
2 tablespoons oil
½ teaspoon thyme
juice of 1 lemon

Brush kidneys with oil. Dust with thyme. Broil for 6 minutes on each side. Serve, sprinkled with lemon juice. *Serves 6.*

## BROILED LAMB KIDNEYS AND LAMB

juice of 2 lemons
2 tablespoons parsley, minced
½ teaspoon tarragon
2 onions, grated
2 lamb kidneys, cubed
2 pounds lean lamb (shoulder, leg or loin) cubed

Mix lemon juice, parsley, tarragon and onions. Marinate kidney and lamb for 30 minutes. Drain. Skewer kidney and lamb. Broil, turning to brown on all sides. *Serves 6.*

## VEAL KIDNEYS IN CRANBERRY JUICE

2 veal kidneys, sliced thin
2 tablespoons wholewheat flour
3 tablespoons oil
½ cup cranberry juice
½ teaspoon salt
2 tablespoons nutritional yeast
1 tablespoon parsley, minced
2 tablespoons sour cream*

Heat oil. Dredge kidneys in flour and sauté for 4 minutes. Remove kidneys from pan and keep hot. Blend cranberry juice, salt, yeast and parsley in pan in which kidneys were cooked and heat thoroughly. Remove pan from heat and stir in sour cream. Pour over kidneys. *Serves 6.*

## BRAISED KIDNEY

2 tablespoons oil
1½ pounds beef or pork kidney, sliced thin
½ cup onion, chopped
¾ cup sweet cider
¼ teaspoon salt
2 tablespoons nutritional yeast
1 tablespoon parsley, minced

Heat oil. Sauté kidneys for 2 minutes. Remove from pan. Sauté onion in same pan. Add kidney and remainder of ingredients to onion in pan. Cover and cook for 3 minutes. *Serves 6.*

## KIDNEYS AND MUSHROOMS

3 tablespoons oil
2 veal kidneys, split
½ cup mushrooms, sliced
1 onion, sliced
1 tablespoon parsley, minced
¼ cup sweet cider
¼ cup stock
½ teaspoon salt
2 tablespoons nutritional yeast
1 teaspoon soy flour

Heat oil. Sauté kidneys for 2 minutes. Add mushrooms and onions and sauté for 1 minute more. Add remaining ingredients and blend well. Cover. Simmer for 10 minutes. *Serves 6.*

## KIDNEYS CREOLE

1½ pounds beef kidney, sliced thin
2 tablespoons wholewheat flour
2 tablespoons oil
2 onions, chopped
1 green pepper, chopped
1 stalk celery and top, chopped
2 cups tomatoes, stewed

½ teaspoon salt
2 tablespoons nutritional yeast
¼ cup soy grits, soaked in
¼ cup stock
½ teaspoon tarragon
½ teaspoon savory
juice of 1 lemon
2 slices bacon, broiled, minced

Dredge kidney in flour and sauté in hot oil. Remove and set aside. Sauté onion, green pepper and celery in same pan. Add rest of ingredients except bacon. Combine kidney with mixture in pan and cover. Simmer until thoroughly heated. Garnish with bacon bits just before serving. *Serves 6.*

## LAMB KIDNEYS, FRENCH STYLE

12 lamb kidneys, sliced thin
3 tablespoons wholewheat flour
3 tablespoons oil
1 tablespoon meat stock
½ cup cider
½ teaspoon tarragon
½ teaspoon salt
2 tablespoons nutritional yeast

Heat oil. Dredge kidneys in flour and sauté. Remove from pan and keep warm. Add remaining ingredients to pan and bring to boil; lower heat and simmer for 5 minutes. Pour sauce over kidneys. Serve on wholewheat toast. *Serves 6.*

## VEAL KIDNEY SAUTÉ

2 veal kidneys, sliced thin
3 tablespoons wholewheat flour
3 tablespoons oil
1 onion, chopped
¼ cup sweet cider
1 tablespoon honey
pinch of mace, ground
pinch of nutmeg, ground
1 teaspoon salt
3 teaspoons nutritional yeast

½ cup sour cream*
3 tablespoons chives, minced

Dredge kidneys in flour and sauté briefly in hot oil. Remove from pan and set aside. Sauté onion in same pan; set aside. Blend cider, mace, nutmeg, salt and yeast in pan. Cover and bring to boil. Remove from heat. Let stand for a few minutes, then stir in sour cream. Add kidneys and onions to sauce and cook gently until thoroughly heated. Serve garnished with chives. *Serves 6.*

## ENGLISH BEEF-KIDNEY CASSEROLE

2 veal kidneys, cubed
2 tablespoons wholewheat flour
3 tablespoons oil
¾ pound round steak, cubed
½ cup mushrooms, sliced
2 onions, sliced
1 cup stock
1 bay leaf
1 tablespoon parsley, minced
¼ cup celery leaves, chopped
½ teaspoon salt
3 tablespoons nutritional yeast
½ teaspoon marjoram
¼ cup soy grits, soaked in
¼ cup stock
½ cup carrots, cooked, cubed
pastry dough

Heat oil. Dredge kidneys in flour and sauté. Remove from pan and set aside. Sauté round steak in same pan. Take out, and sauté mushrooms and onions. Remove. Add to pan all remaining ingredients except pastry dough. Blend and heat until mixture boils. Remove from heat and combine with kidneys, round steak, mushrooms and onions. Turn into oiled casserole and top with pastry (see under Pastries for suggested recipes). Bake at 425°

[Recipe continued on next page]

[Recipe continued from previous page]
F. for 30 minutes, or until pastry is crisp and brown. *Serves 6.*

## SAVORY LAMB KIDNEY SAUTÉ

12 lamb kidneys, sliced thin
3 tablespoons wholewheat flour
3 tablespoons oil
3 cups stock, hot
2 teaspoons Essence of Sweet Herbs
1 teaspoon salt
3 tablespoons nutritional yeast
½ teaspoon tarragon
1 tablespoon parsley, minced
wholewheat toast

Dredge kidneys in flour. Heat oil. Sauté kidneys in oil and remove kidneys from pan. Keep hot. Add stock, essence of sweet herbs, salt, yeast and tarragon to pan in which kidneys were cooked. Blend well. Cover and simmer for 10 minutes. Arrange kidneys on toast and pour sauce over. Garnish with parsley and serve. *Serves 6.*

## FRENCH KIDNEY CASSEROLE

1 beef kidney, sliced
3 tablespoons wholewheat flour
3 tablespoons oil
1 quart tomatoes, stewed
1 teaspoon salt
3 tablespoons nutritional yeast
½ teaspoon tarragon
1 teaspoon honey
1 bay leaf
¼ teaspoon celery seeds
1 tablespoon parsley, minced
1 onion, grated
1 clove garlic, minced
¼ teaspoon cinnamon, ground
1 green pepper, minced
½ cup celery leaves, chopped
¼ cup mushrooms, sliced
¼ cup soy grits, soaked in
¼ cup stock

Dredge kidney in flour and sauté

in oil. Put in oiled casserole. Combine remaining ingredients and pour over kidney. Cover. Bake at 250° F. for about 1½ hours, until kidney is tender. *Serves 6.*

## ENGLISH KIDNEY STEW

2 beef kidneys or 8 lamb kidneys, sliced thin
3 cups stock
2 onions, sliced
6 slices bacon, broiled, chopped
1 bay leaf
½ teaspoon salt
3 tablespoons nutritional yeast
2 tablespoons wholewheat flour
½ teaspoon savory
¼ cup soy grits, soaked in
¼ cup stock
3 tablespoons parsley, minced

Combine all ingredients, except parsley, in pot. Simmer until kidneys are tender. Garnish with parsley. *Serves 6.*

VARIATIONS:
Mushrooms and/or sliced potatoes may be added.
Stewed tomatoes may be substituted for part of the stock.

## ONIONS STUFFED WITH KIDNEYS (in blender)

6 large onions
3 cups stock
6 lamb kidneys, chopped
¼ teaspoon nutmeg, ground
¼ teaspoon tarragon
¼ teaspoon thyme
1 tablespoon parsley
1 teaspoon salt
3 teaspoons nutritional yeast
6 cloves, whole

Cover onions with stock. Simmer for 20 minutes. Cool. Scoop out centers leaving a shell about ½-inch thick. Purée scooped-out onion with kidneys in blender, adding small amount of stock to blend smoothly. Add all flavorings except cloves and blend again. Pack mixture into onions. Stick 1 clove in each onion. Arrange onions in shallow baking dish. Pour in stock, cover and bake at 350° F. for 40 minutes. *Serves 6.*

## ITALIAN KIDNEY-RICE CASSEROLE

3 tablespoons oil
1 onion, chopped
1 leek, chopped
1 tablespoon parsley, minced
3 veal kidneys
4 small zucchini, sliced thin
2 cups brown rice, cooked
1¼ cups stock
1 teaspoon salt
3 tablespoons nutritional yeast
1 teaspoon soy flour
¼ cup Parmesan cheese, grated

Heat oil and lightly sauté onion, leek and parsley. Add kidneys and sauté for 3 minutes more. Add remainder of ingredients, except cheese. Cover. Simmer 10 minutes. Turn mixture into oiled casserole. Sprinkle cheese on top. Bake uncovered at 375° F. for 20 minutes. *Serves 6.*

## BAKED KIDNEY LOAF
(in blender)

1 cup milk
2 eggs
1 pound kidney, cut in pieces
1 onion
1 green pepper
1 sprig parsley
1 teaspoon salt
3 tablespoons nutritional yeast
½ teaspoon sage
½ cup milk powder

1 teaspoon soy flour
1½ cups wholewheat bread crumbs

Blend milk, eggs, kidney, onion, green pepper and parsley until smooth. Combine with remaining ingredients. Mix thoroughly. Pack into oiled 5- x 9-inch loaf pan. Bake at 350° F. for 1½ hours. *Serves 6.*

# Leftover Kidney

## KIDNEY HASH

2 tablespoons oil
2 onions, sliced
2 cups kidney, cooked, ground
½ teaspoon salt
2 tablespoons nutritional yeast
1 cup potatoes, cooked, cubed
½ teaspoon thyme
1 tablespoon parsley, minced
½ cup Soybeans, Roasted, ground
½ cup stock

Heat oil. Sauté onions. Blend with remaining ingredients. Pack into oiled baking dish. Bake in 300° F. oven for 20 minutes. *Serves 6.*

## KIDNEY SOUFFLÉ

3 tablespoons oil
3 tablespoons wholewheat flour
1 cup stock, hot
½ teaspoon salt
2 tablespoons nutritional yeast
½ teaspoon oregano
5 egg yolks, beaten
1 cup kidney, cooked, ground
¼ cup sunflower seeds, ground
5 egg whites, beaten stiff

Heat oil. Blend in flour. Gradually add stock and cook over low heat, stirring until smooth and thickened. Add salt, yeast and oregano. Remove from heat. Cool. Blend in yolks, kidney and sunflower seeds. Fold in egg whites. Turn mixture

[Recipe continued on next page]

[Recipe continued from previous page]
into oiled casserole or oiled individual custard cups. Bake at 350° F. for 30 minutes. *Serves 6.*

## KIDNEY OMELET (in blender)

6 egg yolks
3 tablespoons oil
¼ teaspoon salt
2 tablespoons nutritional yeast
2 tablespoons parsley
1 cup kidney, cooked, cubed
1 teaspoon soy flour
¼ teaspoon thyme
6 egg whites, beaten stiff
3 tablespoons chives, minced

Combine egg yolks, oil, salt, yeast, parsley, kidney, soy flour and thyme in food blender. Blend until smooth. Turn into bowl. Fold in egg whites. Turn into oiled casserole. Bake at 300° F. for about 20 minutes, until set. Garnish with chives. *Serves 6.*

OTHER KIDNEY RECIPES
See: Kidney-Cheese Spread; Russian Kidney Soup; German Kidney Soup; Liver-Kidney Kebab.

# Tripe

HINTS:
Plain tripe averages 7 pounds; honeycomb tripe, 1½ pounds. 1½ pounds of tripe serves 6.
Tripe may be broiled, simmered, or baked in a casserole.

## BROILED BREADED TRIPE

1 egg
1 tablespoon milk
2 tablespoons oil
¼ teaspoon sweet basil
¼ teaspoon salt
1½ pounds tripe, cut into pieces
½ cup wheat germ
3 tablespoons parsley, minced

Blend milk, egg, oil, basil and salt together. Dip pieces of tripe in this mixture, then in wheat germ. Arrange in shallow pan. Broil. Garnish with parsley. *Serves 6.*

## BROILED TRIPE

1½ pounds tripe, cut into pieces
3 tablespoons oil
3 tablespoons parsley, minced
1 lemon, in wedges

Brush tripe with oil on both sides. Arrange in shallow pan. Broil for 5 minutes on each side. Garnish with parsley and lemon wedges. *Serves 6.*

## CREOLE TRIPE CASSEROLE

1½ pounds tripe, cut into pieces
hot stock to cover
½ pound bacon
1 stalk celery and top, chopped
2 onions, sliced
1 carrot, chopped
1 green pepper, chopped
1 leek, chopped
2 bay leaves
1 clove garlic, minced
5 cloves, whole
3 sprigs parsley, minced
1 sprig thyme, minced
1 teaspoon rosemary
1 teaspoon salt
3 tablespoons nutritional yeast
2 cups sweet cider*
1 calf's foot, split in two

Pour boiling stock over tripe. Cover. Let stand for 5 minutes. Drain, reserving stock. Line large oiled casserole with half the bacon, half the vegetables, and half the tripe. Repeat, using rest of bacon, vegetables and tripe. Combine stock with cider and all flavorings. Pour this mixture into casserole. Place calf's foot on

top. Cover tightly. Bake at 250° F.
for about 5 hours. *Serves 6.*

## ITALIAN STEWED TRIPE

1½ pounds veal tripe
2 quarts stock
1 teaspoon salt
1 stalk celery and top, chopped
2 cloves
3 tablespoons oil
2 onions, chopped
2 carrots, diced
1 green pepper, chopped
¼ pound bacon, broiled, minced
1 cup tomatoes, stewed
1 cup red beans, cooked
½ small cabbage, sliced thin
3 large potatoes, cooked, diced
1 pinch saffron
½ teaspoon sage, ground
3 tablespoons nutritional yeast
¼ cup Parmesan cheese, grated

Place tripe, stock, salt, celery and
cloves in large pot. Cover and simmer for 2 hours. Remove tripe from
stock. Cut into thin strips. Heat oil.
Sauté onions, carrots and green
peppers. Return tripe to pot with
sautéed vegetables and tomatoes.
Cover and simmer for 5 minutes.
Add beans, cabbage, potatoes, cover
again and simmer for 20 minutes
more. Add saffron, sage and yeast,
and simmer 5 minutes longer. Garnish with cheese and serve. *Serves 6.*

## RUMANIAN STEWED TRIPE

1½ pounds tripe, cut into pieces
1 marrow bone
stock to cover
1 onion, chopped
3 carrots, diced
½ cup celery and tops, chopped
½ cup brown rice, raw
¼ cup soy grits, soaked in
½ cup stock
1 teaspoon salt
3 tablespoons nutritional yeast

juice of 1 lemon
1 egg yolk, beaten

Put tripe, marrow bone and stock
into pot and cover. Simmer for 2
hours. Add onion, carrots and celery. When mixture simmers again,
slowly add rice and stir. Add soy
grits, salt and yeast and cover again.
Continue simmering until rice is
tender; remove from heat. Take out
marrow bone. Gradually blend in
egg yolk. Just before serving, add
lemon juice. *Serves 6.*

## CHINESE STEWED TRIPE

1½ pounds beef tripe
3 cups stock
1 scallion, chopped
3 tablespoons Essence of Sweet
    Herbs
½ teaspoon salt
3 tablespoons nutritional yeast
3 tablespoons sweet cider
carrot strips, very thin
green pepper strips, very thin
½ cup mung bean Sprouts

Cover tripe with stock. Cover. Simmer 2 hours. Remove tripe. Cut
into strips ½-inch wide and 1½-
inches long. Return to pot. Add
scallions, essence of sweet herbs,
salt, yeast and cider. Cover. Simmer
1 hour longer. During last 5 minutes, add carrot and green pepper
strips. Remove from heat. Garnish
with mung bean sprouts. *Serves 6.*

# Leftover Tripe

## CREAMED TRIPE

2 tablespoons oil
2 cups tripe, cooked, cut up
1 cup peas, cooked
1 cup carrots, cooked, cubed
1 cup Soybeans, Roasted, ground
1 cup white sauce (see Sauces for
    Vegetables)

[Recipe continued on next page]

[Recipe continued from previous page]

Heat oil and sauté tripe. Blend in remaining ingredients and heat thoroughly. *Serves 6.*

## TRIPE À LA KING

2 tablespoons oil
1 onion, chopped
2 cups tripe, cooked, in pieces
1 cup brown rice, cooked
1 cup chicken stock
3 tablespoons nutritional yeast
⅛ teaspoon cinnamon, ground
juice of 1 lemon
6 slices wholewheat bread, toasted
3 tablespoons parsley, minced

Heat oil. Sauté onion. Blend in tripe, rice, stock, yeast, cinnamon and lemon juice. Heat thoroughly, garnish with parsley, and serve on toast. *Serves 6.*

## ITALIAN TRIPE

2 tablespoons oil
1 onion, chopped
1 clove garlic, minced
1 sprig parsley, minced
¼ cup tomato juice
1 cup stock
½ teaspoon salt
3 tablespoons nutritional yeast
1 sprig mint, minced
1½ pounds tripe, cooked, sliced
    thin
2 slices bacon, broiled, minced
½ cup Parmesan cheese, grated

Heat oil. Sauté onions, garlic and parsley. Add tomato juice, stock, salt, yeast and mint. Cover. Simmer for 10 minutes. Add tripe and bacon, cover again and simmer 10 minutes longer. Serve garnished with cheese. *Serves 6.*

OTHER TRIPE RECIPES
See: Tripe Soup, Philadelphia; Tripe Soup, Turkish.

# Sweetbreads

HINTS:
Sweetbreads average ⅛ pound; 1½ pounds of sweetbreads serve 6. Sweetbreads need not be soaked before cooking. They may be prepared without precooking. They are, however, extremely perishable and if they are not to be used immediately, precooking is necessary. To precook: Simmer for 15 minutes in water or stock, to which 1 teaspoon of salt and 1 tablespoon of lemon juice or cider vinegar have been added for every quart of liquid. Cool. Remove loose membrane. Store in refrigerator and use as soon as possible.

## BRAISED SWEETBREADS

1½ pounds sweetbreads
3 tablespoons wholewheat flour
2 tablespoons oil
stock to cover

Wash sweetbreads and remove membrane. Dredge in flour. Heat oil and sauté briefly. Pour stock over and cover pan. Simmer for 20 minutes. *Serves 6.*

## BRAISED SWEETBREADS WITH VEGETABLES

1½ pounds sweetbreads
3 tablespoons wholewheat flour
3 tablespoons oil
1 onion, chopped
1 carrot, cooked, cubed
2 strips bacon, broiled, minced
2 sprigs parsley, minced
1 teaspoon salt
1 bay leaf
2 cups stock

Wash sweetbreads. Remove membrane. Dredge sweetbreads in flour and sauté briefly in hot oil. Remove from pan. Sauté onion. Mix all ingredients together and turn into oiled casserole. Bake, covered, at 350° F. for 20 minutes; uncover and bake an additional 10 minutes. *Serves 6.*

## FRENCH BRAISED SWEETBREADS

1½ pounds sweetbreads
3 tablespoons wholewheat flour
3 tablespoons oil
1 onion, sliced
1½ cups sweet cider
1 bay leaf
½ teaspoon thyme
½ teaspoon rosemary
pinch of mace, ground
1 teaspoon salt
3 tablespoons nutritional yeast
1 cup peas, raw

Wash sweetbreads. Remove membrane. Dredge in flour. Heat oil and briefly sauté sweetbreads. Remove from pan. Sauté onion in same pan. Mix all ingredients together except peas. Turn into oiled casserole. Bake, covered, at 350° F. for 40 minutes, adding peas for last 3 minutes of baking. *Serves 6.*

## BROILED BREADED SWEETBREADS

1½ pounds sweetbreads, precooked
1 tablespoon oil
wheat germ
2 tablespoons additional oil
2 tablespoons wholewheat flour
1 cup milk, hot
½ teaspoon salt
2 tablespoons nutritional yeast
2 tablespoons lemon juice
2 tablespoons chives, minced

Brush sweetbreads with oil. Roll in wheat germ. Broil. Meanwhile,

heat additional oil. Blend in flour. Gradually add hot milk. Continue to cook, stirring meanwhile, until thickened. Add salt, yeast and lemon juice. Blend thoroughly. Pour sauce over sweetbreads. Garnish with chives. *Serves 6.*

## BROILED SWEETBREADS

1½ pounds sweetbreads, precooked
1 tablespoon oil
¼ teaspoon salt
¼ teaspoon rosemary

Split sweetbreads crosswise. Brush with oil. Sprinkle with salt and rosemary. Broil for 5 minutes. *Serves 6.*

## BROILED SWEETBREADS-PINEAPPLE-BACON

6 slices Canadian bacon, cut
    ¼ inch thick
1½ pounds sweetbreads, precooked
2 tablespoons oil
6 slices fresh pineapple
3 tablespoons parsley, minced

Broil bacon 3 inches from heat, 4 minutes on each side. Drain fat. Set bacon aside. Add sweetbreads to pan and brush each side with oil. Add pineapple slices. Broil 3 minutes on each side. Add bacon and garnish with parsley. *Serves 6.*

## SWEETBREADS EN BROCHETTE

1½ pounds sweetbreads, precooked
1 green pepper, cut for skewering
1 tomato, in wedges
1 onion, sliced or in wedges
½ pound mushrooms, whole
1 tablespoon oil

Cut sweetbreads into chunks. Thread all ingredients on skewers.

[Recipe continued on next page]

[Recipe continued from previous page]
Brush with oil. Broil on all sides.
*Serves 6.*

## SWEETBREADS-MUSHROOM CASSEROLE

3 tablespoons oil
2 cups mushrooms, diced
¾ cup milk, hot
¼ cup milk powder
½ teaspoon salt
3 tablespoons nutritional yeast
½ cup sweet cider
1½ pounds sweetbreads, precooked, cubed

Heat oil. Sauté mushrooms and set aside. Gradually add milk to oil in pan and blend until smooth. Add milk powder, salt, yeast and cider and blend again. Return mushrooms to pan with sweetbreads. Turn into oiled casserole and bake at 300° F. for 15 minutes. *Serves 6.*

## SWEETBREADS-PANCAKE CASSEROLE

FILLING:

3 tablespoons oil
3 tablespoons wholewheat flour
1½ cups milk, hot
½ cup milk powder
1 teaspoon salt
3 tablespoons nutritional yeast
½ teaspoon rosemary
1½ pounds sweetbreads, precooked, cubed

Heat oil and blend in flour. Keeping over low heat, gradually add milk and stir until smooth and thickened. Add milk powder, salt, yeast and rosemary and blend again. Combine sweetbreads with mixture and cook for 5 minutes more.

PANCAKE BATTER:
(in blender)

1½ cups milk
3 eggs
1 tablespoon oil
1⅓ cups wholewheat flour, sifted
½ teaspoon salt
1 teaspoon soy flour

Combine all ingredients in blender. Blend until smooth; batter should be quite thin. Pour batter onto hot, unoiled soapstone griddle or into heated, oiled pan.

Arrange a layer of pancakes on the bottom of an oiled casserole. Top with a layer of creamed sweetbreads. Continue alternating layers, ending with sweetbreads. Cover. Bake at 400° F. for about 15 minutes, until sauce begins to bubble. *Serves 6.*

# Leftover Sweetbreads

## RAGOÛT OF SWEETBREADS

3 tablespoons oil
1 clove garlic, minced
3 tablespoons wholewheat flour
2 cups beef stock, hot
1 cup cream
¼ cup milk powder
1 teaspoon salt
3 tablespoons nutritional yeast
2 egg yolks, beaten
¼ cup sweet cider
2 cups asparagus, cooked, diced
1 cup sweetbreads, cooked, diced
1 cup brown rice, cooked
3 tablespoons parsley, minced

Heat oil and blend in garlic and flour. Gradually add stock and cook, stirring meanwhile, until thickened. Add cream, milk powder, salt and yeast and blend well. Remove from heat. Stir in yolks and cider. Add remaining ingredients, except parsley, and mix. Return to heat and when piping hot, garnish with parsley and serve. *Serves 6.*

## FRENCH SWEETBREADS

3 tablespoons oil
5 cooking apples, sliced
2 cups sweetbreads, cooked, diced
½ pound mushrooms, sliced
½ cup sweet cider, hot
1 cup top milk
2 egg yolks
1 teaspoon salt

Sauté apples in hot oil and set aside. Sauté mushrooms and sweetbreads in same oil. Set these aside as well. Blend cider with oil and juices in pan, keeping hot. In a bowl, mix milk, egg yolks and salt. Gradually stir this mixture into hot cider. Cook, stirring constantly, until sauce thickens but does not boil. Remove from heat. Again add sweetbreads, apples and mushrooms to pan, mix thoroughly and reheat. *Serves 6.*

## SWEETBREADS WITH VEGETABLES

2 cups sweetbreads, cooked, cubed
½ cup mushrooms, sliced
4 onions, small
1 stalk celery and top, chopped
1 green pepper, chopped
1 cup stock
½ cup sweet cider
1 egg yolk
1 teaspoon lemon juice
1 sprig parsley, minced

Combine all ingredients in pot and cover. Simmer for 20 minutes. *Serves 6.*

OTHER SWEETBREAD RECIPES
See: Sweetbread Salad; Sweetbread-Chicken Salad; Brain-Sweetbread Salad.

# Brains

HINTS:
Brains average ⅜ pound; 1½ pounds serve 6.
Brains are pinkish grey when fresh. As they are extremely perishable, they should be precooked if not used immediately. To precook: Cover brains with cold water, to which 1 teaspoon salt and 1 tablespoon lemon juice or cider vinegar have been added for each quart of liquid. Soak for 15 minutes. Remove and discard membrane. Simmer brains in salted water for 20 to 30 minutes. Drain, cool and refrigerate. Use as soon as possible.

## BRAISED BRAINS

6 lamb's brains, precooked
3 tablespoons wholewheat flour
3 tablespoons oil
½ cup milk, hot
⅛ teaspoon nutmeg, ground
juice of 1 lemon

Cut brains in half, lengthwise. Dredge in flour. Heat oil. Sauté brains and set aside. Gradually add remaining ingredients to pan and blend thoroughly. Continue to cook, stirring until thickened. Return brains to pan, cover and simmer for 20 minutes. *Serves 6.*

## CALF'S BRAINS, SAUTÉED

1½ pounds calf's brains, precooked
2 eggs
1 teaspoon salt
3 tablespoons nutritional yeast
⅛ teaspoon mace, ground
½ cup sunflower-seed meal
3 tablespoons oil
3 tablespoons chives, minced

[Recipe continued on next page]

[Recipe continued from previous page]

Dice brains. Blend eggs, salt, yeast and mace. Dip brains in mixture, then coat with sunflower-seed meal. Sauté brains in hot oil until golden brown on all sides. Serve garnished with chives. *Serves 6.*

## BROILED BRAINS

1½ pounds brains, precooked
2 eggs, beaten
2 teaspoons water, cold
¼ teaspoon salt
3 tablespoons nutritional yeast
2 tablespoons oil
juice of 1 lemon
wheat germ
1 tablespoon parsley, minced
¼ cup water cress, minced

Cut brains into 2- or 3-inch pieces. Blend together eggs, water, salt, yeast, oil and lemon juice. Dip brains in mixture, then roll in wheat germ. Broil. Garnish with parsley and water cress. *Serves 6.*

## BRAINS AU GRATIN

2 cups brown rice, cooked
1½ pounds brains, precooked
3 eggs, hard-cooked, sliced
½ cup cheddar cheese, grated
¼ cup stock
2 tablespoons oil
3 tablespoons nutritional yeast
1 tablespoon lemon juice
3 tablespoons parsley, minced
⅛ teaspoon mace, ground

In bottom of oiled casserole arrange a layer of rice, a layer of sliced brains, a layer of eggs and a layer of cheese. Repeat layers, ending with rice. Blend remaining ingredients together and pour over mixture in casserole. Cover and bake at 300° F. for 20 minutes; for last 3 minutes of baking time, remove cover, and put under broiler to brown top. *Serves 6.*

## RUSSIAN VEAL CHOPS WITH BRAINS

6 veal chops
1 pair calf's brains, precooked
¼ teaspoon salt
3 tablespoons nutritional yeast
½ cup wheat germ
1 onion, sliced and sautéed
3 tablespoons parsley, minced
1 tablespoon wholewheat flour
3 tablespoons sour cream*
2 egg yolks, diluted with
few tablespoons stock

Broil chops briefly. Arrange at bottom of large casserole. Cover each chop with a slice of brain. Blend salt, yeast and wheat germ together. Dust tops of brains with mixture. Cover and bake at 375° F. for 25 minutes. Meanwhile, combine remaining ingredients in saucepan and cook over gentle heat. When sauce is hot and slightly thick, pour over casserole. Bake for an additional 15 minutes. *Serves 6.*

## BRAINS IN SAVORY SAUCE

3 tablespoons oil
3 tablespoons wholewheat flour
2 cups milk, hot
½ cup celery and tops, chopped
2 green peppers, chopped
1 onion, grated
1 carrot, grated
2 tablespoons parsley, minced
3 tablespoons nutritional yeast
pinch of allspice, ground

1½ pounds brains, precooked,
   cubed
6 slices wholewheat toast

Heat oil. Blend in flour. Gradually
add milk and cook, stirring until
thickened. Add all ingredients except toast. Mix well. Simmer until
hot. Serve on toast. *Serves 6.*

## BRAINS IN TOMATO SAUCE

3 tablespoons oil
1 onion, sliced
2 cups tomatoes, stewed
½ cup celery and tops, chopped
1 teaspoon oregano
1 bay leaf
1 tablespoon wholewheat flour
1 teaspoon soy flour
½ teaspoon salt
3 tablespoons nutritional yeast
¼ cup soy grits, soaked in
½ cup stock
1½ pounds brains, precooked,
   cubed

Heat oil in pan and sauté onion.
Add tomatoes, celery, oregano and
bay leaf. Cover and simmer for 15
minutes. Blend in flours, salt and
yeast. Add soy grits and brains and
simmer until thoroughly heated.
*Serves 6.*

## BRAINS WITH SPINACH
(in blender)

1½ pounds brains, precooked
1 egg, beaten
Soybeans, Roasted, ground
1 pound spinach, cooked, drained
¼ teaspoon salt
3 tablespoons nutritional yeast
2 tablespoons oil
½ cup sour cream*

Cube brains. Dip into egg and then
into ground Soybeans. Brush with
oil and broil. Meanwhile, purée
spinach in blender. Add salt, yeast,

oil and sour cream and blend again
until smooth. Turn spinach mixture
into saucepan and heat. Pour over
brains. *Serves 6.*

# Leftover Brains

## BRAINS WITH SCRAMBLED EGGS
(in blender)

6 eggs
¾ cup milk
¼ cup milk powder
½ teaspoon salt
3 tablespoons nutritional yeast
1 teaspoon soy flour
3 tablespoons oil
½ green pepper, minced
1 cup brains, precooked, chopped
   fine
pinch of mace, ground

Blend eggs, milk, milk powder, salt,
yeast and flour in blender until
smooth. Sauté green pepper and
brains in hot oil. Add blended mixture to pan with peppers and brains
and scramble all together. Remove
from heat. Dust with mace. *Serves 6.*

## BRAIN SOUFFLÉ

3 tablespoons oil
3 tablespoons wholewheat flour
1 cup top milk, hot
4 egg yolks, beaten
2 cups brains, precooked, chopped
   fine
¼ teaspoon salt
3 tablespoons nutritional yeast
4 egg whites, beaten stiff

Heat oil. Blend in flour. Gradually
add milk. Cook over gentle heat,
stirring until thickened. Remove
from heat. When cool, add egg
yolks, brains, salt and yeast and mix
well. Fold in egg whites. Turn mixture into oiled casserole or oiled

[Recipe continued on next page]

[Recipe continued from previous page]
individual custard cups. Bake at 350° F., 1 hour in casserole, 45 minutes in custard cups. Do not open oven door while baking. *Serves 6.*

## CZECHOSLOVAKIAN BRAIN PANCAKES

pancakes from favorite recipe (see Chapter 19, Quick Breads)
3 tablespoons oil
3 onions, cut
½ clove garlic, minced
2 cups brains, precooked, cubed
3 eggs, beaten
½ cup top milk
½ teaspoon salt
2 tablespoons nutritional yeast
1 tablespoon parsley, minced

Prepare pancakes. Sauté onions and garlic in hot oil. Add brains. Cover and cook over low heat for 20 minutes. Add remaining ingredients. Simmer until mixture thickens. Arrange a layer of pancakes at the bottom of an oiled casserole. Place a layer of brain mixture on top. Repeat until all pancakes and filling are used. Cover and bake at 350° F. for 10 minutes. Cut diagonally and serve. *Serves 6.*

## TURKISH BRAIN SALAD

lettuce leaves
2 cups lamb's brains, precooked, thinly sliced, chilled
3 tomatoes, cut into wedges
6 radish roses
1 green pepper, cut into strips
juice and rind of 1 lemon
3 tablespoons oil
½ teaspoon salt
1 sprig mint, chopped fine

Arrange lettuce on platter. Top with brains. Garnish with tomatoes, radishes and green peppers. Blend

lemon juice, rind, oil and salt together and drizzle this dressing over top of salad. Garnish with mint. *Serves 6.*

## BRAIN-SWEETBREAD SALAD

1 cup Sprouts
1 cup celery and tops, chopped
1 cup sweetbreads, precooked, diced
1 cup brains, precooked, diced
1 onion, grated fine
favorite salad dressing

Blend all ingredients together. Moisten with dressing. Serve on salad greens. *Serves 6.*

## BRAIN FILLING FOR MEAT PASTRIES

1 pair calf's brains, precooked
2 cups stock
2 bay leaves
3 tablespoons nutritional yeast
1 tablespoon oil
1 tablespoon wholewheat flour
1 tablespoon lemon juice
2 tablespoons sour cream*

Put brains into pot with stock. Add bay leaves and yeast. Cover and simmer for 10 minutes. Cool. Cut brain into small pieces. Heat oil and in it brown flour. Add lemon juice and brains. Sauté briefly. Remove from heat and stir in sour cream. Use as filling for meat pastries.

# Heart

HINTS:
One beef heart averages 4 pounds and will serve 8 to 10. It is usually braised or baked. It will be tender and tasty if allowed 3 to

3½ hours of cooking in liquid over low heat.

One calf heart averages ½ pound and serves 2. Calf heart is usually braised or baked. It requires about 2½ hours' cooking time.

One pork heart averages ½ pound and serves 2. Braise whole or in slices.

One lamb heart averages ¼ pound. Allow 1 lamb heart per serving. Braise whole or in slices.

Heart does not require soaking or precooking. Before cooking, wash, remove valves and trim excess fat. Heart can be stuffed prior to braising or baking. See under Stuffings for additional recipes.

## BRAISED STUFFED HEART

1 beef heart or 3 calf or pork hearts
3 tablespoons wholewheat flour
3 tablespoons oil
1 cup stock
1 cup tomato juice
1 teaspoon soy flour
3 tablespoons nutritional yeast

Slit heart. Remove fat, gristle and blood vessels. Fill with stuffing (see below) and sew up slit. Dredge heart in flour and sauté in hot oil until brown on all sides. Blend remaining ingredients and pour over heart. Cover pan and simmer until tender: 3-3½ hours for beef heart, 2½ hours for calf or pork heart. Or bake in covered casserole at 300° F., allowing same time as for braising.

STUFFING:

1 onion, chopped, sautéed in oil
2 stalks celery and tops, chopped
1 cup wholewheat bread crumbs
1 cup Soybeans, Roasted, ground
1 teaspoon salt
2 tablespoons nutritional yeast
¼ teaspoon thyme
1 tablespoon parsley, minced

Combine all ingredients. If dry, moisten with small amount of stock. Stuff heart. *Serves 6.*

## BROILED HEART

2 pounds heart
stock to cover
½ teaspoon sage
3 tablespoons nutritional yeast
1 tablespoon oil
3 tablespoons parsley, minced

Pour stock over heart in pan. Add sage and yeast. Cover and simmer until tender. Remove heart and cut into ½-inch slices. Save stock for use in other recipes. Brush slices with oil and broil for 3 minutes on each side. Garnish with parsley. *Serves 6.*

## ANDALUSIAN STEWED HEART

2 pounds heart, cubed
1 cup stock
1 teaspoon salt
¼ cup wholewheat flour
1 cup tomato juice
1 tablespoon Essence of Sweet Herbs
½ cup milk
3 tablespoons nutritional yeast
1 teaspoon basil
pinch of allspice, ground
¼ cup soy grits, soaked in ½ cup stock
2 cups brown rice, cooked
2 cups young green peas, raw
¼ pound cheddar cheese, grated

Put heart into pot with stock and salt. Cover. Simmer for 1 hour. Blend flour with tomato juice, Essence of Sweet Herbs, milk, yeast, basil and allspice. Add to heart along with soy grits and rice. Cover. Cook until mixture comes to a boil. Add peas and cook until peas are just tender. Garnish with cheese and serve. *Serves 6.*

## ITALIAN STEWED HEART

3 tablespoons oil
½ pound mushrooms, sliced
2 pounds beef heart, sliced thin
¾ cup stock
¼ cup tomato juice
¼ teaspoon salt
3 tablespoons nutritional yeast
1 teaspoon oregano

Heat oil. Sauté mushrooms and set aside. Sauté heart in same pan and set aside. Combine remaining ingredients and pour into pan in which heart and mushrooms were cooked. Cover. Simmer for 5 minutes. Add mushrooms and heart to liquid, cover again and simmer until heart is tender. *Serves 6.*

## BAKED HEART WITH APPLES

2 pounds heart
3 tablespoons wholewheat flour
3 tablespoons oil
stock to cover
2 tablespoons honey
¼ teaspoon clove, ground
1 teaspoon salt
3 tablespoons nutritional yeast
4 apples, quartered
2 bay leaves

Dredge heart in flour. Heat oil and sauté heart. Place in casserole and pour stock over. Add honey, clove, salt and yeast. Cover and bake at 350° F. When heart is nearly tender, add apples and bay leaf and continue baking until both heart and apples are done. Entire baking time should be 2-3 hours. *Serves 6.*

## SAUTÉED HEART, ITALIAN STYLE

3 tablespoons oil
½ teaspoon salt
3 tablespoons yeast
½ teaspoon basil
2 pounds beef heart, sliced thin
1 lemon, cut into wedges

Mix oil, salt, yeast and basil. Marinate slices of heart in this mixture for 30 minutes, turning them occasionally. Sauté for 8 minutes. Garnish with lemon wedges and serve. *Serves 6.*

## CORATELLA

6 artichokes
3 tablespoons oil
1 onion, sliced
3 lamb's coratella (lungs, heart and liver), sliced thin
½ cup sweet cider
¼ teaspoon salt
3 tablespoons nutritional yeast
1 teaspoon sweet basil
1 tablespoon parsley, minced
1 teaspoon lemon juice
1 lemon, cut into wedges

Remove outer leaves of artichokes. Cut each into 8 wedges. Remove chokes from centers. Heat oil and sauté artichoke pieces. Set aside. Sauté onions and coratella in same pan. Mix remaining ingredients together, except lemon wedges. Pour mixture over coratella. Return artichokes to pan. Cover and simmer until coratella is tender. Garnish with lemon wedges. *Serves 6.*

## BEEF HEART PATTIES
(in blender)

2 cups beef heart, cooked, cubed
1 cup potatoes, cooked, cubed
¼ cup soy grits, soaked in
¼ cup stock
1 teaspoon salt
½ teaspoon sage
3 tablespoons nutritional yeast
3 tablespoons parsley, minced

Grind heart and potatoes in blender. Turn into bowl. Add remaining ingredients, mix well and form into patties. Broil on both sides. *Serves 6.*

LEFTOVER HEART
Grind heart leftovers and use in making stock, soup, meat loaf and stew; use as meat filling in meat pastries.

# Tongue

HINTS:
1 beef tongue averages 3¾ pounds; half a tongue serves 6. 1 veal tongue averages 1½ pounds and serves 4-6. 1 pork tongue averages ¾ pound; allow 2 for 6 servings. 1 lamb tongue averages ½ pound; 2 to 3 lamb's tongues serve 6.
Long, slow cooking in liquid makes tongue tender and flavorful.

## BRAISED TONGUE

1 beef tongue
stock to cover
8 slices bacon
6 carrots, diced
1 onion, chopped
1 teaspoon basil
1 teaspoon savory
1 teaspoon rosemary
1 tablespoon parsley, minced
1 teaspoon salt
3 tablespoons nutritional yeast
2 cloves, whole

Cover tongue with stock. Simmer for 1 hour. Remove skin. Arrange 4 slices of bacon at bottom of deep saucepan. Lay tongue on top. Cover with remaining 4 slices of bacon. Add rest of ingredients and 1 cup of stock in which tongue was cooked. Cover and continue simmering un-

til thoroughly cooked. Split tongue down middle and surround with vegetables. *Serves 10-12.*

## BEEF TONGUE CASSEROLE

3 pounds beef tongue
stock to cover
1 cup carrots, diced
½ cup turnips, diced
1 cup celery and tops, diced
1 cup potatoes, diced
1 cup peas
1 cup beans, cooked
6 small onions
3 tomatoes, sliced
¼ cup soy grits, soaked in
½ cup stock
1 teaspoon salt
3 tablespoons nutritional yeast
3 tablespoons parsley, minced
1 teaspoon rosemary
¼ teaspoon nutmeg, ground

Cover tongue with stock. Simmer for 2 hours. Remove skin and place tongue in large casserole. Surround and cover with vegetables and soy grits. Blend remaining ingredients with stock. Pour mixture over tongue and vegetables. Cover and bake at 300° F., about 2 hours. *Serves 6-8.*

# Leftover Tongue

## TONGUE EN GÉLÉ

2 envelopes or 2 tablespoons unflavored gelatin
½ cup tomato juice
2 cups stock in which tongue was simmered, seasoned, hot
1 pound tongue, cooked, sliced thin
1 cup carrot, sliced thin, cooked
1 cup green peppers, sliced thin
½ cup onion rings, sliced thin
10 radish roses

Soften gelatin in tomato juice. Dissolve in hot stock. Put slices of

[Recipe continued on next page]

[Recipe continued from previous page]

tongue in bottom of shallow dish. Arrange carrots, peppers and onion rings over tongue. Pour liquid over, cool and chill. When firm, unmold, and serve garnished with radish roses. *Serves 6.*

## TONGUE AU GRATIN

12 slices tongue, cooked
¼ cup stock
½ teaspoon chervil
½ teaspoon tarragon
3 tablespoons parsley, minced
1 tablespoon shallots, chopped
3 tablespoons nutritional yeast
¼ cup sunflower seeds, ground

Arrange slices of tongue in shallow baking pan. Mix stock with herbs and yeast and pour over tongue. Broil for 5 minutes. Garnish with sunflower seeds. *Serves 6.*

## TONGUE IN SWEET-SOUR SAUCE

2 tablespoons oil
2 tablespoons wholewheat flour
1 cup stock, hot
3 tablespoons honey
3 tablespoons cider vinegar
½ cup seedless raisins
½ cup blanched almonds
1 onion, grated
12 slices tongue, cooked
2 cups brown rice, cooked

Heat oil. Blend in flour. Gradually add stock and cook, stirring, until smooth and thick. Add honey, vinegar, raisins, almonds and onions. Cover and simmer for 10 minutes. Arrange 6 slices of tongue at bottom of oiled casserole. Put half the rice on top. Repeat with layers of tongue and rice and pour sauce over. Cover again and bake at 350° F. for 20 minutes. *Serves 6.*

# Lungs

HINTS:

Lungs are especially good combined in a stew with beef heart or beans.

One beef lung, whole, with an equal weight of beef heart requires 4 to 5 hours cooking time. Veal lung is tenderer and requires less cooking time.

## ITALIAN LUNG-BEAN STEW

3 tablespoons oil
1 onion, sliced
1 clove garlic, minced
1 sprig parsley, minced
1 stalk celery and top, chopped
2 pounds veal lungs, cubed
¼ cup cranberry juice
¼ cup stock
1 cup tomatoes, stewed
¼ teaspoon salt
3 tablespoons nutritional yeast
½ teaspoon sweet basil
1 cup kidney beans, cooked
2 strips bacon, broiled, minced

Heat oil. Sauté onion, garlic, parsley, celery and lungs. Add cranberry juice, stock, tomatoes, salt and yeast. Cover. Simmer for 20 minutes. Add sweet basil and beans. Cover again and simmer for 1 hour longer. Garnish with bacon bits. *Serves 6.*

## RUSSIAN POT ROAST OF LUNGS

2 tablespoons oil
2 stalks celery and tops, chopped
4 onions, chopped
2 pounds lungs, cut into 2-inch
    pieces
2 cups stock
1 bay leaf
2 tablespoons celery seeds, ground
1 teaspoon salt
3 tablespoons nutritional yeast
¼ cup soy grits, soaked in
½ cup stock
3 tablespoons parsley, minced

Heat oil. Sauté celery and onions. Add rest of ingredients except parsley and cover pot. Simmer until lung is tender. Garnish with parsley. *Serves 6.*

# 10

# SEA FOOD

*Since many nutritious sea-food rec-
ipes are available in standard cookbooks, only a limited number are
included here.*

HINTS:

An average serving of fish is generally anywhere from ⅓ to ½
pound of edible flesh. If the whole
fish is served individually, allow
1 pound per person. For dressed
fish, allow ½ pound per person;
for steaks or fillets, ⅓ pound per
person.

Dulse, or sea kelp, may be added
to many sea-food recipes. In that
case, reduce salt in recipe.

Salt-free diets can take advantage
of such fresh-water fish as whitefish, pike, carp, mullet, lake her-
rings, etc.

Low-fat diets can include many
varieties of shellfish and lean fish.
Such diets should, however, avoid
the fat fishes: such salt-water varieties as butterfish, eels, sea her-
ring, Florida mackerel, king mackerel, common mackerel, pompano,
salmon, shad, smelt and tuna; and
such fresh-water fish as brook
trout, chub, lake trout and whitefish.

When buying fish, look for bright,
bulging eyes, reddish gills, shiny
scales tight to the skin. Flesh

should be firm and elastic and
should spring back when pressed.
The shells of oysters, clams and
mussels should be tightly shut
when purchased.

Fish flesh is naturally tender and
should be cooked only a short
time to coagulate the protein and
bring out the flavor. Overcooking
dries and toughens fish.

To wash fish before cooking, dip in
cold salted water and wipe with
a damp cloth or paper towel.
Avoid holding fish under running
water, which leaches it of nutritive values.

Broiling, baking, steaming and
poaching are good methods of
cooking sea food. Oysters and
clams retain all their nutritive
values when served raw.

*Broiling:* Fish fillets require 5 to
10 minutes without turning; fish
steaks, 3 to 5 minutes on each
side; whole dressed fish, 3 to 10
minutes on each side; split fish,
6 to 12 minutes on each side.
Leave bones in, for juice and
flavor.

*Baking:* Leave fish heads on; this

seals in flavor and juices and prevents the flesh from becoming dry and tough. Fish may be marinated prior to baking, or basted while being baked.

*Steaming:* Use minimum of liquid and cover pot tightly. Wrap fish in cheesecloth or muslin to avoid breaking when removing from pot. Time carefully. Fish less than 2 inches thick requires 1 minute of steaming for each ounce. Fish over 2 inches thick requires more time, depending on the variety. Herbs, celery, onions and other seasonings should be added at the beginning so that the flavors have a chance to permeate the fish. Salt, vinegar or lemon juice should be added after the steaming is completed. Save liquid at the bottom of the steamer and add to fish stock.

*Poaching:* Place fish in oiled casserole and cover with fish stock. Cover casserole. Bake in 350° F. oven, allowing 5 to 10 minutes per pound. The fish may be served in its juice, or the juice may be used as a base for sauce.

## CLAMS ON SHELL (uncooked)

clams, raw, shells opened
1 onion, grated fine
¼ cup lemon juice
3 tablespoons parsley, minced

Drain juice from clams, reserving for fish stock. Blend onion, lemon juice and parsley and pour over clams. Serve.

## OYSTERS ON SHELL (uncooked)

oysters, raw, shells opened
¼ cup lemon juice

2 shallots chopped fine
3 tablespoons water cress, minced

Drain juice from oysters and reserve for fish stock. Blend lemon juice, shallots and water cress, pour over oysters. Serve.

## BROILED FISH FILLETS

2 pounds fresh fish fillets
½ teaspoon fennel seeds, ground
2 tablespoons parsley, minced
2 tablespoons oil
juice of 1 lemon
¼ cup soy grits, soaked in
½ cup fish stock

Arrange fish fillets in shallow, oiled baking pan. Blend remaining ingredients together and spoon over fish. Broil without turning, for 5 to 10 minutes. *Serves 6.*

## FISH BAKED IN SWEET-SOUR SAUCE

2 cups stock
1 tablespoon ginger, ground
3 tablespoons wholewheat flour
1 teaspoon soy flour
¼ teaspoon nutmeg, ground
¼ teaspoon allspice, ground
¼ teaspoon cinnamon, ground
¼ teaspoon mace, ground
1 bay leaf
¼ cup molasses
¼ cup cider vinegar*
3 tablespoons nutritional yeast
1 onion, grated
¼ cup seedless raisins
¼ cup almonds, blanched
2 pounds fresh fish fillets, raw

Blend all ingredients together in a saucepan, except fish fillets. Cover. Heat gradually, bringing to boil, then simmer for 10 minutes. Place fillets in bottom of casserole and pour mixture over fish. Cover and

[Recipe continued on next page]

[Recipe continued from previous page]
bake at 350° F. for 30 minutes. *Serves 6.*

## FISH KEBABS

juice of 2 lemons
2 tablespoons oil
½ teaspoon salt
2 tablespoons parsley, minced
½ teaspoon chervil
1½ pounds fresh fillets, cut into chunks
4 slices bacon, cut into squares
½ pound mushrooms, whole
2 green peppers, cut into pieces
2 onions, sliced or cut into wedges

Mix lemon juice, oil, salt, parsley and chervil together. Marinate fish in this mixture for 1 hour. Drain. String fish, bacon, mushrooms, peppers and onions on skewers. Brush with marinade. Broil 3 inches from heat for 5 minutes. Brush again with marinade, turn and broil 3 to 5 minutes longer. *Serves 6.*

## NORWEGIAN FISH LOAF

2½ pounds fresh fish (sole, haddock, flounder, scrod, cod, whitefish, etc.)
3 tablespoons wholewheat flour
3 tablespoons nutritional yeast
1 teaspoon salt
¼ teaspoon nutmeg, ground
1 teaspoon dulse, chopped fine
2 cups milk, scalded, cooled
1 cup cream, scalded, cooled

Remove skin and bones from fish with sharp knife and reserve for fish stock or bisque. Put raw fish through food grinder, using fine blade. Then pound pulp for 10 minutes with mallet or edge of a saucer. Add flour, yeast, nutmeg, salt, dulse and knead for 5 minutes. Add milk and cream gradually,

kneading after each addition. Turn into well-oiled loaf pan. Bake at 325° F. until firm, about 1 hour. Cool. Unmold. This loaf may be served hot or cold. *Serves 6.*

## FISH-VEGETABLE CASSEROLE

3 potatoes, cooked, sliced
2 pounds fresh fish fillets, raw
1 cup tomatoes, stewed
½ cup celery and tops, chopped
½ green pepper, chopped
1 onion, sliced
¼ cup soy grits, soaked in
½ cup stock
½ teaspoon thyme
½ teaspoon basil
1 tablespoon dulse, minced
3 tablespoons nutritional yeast

Arrange potatoes at bottom of oiled casserole. Place fish on top. Cover with tomatoes, celery, pepper and onion. Blend remaining ingredients and spoon over top. Cover and bake at 350° F. for 20 minutes. *Serves 6.*

## SEA FOOD POT PIE

3 tablespoons oil
4 mushrooms, sliced
1 onion, sliced
1 tablespoon wholewheat flour
1 cup milk, scalded
juice of 1 lemon
1 tablespoon parsley, minced
½ teaspoon chervil
½ teaspoon chives, minced
½ teaspoon marjoram
3 tablespoons nutritional yeast
1 tablespoon dulse, minced
2 pounds fresh sea food (fish, shellfish, or both, cut in serving pieces)
3 potatoes, cooked, cubed
½ cup carrots, cooked, cubed

Sauté mushrooms and onions in hot oil. Remove and set aside. Add flour to pan and blend with remaining oil and juices. Gradually add milk and continue to cook, stirring until mixture thickens. Remove from heat and return mushrooms and onions to pan. Mix lemon juice with herbs, yeast and dulse and blend with mushroom-onion sauce. Arrange fish, potatoes and carrots in oiled casserole and pour sauce over. Top with pastry crust, if desired or leave plain and cover casserole. Bake at 375° F., 40 minutes with pastry top, and 30 minutes at 350° F. without pastry. *Serves 6.*

## SHRIMP IN PIQUANT SAUCE

3 tablespoons oil
2 carrots, diced
1 green pepper, diced
2 onions, sliced
½ clove garlic, minced
1 tablespoon wholewheat flour
1 teaspoon soy flour
1½ cups fish stock, hot
½ cup almonds, blanched
½ teaspoon salt
¼ teaspoon thyme
¼ teaspoon rosemary
1 tablespoon celery seeds, ground
3 tablespoons nutritional yeast
1 teaspoon dulse, minced
1½ pounds fresh shrimp, cooked, cleaned
½ cup yoghurt*
1 cup Sprouts

Heat oil and sauté carrots, green pepper, onion and garlic. Remove from pan and set aside. Put flours into pan and blend well. Gradually add stock and continue to cook, stirring until thickened. Return sautéed vegetables to pan and add almonds. Mix all seasonings, yeast and dulse, combine with sauce and vegetables in pan. Cover and simmer for 20 minutes. Add shrimp and simmer 5 minutes longer. Remove from heat and blend in yoghurt. Sprinkle Sprouts on top. *Serves 6.*

## ESCABECHE OF FLOUNDER

2 pounds fillets of flounder
cider vinegar* to cover
3 tablespoons wholewheat flour
3 tablespoons oil
1 clove garlic, minced
3 tablespoons lemon juice
⅓ cup fresh orange juice
3 tablespoons chives, minced
¼ teaspoon coriander seeds, ground
¼ teaspoon salt
1 teaspoon dulse, minced
2 tablespoons nutritional yeast

Arrange fillets in shallow dish. Cover with vinegar. Marinate for 10 minutes. Drain fish and dredge in flour. Heat oil and sauté fish briefly. Put again into shallow dish. Mix remaining ingredients in a bowl and pour over fish. Marinate in refrigerator for 24 hours. *Serves 6.*

## STUFFED MUSSELS

24 fresh mussels
1 cup fish stock
½ cup sweet cider
¼ teaspoon salt
3 tablespoons oil
1 onion, chopped
½ clove garlic, minced
½ cup brown rice, raw
½ teaspoon allspice, ground
¼ cup pignolias
¼ cup currants, dried
2 tablespoons parsley, minced
¼ cup soy grits, soaked in
¼ cup stock
2 tablespoons nutritional yeast

Remove "beards" and scrub mussels well. Put in pot and add stock, cider and salt. Cover. Simmer for 10 minutes. Discard any mussels which do not open. Drain mussels, remove from shells and set aside. Save shells.

[Recipe continued on next page]

[Recipe continued from previous page]

Let stock stand until any sand settles to bottom. Heat oil and in it sauté onion, garlic and rice for 3 minutes. Add stock to this, pouring carefully to avoid disturbing sand at bottom. Cover and simmer for 15 minutes. Add remaining ingredients and simmer 5 minutes longer. Let cool. Chop mussels and combine with rice mixture. Pack into mussel shells. Serve cold or reheat if desired. *Serves 6.*

## Leftover Sea Food

### SEA FOOD JAMBALAYA

¾ pound fish, cooked, flaked
¼ cup bacon, broiled, chopped
3 tablespoons onion, grated
3 tablespoons green pepper, chopped
½ clove garlic, minced
¼ cup soy grits, soaked in
½ cup stock
1 tablespoon dulse, minced
1 teaspoon Essence of Sweet Herbs
2 cups tomatoes, stewed
2 tablespoons nutritional yeast
2 cups brown rice, cooked
½ teaspoon basil
½ teaspoon oregano
1 teaspoon celery seeds, ground

Blend all ingredients together. Simmer in covered saucepan until thoroughly heated. *Serves 6.*

### BAKED FISH OMELET
(in blender)

4 egg yolks
½ cup milk
1 teaspoon soy flour
2 cups fish, cooked, flaked
1 tablespoon lemon juice
rind of 1 lemon
2 tablespoons oil

1 onion
½ green pepper
1 sprig parsley
2 tablespoons nutritional yeast
1 teaspoon dulse
½ teaspoon sage
4 egg whites, beaten stiff

Place all ingredients, except egg whites, in blender and blend until smooth. Turn into bowl. Fold in stiffly beaten whites. Put mixture into oiled pie plate and bake at 300° F. until top is firm and dry, about 20 minutes. *Serves 6.*

### FISH SOUFFLÉ

3 tablespoons oil
3 tablespoons wholewheat flour
1 teaspoon soy flour
¾ cup milk, hot
1½ cups fish, cooked, flaked
4 egg yolks, beaten
1 teaspoon dulse, minced
3 tablespoons nutritional yeast
1 tablespoon parsley, minced
1 sprig dill, minced
1 teaspoon dill seeds, ground
4 egg whites, beaten stiff

Heat oil and blend flours in pan with oil. Gradually add milk and cook over low heat, stirring until thickened. Remove from heat. Add remaining ingredients, except egg whites, and blend thoroughly. Fold in egg whites. Turn mixture into oiled 2-quart casserole or oiled individual custard cups. Bake at 375° F., 40 minutes in casserole, 30 minutes in custard cups. *Serves 6.*

### FISH-CORN CASSEROLE

½ cup wheat germ
1 cup wholewheat bread crumbs
¼ cup soy grits, soaked in
½ cup stock

3 tablespoons nutritional yeast
1 teaspoon dulse, minced
3 tablespoons oil
2 cups corn, cooked
2 cups fish, cooked, flaked
juice of 1 lemon
1⅓ cups milk
2 eggs, beaten
½ teaspoon salt
½ teaspoon rosemary
½ teaspoon celery seeds, ground

Combine wheat germ, bread crumbs, soy grits, yeast, dulse and oil. Place half of mixture in bottom of oiled casserole. Add layer of corn, then the fish. Sprinkle with lemon juice. Top with rest of bread-crumb mixture. Combine remaining ingredients and pour over casserole. Cover and bake at 350° F. for 30 minutes. *Serves 6.*

## BAKED FISH LOAF

⅔ cup milk
1 egg, beaten
½ cup wholewheat flour
3 tablespoons soy flour
¼ cup Soybeans, Roasted, ground
2 cups fish, cooked, flaked
1 teaspoon dulse, minced
3 tablespoons nutritional yeast
¼ teaspoon nutmeg, ground
½ cup cheddar cheese, grated

Blend all ingredients thoroughly. Turn into oiled loaf pan. Bake at 350° F. for 50 to 60 minutes, until loaf is firm. This may be served hot or cold. *Serves 6.*

## FISH-CORNMEAL MUFFINS

1 cup stock, cold
1 cup cornmeal
1 cup stock, hot
¼ cup soy grits, soaked in
½ cup stock
2 eggs, beaten
2 cups fish, cooked, flaked

3 tablespoons oil
½ teaspoon tarragon
½ teaspoon salt
3 tablespoons nutritional yeast
1 teaspoon dulse, minced
½ cup wheat germ

Thoroughly mix cornmeal in cold stock. Combine with hot stock. Cover and cook over hot water in double boiler until it is consistency of cornmeal mush. Remove from heat and allow to cool. Blend with remaining ingredients. Turn into oiled muffin pans. Bake at 350° F. for 20 minutes. *Serves 6.*

Small amounts of leftover sea food may be used in making chowders, fish soups, bisques, salads, aspics, sauces, sandwich spreads, stuffings; stuffed tomatoes, green peppers, eggplant; combined with hard-cooked eggs, Sprouts, nuts.

GARNISHES FOR THE FISH PLATTER:
*Cucumber:* Score the skin of a cucumber lengthwise with a fork. Cut crosswise into paper-thin slices. Marinate in tarragon vinegar. Arrange slices of cucumber on top of whole fish.
*Lemon:* Cut lemon (or lime) into 6 lengthwise wedges. Dip in finely chopped water cress or parsley to coat ridges along top. Serve on fish platter.
*Water Cress-Carrot Bouquets:* Cut carrots crosswise into ¼-inch slices. With an apple corer, cut out centers (save for salads). Slip a sprig of water cress (or parsley) through carrot ring. Arrange on fish platter.
*Hard-Cooked Egg:* Rub 2 hard-cooked eggs through a sieve. Sprinkle over fish. Top with minced chives.

[Continued on next page]

[Continued from previous page]

OTHER GARNISHES:
Beets—whole or sliced (cooked)
Carrots—slivers, sticks, curls, shreds
Celery—tops, hearts, sticks
Green pepper—rings, strips
Radishes, whole, sliced or roses
Parsley, water cress, dill—sprigs or
  minced
Cranberry relish

See also: Butter, Lemon-Herb
  For stuffing recipes for whole fish,
    see Stuffings.
  See recipe for Flourless Batter
    Base for sea-food casseroles.

# Sea Food Sauces

## CREOLE SAUCE

3 tablespoons oil
1 onion, chopped
1 stalk celery and tops, chopped
3 tablespoons wholewheat flour
1 teaspoon soy flour
1 cup tomatoes, stewed, puréed
¼ teaspoon salt
2 tablespoons nutritional yeast
¼ teaspoon oregano
¼ teaspoon basil
1 teaspoon dulse, minced
1 bay leaf

Sauté onion and celery in oil, then
remove and set aside. Blend flours
with remaining oil in pan until
smooth. Combine tomato mixture,
onion-celery mixture and rest of ingredients with flour in same pan.
Cover and simmer for 30 minutes.
Remove bay leaf. *Serves 6.*

## COLD CUCUMBER SAUCE
(in blender)

2 cucumbers, in chunks
1 onion, sliced

¼ cup yoghurt*
1 teaspoon cider vinegar*
¼ teaspoon celery seeds, ground
pinch of salt
1 tablespoon parsley
1 tablespoon dill
1 teaspoon dulse
1 teaspoon mint

Blend all ingredients. Chill. Serve
with fish salad. *Serves 6.*

## SHRIMP SAUCE

2 tablespoons oil
½ pound shrimps, cooked, chopped
2 tablespoons wholewheat flour
1 teaspoon soy flour
1 cup milk, hot
½ teaspoon salt
1 teaspoon dulse, minced
2 tablespoons nutritional yeast
¼ teaspoon thyme
¼ teaspoon savory
3 tablespoons parsley, minced
3 hard-cooked eggs, chopped

Heat oil. Sauté shrimps and set
aside. Blend flours in pan in which
shrimps were cooked. Gradually add
milk and cook over low heat, stirring, until thickened. Blend remaining ingredients, except eggs and
add to milk mixture. Cover and
simmer for 10 minutes. Add shrimps
and eggs. When hot, serve over
plain steamed fish. *Serves 6.*

## SWEET-SOUR LENTIL SAUCE

2 cups lentils, cooked
3 tablespoons honey
3 tablespoons cider vinegar*
3 tablespoons parsley, minced

Combine all ingredients. Simmer
for 10 minutes in covered saucepan.
Good with plain steamed fish. *Serves
6.*

## DILL SAUCE
(in blender, uncooked)

3 tablespoons oil
2 sprigs dill
1 sprig parsley
1 tablespoon chives
½ teaspoon salt
1 teaspoon dill seeds
1 teaspoon dulse
juice and rind of 1 lemon

Blend all ingredients. Serve over broiled fish. This sauce is especially good with halibut, mackerel and salmon. It also adds flavor to boiled potatoes or steamed vegetables. *Serves 6.*

## CLAM SAUCE

3 tablespoons oil
1 clove garlic, minced
2 tablespoons wholewheat flour
1 teaspoon soy flour
1 cup clam juice, hot

2 sprigs parsley, minced
¼ teaspoon salt
2 tablespoons nutritional yeast
1 teaspoon dulse, minced
pinch of thyme
pinch of mace, ground
1 dozen small clams, steamed,
    minced

Sauté garlic in oil and blend flours in. Gradually add clam juice. Continue to cook, stirring, until thickened. Add remaining ingredients, except clams, and cover. Simmer for 15 minutes. Add clams and cook only until heated through. Serve over plain steamed fish. *Serves 6.*

OTHER SEA FOOD RECIPES
See under Fish: Balls; -Cornmeal Balls; Bisque; Chowder, Italian; Spreads; Stock. See also: Bouillabaisse; Sea Food Mold; Clam Dip; Oyster Stuffing; Shrimp Stuffing.

# 11

# FOWL
# AND STUFFINGS

*Since many recipes for nutritious fowl dishes are available in standard cookbooks, fowl is given limited consideration here.*

## CHICKEN EN CASSEROLE

1 large chicken, cut into 6 serving
 pieces
1 clove garlic
3 tablespoons oil
½ pound mushrooms, sliced
1½ cups sweet cider
1 dozen small white onions, stuck
 with cloves
2 carrots, diced
1 stalk celery and tops, chopped
¼ cup soy grits, soaked in
½ cup stock
1 bay leaf
¼ teaspoon basil
¼ teaspoon tarragon
¼ teaspoon thyme
3 tablespoons parsley, minced
1 teaspoon salt
3 tablespoons nutritional yeast
1 tablespoon soy flour

Rub chicken with garlic and sauté in hot oil. Remove chicken and sauté mushrooms in same pan. Arrange chicken and mushrooms at bottom of casserole. Blend remaining ingredients together. Pour over chicken and mushrooms and cover casserole. Bake at 350° F. until

chicken is tender, about 1 hour. *Serves 6.*

## CHICKEN WITH YOGHURT

1 large chicken, cut into 6 serving
 pieces
3 tablespoons oil
2 onions, sliced
2 cups stock
3 tablespoons wholewheat flour
¼ teaspoon salt
3 tablespoons nutritional yeast
2 teaspoons tarragon
1 tablespoon parsley, minced
1 pint yoghurt*

Brush chicken with oil. Broil lightly on each side. Arrange chicken pieces in casserole. Surround with onions. Blend stock, flour, salt, yeast, tarragon and parsley together. Pour mixture over chicken and onions. Cover. Bake at 350° F. until chicken is tender, about 1 hour. Remove casserole from oven. Pour out liquid and gradually blend yoghurt into it. Return to casserole and reheat briefly if necessary. *Serves 6.*

## CHICKEN FROM ARLES

1 large chicken, cut into 6 serving
  pieces
3 tablespoons wholewheat flour
1 clove garlic, minced
3 tablespoons oil
1 eggplant, diced
1½ cups tomatoes, stewed
1 teaspoon salt
3 tablespoons nutritional yeast
½ cup sweet cider
3 tablespoons parsley, minced
1 teaspoon oregano
1 teaspoon celery seeds, ground

Dredge chicken in flour mixed with garlic and sauté in hot oil. Add remaining ingredients. Cover. Simmer until chicken is tender. *Serves 6.*

# Stuffings

Some of these stuffings are primarily for fowl. Others can be used for stuffing fish, heart, or vegetables such as tomatoes, green peppers, eggplant, squash, onion.

## OYSTER STUFFING

1 pint oysters in their juice
3 tablespoons oil
1 onion, sliced
1 tablespoon parsley, minced
2 stalks celery and tops, chopped
1 teaspoon dulse, minced
½ cup soy grits, soaked in
½ cup stock
1 teaspoon celery seeds, ground
1 cup sunflower seed meal
¼ teaspoon marjoram
¼ teaspoon thyme
3 tablespoons nutritional yeast

Heat oysters in their juice over low heat. Heat oil. Sauté onion, parsley and celery. Add remaining ingredients to sautéed vegetables. Blend thoroughly. Add oysters and only

enough liquid to blend. This will stuff a 4- to 5-pound fowl.

## LENTIL STUFFING

2 cups lentils, cooked, puréed
½ cup cheddar cheese, grated
2 tablespoons oil
1 tart apple with skin, grated
½ teaspoon sage
2 tablespoons nutritional yeast
¼ teaspoon salt
pinch of nutmeg, ground
½ teaspoon cumin seeds, ground
¼ cup wheat germ

Thoroughly blend all ingredients. Good for stuffing vegetables.
  See also Basic Soybean Filler.

## SOY GRITS STUFFING

3 tablespoons oil
1 cup celery and tops, chopped
½ cup parsley, minced
1 onion, minced
½ teaspoon savory
½ teaspoon oregano
½ cup soy grits, soaked in
1 cup stock
½ teaspoon salt
3 tablespoons nutritional yeast
1 cup wheat germ
2 cups wholewheat bread crumbs
1 egg, beaten

Heat oil. Sauté celery, parsley and onion. Combine with rest of ingredients. Blend thoroughly. Good for stuffing vegetables.

## RICE-MUSHROOM STUFFING

2 cups brown rice, cooked
¼ cup mushrooms, sautéed
2 onions, sliced, sautéed
½ teaspoon dill seeds, ground
2 tablespoons nutritional yeast
½ teaspoon thyme
½ teaspoon salt
stock

[Recipe continued on next page]

[Recipe continued from previous page]

Blend all ingredients together. Add only enough stock to moisten.

## SHRIMP STUFFING

3 tablespoons oil
1 onion, chopped
2 tablespoons parsley, chopped
½ pound shrimps, cooked, chopped
2 eggs, beaten
¼ cup soy grits, soaked in
½ cup stock
½ teaspoon salt
½ teaspoon thyme
2 tablespoons nutritional yeast
1 teaspoon dulse, minced
1 teaspoon celery seeds, ground
1 cup wheat germ

Heat oil. Sauté onions. Mix well with rest of ingredients. This will stuff a 4-pound fowl.

## BRAZIL NUT STUFFING

1 cup Brazil nuts, ground
1 cup wholewheat bread crumbs
¼ cup stock
2 stalks celery and tops, chopped
2 onions, grated
¼ cup soy grits, soaked in
½ cup stock
3 tablespoons nutritional yeast
1 teaspoon salt
½ teaspoon rosemary
¼ teaspoon thyme
¼ teaspoon basil
3 tablespoons oil

Blend all ingredients. Use in stuffing vegetables, fish or fowl.

## ALMOND STUFFING

¼ cup almonds, blanched, ground
2 tablespoons oil
¼ cup wheat germ
1 egg, beaten
¼ cup soy grits, soaked in
½ cup stock
1 cup wholewheat bread crumbs

½ cup milk
¼ cup milk powder
1 teaspoon salt
3 tablespoons nutritional yeast
¼ teaspoon savory
1 teaspoon coriander seeds, ground

Blend all ingredients together. This will stuff a 4- to 5-pound fowl.

## NUT-BUCKWHEAT STUFFING

2 cups boiling stock
1 cup buckwheat
½ teaspoon salt
3 tablespoons nutritional yeast
½ teaspoon basil
½ teaspoon sweet marjoram
1 teaspoon celery seeds, ground
½ cup parsley, minced
1 onion, grated
2 stalks celery and tops, chopped
¼ cup nuts, ground
¼ cup Soybeans, Roasted, ground

Pour boiling stock over buckwheat. Stir. Cover. Let stand for 15 minutes. Add remaining ingredients and blend well. This will stuff a 4- to 5-pound fowl.

## CORNBREAD STUFFING

3 tablespoons oil
1 onion, chopped
1 cup dry cornbread crumbs
½ cup soy grits, soaked in
½ cup stock
2 eggs, beaten
¼ teaspoon salt
3 tablespoons nutritional yeast
¼ teaspoon sage
¼ teaspoon thyme
1 teaspoon Essence of Sweet Herbs
1 teaspoon caraway seeds, ground
milk powder

Heat oil. Sauté onions. Add rest of ingredients, using enough milk powder to bind mixture to good consistency. This will stuff a 4- to 5-pound fowl.

## BULGUR STUFFING

¼ cup oil
2 cups bulgur
1 quart stock, hot
1 onion, grated
1 green pepper, chopped
2 stalks celery and tops, chopped
1 teaspoon salt
2 tablespoons nutritional yeast
3 tablespoons parsley, minced
¼ teaspoon tarragon
¼ teaspoon thyme
¼ teaspoon basil

Heat oil. Sauté bulgur. Gradually add stock. Cover. Simmer for 10 minutes. Add remaining ingredients. Simmer for 5 minutes more. Let cool.

This will stuff a 4- to 5-pound fowl. It is also good for stuffed vegetables.

## RICE-ALMOND STUFFING

giblets from chicken or turkey
3 cups stock
3 tablespoons oil
1 cup onions, chopped
1½ cups brown rice, raw
1 teaspoon salt
3 tablespoons nutritional yeast
¼ cup almonds, blanched, chopped
3 tablespoons parsley, minced
1 teaspoon tarragon

Put giblets with stock into pot and cover. Simmer until tender. Heat oil. Sauté onion and rice slowly for 10 minutes. Drain giblets and chop fine, reserving stock. Combine giblets and stock with rice and onions. Cover pot. Cook slowly for 20 minutes, or until all stock is absorbed. Add rest of ingredients. Blend well.

This will stuff a 4- to 5-pound

roasting chicken. For turkey, double the recipe.

## WILD RICE STUFFING

3 tablespoons oil
½ pound mushrooms, sliced
1 onion, sliced
3 cups wild rice, cooked
¼ teaspoon salt
3 tablespoons nutritional yeast
¼ cup wheat germ
3 tablespoons parsley, minced
¼ teaspoon basil
1 teaspoon cumin seeds, ground

Heat oil. Sauté mushrooms and onion. Combine remaining ingredients and mix well.

This will stuff a 4- to 5-pound fowl. It is also good for stuffed vegetables.

## YAM STUFFING

2 cups yams, cooked, puréed
½ pound pork sausage, cooked, drained of fat
4 stalks celery and tops, chopped
2 cups wholewheat bread crumbs
3 tablespoons nutritional yeast
pinch of allspice, ground
1 cup dried apricots, chopped fine
1 onion, grated
1 cup stock

Thoroughly blend all ingredients. Will stuff a 4- to 5-pound fowl.

## APPLE-PRUNE STUFFING
## (flourless)

1 cup prunes
water to cover
3 apples
pinch of cinnamon, ground

Soak prunes overnight. Remove pits. Retain liquid as fruit stock. Chop prunes in small pieces. Core and

[Recipe continued on next page]

[Recipe continued from previous page]
cut apples into small pieces, leaving skins on. Mix both fruits. Add cinnamon. This will stuff a 4- to 5-pound fowl.

## VEGETABLE STUFFING

2 cups carrots, grated fine
1 cup celery and tops, chopped fine
1 onion, grated
1 cup summer squash, cubed, raw
2 apples with skins, grated
½ cup raisins, chopped
1 teaspoon Essence of Sweet Herbs
½ teaspoon rosemary
1 cup Soybeans, Roasted, ground
1 green pepper, chopped
¼ cup wheat germ
¼ cup soy grits, soaked in
½ cup stock
½ teaspoon salt
3 tablespoons nutritional yeast
2 eggs, beaten
1 teaspoon dill seeds, ground

Combine all ingredients and blend well. This will stuff a 4- to 5-pound fowl.

## CHESTNUT STUFFING

3 tablespoons oil
1 onion, chopped
1½ cups chestnuts, cooked, puréed
½ cup wheat germ
¼ teaspoon salt
3 tablespoons nutritional yeast
¼ cup milk
3 tablespoons parsley, minced
1 teaspoon marjoram
1 teaspoon Essence of Sweet Herbs
pinch of mace, ground
1 potato, cooked, mashed
stock

Heat oil. Sauté onion. Blend with all remaining ingredients. Add only enough stock to bind mixture to good consistency. This will stuff a 4- to 5-pound fowl.

## POTATO STUFFING

2 cups potatoes, cooked, mashed
1 onion, grated
2 eggs, beaten
¼ cup wholewheat bread crumbs
¼ cup soy grits, soaked in
½ cup stock
¼ teaspoon rosemary
¼ teaspoon basil
½ teaspoon salt

Thoroughly blend all ingredients. This will stuff a 4- to 5-pound fowl.

## APPLE STUFFING

3 tart apples with skins, grated
½ cup seedless raisins
½ cup onions, grated
1 clove garlic, minced
2 eggs, beaten
¼ cup soy grits, soaked in
½ cup stock
1 cup wholewheat bread crumbs
½ cup celery and tops, chopped
2 tablespoons nutritional yeast
1 teaspoon salt
3 tablespoons parsley, minced
pinch of clove, ground

Thoroughly blend all ingredients. Will stuff a 4- to 5-pound fowl.

## APPLE-SAGE STUFFING

3 tablespoons oil
3 onions, grated
4 tart apples with skins, grated
2 cups wholewheat bread crumbs
½ cup wheat germ
¼ cup soy grits, soaked in
½ cup stock
2 teaspoons sage
1 tablespoon cider vinegar*
½ cup yoghurt*
½ teaspoon salt
2 tablespoons nutritional yeast
1 egg, beaten

Heat oil. Sauté onions and apples. Combine with remaining ingredients. Blend thoroughly. Will stuff a 4- to 5-pound fowl.

## APRICOT STUFFING

3 tablespoons oil
½ cup mushrooms, sliced
1 onion, sliced
3 tablespoons parsley, minced
3 cups brown rice, cooked
½ pound dried apricots, chopped
1 cup fresh orange juice
½ teaspoon savory
pinch of mace, ground
pinch of cinnamon, ground
¼ teaspoon salt
3 tablespoons nutritional yeast

Heat oil. Sauté mushrooms, onion and parsley. Add to remaining ingredients and blend thoroughly.

This stuffing is especially good for duck.

## ORANGE STUFFING

2 tablespoons oil
1 onion, chopped
3 cups brown rice, cooked
½ cup stock, hot
juice and grated rind of 2 large
    oranges
4 stalks celery and tops, chopped
¼ teaspoon salt
3 tablespoons nutritional yeast
1 egg, beaten
1 tablespoon parsley, minced
1 tablespoon honey
¼ cup raisins, seedless
¼ teaspoon ginger, ground

Heat oil. Sauté onion. Add to remaining ingredients. Blend thoroughly. This stuffing is especially good for duck.

# 12

# EGGS

*Since many recipes for nutritious egg dishes are available in standard cookbooks, they are given limited consideration here.*

HINTS:

To preserve texture and flavor, eggs and dishes in which they predominate should be cooked slowly, at moderate, even heat. For oven baking, set oven at 250° F. to 300° F.; for poaching or boiling, keep temperature just below boiling point.

## EGGS POACHED IN CORNMEAL MUSH

1 cup cornmeal
1 cup stock, cold
2 cups stock, hot
1 teaspoon salt
3 tablespoons nutritional yeast
3 tablespoons oil
6 eggs
1 tablespoon chives, minced

Mix cornmeal in cold stock. Combine with hot stock, salt and yeast and blend thoroughly. Cook over hot water in double boiler for 30 minutes. Rinse shallow pan with cold water; then pour cornmeal mush into pan to depth of ¾-inch. Let stand overnight. Cut into 6 large squares. Heat oil. Sauté mush squares until light brown on each side. Remove from heat. With spoon, make hollow in center of each square. Break an egg into each hollow. Replace squares in pan. Cover. Cook over low heat until eggs are firm (about 5 minutes). Garnish with chives. *Serves 6.*

## EGGS FLORENTINE (in blender)

2 pounds spinach, washed, trimmed
milk to moisten
¼ cup milk powder
6 eggs
3 tablespoons oil
3 tablespoons nutritional yeast
pinch of nutmeg, ground
¼ cup Parmesan cheese, grated

Put spinach with small amount of milk into blender and blend until smooth. Add milk powder. Blend again. Turn mixture into oiled casserole. Cover and bake at 300° F. for 15 minutes. Slip eggs onto spinach mixture. Drizzle with oil. Mix yeast, nutmeg and cheese together. Sprinkle mixture over eggs. Bake for 5 to 10 minutes more. *Serves 6.*

## BAKED FLUFFY OMELET

6 egg yolks
3 tablespoons stock
½ teaspoon salt
1 tablespoon nutritional yeast
¼ teaspoon chervil
¼ teaspoon marjoram
2 tablespoons oil
6 egg whites, beaten stiff

Beat egg yolks until lemon yellow. Thoroughly blend all ingredients, except egg whites. Fold in egg whites. Preheat oiled pie plate. Turn mixture into this and bake at 300° F. for 15 to 20 minutes. *Serves 6.*

## CHICKEN LIVER OMELET

3 tablespoons oil
3 chicken livers, chopped
4 eggs, separated
¼ teaspoon salt
2 tablespoons nutritional yeast
3 tablespoons chives, chopped

Heat oil. Lightly sauté livers. In a bowl, beat egg whites until stiff, and in another, beat egg yolks. Add salt, yeast and chives to yolk. Add livers and blend well. Fold in egg whites. Turn mixture into oiled casserole. Bake uncovered at 350° F. for 15 minutes. *Serves 6.*

## GERMAN BAKED PANCAKE
(in blender)

3 eggs
½ cup milk
½ teaspoon salt
2 tablespoons nutritional yeast
2 tablespoons oil
¼ cup milk powder
½ cup wholewheat flour
1 teaspoon soy flour

Put all ingredients in blender and blend until smooth. Turn into cold, oiled pie plate. Bake for 10 minutes at 450° F., decrease heat to 350° F. and bake 10 minutes longer. When done, pancake will puff up at sides and be crisp and brown. Serve plain or garnish with one of the following mixtures:

Lemon juice, cinnamon, honey
Finely chopped raw apple with skin, chopped walnuts, nutmeg
Stewed fruit          *Serves 6.*

## EGG FOO YONG

3 tablespoons oil
3 stalks celery and tops, chopped
2 scallions, chopped
8 eggs
3 tablespoons nutritional yeast
1 tablespoon honey
1 tablespoon Essence of Sweet Herbs
½ cup meat, fowl or sea food, sliced thin (leftovers)
1 cup mung bean Sprouts

Heat oil. Sauté celery and scallions. Remove from pan and reserve. Blend eggs, yeast, honey, essence of sweet herbs together and pour mixture into pan. Cover. Cook over low heat for 1 minute. While eggs are still partly liquid, add meat or fish and sautéed vegetables. Let cook over low heat until firm; turn and cook other side for ½ minute. Garnish with sprouts. *Serves 6.*

## SCRAMBLED HERBED EGGS

12 eggs
¼ teaspoon salt
2 tablespoons nutritional yeast
3 tablespoons milk
3 tablespoons any combination herbs desired: basil, marjoram, savory, tarragon, thyme, chervil, dill, parsley, etc.
¼ cup milk powder

[Recipe continued on next page]

[Recipe continued from previous page]
Blend all ingredients. Turn into heated, oiled pan. Cook, covered, over low heat, stirring occasionally, until eggs are set. *Serves 6.*

## PENNSYLVANIA DUTCH EGGS

6 eggs, hard-cooked, shelled
beet juice to cover
juice of 1 lemon
¼ teaspoon salt
1 clove garlic, minced
1 tablespoon dill, minced

Place all ingredients in a glass jar. Cover. Refrigerate for 3 days. Lift out eggs, slice or quarter and use in salads or as garnishes.

VARIATION:
Add raw onion rings to marinating liquid. These too can be used as garnishes.

## STUFFED HARD-COOKED EGGS

Cut cooked eggs in half and scoop out yolks. Sieve or mash yolks and blend with any of the following:

One of the spreads from chapter on Spreads; ground cumin seeds, caraway seeds, dill seeds or celery seeds; any desired combination of minced herbs.

Moisten with favorite dressing. Heap mixture into hollowed egg white. Garnish with chopped chives. Chill.

LEFTOVER EGGS
Add leftover egg yolks (uncooked) to recipe for Zabaglione, soufflés, custards, puddings, soup garnishes.
Add leftover egg whites (uncooked) to recipe for Macaroons, soufflés, omelets, meringues.
Slice or chop leftover hard-cooked eggs and add to spreads, meat and fish sauces, or use as garnish.

OTHER EGG RECIPES
See: Egg Spreads; Italian Egg Soup

# 13

# CHEESE

*Since many recipes for nutritious cheese dishes are available in standard cookbooks, they are given limited consideration here.*

## Homemade Cheeses

### HOMEMADE CREAM CHEESE

Allow fresh cream to sour at room temperature. This will take about 2 days. Pour the soured cream into a clean cheese bag and let liquid drain. Remove solid cheese from bag. Chill. Form into flat cakes. Serve as dessert with fresh fruit, or use in recipes such as Honey Bonbons.

See also: Coeur à la Crème; Cheese Pastry; Cream Cheese Piecrust; Cream Cheese Cake; Cream Cheese Cookies; Yoghurt-Cream Cheese Pie Filling.

### HOMEMADE COTTAGE CHEESE

¼ tablet junket (rennet)
½ cup water, cold
1 gallon skim milk
¼ cup buttermilk or acidophilus milk

1½ teaspoons salt
⅓ cup cream

Dissolve junket tablet in water Combine milk and buttermilk and heat to 70° F. Add junket solution and stir well. Cover with towel. Let stand at room temperature 12 to 18 hours, or until smooth, firm curd forms. Cut curd into ½-inch pieces, using a long knife. Heat curd slowly in pan of hot water until temperature reaches lukewarm (110° F.). Keep curd at this temperature for 20 to 30 minutes, stirring at 5-minute intervals to heat all curd uniformly. When curd is sufficiently firm, pour mixture onto fine cheesecloth in colander to allow whey to drain off. Shift curd around occasionally by lifting corners of cloth. After whey has stopped draining off, draw ends of cheesecloth together. Immerse in cold water. Work with spoon until curd is entirely free of whey. Add salt and cream. Mix thoroughly. Chill.

## RUSSIAN COTTAGE CHEESE PANCAKES

2 cups cottage cheese (see above)
6 eggs, beaten
3 tablespoons oil
½ cup wholewheat flour
½ teaspoon salt
½ cup milk powder
1 tablespoon nutritional yeast
1 teaspoon cumin seeds, ground

Blend all ingredients together. Form patties. Bake in shallow, oiled baking dish until delicately brown. Serve with sour cream on top or honey blended with stewed apricots, peaches or plums. *Serves 6.*

## COTTAGE CHEESE WITH HERBS

1 pound cottage cheese ( see p. 135)
1 teaspoon chives, minced
¼ teaspoon poppy seeds
¼ teaspoon caraway seeds
½ teaspoon sesame seeds
2 tablespoons cream
1 teaspoon oil
1 sprig marjoram, minced
1 sprig basil, minced
1 sprig thyme, minced
1 sprig sage, minced
1 sprig parsley, minced
1 sprig dill, minced
3 tablespoons nutritional yeast

Blend all ingredients in bowl and let stand at least 1 hour before using. Use as dip, spread, in salad, etc.

## TANGY COTTAGE CHEESE-FILLED PANCAKES

BATTER:

4 eggs, beaten
1 cup wholewheat flour
½ teaspoon salt
1 cup milk
¼ cup milk powder
1 tablespoon nutritional yeast

Blend all ingredients together until smooth. Batter should be thin. Pour onto hot, unoiled soapstone griddle or into heated, oiled pan. Brown lightly on both sides.

FILLING:

1½ cups cottage cheese (see p. 135)
2 egg yolks, beaten
½ teaspoon caraway seeds, ground
½ teaspoon celery seeds, ground
¼ teaspoon sage, ground
3 tablespoons chives, minced

Mix all ingredients together. Place 1 tablespoon of the filling in the center of each pancake. Fold edges of pancakes into envelopes. Arrange filled pancakes in shallow, oiled baking dish. Bake at 250° F. for 10 minutes. Serve hot or cold, garnished with sour cream or yoghurt. *Serves 6.*

VARIATIONS:
Substitute chopped mint for seed flavorings, sage and chives and garnish with fresh or stewed fruit.
See also Pancakes Filled with Cottage Cheese.

## HOMEMADE KOCH KAESE

1 quart cottage cheese (see p. 135)
1 teaspoon salt
3 tablespoons caraway seeds, whole
1 tablespoon oil
1½ cups water
1 egg yolk, beaten

Blend cheese, salt and caraway seeds. Place in bowl. Cover and set in warm place. Stir with fork every day for 1 week, until cheese is "ripe" and clear. Heat oil and water. Add cheese. Cover. Simmer for 20 minutes, stirring constantly. Remove from heat. When cool, blend in egg yolk. Beat until glossy. Chill. *Serves 6.*

OTHER RECIPES USING
COTTAGE CHEESE

See: Cottage Cheese Dessert; Molded
Cottage Cheese Dessert; Cottage
Cheese Sherbet; Cottage Cheese
Cake; Cottage Cheese-Yoghurt
Cake; Cottage Cheese Pie Filling;
Cottage Cheese Pie Filling, Re-
frigerated; Russian Cheese Tarts;
Coventry Tart Filling; Cottage
Cheese Dressing; Corn-Cottage
Cheese Casserole.

## HOMEMADE IRISH MOSS CHEESE

¼ cup Irish moss (carrageen)
2 cups water
1 quart sour milk*
1 teaspoon celery seeds, ground
1 cup tomatoes, stewed and puréed
1 tablespoon parsley, minced

Bring Irish moss and water to boil.
Cool. Mix with sour milk. Pour into
muslin bag. Drain off whey. Empty
solid cheese into bowl. Beat remaining ingredients into cheese. Turn
into shallow pan. When set, cut into
squares.

## HOMEMADE SOY CHEESE

Soy cheese is also known as soybean
curd or *tofu.* It may be used the
same way as cottage cheese. The
fresh cheese is fragile. To keep,
wrap in clean cheesecloth, place in
a bowl, cover with cold water and
refrigerate.

When making soy cheese, save
soybean residue for use in bread
dough, cookies, meat, fish or nut
loaves, casserole and soup.

*Method No. 1* (from soy milk)
3 cups soy milk*
juice of 2 lemons

Heat soy milk over hot water in
double boiler. Bring to boil. Add
lemon juice and stir only long
enough to blend thoroughly. Remove from heat. Allow mixture to
cool slowly with top saucepan remaining in hot water. When mixture coagulates, strain through fine
cheesecloth.

*Method No. 2* (from soy flour)
1 cup soy flour (use full-fat soy
    flour)
1 cup water, cold
2 cups water, boiling
juice of 2 lemons

Beat soy flour into cold water until
it forms a smooth paste. Add to boiling water and cook for 5 minutes.
Add lemon juice. Remove from heat
and let cool. When it coagulates,
strain through fine cheesecloth.

# Recipes Using Other Natural Cheeses

## CHEESE SOUFFLÉ

3 tablespoons oil
3 tablespoons wholewheat flour
1 teaspoon soy flour
2 cups milk, hot
½ cup milk powder
½ teaspoon salt
3 tablespoons nutritional yeast
½ teaspoon thyme
6 eggs, separated
½ cup hard cheese, grated

Heat oil. Blend in flours. Gradually
add milk and cook over gentle heat,
stirring, until smooth and thickened.
Blend in milk powder, salt, yeast,
and thyme. Remove from heat.
When cool, blend in beaten egg
yolks and cheese. Fold in stiffly
beaten egg whites. Turn into oiled

[Recipe continued on next page]

[Recipe continued from previous page]
casserole or oiled individual custard cups. Bake uncovered at 350° F., 1 hour for casserole, 45 minutes for individual custard cups. Do not open oven door while baking. *Serves 6.*

VARIATION:
Before baking, add to mixture ½ to 1 cup of leftover meat, fish, fowl or vegetables, minced fine.

## CHEESE FONDUE

6 eggs, beaten
3 cups milk
½ cup milk powder
3 cups wholewheat bread crumbs
3 cups hard cheese, grated
2 tablespoons oil
3 tablespoons nutritional yeast
½ teaspoon basil
½ teaspoon sweet marjoram
¼ teaspoon salt

Blend all ingredients together. Mix lightly. Turn into oiled casserole. Bake at 350° F. for about 30 minutes, until lightly browned. *Serves 6.*

## CHEESE-SOY SOUFFLÉ

3 tablespoons oil
¼ cup soy flour
1⅔ cups milk, hot
½ teaspoon salt
3 tablespoons nutritional yeast
1 teaspoon tarragon
1½ cups hard cheese, grated
6 eggs, separated

Heat oil. Blend in flour. Gradually add milk. Stir until smooth and thickened. Blend in salt, yeast, tarragon and cheese. Remove from heat. When cool, blend in egg yolks. Fold in stiffly beaten egg whites. Turn mixture into oiled casserole, or oiled individual custard cups. Bake uncovered at 350° F., 45 min-

utes for casserole, 30 minutes for custard cups. Do not open oven door while baking. *Serves 6.*

## CORNMEAL-CHEESE SOUFFLÉ

½ cup cornmeal
½ cup milk powder
½ teaspoon salt
3 tablespoons nutritional yeast
½ teaspoon rosemary
1½ cups milk
6 eggs, separated
1½ cups hard cheese, grated

Mix cornmeal, milk powder, salt, yeast and rosemary. Beat into milk. Cook in double boiler over hot water until mixture thickens slightly. Remove from heat. Cool. Blend in egg yolks and cheese. Fold in stiffly beaten egg whites. Turn mixture into oiled casserole, or oiled individual custard cups. Bake uncovered at 325° F., 1 hour for casserole, 45 minutes for custard cups. *Serves 6.*

## BAKED CHEESE-CORNMEAL CASSEROLE

½ cup cornmeal
½ cup milk powder
1 teaspoon salt
3 tablespoons nutritional yeast
½ teaspoon sage, ground
1 cup milk, cold
1 cup milk, scalded and hot
3 tablespoons oil
1½ cups hard cheese, grated
½ cup Soybeans, Roasted, ground

Mix cornmeal, milk powder, salt, yeast and sage. Beat into cold milk. Gradually add hot milk and cook, covered, in double boiler over hot water. Stir occasionally. When it thickens into mush, add oil and cheese and stir until smooth. Turn into oiled 8-inch-square pan and let cool. Sprinkle with Soybeans. Bake, uncovered, at 350° F. for 15 minutes. Cut into squares before serving. *Serves 6.*

## CHEESE CASSEROLE WITH WHOLEWHEAT BERRIES

3 cups tomato juice
½ cup wholewheat flour
1 tablespoon soy flour
1 onion, grated
1 teaspoon salt
3 tablespoons nutritional yeast
½ teaspoon oregano
1 cup hard cheese, grated
3 cups wholewheat berries, cooked
6 slices bacon, broiled, minced

Blend tomato juice, flours, onion, salt, yeast and oregano. Cook, covered, over low heat until mixture simmers. Remove from heat. Add cheese. Put wholewheat berries into oiled casserole and pour sauce over. Garnish with bacon bits. Bake uncovered at 350° F. for 45 minutes. *Serves 6.*

## CHEESE PIE

piecrust for 9-inch pie (for recipes, see under Piecrust)
½ pound hard cheese, grated
2 tablespoons wholewheat flour
½ teaspoon salt
3 tablespoons nutritional yeast
½ teaspoon marjoram
6 eggs
1½ cups milk

Line pie plate with pastry. Blend cheese, flour, salt, yeast and marjoram. Spread over pastry. Blend eggs and milk. Pour over cheese mixture. Bake until knife inserted in center of cheese comes out clean: at 400° F. for 15 minutes, then at 300° F. for 15 minutes, then at 300° F. for 30 minutes. Serve hot or cold. *Serves 6.*

VARIATION:
Individual cheese tartlets may be made in the same manner. Decrease baking time to 20-25 minutes.
See also Cheese-Onion Pie.

## ROQUEFORT MOUSSE

½ pound Roquefort cheese
½ cup milk
1 cup cream, whipped
1 tablespoon chives, minced

Press cheese through coarse sieve. Add milk. Blend. Cook in double boiler over hot water until mixture is smooth. Cool. Fold in whipped cream. Turn into flat shallow mold. Chill until firm. Unmold on salad greens. Garnish with chives. *Serves 6.*

## CHEESE TURNOVERS

2 cups hard cheese, grated
2 cups Soybeans, Roasted, grated
milk
favorite pastry dough (see under Pastries)

Mix cheese and soybeans together. Add enough milk to moisten. Roll pastry thin. Cut into rounds. Fill with stuffing. Fold in half. Seal edges. Prick tops. Arrange on oiled cooky sheet. Bake at 450° F. for about 8 minutes. *Serves 6.*

## BAKED CHEESE CHARLOTTE

6 slices wholewheat bread
2½ cups milk, scalded
4 egg yolks, beaten
½ cup milk powder
½ teaspoon salt
3 tablespoons nutritional yeast
¼ teaspoon nutmeg, ground
1 cup hard cheese, grated
4 egg whites, beaten stiff
¼ cup sunflower seeds

[Recipe continued on next page]

[Recipe continued from previous page]

Cut 4 slices of bread in half. Dip into milk and arrange in shallow, oiled baking pan. Cut remaining slices of bread into cubes and soak in milk. Meanwhile, blend egg yolks, milk powder, salt, yeast, nutmeg and cheese together. Add cubed bread to mixture; fold in egg whites. Pour mixture over bread in pan. Bake at 350° F. for about 30 minutes. Garnish with sunflower seeds. *Serves 6.*

## BAKED CHEESE SANDWICHES (in blender)

2 cups milk
2 eggs
½ cup milk powder
½ teaspoon salt
3 tablespoons nutritional yeast
1 onion, chopped
1 sprig dill
12 slices wholewheat bread
1 tablespoon oil
1 pound hard cheese, sliced

Put into blender milk, eggs, milk powder, salt, yeast, onion and dill and blend until smooth. Arrange 6 slices of bread close together in bottom of shallow, oiled baking pan. Top with cheese. Close sandwiches with remaining bread. Pour milk mixture over sandwiches. Bake at 350° F. for about 20 minutes, putting under broiler during the last few minutes to brown. Cut into 6 portions. *Serves 6.*

OTHER RECIPES USING CHEESE

See: Cheese Spreads; Soy Cheese Spread; Cheese Crackers; New England Cheese Soup; Baked Eggplant Slices; Eggplant Casserole; Cheese Pastry; Eggs Florentine; Walnut Cheese Loaf; Risotto; Cheese Bread; Soy Cheese Sherbet; cheese-cake recipes under *Cake;* cheese piecrusts under *Piecrust.*

# 14

# DRIED BEANS
# AND PEAS

HINTS:

1½ cups of dried beans will serve 6.
Split peas, lentils, pinto beans and black-eye peas can be cooked without soaking. Other legumes should be soaked first.

The volume of dried legumes is increased by soaking and cooking. Some double in size; lentils more than double in size; soybeans increase their original volume 2½ to 3 times.

To retain nutritive values and develop full, natural flavor, simmer legumes in water in which they were soaked. Gentle cooking, with a minimum of stirring, will keep them firm and unbroken. Their flavor is enhanced if salt, onions and herbs are added to soaking and simmering water.

After soaking overnight, most beans require 2 to 2½ hours of simmering. Soaking time may be reduced as follows:

1. Plunge dried beans into boiling water and cook for 2 minutes. Remove from heat and soak for 1 hour. Then complete cooking.
2. Grind dried beans in a home flour grinder. Bean flour can then be cooked immediately in a double boiler. Preliminary soaking is eliminated and cooking time reduced.

When beans are soaked overnight (especially soybeans), refrigerate to prevent any possible fermentation.

In making bean pulp, sieve beans while they are still hot. They are easier to purée, and less residue remains, if they are not too well drained beforehand. One cup of purée plus a little bean stock will almost equal the original measure of cooked beans. Any remaining stock should be saved for soup.

Prepare enough dried legumes at one time to use in several dishes.

For variety, try some of the following in recipes: pea beans (navy), jumbo marrow, fat marrow, yellow eyes, red kidney, Great Northern, California small white, pinto, cranberry, fava, Salonica, mung (Kalamata) beans; large and baby limas; green split peas, yellow split peas, green whole peas, yellow whole peas, cowpeas, chick peas (garbanzos), black-eyed peas; different varieties of lentils and soybeans, etc.

# Soybeans

## BASIC SOYBEAN FILLER

1 cup soybeans, dried
3 cups stock

Soak soybeans in stock and refrigerate overnight. Drain beans. Grind in food grinder with medium knife. Place ground soybeans in pan with stock in which they were soaked. Simmer 1½ to 2 hours, or until tender, stirring occasionally. Use this filler in bread dough, cereal, soup, meat, fish, fowl, vegetable or nut casseroles or loaves, stuffed tomatoes, eggplants, peppers, onions.

## BROILED SOYBURGERS

2 cups soybeans, cooked, puréed
1 onion, grated
1 clove garlic, minced
1 carrot, grated
1 stalk celery and tops, chopped
½ cup wheat germ
2 eggs, beaten
¼ cup soy grits, soaked in
½ cup stock
3 tablespoons oil
3 tablespoons nutritional yeast
½ teaspoon salt
½ cup brown rice, cooked
½ teaspoon dill seeds, ground
1 sprig dill, minced

Blend all ingredients and mold into patties. Broil until brown on each side. *Serves 6.*

## SOYBEAN RING (in blender)

¼ cup stock
½ cup tomato juice
2 eggs
2 tablespoons oil
2 cups soybeans, cooked
2 stalks celery and tops, chopped
¼ green pepper
½ teaspoon salt

3 tablespoons nutritional yeast
½ teaspoon sage
1 sprig parsley
1 cup buckwheat, cooked

Blend all ingredients except buckwheat in food blender until smooth. Combine with buckwheat. Turn into oiled ring mold and bake at 350° F. for 45 minutes. Unmold and serve. *Serves 6.*

## BAKED SOYBEAN CROQUETTES

1 cup tomatoes, stewed, puréed
2 tablespoons oil
1 onion, grated
1½ cups celery and tops, chopped
1 teaspoon salt
1 teaspoon oregano
5 tablespoons wholewheat flour
3 tablespoons nutritional yeast
3 cups soybeans, cooked, puréed
1 egg, beaten with
2 tablespoons milk
cornmeal
3 tablespoons parsley, minced

Mix tomatoes, oil, onion, celery, salt and oregano together in pot. Cover. Slowly bring to boil. Add flour and continue to cook over low heat, stirring occasionally, until thickened. Let cool and blend with yeast and soybean purée. Shape into 12 croquettes. Dip in egg mixture and roll in cornmeal. Arrange in oiled baking pan. Bake at 300° F. for 20 to 30 minutes. Garnish with parsley. *Serves 6.*

## SOYBEAN CASSEROLE

2 cups soybeans, cooked
2 cups corn, cooked
¼ cup hard cheese, grated
2 cups tomatoes, stewed
¼ cup stock
3 tablespoons oil
1 bay leaf, crushed

3 tablespoons parsley, minced
½ teaspoon thyme
¼ cup wheat germ

In oiled casserole alternate a layer of beans, a layer of corn, a layer of cheese and a layer of tomatoes. Repeat until all ingredients are used. Mix stock with oil, bay leaf, parsley and thyme and pour into casserole. Garnish with wheat germ. Bake, covered, at 350° F. for 30 minutes. *Serves 6.*

## BAKED SOYBEANS

4 cups soybeans, cooked
1 onion, grated
½ green pepper, chopped
1 carrot, grated
½ cup celery and tops, chopped
3 tablespoons molasses
3 tablespoons nutritional yeast
3 tablespoons parsley, minced
¼ teaspoon thyme
¼ teaspoon summer savory
4 slices bacon, broiled, minced
tomato juice, as needed

Mix all ingredients except bacon and tomato juice. Turn mixture into oiled casserole. Cover with bacon bits. Cover casserole and bake at 350° F., 1¾ to 2 hours, adding tomato juice from time to time, as needed. Uncover casserole for last 30 minutes of baking. *Serves 6.*

## SOYBEAN-LENTIL LOAF

1 cup soybeans, cooked
1 cup lentils, cooked
1 cup brown rice, cooked
½ cup wheat germ
¼ cup soy grits, soaked in
½ cup stock
2 cups milk
3 tablespoons nutritional yeast
1 tablespoon mint, minced
2 tablespoons parsley, minced
1 teaspoon celery seeds, ground

Blend all ingredients. Turn into oiled loaf pan. Bake at 350° F. for 30 minutes. *Serves 6.*

## STEWED SOYBEANS

3 cups soybeans, cooked
1 cup tomatoes, stewed
3 tablespoons nutritional yeast
½ teaspoon salt
1 cup celery and tops, chopped
1 onion, grated
1 bay leaf
¼ teaspoon sage, ground

Mix all ingredients together. Simmer for 10 minutes. *Serves 6.*

## SOYBEAN SOUFFLÉ

3 tablespoons oil
3 tablespoons wholewheat flour
1 cup milk, hot
1 cup soybeans, cooked, puréed
1 onion, grated
3 tablespoons nutritional yeast
½ teaspoon salt
½ teaspoon sage, ground
4 egg yolks, beaten
4 egg whites, beaten stiff

Heat oil. Blend in flour. Gradually add milk and continue to cook, stirring, until thickened. Remove from heat. Add soybeans, onion, yeast, salt and sage. When cool, blend in egg yolks and fold in egg whites. Turn mixture into oiled casserole or oiled individual custard cups. Bake at 300° F. about 50 minutes for casserole, 35 minutes for custard cups, until firm. *Serves 6.*

## SOYBEAN SQUARES

5 cups soybeans, cooked, puréed
2 tablespoons oil
1 teaspoon salt
3 tablespoons nutritional yeast
½ teaspoon summer savory
½ teaspoon basil

[Recipe continued on next page]

[Recipe continued from previous page]

Blend all ingredients. Turn into shallow, oiled pan to depth of 2 inches. Bake at 300° F., 1½ to 2 hours, or until firm. Cut into squares. Serve with tomato or mushroom sauce. Leftovers may be used as basis for spreads. *Serves 6.*

## ROASTED SOYBEANS

¼ cup soybeans, dry
1 cup cold water

Soak soybeans overnight and keep in refrigerator. The next day, drain liquid and reserve as stock. Dry soybeans between towels. Spread out on shallow pan and roast for 2 hours in 200° F. oven. Then place under broiler and continue to cook, stirring frequently, until soybeans are brown. They may then be used just as they are, or oiled and seasoned. Leave whole or grind, if desired, in blender or food grinder and use as topping the same way as nuts.

LEFTOVER SOYBEANS

Use small amounts of cooked soybeans in sandwich spreads; stuffed eggs and tomatoes, green peppers, eggplants, or onions; as a filler in meat, fish, fowl, vegetable or nut loaves, casseroles or patties; stews and soups.

## Lentils

### BAKED LENTIL LOAF

2½ cups lentils, cooked
1 cup millet, cooked
1 egg, beaten
2 slices bacon, broiled, chopped
2 onions, grated
1 clove garlic, minced
½ teaspoon salt

3 tablespoons nutritional yeast
¼ cup parsley, minced
¼ teaspoon thyme
pinch of nutmeg, ground
stock

Blend all ingredients, adding only enough stock to moisten. Turn into oiled loaf pan. Bake at 375° F. for 40 to 45 minutes. Serve with favorite sauce. *Serves 6.*

## LENTIL ROAST

3 cups lentils, cooked, puréed
1 cup potatoes, cooked, puréed
½ cup soy grits, soaked in
1 cup stock
1 egg
1 onion, grated
½ teaspoon sage, ground
3 tablespoons oil
1 teaspoon salt
3 tablespoons nutritional yeast
3 tablespoons parsley, minced
juice of 1 lemon
stock

Blend all ingredients, adding enough stock to give mixture a good consistency. Turn into oiled casserole. Cover and bake at 350° F. for 30 minutes. *Serves 6.*

## LENTILS BAKED IN SWEET-SOUR SAUCE

2 tablespoons oil
2 tablespoons wholewheat flour
1 cup stock, hot
¼ teaspoon salt
2 tablespoons nutritional yeast
3 tablespoons cider vinegar *
3 tablespoons molasses
3 cups lentils, cooked

Heat oil. Blend in flour. Gradually add stock. Stir until thickened. Add salt, yeast, vinegar and molasses. Blend thoroughly. Cover. Simmer 5 minutes. Add lentils. Turn mixture into oiled casserole. Bake, covered, at 350° F. for about 20 minutes, until liquid is absorbed. *Serves 6.*

## LENTIL TIMBALES

2 cups lentils, cooked, puréed
1 cup bulgur, cooked
1 cup sunflower-seed meal
3 tablespoons nutritional yeast
½ teaspoon salt
¼ teaspoon basil

Thoroughly blend all ingredients. Turn into oiled muffin pans. Bake at 300° F. for 30 to 40 minutes. Serve with favorite sauce. *Serves 6.*

## LENTIL RISSOLES

3 cups lentils, cooked, puréed
1 cup cornmeal mush, cooked
½ cup soy grits, soaked in
1 cup stock
2 tablespoons oil
3 tablespoons parsley, minced
¼ teaspoon sage, ground
¼ teaspoon savory
¼ teaspoon rosemary
½ teaspoon salt
3 tablespoons nutritional yeast
1 egg, beaten with
2 tablespoons milk
wheat germ

Blend all ingredients together except egg mixture and wheat germ. Form into cones, cylinders, or any other desired shape. Dip into egg mixture and roll in wheat germ. Broil until brown on all sides. *Serves 6.*

## EAST INDIAN LENTIL KEDGEREE

2 tablespoons oil
1 onion, chopped
1 clove garlic, minced
1½ quarts stock
2 bay leaves

½ teaspoon cinnamon, ground
12 cardamom seeds, ground
¼ teaspoon mace, ground
6 cloves, whole
3 tablespoons nutritional yeast
1 cup lentils, soaked overnight
1 cup brown rice, raw

Heat oil in large pot. Sauté onion and garlic. Add rest of ingredients, except rice, to pot and cover. Simmer for 1½ hours. Then add rice. Cover again and simmer for an additional 30 minutes. Drain off any remaining liquid. Steam lentil-rice mixture until rice is dry and fluffy. *Serves 6.*

## SPANISH LENTILS

3 cups lentils, cooked
2 cups tomatoes, stewed
3 tablespoons oil
1 onion, chopped
1 green pepper, chopped
1 teaspoon soy flour
1 teaspoon salt
3 tablespoons nutritional yeast
1 teaspoon oregano
1 teaspoon celery seeds, ground

Combine all ingredients. Cover and simmer until thoroughly heated. *Serves 6.*

## ASIAN LENTILS

3 tablespoons oil
1 onion, grated
1 clove garlic, minced
1 tablespoon honey
3 tablespoons nutritional yeast
1 teaspoon tarragon
4 cups lentils, cooked, puréed
½ cup hard cheese, grated

Heat oil. Sauté onion and garlic. Blend in remaining ingredients except cheese. Cover and heat thoroughly. Garnish with cheese. *Serves 6.*

## Other Legumes

### BEAN LOAF

3 tablespoons oil
1 onion
3 cups cranberry beans, cooked
1 egg, beaten
1 carrot, grated
½ teaspoon salt
3 tablespoons nutritional yeast
1 teaspoon savory
1 cup wholewheat bread crumbs
½ cup nuts, ground

Heat oil and sauté onions. Combine with remaining ingredients and blend thoroughly. Turn into oiled loaf pan. Bake at 350° F. until well browned, about 1 hour. Serve with favorite sauce. *Serves 6.*

### SAVORY LIMA BEANS

4 cups lima beans, cooked
1 cup tomatoes, stewed
1 cup celery and tops, chopped
1 onion, minced
1 clove garlic, minced
½ teaspoon salt
3 tablespoons nutritional yeast
¼ cup soy grits, soaked in
½ cup stock
1 teaspoon chervil
3 slices bacon, broiled, minced

Combine all ingredients except bacon bits. Cover. Simmer for 15 minutes. Serve garnished with bacon bits. *Serves 6.*

### BEANS IN CHEESE SAUCE

2 tablespoons oil
2 tablespoons wholewheat flour
1½ cups milk, hot
½ teaspoon salt
3 tablespoons nutritional yeast
1½ cups hard cheese, grated
3 cups fava beans, cooked
3 tablespoons chives, minced

Heat oil. Blend in flour. Gradually add milk and cook over gentle heat. When thickened, add salt, yeast and cheese, blend and continue to cook until cheese is melted and sauce is smooth. Add beans. When thoroughly heated, garnish with chives and serve. *Serves 6.*

### MEXICAN FRIJOLES

3 cups pinto beans, cooked, puréed
1 clove garlic, minced
1 onion, grated
3 tablespoons nutritional yeast
1 tablespoon Essence of Sweet Herbs
½ cup hard cheese, grated

Mix all ingredients. Heat in double boiler until cheese is melted and blended. *Serves 6.*

### LIMA BEAN CASSEROLE

3 cups lima beans, cooked
¼ cup soy grits, soaked in
½ cup stock
3 carrots, cooked, cubed
1 onion, minced
½ teaspoon salt
3 tablespoons nutritional yeast
stock
4 slices bacon, broiled, minced

Combine all ingredients except bacon, adding enough stock to moisten. Turn into oiled casserole. Cover and bake at 350° F. for 30 minutes. Garnish with bacon. *Serves 6.*

### BEAN-LENTIL CROQUETTES

2 cups beans, cooked, puréed
2 cups lentils, cooked, puréed
¼ cup soy grits, soaked in
½ cup stock
1 teaspoon salt
3 tablespoons nutritional yeast
1 teaspoon chervil
1 egg, beaten with

2 tablespoons milk
Soybeans, Roasted, ground

Blend all ingredients except egg mixture and soybeans. Shape into croquettes. Dip in egg batter and roll in soybeans. Brush with oil and broil, turning a few times to brown on all sides. *Serves 6.*

## BEAN AND MEAT STEW

3 tablespoons oil
1 onion, chopped
½ pound lean meat, freshly ground
3 cups tomatoes, stewed
3 cups beans, cooked
1 teaspoon salt
3 tablespoons nutritional yeast
1 bay leaf
1 teaspoon oregano
1 sprig parsley, minced

Heat oil. Sauté onion and meat. Add remaining ingredients. Cover and simmer for 15 minutes. *Serves 6.*

## BEANS AND SUCCOTASH

3 tablespoons oil
1 onion, chopped
1 clove garlic, minced
½ green pepper, chopped
2 cups corn, cooked
2 cups beans, cooked
1 teaspoon salt
3 tablespoons nutritional yeast
1 teaspoon savory
stock

Heat oil. Sauté onion, garlic and pepper. Add remaining ingredients, using enough stock to moisten.

Cover pot and simmer for 20 minutes. *Serves 6.*

## SOUTHERN HOPPING JOHN

2 cups ham stock
3 cups black-eye peas, cooked
1 cup ham, cooked, cubed
1 cup brown rice, cooked
3 tablespoons nutritional yeast
3 tablespoons parsley, minced

Combine all ingredients. Cook until thoroughly heated. *Serves 6.*

LEFTOVER DRIED BEANS AND PEAS
Add small amounts of cooked beans or peas, whole or puréed, to spread, soups, salads, meat, fish, fowl, nut or vegetable loaves or casseroles.

OTHER RECIPES USING DRIED BEANS AND PEAS
See: Egg-Lentil Spread; Soybean Spread; Soy Milk and Soy Milk, Spiced; Winter Salad; Soybean-Cheese Salad; Soybean-Vegetable Salad; Soybean Molded Salad; Italian Lung-Bean Stew; Sweet-Sour Lentil Sauce; Lentil Stuffing; Homemade Soy Cheese; Barley-Lentil Kasha; Barley Soybean Casserole; Soy Bread; Wholewheat-Soy Piecrust; Spiced Soybean Pie Filling; see under *Soup:* Soybean Soup; Cream of Soy Soup; Lentil Soup; Lima Bean Soup; Black Bean Soup.
See also: Sprouts, for sprouting of dried beans and peas.

# 15

# NUT ENTREES

HINTS:

Use fresh, raw, unoiled, unsalted nuts.

Grind small quantities as needed.

Experiment with different varieties in recipes such as: almonds, beechnuts, Brazil nuts, butternuts, cashews, coconuts, filberts (hazelnuts), hickory nuts, peanuts, pecans, pine (pignolia) nuts, pistachio nuts, walnuts (English and black).

## PECAN LOAF

2 cups pecans, ground
1 cup wholewheat bread crumbs
¼ cup soy grits, soaked in
½ cup stock
2 eggs, beaten
2 onions, grated
¼ cup mushrooms, chopped
¼ cup celery and tops, chopped
½ green pepper, chopped
1 cup milk
½ cup milk powder
½ teaspoon salt
3 tablespoons parsley, minced
½ teaspoon sage
3 tablespoons nutritional yeast

Blend all ingredients. Turn into oiled loaf pan. Bake at 350° F. for 30 minutes. Serve with favorite sauce. *Serves 6.*

## CASHEW-ALMOND LOAF

1 cup cashews, ground
1 cup almonds, blanched and ground
1 cup brown rice, cooked
¼ cup soy grits, soaked in
½ cup stock
1 egg, beaten
2 onions, grated
¼ cup parsley, minced
¼ cup wheat germ
½ teaspoon salt
3 tablespoons nutritional yeast
½ teaspoon thyme

Blend all ingredients. Turn into oiled loaf pan. Bake at 350° F. for 30 minutes. Serve with favorite sauce. *Serves 6.*

## WALNUT-CHEESE LOAF

1 cup walnuts, ground
1 cup hard cheese, ground
½ cup wheat germ
¼ cup soy grits, soaked in
½ cup stock
2 onions, chopped and sautéed

juice of ½ lemon
2 eggs, beaten
¼ teaspoon salt
3 tablespoons nutritional yeast
1 teaspoon caraway seeds, ground

Combine all ingredients. Turn into oiled loaf pan. Bake at 350° F. for 30 minutes. Serve with favorite sauce. *Serves 6.*

## FILBERT-POTATO LOAF

1 cup filberts, ground
3 cups potatoes, cooked, puréed
1 cup celery and tops, chopped
1 onion, chopped and sautéed
1 teaspoon salt
3 tablespoons nutritional yeast
¼ cup soy grits, soaked in
½ cup stock
1 egg, beaten
¼ teaspoon nutmeg, ground
3 tablespoons parsley, minced

Combine all ingredients. Turn into oiled loaf pan. Bake at 350° F. for 30 minutes. Serve with favorite sauce. *Serves 6.*

## NUT-CORNMEAL PATTIES

1½ cups cornmeal
½ cup stock, cold
1 cup stock, hot
1 stalk celery and tops, chopped
1 onion, grated
1 green pepper, chopped
1 carrot, grated
¼ cup soy grits, soaked in
½ cup stock
¼ teaspoon sage, ground
¼ teaspoon rosemary
¼ teaspoon savory
½ teaspoon salt
3 tablespoons nutritional yeast
2 cups nuts, ground

Mix cornmeal in cold stock. When blended, combine with hot stock in top of double boiler and cook over direct heat, stirring constantly, until mixture comes to a boil. Cover and set over bottom of double boiler, to which hot water has been added. Continue cooking for 30 minutes, or until thickened into mush. Add remaining ingredients except nuts. Cook 20 minutes longer. Remove from heat. When cool, add nuts. Shape mixture into patties. Broil until brown on each side. *Serves 6.*

## PEANUT-SPINACH LOAF
### (in blender)

1 egg
1 onion, chopped
1 pound spinach, cooked, cold
1 cup peanuts
1 sprig parsley
1 clove garlic
1 cup wholewheat bread crumbs
½ teaspoon salt
3 tablespoons nutritional yeast
pinch of mace, ground

Gradually blend egg, onion, spinach, peanuts, parsley and garlic in blender until smooth. Pour into bowl. Add remaining ingredients and mix well. Turn into oiled loaf pan. Bake at 350° F. for 30 minutes. *Serves 6.*

## NUT-OATMEAL CASSEROLE

3 tablespoons oil
1 onion, sliced
¼ cup mushrooms, sliced
3 eggs, beaten
1 cup oatmeal, cooked
1 cup nuts, ground
½ cup wheat germ
½ teaspoon salt
3 tablespoons nutritional yeast
1 tablespoon Essence of Sweet Herbs
3 tablespoons parsley, minced
¼ teaspoon sage, ground
½ cup milk powder
stock

[Recipe continued on next page]

[Recipe continued from previous page]

Heat oil. Sauté onion and mushrooms. Blend with remaining ingredients, adding enough stock to moisten. Bake at 325° F. for 45 minutes, adding more stock if needed. *Serves 6.*

LEFTOVER NUT ENTREES

Moisten with favorite dressing and use as spread.

Add to soups and meat, sea food, fowl or vegetable loaves or casseroles.

ADDITIONAL RECIPES USING NUTS

See: Nut Cream; Nut Butters; Nut Spreads; Nut Milk; East Indian Coconut Soup; Squash-Chestnut Soup; Nut Dumplings; Vegetable-Chestnut Stew; nut stuffings listed under *Stuffing;* Sprouted Wheat Patties, Broiled; Chestnut Purée; Chestnut Soufflé; Nut Ice Cream; Almond Sauce; nut cakes listed under *Cakes;* Almond Filling; nut cookies listed under *Cookies;* Nut Crumb Pie Shell; Chestnut Pie Filling; Coconut Shreds.

# 16
# GRAINS

The whole-grain dishes made from the following recipes can be served the same way as potatoes or other starch foods.

## Wholewheat

### STEAMED WHOLEWHEAT BERRIES

4 cups seasoned stock
2 cups wholewheat berries, raw
2 tablespoons oil
3 tablespoons nutritional yeast
3 tablespoons parsley, minced

Bring stock to boil in top of double boiler, over direct heat. Add wholewheat, oil and yeast, cover and set on bottom of double boiler to which hot water has been added. Cook over gentle heat until grains have absorbed all liquid. Garnish with parsley and serve. Leftovers may be reheated and added to soup, cereal or bread dough. *Serves 6.*

### BROILED SPROUTED WHEAT PATTIES (in blender)

2 cups wholewheat berries, Sprouted
1 cup nuts

1 onion
1 cup milk
1 tablespoon soy flour
1 teaspoon salt
3 tablespoons nutritional yeast
1 sprig parsley
1 egg
2 cups whole-grain bread crumbs (about)

Blend all ingredients, except bread crumbs, in blender until smooth. Turn into bowl. Add enough bread crumbs to make mixture stiff. Shape into patties. Arrange on oiled cookie sheet. Broil on each side until golden brown. *Serves 6.*

### WHOLEWHEAT SOUFFLÉ

1½ cups seasoned stock
½ cup cracked wheat
3 tablespoons nutritional yeast
2 tablespoons oil
¾ cup milk
3 eggs, separated
½ cup cheese, grated
½ teaspoon celery seeds, crushed

Heat stock in top of double boiler over direct heat. When boiling, add wheat, yeast and oil. Cover. Place over bottom of double boiler, to

[Recipe continued on next page]

[Recipe continued from previous page]
which hot water has been added. Cook over gentle heat until wheat has absorbed liquid. Cool to lukewarm. Stir in milk, egg yolks, cheese and celery seeds. Fold in stiffly beaten egg whites. Turn into oiled custard cups. Bake at 350° F. for 30 minutes. *Serves 6.*

OTHER RECIPES USING WHOLEWHEAT BERRIES

See: Wholewheat Berry Chowder; Wholewheat Berry Cereal Soup; Armenian Meat Balls; Meat Loaf with Wholewheat Berries; Cheese Casserole with Wholewheat Berries; Wholewheat Sprouts; Soaked Wholewheat Bread; Baked Wholewheat Berry Pudding.

# Bulgur

## BASIC BULGUR

2 tablespoons oil
2 cups bulgur, raw
4 cups stock, hot, seasoned

Heat oil. Sauté bulgur, making sure all grains are coated with oil. Add stock gradually to bulgur. Cover tightly. Simmer gently for 15 minutes or until bulgur has absorbed all liquid. *Serves 6.*

VARIATIONS:
Substitute tomato juice for stock.
Add any of the following ingredients to the bulgur mixture as it simmers: diced green peppers; sliced onion; chopped scallions; diced celery; grated carrot; sliced mushrooms; minced garlic; minced parsley, dill or other herbs.
Nutritional yeast may be added to stock.

OTHER RECIPES USING BULGUR
See: Bulgur Stuffing; Bulgur Raisin Pudding.

# Rye

## STEAMED WHOLE RYE

4 cups seasoned stock
2 cups whole rye grains, raw
2 tablespoons oil
3 tablespoons nutritional yeast
3 tablespoons parsley, minced

Heat stock in top of double boiler over direct heat. When boiling, add rye, oil and yeast. Cover. Place over bottom of double boiler, to which hot water has been added. Cook over gentle heat until grain has absorbed all liquid. Garnish with parsley before serving. Leftovers may be reheated, added to soup, cereal or bread dough. *Serves 6.*

## RYE SOUFFLÉ

1½ cups seasoned stock
½ cup cracked rye
3 tablespoons nutritional yeast
2 tablespoons oil
¾ cup milk
3 eggs, separated
½ cup cheese, grated
½ teaspoon caraway seeds, crushed

Heat stock in top of double boiler over direct heat. When boiling, add rye, yeast and oil. Cover. Place over bottom of double boiler, to which hot water has been added. Cook over gentle heat until rye has absorbed liquid. Remove from heat and cool to lukewarm. Stir in milk, egg yolks, cheese and caraway seeds. Fold in stiffly beaten egg whites. Turn into oiled custard cups. Bake at 350° F. for 30 minutes. *Serves 6.*

OTHER RECIPES USING RYE
See: Mix-Your-Own-Cereal Blend; Cereal Soup; breads listed under *Rye Bread;* Rye Pancakes; Rye Bread Torte; Boston Brown Bread; Rye-Honey Cookies; Rye Pie Shell; Rye-Rice Piecrust.

# Rice

## STEAMED RICE

2 cups seasoned stock
1 cup brown rice, raw
2 tablespoons oil
3 tablespoons nutritional yeast
3 tablespoons parsley, minced
1 teaspoon marjoram

Heat stock in top of double boiler over direct heat. When boiling, add rice, oil and yeast. Place over bottom of double boiler, to which hot water has been added. Cook gently for 30-40 minutes, or until grains have absorbed all liquid. Garnish with parsley and marjoram. Leftovers may be reheated, added to soup, cereal or bread dough. *Serves 6.*

VARIATIONS:
If rice is to be cooked for use in desserts, substitute 2 cups of milk for stock. Omit parsley and marjoram and add ½ teaspoon crushed anise.

## RISOTTO

2 tablespoons oil
1 onion, chopped
1 clove garlic, minced
1 cup brown rice, raw
2 cups seasoned stock, hot
3 tablespoons nutritional yeast
½ teaspoon rosemary
3 tablespoons parsley, minced

pinch of saffron
½ cup cheese, grated

Heat oil and sauté onion and garlic. Add rice and cook for 3 minutes more, stirring constantly. Each grain should be golden. Dissolve yeast, herbs and saffron in stock. Pour ½ cup of stock into rice mixture. Cover and simmer gently, gradually adding rest of stock as liquid is absorbed (rice should be tender in about 30 minutes). Add ¼ cup cheese a few minutes before rice is done. When cheese is melted through, remove from heat. Top with remaining cheese and serve. *Serves 6.*

## RICE PATTIES

1 cup brown rice, cooked
1 cup sweet potatoes, cooked, puréed
1 tablespoon oil
1 tablespoon nutritional yeast
⅛ teaspoon mace
milk powder

Combine all ingredients and bind with as much milk powder as mixture will hold. Shape into patties and arrange in oiled baking pan. Broil each side until browned. *Serves 4-6.*

## RICE-CHEESE CASSEROLE

3 tablespoons oil
1 onion, chopped
1 clove garlic, minced
2 cups brown rice, cooked
2 cups soy milk*
1 tablespoon nutritional yeast
1 teaspoon basil
1 cup cheese, grated
3 tablespoons parsley, minced

Heat oil and in it sauté onion and garlic. Combine with rice, soy milk, yeast, basil and half the cheese.

[Recipe continued on next page]

[Recipe continued from previous page]

Mix well and turn into oiled casserole. Sprinkle remaining cheese on top. Bake at 350° F. for 30 minutes. Garnish with parsley. *Serves 4-6.*

## PILAU

4 tablespoons oil
1 onion, chopped
1 clove garlic, minced
1 cup brown rice, raw
2 cups seasoned stock, hot
3 tablespoons nutritional yeast
¼ teaspoon cloves, ground
3 cardamom seeds, crushed
½ teaspoon allspice, ground
½ teaspoon cinnamon, ground
¼ cup almonds, slivered
¼ cup raisins

Heat oil and sauté onion and garlic. Add rice and cook, stirring constantly until each grain is transparent. Dissolve yeast and spices in hot stock. Add ½ cup of stock to rice mixture. Cover and simmer gently, gradually adding rest of stock as liquid is absorbed. Add almonds and raisins. Rice should be tender in 30 to 40 minutes. *Serves 6.*

## CHINESE RICE

4 cups brown rice, cooked
3 tablespoons oil
1 onion, chopped
½ teaspoon salt
1 tablespoon nutritional yeast
1 tablespoon Essence of Sweet Herbs
½ cup cooked meat, diced
3 tablespoons celery and tops,
    chopped fine
3 eggs, beaten
½ cup bean Sprouts

Sauté rice in oil in large pan. Add onion, salt, yeast, essence, meat and celery and mix thoroughly. Make hollow in center of mixture and pour beaten eggs into this. Cover. When eggs are half cooked, stir to distribute throughout mixture. Cook a few seconds more. Garnish with bean sprouts before serving. *Serves 6.*

## RICE-CARROT CASSEROLE

2 cups brown rice, cooked
2 cups carrots, shredded, raw
2 eggs, beaten
1 cup seasoned stock
1 tablespoon nutritional yeast
1 cup cheese, grated
½ onion, minced
1 teaspoon tarragon

Blend all ingredients. Turn into oiled casserole and set in pan of hot water. Bake at 350° F. for about 45 minutes. *Serves 6.*

## RICE-PUMPKIN CASSEROLE

3 tablespoons oil
6 onions, sliced thin
1 cup brown rice, raw
2 cups pumpkin, cooked, puréed
2 cups seasoned stock
¼ teaspoon cinnamon, ground
¼ teaspoon allspice, ground
3 tablespoons yeast

Sauté onions in hot oil. Add rice and cook, stirring constantly, until rice is golden brown. Remove from heat. Combine with rest of ingredients and turn into oiled casserole. Bake at 350° F. for 40 minutes. *Serves 6.*

OTHER RECIPES USING RICE
See: Mix-Your-Own-Cereal Blend; Herbed Brown Rice Soup; Rice Squares (garnishes); Stuffed Cabbage Rolls; Oriental Congee; Rice Ring with Liver; Rice-Al-

mond Stuffing; Rice-Mushroom Stuffing; Rice Ring, Baked; Rice Puddings.

# Wild Rice

## BASIC WILD RICE

*Method No. 1*
3 cups boiling stock
1½ cups wild rice, washed in cold
    water

Pour boiling stock over washed rice. Stir and cover. Let stand overnight to absorb liquid. Reheat to serve. *Serves 6.*

*Method No. 2*
3 cups boiling stock
1½ cups wild rice, washed in cold
    water

Pour boiling stock over washed rice. Stir. Cover and let cool. Drain stock off and boil again, pour over rice, stir, cover and let cool. Repeat this procedure three times in all. Rice will open and be thoroughly cooked. *Serves 6.*

## WILD RICE AND MUSHROOMS

3 tablespoons oil
1 onion, sliced
½ pound mushrooms, sliced
1 teaspoon salt
1 tablespoon parsley, minced
2 tablespoons nutritional yeast
1½ cups wild rice, washed in cold
    water
2 cups boiling stock
1 cup sweet cider
½ cup yoghurt*

Heat oil. Sauté onions and mushrooms. Add salt, parsley, yeast and rice. Stir well to coat grains with oil and blend all ingredients. Add one cup of hot stock. Cover tightly. Cook over low heat until liquid has been absorbed, add rest of stock and cook until this too has been absorbed; then add sweet cider, continue cooking until cider has been absorbed and rice is done. Keep covered during cooking process. Remove from heat and blend in yoghurt. *Serves 6.*

# Millet

HINT:
In recipes calling for cornmeal, millet may be used instead. Substitute one cup of millet for one cup of cornmeal.

## BASIC MILLET

4 cups seasoned stock
1 cup millet, raw
2 tablespoons oil
3 tablespoons nutritional yeast
3 tablespoons dill
3 tablespoons parsley, minced

Heat stock in top of double boiler over direct heat. When boiling, add millet, oil and yeast. Stir. Cover and boil for 2 minutes. Add dill. Put over bottom of double boiler, to which hot water has been added. Cover. Cook gently for about 30 minutes or until all liquid has been absorbed. Garnish with parsley before serving. Leftovers may be reheated, added to soup, cereal or bread dough. *Serves 6.*

VARIATION:
If cooked millet is to be used for a dessert, substitute 4 cups milk for 4 cups stock and omit parsley and dill. Add ½ teaspoon crushed fennel seeds.

## MILLET SOUFFLÉ

1 cup milk
4 eggs, separated
2 cups millet, cooked in milk
½ teaspoon dill seeds, crushed
1 tablespoon nutritional yeast
½ cup cheese, grated

Combine milk and egg yolks. Blend in rest of ingredients except egg whites. Beat egg whites until stiff and fold in. Turn into oiled custard cups. Bake at 350° F., about 20 minutes. *Serves 6.*

### LEFTOVER MILLET

Sauté in oil. Garlic and/or onions, cheese and stewed tomatoes may be added.

Slices of leftover millet can be added to soups, stews, or casseroles.

### OTHER RECIPES USING MILLET

See: Millet Cereal; Mix-Your-Own-Cereal Blend; Millet Crackers; Cereal Soup; Oriental Congee; Chewy Meal Cakes; Millet Waffles; Millet-Oat Waffles; Millet Pudding.

## Oats

### HINTS:

Finely ground oatmeal may be used in recipes calling for wholewheat. Use 1½ cups of oatmeal for each cup of wholewheat.

Cooked oatmeal may be substituted for breadcrumbs as binder for loaves and patties of meat, fish or nuts.

### STEAMED OATS

2 cups seasoned stock
1 cup whole oats, raw
2 tablespoons oil
3 tablespoons nutritional yeast
1 teaspoon caraway seeds, crushed
3 tablespoons parsley, minced

Heat stock in top of double boiler over direct heat. When boiling, add rice, oil, yeast and seeds. Place over bottom of double boiler, to which hot water has been added. Cover. Cook gently for about 30 minutes, or until all liquid has been absorbed. Garnish with parsley before serving. Leftovers may be reheated, added to soup, cereal or bread dough. *Serves 6.*

### VARIATION:

If cooked oats are to be made into a dessert, substitute 2 cups of milk for stock. Omit caraway seeds and parsley and add ½ teaspoon crushed cardamom seeds.

## OATMEAL SOUFFLÉ

1½ cups seasoned stock
1 tablespoon nutritional yeast
¼ teaspoon cloves, ground
½ cup oatmeal
½ cup cheese, grated
¾ cup milk
1 tablespoon soy flour
3 eggs, separated

Heat stock in top of double boiler over direct heat. When boiling, add yeast, cloves and oatmeal. Cover. Place over bottom of double boiler, to which hot water has been added. Cook over gentle heat for 20 minutes, or until oatmeal has absorbed liquid. Remove from heat. Gradually stir in cheese, milk, soy flour and egg yolks and blend well. Beat egg whites stiff and fold in. Turn into oiled custard cups. Bake for about 30 minutes in 350° F. oven. *Serves 6.*

### OTHER RECIPES USING OATS

See: Swiss Breakfast; Cereal Soup; Oat Breads; Cornmeal-Oatmeal Rolls; Unraised Wholewheat-Oatmeal Biscuits; Oat Pancakes; Oatmeal Pudding; Oatmeal Cake; Rye-Oatmeal Squares; Oatmeal Shortbread; Oatmeal Fruit Squares; Oatmeal Cookies; Oatmeal Macaroons.

# Cornmeal

HINT:
When cornmeal is substituted for wholewheat, use ¾ cup cornmeal to replace 1 cup of wholewheat flour.

## HASTY PUDDING

1 cup cornmeal
2 tablespoons nutritional yeast
3 cups seasoned stock

Blend cornmeal, yeast and ½ cup of stock into a smooth paste. Heat remainder of stock in top of double boiler, over direct heat. When boiling, add cornmeal mixture and stir until smooth. Place over bottom of double boiler, to which hot water has been added. Cover. Cook over gentle heat until all liquid has been absorbed. *Serves 6.*

VARIATION:
Substitute 3 cups of milk for stock.

## CORNMEAL YORKSHIRE PUDDING

½ cup cornmeal
1 teaspoon salt
3 tablespoons nutritional yeast
½ teaspoon marjoram
2 cups milk
4 eggs, beaten
½ teaspoon oil for each muffin well or custard cup

Stir to a paste cornmeal, salt, yeast, marjoram and ½ cup milk. Heat rest of milk in top of double boiler, over direct heat. When just at boiling point, add cornmeal mixture. Stir until smooth. Place over bottom of double boiler, to which hot water has been added. Cover. Cook over gentle heat until all liquid has been absorbed. Remove from heat. When lukewarm, blend in eggs. Put ¼ teaspoon of oil in bottom of already oiled muffin pans or custard cups and preheat in oven. Turn cornmeal mixture into heated pans, filling only half full. Bake for 10 minutes at 350° F. Remove from oven and dot each pudding with remaining ¼ teaspoon of oil. Return to oven and bake for 15 minutes longer. *Serves 6.*

## CORNMEAL SOUFFLÉ

½ cup cornmeal
1 teaspoon salt
3 tablespoons nutritional yeast
½ teaspoon thyme
2 cups milk
2 tablespoons oil
½ cup cheese, grated
4 eggs, separated

Stir cornmeal, salt, yeast and thyme into ½ cup milk. Blend into paste. Heat remaining milk in top of double boiler, over direct heat. When almost boiling, add cornmeal paste, oil and cheese. Stir until smooth and place over bottom of double boiler, to which hot water has been added. Cover. Cook over gentle heat until all liquid is absorbed. Remove from heat and when cooled to lukewarm, blend in egg yolks. Fold in stiffly beaten egg whites. Turn into oiled custard cups. Bake at 350° F., about 25 minutes, or until slightly crusty on top. *Serves 6.*

## POLENTA

1 cup cornmeal
1 tablespoon soy flour
2 tablespoons nutritional yeast
3 cups seasoned stock
1 cup cheese, grated
1 egg, beaten

Stir cornmeal, soy flour, and yeast into ½ cup of stock. Blend into paste. Heat remainder of stock in top of double boiler, over direct heat. When boiling, add cornmeal mixture and cheese. Stir until smooth. Place over bottom of double boiler, to which hot water has been added. Cover. Cook over gentle heat until all liquid has been absorbed. Remove from heat. Cool to lukewarm. Add egg. Drop by spoonfuls onto oiled cooky sheet. Broil until brown on both sides. *Serves 4-6.*

OTHER RECIPES USING CORNMEAL
See: Fish-Cornmeal Balls; Polenta with Chicken Livers; Cornmeal Pie; Cornbread Stuffing; Eggs Poached in Cornmeal Mush; Cornbreads; Spoon Breads; Cornmeal Pancakes; Indian Pudding; Cornmeal Puffs; Boston Brown Bread; Cornmeal Pie Shell.

# Buckwheat

## BASIC BUCKWHEAT

2 cups buckwheat groats
hot seasoned stock, to cover
1 tablespoon soy flour
3 tablespoons nutritional yeast
2 tablespoons oil

Place buckwheat in top of double boiler. Pour hot stock over it. Add soy flour, yeast and oil. Blend.

Cover. Cook gently over hot water 15 minutes or until buckwheat has absorbed all liquid. Garnish with parsley, minced. Leftovers may be reheated, added to soup, cereal or bread dough. *Serves 6.*

## KASHA

2 cups buckwheat groats
3 tablespoons oil
hot seasoned stock, to cover
1 tablespoon soy flour
3 tablespoons nutritional yeast
yoghurt *

Sauté buckwheat in oil in top of double boiler over direct heat, stirring constantly, until all grains are well coated with oil. Pour boiling stock over and add soy flour and yeast. Mix well. Drain off stock, leaving only enough to cover buckwheat to depth of ½ inch. Reserve poured-off stock. Cover buckwheat and place over bottom of double boiler, to which hot water has been added, and cook gently for 15 minutes. Add reserved stock as needed. When buckwheat is tender, moisten with yoghurt and serve. *Serves 6.*

## BUCKWHEAT BLINTZES

DOUGH:

1 cup wholewheat flour
1 tablespoon soy flour
2 eggs, beaten
1 tablespoon oil
2 tablespoons cold seasoned stock
  (about)

Blend all ingredients, adding enough stock to make stiff dough. Chill. Roll out very thin. Cut into 4-inch squares. Place spoonful of filling in center of each square. Fold squares into envelopes. Bake at 350° F. for 30 minutes.

FILLING:

2 cups buckwheat groats (or other whole grain)
hot seasoned stock, to cover
1 teaspoon caraway seeds, crushed
3 tablespoons nutritional yeast
2 onions, chopped, sautéed
1 egg, hard-cooked, chopped

Combine buckwheat and hot stock in top of double boiler. Blend in caraway seeds and yeast. Cover and cook gently over hot water for 15 minutes or until buckwheat has absorbed all liquid. Remove from heat. Blend in onions and egg. *Serves 6.*

OTHER BUCKWHEAT RECIPES

See: Buckwheat and Potato Soup; Cereal Soup; Oriental Congee; Russian Meat Balls with Buckwheat; Nut-Buckwheat Stuffing; Raised Buckwheat Pancakes.

# Barley

HINTS:

Use whole, hulled barley that has not been pearled.
Barley may be substituted in recipes calling for rice, millet or buckwheat.

## BARLEY PILAFF

1 pound mushrooms, sliced
4 tablespoons oil
2 onions, sliced
1¾ cups whole barley, hulled, raw
1 quart hot seasoned stock (about)
3 tablespoons nutritional yeast
1 tablespoon dill

Sauté mushrooms in oil for 5 minutes. Set mushrooms aside, sauté onions until golden and remove these too. Cook raw barley in same oil, stirring constantly, until grains are well coated with oil. Remove from heat. Mix mushrooms and onions with barley and blend in remaining ingredients. Turn all into oiled casserole. Cover and bake at 350° F. for 30 minutes, adding more stock, if needed. *Serves 6-8.*

## BARLEY-LENTIL KASHA

½ cup whole barley, hulled, raw
1 cup lentils, soaked
¼ cup soy grits
hot seasoned stock, to cover
3 tablespoons nutritional yeast
1 onion, sliced and sautéed
3 tablespoons parsley, minced
1 teaspoon rosemary

Combine barley, lentils and soy grits in saucepan. Cover with stock to depth of ½ inch above mixture. Cover. Simmer gently for 30 minutes, until barley and lentils are tender. Add rest of ingredients and, if necessary, more stock. Simmer 10 minutes longer. *Serves 6.*

## BARLEY-SOYBEAN CASSEROLE

½ cup whole barley, hulled, soaked
2 cups cooked soybeans
2 boiled potatoes, diced
2 stalks celery and tops, diced
2 onions, sliced
1 carrot, grated
1 cup stewed tomatoes
1 teaspoon salt
3 tablespoons nutritional yeast
½ teaspoon savory
½ teaspoon chervil
1 teaspoon dill seeds, crushed
1 bay leaf

Blend all ingredients. Turn into oiled casserole. Bake at 350° F. for about 30 minutes. *Serves 6.*

OTHER BARLEY RECIPES
See: Mix-Your-Own-Cereal Blend:
Cereal Soup; Oriental Congee;
Bacon-Barley Puffs; Barley Meal
Scones, Scottish; Barley-Apple
Pudding.

# Breakfast Dishes, Uncooked

## BREAKFAST SALAD

2½ cups wholewheat Sprouts
1 cup sunflower seeds, hulled
3 apples with skins, grated
3 bananas, sliced
½ cup raisins
½ cup yoghurt *

Blend all ingredients together.
*Serves 6.*

## SWISS BREAKFAST

½ cup whole oats, raw
1 cup water
juice of 3 lemons
½ cup yoghurt *
12 apples with skins, shredded
3 tablespoons honey

Soak oats overnight in water. In
morning, mix with rest of ingredients. *Serves 6.*

## VIM AND VIGOR BREAKFAST

1 cup Sprouts
1 cup sunflower seeds, hulled
juice of 3 lemons
3 tablespoons nutritional yeast
3 tablespoons honey
½ cup powdered milk
6 apples with skins, grated
½ cup wheat germ

Blend all ingredients. *Serves 6.*

## GLORIFIED SWISS BREAKFAST

½ cup rolled oatmeal
1 cup yoghurt *
3 tablespoons honey
¼ cup nuts, ground
juice of 2 lemons
1 quart fresh fruit or berries

Blend all ingredients. *Serves 6.*

# Porridge

HINTS:
Add soy grits to cereal in a proportion of 2 tablespoons to each cup
of uncooked cereal.
Wheat germ may be added to cereal
in any proportion up to ½ the
amount of uncooked cereal. Mix,
dry, with the cereal before cooking, or stir in shortly before serving. Wheat germ may also be
sprinkled over the top of any
cooked cereal.
Add rice polishings to cereal in any
proportion up to ¼ the amount
of uncooked cereal. Combine polishings with extra milk or water
and stir into hot cereal mixture
in top of double boiler before
completing cooking over hot water.
Use potato water (water in which
potatoes have been boiled) or
milk for all or part of the liquid
in which cereal is cooked. Cook
cereal in a double boiler. Put top
over direct heat only long enough
to thicken; then set over bottom
of double boiler, to which hot
water has been added, to complete cooking. When milk is used,
a little more liquid is required
than when using water. Soy or
powdered milk can substitute for
liquid cow's milk. Combine powdered milk dry with uncooked

cereal, using ¼ cup to one cup of cereal. Then add liquid as necessary.

Cook whole-grain cereals at night in a double boiler. Cover the cereal with water to prevent crusting. Pour off the water before reheated in the morning.

## MIX-YOUR-OWN-CEREAL BLEND

4 cups barley
4 cups rye
4 cups brown rice
4 cups wholewheat berries
4 cups oats
4 cups cornmeal
2 cups millet
2 cups buckwheat
2 cups soy grits
2 cups bran
2 cups rice polishings

Mix all ingredients. Store in tightly closed container in cool, dry place. 2 cups of this mix makes 6 servings. Grains may, of course, be mixed in any proportion desired.

## WHOLE GRAIN CEREAL

Whole grains require longer cooking than cracked grains. Use 1 cup of grains to 2-3 cups of water. They may be cooked in several ways:
1. Slow-baked dry as part of the cooking process
2. Slow-baked in oven after water is added
3. Cooked in deep well in stove or with fuelless cooker
4. Cooked in an electric cooker or bean pot
5. Cooked in a wide-mouth thermos: In morning, soak whole grains in enough water to cover. The same evening, drain off water into measuring cup, adding more water, if necessary, to make

3 cups. Heat water to boiling, add soaked grain and bring to active boil. Pour hot grain and water into preheated thermos. Cap tightly. Turn thermos on side overnight. Serve the following morning.

## CRACKED GRAIN CEREAL

Crack freshly if home grinding mill is available. Cracked grain requires shorter cooking time than whole grain. Use 1 cup grain to 2-3 cups of water. Cook in a heavy pan with tight lid. To serve 6, stir 2 cups of grain into 4-6 cups of boiling water, potato water or milk. Cover pan and cook over low heat 7-10 minutes, or cook in double boiler over hot water for 15-20 minutes.

## CRACKED WHEAT CEREAL
(uncooked)

2 cups cracked wheat, raw
4 cups milk, water or fruit juice

Soak wheat in liquid overnight. *Serves 6.*

## MIXED SEED-FLOUR CEREAL

1 tablespoon sesame seeds
1 tablespoon sunflower seeds
½ cup wholewheat flour
½ cup oatmeal
¼ cup barley flour
¼ cup rye flour
¼ cup soy flour
¼ cup cornmeal
¼ cup brown rice
1 teaspoon salt
4 tablespoons honey
4 tablespoons oil
2 cups water, boiling

Combine seeds, flours, grain and salt. Blend honey and oil in water

[Recipe continued on next page]

[Recipe continued from previous page]

and pour over dry mixture. Mix all and turn into oiled casserole. Bake at 325° F., about 30 minutes. Turn off heat but leave in oven to keep hot, stirring occasionally, till all liquid has been absorbed. *Serves 6.*

## SOY-OATMEAL PORRIDGE

½ cup soy grits
1½ cups oatmeal
4 cups water, potato water or milk

Soak soy grits and oatmeal overnight in liquid, in top of double boiler. In morning, place over bottom of double boiler, to which hot water has been added, and cook. *Serves 6.*

## SOY-CORNMEAL PORRIDGE

½ cup soy grits
1½ cups cornmeal
1 teaspoon salt
2 tablespoons nutritional yeast
1 cup cold water, potato water or milk
3 cups hot water, potato water or milk

Mix soy grits, cornmeal, salt and yeast with cold water to make smooth paste. Stir mixture into boiling liquid in top of double boiler. Cook over direct heat for 5 minutes, stirring constantly. Cover.

Place over bottom of double boiler, to which hot water has been added. Cook for one hour. *Serves 6.*

SUGGESTED TOPPINGS FOR COOKED PORRIDGE:
fresh fruit
dried fruit
nuts, ground
bran
wheat germ
Soybeans, Roasted, ground
Nut Butters
Nut Creams
bone meal
whole-grain bread crumbs
nutritional yeast
sesame seeds
sunflower seeds or meal
carob powder
Coconut Shreds
Powdered Fruit Rind

LEFTOVER PORRIDGE
Reheat and serve with cheese or tomato sauce as starch dish.
Blend into meat or fish loaf, egg or vegetable casseroles.
Add to soups instead of rice or barley.
Add (up to 1 cup) to bread dough, cooky dough, quick bread dough.
Blend with ground nuts or Roasted Soybeans, with mushrooms and herbs, shape into patties and broil.

# 17

# SPROUTS

Seeds contain the elements necessary to grow new plants. When given heat and moisture, they become rich in vitamins, particularly B-complex.

The following seeds, whole grains, dried beans and peas (*untreated*) can be sprouted successfully:

SEEDS—alfalfas, unhulled sesame, unhulled sunflower, radishes, mustard, red clover, fenugreek

WHOLE GRAINS—wheat, rye, oats, corn, barley

WHOLE DRIED BEANS AND PEAS—soybeans, lentils, green peas, lima beans, mung beans, chick peas, marrow beans, kidney beans, pinto beans, cranberry beans, fava beans

## METHOD OF SPROUTING

1. Select clean, whole seeds, grains or beans. Remove any debris and broken seeds. Soak a small quantity at a time—remember that ¼ cup dried seeds, grains or beans will swell to ½ cup after soaking and to 2 cups after sprouting. Soak overnight.
2. Next morning, drain off water and reserve as stock. Put seeds in

sprouting container (see below). Be sure cover fits loosely; sprouts need ventilation to develop.
3. Keep sprouts moist, warm and dark. A kitchen cupboard usually assures even warm heat. Sprouts will be ready to eat in 3 to 6 days, depending on variety of plant as well as on temperature.

## CONTAINERS SUITABLE FOR SPROUTING
### (with natural drainage)

Use a new container wherever possible and reserve exclusively for sprouting.

UNGLAZED FLOWERPOT:
Soak pot thoroughly by submerging in water. Plug drainage hole with cheesecloth, screen, cork or absorbent cotton. Place drained seeds (see above) at bottom. Cover with saucer or pot cover. Place in shallow pan of water.

The old-fashioned unglazed butter dish popular prior to the introduction of electric refrigerators, and still sold in Europe, can also be used. Discard inner glass dish; treat unglazed outside dish in same manner as flowerpot, except that there will be no drainage hole.

UNGLAZED FLOWERPOT SAUCER:

Soak saucer thoroughly by submerging it in water. This container works well for small seeds. Place drained seeds such as alfalfa, radish or mustard in saucer. Cover with another saucer or a pot cover and set in shallow pan of water.

COLANDER:

Suitable for large seeds, grains and beans (corn, lentils, soybeans, whole peas and lima beans). Place drained seeds in colander and set in large saucepan or bowl. Cover. Small seeds can also be sprouted in a colander by lining it with cheesecloth.

TRIANGULAR SINK STRAINER:

Strainer should be the kind designed to hold peelings and other waste matter. Place drained seeds in strainer and set in large saucepan or bowl. Cover. Good for sprouting large seeds or, if lined with cheesecloth, small seeds as well.

TEA STRAINER:

Especially useful for sprouting small seeds for one or two servings. Place drained seeds in strainer and set strainer in teacup or teapot. Cover.

COFFEE PERCOLATOR:

Carefully scour discarded coffee percolator, especially inner strainer that holds coffee grounds. Place drained seeds in strainer and lower into pot. Cover. Especially good for small seeds.

TURKISH TOWEL:

Soak Turkish towel in water and wring out. Place drained seeds on top of towel. Roll up. Use for large seeds, grains or beans.

SPONGES:

Use two new synthetic utility sponges. Soak sponges in water and wring out. Place drained seeds between sponges. Good for small seeds.

BLOTTING PAPER:

Soak two new sheets of blotting paper in water. Drain off excess water. Place drained seeds between sheets.

## CONTAINERS SUITABLE FOR SPROUTING
(without drainage)

Household containers without natural drainage may also be utilized for sprouting; if care is exercised, results will be successful. Seeds, grains or beans should be rinsed thoroughly with tepid water twice a day, to compensate for lack of drainage in such containers. The following may be used:

SAUCEPAN: Place drained seeds in saucepan. Cover should fit loosely.

GLAZED COVERED CASSEROLE: Place drained seeds in casserole. Cover should fit loosely.

CROCKERY BOWL: Place drained seeds in bowl. Cover with plate or loosely fitting pot cover.

MILK BOTTLE OR FRUIT JAR: Use bottle or jar with wide mouth. Place drained seeds at bottom. Cover mouth with cheesecloth or screen and fasten securely with rubber band or string. Each time sprouts are rinsed, invert jar afterward for a few seconds to drain thoroughly.

COMMERCIAL SPROUTING CONTAINERS:

For suggestions as to where these may be purchased, see p. 269. Follow the accompanying directions.

## SPECIAL HINTS FOR SOYBEANS

Soybeans are sometimes difficult to sprout, especially in warm weather.

The varieties that sprout best are Chief, Ebony, Illini, Lincoln and Richland. Beans older than one year will not germinate well. Try to use only those from the current year's crop. As they germinate, remove any that are decaying.

SPROUTS ARE READY TO EAT WHEN:
the wheat sprout is the length of the seed;
the mung bean sprout is 1½ to 3 inches long;
the alfalfa sprout is 1 to 2 inches long;
the lentil sprout is 1 inch long;
the soybean or pea sprout is 2 inches long.

Use sprouts as soon as they are ready, if possible. They are best served raw. If not used immediately, they should be stored in a covered container in the refrigerator and used within a few days, as any fresh food. To preserve their crispness and nutritive value, add them to any hot dish immediately before serving. Use both the bean and the sprout. The skins of mung beans may also be eaten.

## WAYS TO SERVE SPROUTS

raw, as separate dish
in tossed salads
garnish for soups, casseroles, stews
blended into beverages
blended into sandwich spreads
in meat, fish or nut loaves
with scrambled eggs or omelets
in bread, muffins and waffle batters
in breakfast dishes
in vegetable casseroles
in soufflés
stewed with tomatoes
in sauces
in desserts

## SAUTÉED SPROUTS

2 tablespoons oil
1 cup Sprouts
stock to cover

Sauté sprouts briefly. Add stock. Cover pan and cook over low heat for 3 minutes.

If desired, add one or more of the following while cooking: sliced mushrooms, onions, scallions and green peppers, diced celery; shredded carrots, radishes and turnips; soy grits. Flavor with Essence of Sweet Herbs, fresh or dried herbs, nutritional yeast.

## STEAMED SPROUTS

Steam Sprouts briefly in stock.

OTHER RECIPES USING SPROUTS
See: Vim and Vigor Breakfast; Combination Salads, Golden Slaw, Sweetbread Salad and others under *Salad;* Bean Sprout Soup; American Chop Suey; Chinese Egg Rolls; Egg Foo Yong; Sprouted Wheat Patties, Broiled; Wholewheat Bread with Sprouted Wheat; Sprouted Wheat Balls.

# 18

# BREADS (YEAST, SOUR DOUGH, UNLEAVENED)

HINTS:
Have bread-baking ingredients at room temperature.

Use freshly ground whole-grain flours. A home flour grinder is desirable for this purpose.

When preparing whole-grain bread, all ingredients except yeast may be mixed at night for the first rising. Allow mixture to stand overnight; this softens the bran in the flour. In the morning, soften yeast in warm water, add to flour mixture and proceed as usual.

Dough is ready to be kneaded when flour and liquid are mixed thoroughly and dough no longer sticks to the sides of the bowl. Avoid overkneading, which may injure the baking quality of the gluten and result in poor texture and volume. Do not knead additional flour into dough after fermentation has begun.

After proper kneading, oil surface of dough. This will prevent it from drying out or cracking as it rises.

Don't let dough stand too long before punching down, as this, too, may injure gluten. If dough is allowed to rise too high in the pans before baking it will result in coarse-grained bread. If dough fails to rise sufficiently in the pans before baking, the bread will be heavy.

To shape breads into a compact loaf, press or roll each loaf into a flat, oblong sheet. Fold 1/3 of dough over and press it with the palm of the hand to seal. Fold opposite side to overlap the first. Press and seal. Fold 1/3 of dough over open end. Press and seal. Fold over other side to overlap the first. Press and seal. Roll dough up lengthwise, like a jelly roll. Place in oiled bread pan with overlap at bottom.

Oil bread pans with soy lecithin spread, for easy removal of loaves.

Bake breads on center rack in preheated oven.

When loaves of bread are taken out of the oven, brushing tops with milk or oil will heighten the color of the crust and make it glossier and more tender; it will, however, be less crisp.

To adapt bread recipes, follow these general rules, except where otherwise indicated in recipe.

(1) For each cup of white flour,

use only ¾ cup whole-grain flour.

(2) For each 3 tablespoons of oil in recipes using white flour, use 2 tablespoons oil with whole-grain flour.

(3) As much as ¼ cup more liquid may be required in making whole-grain bread. It depends on the texture of the flour.

(4) Use milk, soy milk, potato water or stock for liquid. Reduce salt if stock is already seasoned. Use 1 quart liquid to 3 pounds flour.

(5) To substitute oil for butter, use in the same quantity. If, however, sesame butter is used instead of dairy butter, double the quantity.

(6) For each measure of white sugar, use only ⅔ as much honey or molasses.

(7) For each cup of whole-grain flour, add 1 tablespoon soy flour, 1 tablespoon milk powder, 1 tablespoon wheat germ and 1 teaspoon nutritional yeast.

Whole-grain breads may be made with a mixture of the following whole grains, in any proportion desired: wholewheat, rye, corn, oats, millet, brown rice, buckwheat, barley, soy. Some wholewheat in the mixture is desirable, because of its gluten. Oatmeal will enhance the texture of bread. Soy-flour baked goods brown faster and stay fresh longer.

SUGGESTED ADDITIONS TO
YEAST BREADS:
peanut flour
lima-bean flour
potato flour
gluten flour

cottonseed flour
soy grits
Soybeans, Roasted, ground
sunflower-seed meal
bone meal
white potatoes, cooked and puréed
sweet potatoes, cooked and puréed
lentils, cooked and puréed
soybeans, cooked and puréed
fennel seeds, whole or ground
anise seeds, whole or ground
cardamom seeds, ground
carob powder
lemon peel, grated or Powdered
orange peel, grated or Powdered
honeyed fruit
cooked porridge
rice polishings
bran
sesame seeds, whole or ground
dill seeds, whole or ground
celery seeds, whole or ground
caraway seeds, whole or ground
raisins, seedless
currants, dried
figs, chopped
dates, chopped
prunes, pitted and chopped
apricots, dried and chopped
nuts, ground
hard cheese, grated
eggs, raw
fruit juice (as liquid in dough)
whole grains, soaked
whole grains, Sprouted

## Yeasts

Home-grown yeast may be used as a starter from one baking to the next. This mixture is sometimes called a sponge or ferment. Yeast functions best at temperatures between 80° and 85° F. Above 85° F., conditions become favorable to the growth of undesirable organisms.

## LIQUID YEAST

3 potatoes, raw (¾ pound)
1¼ cup water, boiling
¼ cup honey
1½ tablespoons salt
1½ cups water, cold (approximately)
1 cup starter, or 1 cake or 1 table-
    spoon dried yeast, soaked in
1 cup lukewarm water

Choose sound, clean potatoes. Pare and cube. Place in pot with boiling water. Cover and simmer until tender. Remove from heat. Purée potatoes and blend with potato water, honey, salt and enough cold water to make 3¼ cups liquid. Cool mixture to lukewarm (82°F.). Add starter reserved from last baking, or dried yeast soaked in water. Allow mixture to stand overnight. The following morning, stir and reserve 1 cup as starter for next baking. Store starter in clean, scalded, loosely covered jar and keep in cool place. Do not allow to freeze. Use remainder for soft wheat-flour bread dough. This liquid yeast may be used in yeast breads, muffins, cakes, griddle cakes, etc. Should the mixture develop any unusual appearance or odor, discard. Prepare new starter with fresh ingredients and scalded utensils.

## FARMERS' YEAST

1 quart water, boiling
1 cup hops, with pollen
4 potatoes, pared, cubed
wholewheat flour
1 teaspoon salt
½ cup honey
2 cakes or 2 tablespoons dried yeast,
    soaked in
¼ cup lukewarm water

Mix water, hops and potatoes in pot. Cover and simmer until pota-toes are tender. Strain out hops. Purée potatoes. Add enough flour to make thick batter, and salt and honey. Gradually heat to boiling point, stirring constantly. Remove from heat and cool to lukewarm. Add soaked yeast. Stir. Allow mixture to stand 2 or 3 days, until light and spongy. Use and store as above.

## SOUR DOUGH STARTER

1 cup rye flour
½ cup lukewarm water
½ cake or ½ tablespoon dried yeast,
    soaked in
½ cup lukewarm water

Combine all ingredients. Cover. Without stirring, allow mixture to rise and fall. Keep at room temperature 2 or 3 days, until it attains desired sourness. Combine with bread dough. After dough has been mixed, reserve 1 cup as starter for next batch.

# Wheat Breads

HINTS:

Spring wheat is preferable for bread, winter wheat for cakes. Bread-making values of different types of wheat depend on quantity and quality of gluten in their flour. Methods of milling, as well as variety of wheat, influence the nature and quantity of the gluten. Flours are "strong" if they have a comparatively large quantity of gluten. Wheats grown in the region from the Rocky Mountains to the Mississippi Valley, north and west of Missouri, are usually "hard." Flour from "hard" wheats rises well and can stand more handling than "soft" wheat flours.

When wholewheat flour is sifted, the bran will not go through the sifter. To use bran, simply return to the sifted flour. Where especially fine textures are desired, omit bran and save for use in porridge, casseroles and meat, fish, fowl, nut and vegetable loaves.

## WHOLEWHEAT BREAD

1 cake or 1 tablespoon dried yeast, softened in
¼ cup warm stock
¼ cup oil
1 tablespoon salt
3¾ cups additional stock, warm
6 tablespoons honey
½ cup nutritional yeast
9 cups wholewheat flour (approximately)

Blend 5 cups of the flour with all other ingredients. Cover. Keep in warm room and let rise at least 2 hours. Blend in additional flour until dough is stiff. Knead. Oil dough. Put into bowl, cover and let rise for 1 hour. Punch down. Knead again. Divide dough into 2 loaves. Shape and place in oiled bread pans. Let rise again until double in bulk. Bake at 325° F. for 40 to 50 minutes.

## WHOLEWHEAT BREAD WITH MILK

2½ cups milk, scalded
¼ cup honey
1 tablespoon salt
½ cup nutritional yeast
1 cake or 1 tablespoon dried yeast, softened in
½ cup lukewarm stock
3 tablespoons oil
6 to 8 cups wholewheat flour

Blend milk, honey, salt and nutritional yeast. When cooled to luke-warm, add softened yeast, oil and 3 cups flour. Beat until bubbles rise to surface. Add enough of remaining flour to make a soft dough that comes away clean from sides of mixing bowl. Turn dough onto floured board and let rest for 10 minutes. Then knead until smooth and elastic. Place in oiled bowl, turning dough over a few times to coat with oil. Cover. Let rise in warm place until double in bulk. Punch down. Let rise again. Divide dough into 3 equal portions. Shape into balls, let stand for 5 minutes, then mold into loaves. Place in oiled bread pans. Let rise until nearly doubled in bulk, about 1 hour. Bake at 385° F. for 15 minutes, decrease heat to 350° F. and continue baking for 45 to 55 minutes.

## WHOLEWHEAT BREAD WITH EGGS

2 cups milk, scalded
¾ cup stock
1 tablespoon salt
3 tablespoons nutritional yeast
5 tablespoons oil
¼ cup honey
2 cakes or 2 tablespoons dried yeast, softened in
¼ cup lukewarm stock
3 eggs
9 cups wholewheat flour (approximately)

Combine milk, stock, nutritional yeast, oil and honey. Cool to luke-warm. Combine with yeast mixture and eggs. Add 7 cups of flour and blend thoroughly. Let stand for 10 minutes. Then add enough of remaining flour to knead easily. Knead for 10 minutes. Oil dough, place in bowl and cover. Let rise until double in bulk. Punch down.

[Recipe continued on next page]

[Recipe continued from previous page]

Knead and let rise until again double in bulk. Punch down. Shape into 3 loaves, place in oiled bread pans and let rise for third time. Bake at 400° F. for 15 minutes; lower heat to 375° F. and bake for 30 minutes more.

## WHOLEWHEAT BREAD PLUS

2 cakes or 2 tablespoons dried yeast, softened in
½ cup lukewarm potato water
4 cups milk, scalded
6 tablespoons honey
6 tablespoons oil
1 tablespoon salt
½ cup nutritional yeast
3 tablespoons bone meal
3 tablespoons soy flour
½ cup milk powder
½ cup wheat germ
1 cup porridge, cooked
9 cups wholewheat flour (approximately)

Mix 5 cups of flour with all other ingredients. Blend thoroughly. Let stand 10 minutes. Add enough remaining flour to make stiff dough. Knead until smooth and elastic. Oil dough, place in bowl and cover. Let rise until double in bulk. Punch down. Shape into 3 loaves, place in oiled bread pans and let rise slightly. Bake at 375° F. for 15 minutes, decrease heat to 350° F. and bake about 45 minutes more.

## ONE-HOUR WHOLEWHEAT BREAD

3 cakes or 3 tablespoons dried yeast
3½ to 4½ cups lukewarm stock
1 tablespoon honey
2 teaspoons salt
½ cup nutritional yeast
8 cups wholewheat flour (approximately)

Soften cake or dried yeast in 3½ cups stock. Blend in honey and then the remaining ingredients. Dough should be slippery and glutenous, yet be stiff enough so that a big spoonful will cling to spoon. Dough should not immediately flatten out after mixing and no liquid should show at sides of bowl. Add more stock or flour as needed to achieve this texture. Fill 3 oiled bread pans ⅔ full of dough. Let rise for 15 minutes at 85° F. until it has risen in height by ¼. Bake at 400° F. for 15 minutes, then decrease to 350° F. and bake 15 to 20 minutes longer.

## NO-EXCUSE BREAD

1 cake or 1 tablespoon dried yeast
1 quart milk, lukewarm
3 tablespoons honey
1 tablespoon salt
½ cup nutritional yeast
10½ cups wholewheat flour (approximately)

Soften yeast in ⅓ cup milk. Add honey. Allow to rise and bubble for 10 minutes. Add remaining ingredients. Mix well with large spoon. Dough will be thin, for bread dough. Spoon mixture into 3 oiled bread pans, filling half full. Set in warm place. Cover and let rise until dough has almost reached the top of the pan. Bake at 375° F. for 45 minutes.

## QUICKIE WHOLEWHEAT BREAD

3 cakes or 3 tablespoons dried yeast
4 to 5 cups lukewarm stock
3 tablespoons molasses
1 tablespoon salt
½ cup nutritional yeast
10 cups wholewheat flour

Soften cake or dried yeast in 3 cups stock. Mix with molasses. Let rise and bubble for 10 minutes. Blend thoroughly with remaining ingredients. Add enough stock to work dough with hands and mix until it achieves consistency of modeling clay. Divide into 3 loaves and place in 3 oiled bread pans. Dough should come only halfway up sides of pans. Wet finger tips with cold water and smooth tops of loaves, sealing all cracks. Place bread pans, uncovered, on center rack of 150° F. oven. Allow dough to rise slightly for 15 minutes. Leaving bread pans on center rack, turn oven up to 350° F. and bake for 1 hour at this temperature.

## SOAKED WHEAT BREAD

4 cups wholewheat berries
potato water to cover
3 cups milk, scalded
2 cakes or 2 tablespoons dried yeast
½ cup oil
½ cup molasses
2 tablespoons salt
½ cup nutritional yeast
¼ cup soy flour
6 cups wholewheat flour

Soak wholewheat berries in potato water from 24 to 48 hours. Drain. Grind in food chopper, using finest knife. Cool milk to lukewarm. Soften cake or dried yeast in ½ cup of lukewarm milk. Blend in remaining milk, oil, molasses, salt. Mix nutritional yeast, soy flour and wholewheat flour. Combine soaked, ground wheat, yeast mixture and flour mixture. Mix thoroughly, using hands. Let dough rest for 10 minutes. Oil hands and dough board and knead for 10 minutes. If dough becomes sticky, oil hands and board

again. Place dough in oiled bowl, turn over to coat with oil, and cover. Preheat oven to 150° F. Turn off heat and set dough in oven to rise for about 1 hour. When doubled in bulk, punch down. Divide into 3 loaves and put each in an oiled bread pan. Let rise again until double in bulk. Bake at 325° F. for 1¼ hours.

## NO-KNEAD BREAD

4 cakes or 4 tablespoons dried yeast
4 cups stock, lukewarm
½ cup molasses
¼ cup oil
8 cups wholewheat flour
1 cup soy flour
1 cup wheat germ
1 cup milk powder
2 tablespoons salt
½ cup nutritional yeast

Blend cake or dried yeast in stock. Add molasses, oil and 7 cups of wholewheat flour. Beat 300 strokes or more by hand, or in an electric mixer for 10 minutes on low speed. Combine remaining dry ingredients with last cup of wholewheat flour and add to beaten mixture. Blend thoroughly. Set in warm place. Cover and let rise until double in bulk. Punch down. Divide in half and place in 2 oiled loaf pans. Oil finger tips and smooth tops of loaves. Bake at 350° F. for 1 hour.

## WHOLEWHEAT-GLUTEN BREAD

2 cakes or 2 tablespoons dried yeast
1 quart potato water, lukewarm
3 tablespoons honey
8 cups wholewheat flour (approximately)
2 cups gluten flour
¼ cup oil
1 tablespoon salt
3 tablespoons nutritional yeast

[Recipe continued on next page]

[Recipe continued from previous page]

Soften cake or dried yeast in ½ cup potato water. Add honey. Let rise and bubble for 10 minutes. Then add 2 cups of wholewheat flour and 1 cup gluten flour. Beat well. Cover and set in warm place to rise until double in bulk. Stir in oil, salt and nutritional yeast, and work in enough of remaining flours to make a firm dough. Knead for 10 minutes. Oil dough, place in bowl and cover. Let rise until double in bulk. Punch down. Form 3 loaves and place each in an oiled bread pan. Bake at 375° F. for 15 minutes, then at 350° F. for about 45 minutes.

## WHOLEWHEAT BREAD WITH SPROUTED WHEAT

2 cakes or 2 tablespoons dried yeast
3 cups stock, lukewarm
1 tablespoon salt
¼ cup nutritional yeast
¼ cup honey
3 tablespoons oil
5 cups wholewheat flour (approximately)
2 cups wholewheat Sprouts (whole or ground)

Soften yeast in ½ cup stock. Then add rest of stock, salt, nutritional yeast, honey, oil. Blend well. Stir in 3½ cups flour. Beat dough until elastic. Cover bowl of dough and set in warm place to rise. When it has risen, add sprouts and about 1½ cups of remaining flour. Knead until dough is again smooth and elastic. Place in oiled bowl, turning over to coat with oil. Cover and again let rise in warm place until double in bulk. Punch down. Knead lightly. Divide into 2 loaves and place each in an oiled bread pan. Let rise in warm place until double in bulk. Bake at 375° F. for 25 minutes; then at 300° F. for 35 minutes longer.

## UNLEAVENED WHOLEWHEAT BREAD

½ cup oil
1¼ cups stock
7 cups wholewheat flour (approximately)
1 teaspoon salt

Beat oil while adding water gradually, until it forms an emulsion that looks like beaten egg white. Sprinkle flour over liquid, add salt and knead until dough is smooth and elastic. Let stand overnight. In the morning, knead again. Form 2 loaves and place each in an oiled bread pan. Bake at 325° F. for 1¼ to 1½ hours.

# Rye Breads

HINTS:

Although for bread-baking purposes rye resembles wheat more than any other grain, rye flour makes a stickier and less elastic dough. A satisfactory all-rye loaf is difficult to make and apt to be heavy. All-rye flour is most successful when used in making European-type steamed breads and sour ryes. For lighter loaves, use a combination of wheat and rye.

Rye flour may replace part of the wholewheat flour in wholewheat bread recipes.

For persons allergic to wheat, rye is frequently a satisfactory substitute.

## WHOLE RYE BREAD
## WITH CARAWAY SEEDS

1 cake or 1 tablespoon dried yeast
2 cups milk, scalded, lukewarm
2 tablespoons molasses
1 egg
8 cups rye flour (approximately)
1 tablespoon salt
½ cup nutritional yeast
2 tablespoons caraway seeds, whole

Soften cake or dried yeast in milk. Add molasses and egg. Blend. Add 2 cups of rye flour and other ingredients and mix well. Cover. Let stand in warm place for 30 minutes. Blend in 1½ cups of remaining rye flour, cover again and let stand in warm place an additional 30 minutes. Add remainder of flour as necessary to make dough of good consistency. Knead. Divide in half and place in 2 oiled bread pans. Keep covered and let stand in warm place until dough has doubled in bulk. Bake at 375° F. for about 40 minutes.

## SWISS RYE BREAD

2 cakes or 2 tablespoons dried yeast
2½ cups potato water, lukewarm
8 cups rye flour (approximately)
1 tablespoon salt
2 tablespoons molasses
½ cup nutritional yeast

Soften yeast in ½ cup potato water. Let rise and bubble for 10 minutes. Add remaining potato water, 3 cups of rye flour and other ingredients, and mix well. Cover. Let stand in cool place for 30 hours. Add enough of remaining flour to make dough smooth and elastic. Knead 10 minutes or longer. Oil dough. Place in bowl, cover and set in warm place until doubled in bulk, about 3 to

5 hours. Knead. Divide dough in half and roll each half into a round ball. Oil surface and place each round on an oiled cooky sheet. Set in warm place, until loaves have spread out and risen slightly. Bake at 300° F. for 1 hour or longer.

## SWEDISH LIMPE (ALL-RYE)

½ cup milk, scalded, lukewarm
2 cakes or 2 tablespoons dried yeast
3 tablespoons honey
3 tablespoons oil
1 tablespoon salt
½ cup nutritional yeast
1 tablespoon caraway seeds, ground
1 tablespoon anise seeds, ground
1 tablespoon fennel seeds, ground
1 tablespoon orange rind, grated
2 cups stock, lukewarm
7½ cups rye flour (approximately)

Soften cake or dried yeast in milk. Add rest of ingredients, using enough flour to make dough of good consistency. Knead for 10 minutes. Place in oiled bowl, cover and let stand in warm place. Allow to rise until double in bulk. Punch down. Again let rise until double in bulk and punch down. Shape into 2 round loaves. Place on oiled cooky sheets. Let stand in warm place until loaves have risen somewhat. Bake at 300° F. for 50 to 60 minutes.

VARIATION:
Make with half wholewheat and half rye flour.

## STEAMED DUTCH ROGGEBROOD

2 cups potato water, boiling
½ cup molasses
7 cups rye flour
1 tablespoon salt
½ cup nutritional yeast
2 tablespoons caraway seeds, ground

[Recipe continued on next page]

[Recipe continued from previous page]

Blend all ingredients thoroughly. Dough will be stiff. When cool enough to handle, shape into 2 loaves and place in oiled bread pans with covers to fit. Press dough flat, sealing all cracks on surface. Oil insides of bread-pan covers. Set covered pan in containers filled with water to at least half the depth of the bread pans. Steam, covered, for 3 hours in 250° F. oven. Remove bread pans from water pans, uncover and drain off any accumulation of condensed steam. Bake for another hour, without water. Turn oven off. Remove bread from pans and set on oven racks to continue drying out slowly for 1 hour more. Let cool. When baked, this bread is very dark, heavy and solid. To serve, slice as thin as possible with very sharp knife.

## GERMAN SOUR RYE

1 cup Sour Dough Starter
1½ quarts potato water, lukewarm
10 cups rye flour (approximately)
½ cup molasses
2 tablespoons salt
½ cup nutritional yeast
2 tablespoons caraway seeds, whole
1 cup milk powder

Combine sour-dough starter with all liquids and 6 cups of rye flour and mix well. Cover. Let stand in warm place at least 3 hours (the longer it stands, the more sour the taste). Stir. Set aside and refrigerate 1 cup of mixture as sour-dough starter for next baking. Combine rest of mixture with other ingredients, using enough of remaining flour to make dough of stiff consistency. Knead dough until it is no longer sticky.

Shape into 2 round loaves. Place on oiled cooky sheets. Put dough in warm place to rise 3 to 4 hours, or until about ⅓ more than original size. Bake at 350° F. for 1¼ to 1½ hours.

NOTE:
Since sour dough is a slower rising agent than yeast, allow plenty of time for making this bread.

## RYE-WHEAT BREAD

2 cakes or 2 tablespoons dried yeast
3 cups milk, scalded, cooled to lukewarm
3 tablespoons honey
3 tablespoons oil
1 tablespoon salt
½ cup nutritional yeast
5 cups rye flour, sifted
3 cups wheat flour, sifted

Soften cake or dried yeast in milk. Add 4 cups of rye flour, 2 cups of wholewheat flour, and other ingredients. Mix thoroughly. Add more of both flours as necessary to make dough stiff enough to knead. After kneading, cover with damp cloth and set in warm place to rise until light. Punch down. Let rise 4 times, then shape into 2 loaves. Knead for 5 minutes. Place in oiled bread pans. Cover again with damp cloth, set in warm place and let rise until light. Put a pan of hot water in oven on lower rack and bread pans on rack above. Bake at 300° F. for 1½ hours.

## MILWAUKEE RYE BREAD

1 cake or 1 tablespoon dried yeast
1 quart potato water, lukewarm
2 cups potatoes, cooked, puréed

1 tablespoon salt
½ cup nutritional yeast
1 tablespoon caraway seeds, whole
8 cups rye flour
4 cups wholewheat flour

Soften yeast in ½ cup potato water. Add remaining potato water and other ingredients, stirring in flours gradually. Blend well. Knead until smooth. Oil and place in bowl. Cover. Set in warm place to rise until double in bulk. Shape into 2 balls. Oil again. Place on oiled cooky sheets. Set in warm place and let rise again until double in bulk. Bake at 375° F. for about 1 hour. Brush tops with water and let cool.

### RYE-CORNBREAD

4 cups cornmeal
stock, boiling
4 cups rye flour
½ cup molasses
2 teaspoons salt
½ cup nutritional yeast
½ cup milk powder
1 cup Liquid Yeast

Scald cornmeal with stock, adding enough to wet, but not to thin. Blend in rye flour, molasses, salt, nutritional yeast and milk powder. Add liquid yeast and enough stock so that batter can be stirred with a spoon. Cover. Let batter rise overnight. Next morning, stir down. Turn into 2 oiled bread pans. Wet finger tips with cold water and smooth top of batter. Let rise for 20 minutes. Bake at 325° F. for 40 minutes.

### BANANA RYE BREAD

2 cakes or 2 tablespoons dried yeast
¼ cup stock, lukewarm

1 tablespoon salt
¼ cup nutritional yeast
2 tablespoons honey
3 tablespoons oil
2¼ cups bananas, ripe, puréed
5¼ to 6 cups rye flour

Soften cake or dried yeast in stock. Mix salt, nutritional yeast, honey, oil and bananas, add half of flour and beat until smooth. Beat in yeast mixture. Add remaining flour gradually. Mix thoroughly. Turn dough onto floured board. Knead for 8 minutes. Add enough of remaining flour to keep dough from sticking. Place dough in oiled bowl and turn over to coat all sides with oil. Cover with damp towel. Set in warm place and let rise until double in bulk, for about 2 hours. Turn onto board and knead lightly for 2 minutes. Shape dough into 2 loaves. Place in oiled bread pans. Cover, again set in warm place to rise until double in bulk. This will take about 1 hour. Bake at 425° F. for 10 minutes, then at 350° F. for an additional 40 minutes. Brush tops with water. Cool. Store.

## Oat Breads

HINTS:

Soaked oats may be added to bread in the same way as soaked wheat berries. (See recipe for Soaked Wheat Bread, p. 171, this chapter.)

Oatmeal is best combined with other grains in bread making.

To adapt a white-flour recipe, substitute 1½ cups of oatmeal for every cup of white flour it replaces.

Oatmeal porridge is a good addition to bread dough.

## OATMEAL-WHEAT BREAD

2 cakes or 2 tablespoons dried yeast
3½ cups milk, scalded, cooled to
   lukewarm
4 cups oatmeal
1 tablespoon salt
½ cup nutritional yeast
½ cup honey
¼ cup oil
4 cups wholewheat flour

Soften cake or dried yeast in ½ cup
milk. Add rest of milk to oatmeal,
mix well and blend in salt, nutritional yeast, honey and oil. Combine with yeast mixture and stir in
wholewheat flour. Dough should be
thick—it should just be possible to
beat it with a spoon. Cover. Set in
warm place and let rise until light,
soft, and springy to the touch.
Punch down. Cover and let rise
again in warm place. Turn onto
floured board. Knead for 10 minutes. Form 2 loaves and place in
oiled bread pans. Cover with damp
cloth and let rise in warm place,
until doubled in bulk. Set a pan of
water in the oven on rack beneath
the one holding the bread pans.
Bake at 300° F., 1¼ to 1½ hours.

## NO-KNEAD OATMEAL-WHEAT BREAD

2 cakes or 2 tablespoons dried yeast
3⅔ cups milk, scalded, cooled to
   lukewarm
½ cup honey
¼ cup oil
¼ cup raisins, seedless
¼ cup Soybeans, Roasted, ground
1 tablespoon salt
½ cup nutritional yeast
½ teaspoon mace, ground
½ cup milk powder
5 cups wholewheat flour
2 cups oatmeal

Soften cake or dried yeast in ⅔ cup
milk combined with honey. Stir. Let
rise and bubble for 10 minutes. Add
rest of milk to oil. Blend in raisins,
salt, nutritional yeast, mace, milk
powder. Add softened yeast mixture, then flours, and blend thoroughly. Dough should be soft to
touch but not too wet. Set bowl
of dough in pan of warm water
(85° F.). Cover with heavy towel. Let
rise in warm place for 1½ to 2
hours. Punch down. Turn into 2
oiled bread pans. Cover with towel,
set in warm place and let rise about
45 minutes more. Place bread pans
in cold oven, then turn on heat and
bake for 15 minutes, letting temperature rise to 375° F.; lower to
325° F. and bake for an additional
40 minutes.

## OATMEAL-RYE BREAD

2 quarts milk, scalded, hot
4 cups oatmeal
⅓ cup honey
⅓ cup molasses
1 tablespoon salt
½ cup nutritional yeast
½ teaspoon nutmeg, ground
2 tablespoons oil
1 cake or 1 tablespoon dried yeast
rye flour

Pour 1½ quarts milk over oatmeal.
Add honey, molasses, salt, nutritional yeast, nutmeg and oil. Blend
well. Cover and let stand for 6
hours. At night, warm mixture to
lukewarm. Heat remaining pint of
milk to lukewarm and in it soften
cake or dried yeast. Combine two
mixtures. Add enough rye flour to
make the batter stiff. Cover and
let rise overnight. In the morning,
shape into 2 loaves and place in
oiled bread pans. Bake at 300° F.
for 1½ hours.

## OATMEAL-SOY BREAD

2 cakes or 2 tablespoons dried yeast
1 quart milk, scalded, cooled to lukewarm
¼ cup oil
½ cup honey
1 tablespoon salt
½ cup nutritional yeast
½ cup milk powder
1 cup oatmeal
½ cup soy flour
6 cups wholewheat flour

Soften yeast in ½ cup milk. Stir. Allow to bubble for 10 minutes. Add rest of milk and other ingredients. Blend well. Knead. Oil. Place in bowl, cover and set in warm place. Let rise for 2 hours. Punch down. Shape into 2 loaves and put each in an oiled bread pan. Cover with damp cloth, set in warm place to rise 1 hour longer. Bake at 350° F. for 50 to 60 minutes.

# Cornbreads

HINTS:
Cornmeal is best for bread-making when combined with other grains.
Use freshly ground yellow undegerminated cornmeal.
To adjust a white-flour recipe, substitute ⅞ cup of cornmeal for every cup of white flour it replaces.

## YEAST-RISING CORNBREAD

2 cakes or 2 tablespoons dried yeast
1 cup milk, lukewarm
2 eggs, beaten
3 tablespoons honey
3 tablespoons oil
1 cup cornmeal
½ cup wholewheat flour
¼ cup soy flour
1 teaspoon salt
¼ cup nutritional yeast

Soften yeast in milk. Let stand for 10 minutes. Blend in other ingredients. Turn into oiled 8- x 8-inch pan. Set in warm place and let rise at least 30 minutes. Bake at 350° F. for 30 minutes. Cool slightly and cut into squares. *Serves 6.*

## SALT-RISING CORNBREAD

1 cup milk, scalded, hot
7 tablespoons cornmeal
3 tablespoons honey
1 teaspoon salt
4½ cups wholewheat flour (approximately)
½ cup nutritional yeast
2 cups stock, lukewarm
3 tablespoons oil

Blend milk, cornmeal, 1 tablespoon honey and salt. Put in large covered jar set in dish of hot water and leave in warm place overnight. The next morning, turn mixture into bowl. Add 2 cups of wholewheat flour, yeast, stock, oil and remaining honey. Blend thoroughly. Return mixture to jar and put again into dish of hot water. Set in warm place to rise until light and bubbly. Turn into bowl and add enough flour to make stiff dough. Knead for 10 minutes. Shape into 2 loaves and put into oiled pans. Let rise again in warm place until light. Bake at 425° F. for 15 minutes, decrease heat to 375° F. and bake for 30 minutes more.

## CORNBREAD (in blender)

2 cups buttermilk *
4 eggs
2 tablespoons oil
¼ cup nutritional yeast
1 teaspoon salt
¼ cup soy flour
¼ cup milk powder
2 cups cornmeal

[Recipe continued on next page]

[Recipe continued from previous page]

Gradually blend all ingredients in blender until batter is smooth. Pour mixture into 2 oiled 7- x 3½-inch bread pans. Bake at 400° F. for 30 minutes.

## SOUR CREAM CORNBREAD

3 tablespoons oil
6 eggs, beaten
2 teaspoons salt
¼ cup nutritional yeast
1 quart sour cream *
3 cups cornmeal

Pour oil into 2 9-inch pie plates and heat in preheated oven. Blend remaining ingredients. Pour half the mixture into each pie plate. Bake at 375° F., 25 to 30 minutes. Cut into wedges to serve.

## PLAIN SPOON BREAD

2 cups stock, cold
1 cup cornmeal
1 cup milk
2 eggs, beaten
1 tablespoon oil
1 teaspoon salt

Blend cold stock with cornmeal in saucepan. Heat gradually to boiling point. Remove from heat and blend in remaining ingredients. Turn into oiled square pan. Bake at 400° F., 25 to 30 minutes. Cut into squares. *Serves 6.*

## FLUFFY SPOON BREAD

1 cup cornmeal
3 cups milk, cold
3 egg yolks, beaten
1½ teaspoons salt
¼ cup nutritional yeast
1 tablespoon honey
2 tablespoons oil
⅛ teaspoon mace, ground

3 tablespoons soy flour
3 egg whites, beaten stiff

Blend cornmeal and 1 cup of cold milk together in saucepan. Add rest of milk. Heat gradually to boiling point. Remove from heat and cool to lukewarm. Blend in remaining ingredients except egg whites. When thoroughly mixed, fold in egg whites. Turn into oiled square pan. Bake at 400° F., 45 to 50 minutes. Cool slightly and cut into squares. *Serves 6.*

## MIXED-GRAIN SPOON BREAD

1 cake or 1 tablespoon dried yeast
1¼ cups milk, lukewarm
2 eggs, beaten
¼ cup oil
¼ cup molasses
1 teaspoon salt
¼ cup nutritional yeast
¼ cup milk powder
1 cup cornmeal
½ cup soy flour
½ cup wholewheat flour
½ cup rye flour

Soften cake or dried yeast in ¼ cup of milk. Stir. Let rise for 10 minutes. Add rest of milk, eggs, oil and molasses. Sift remaining ingredients together and stir into liquid mixture. When blended thoroughly, turn into oiled square pan. Set in warm place to rise at least 30 minutes. Bake at 425° F. for 20 minutes, then at 375° F. about 20 minutes longer. Cool slightly and cut into squares. *Serves 6.*

## CHEESE SPOON BREAD

3 cups milk, cold
1 cup cornmeal
1 teaspoon salt
¼ cup nutritional yeast

½ teaspoon dill seeds, ground
3 tablespoons soy flour
1 cup hard cheese, grated
6 eggs, beaten

Blend 1 cup of cold milk with cornmeal in saucepan. When well blended, add remaining milk. Gradually bring to boil. Reduce heat and continue to cook, stirring constantly, until mixture thickens. Add remaining ingredients except eggs. Continue cooking and stirring until cheese is blended with mixture. Remove from heat. When cool, blend in eggs. Turn into oiled casserole. Bake uncovered at 400° F. until fluffy and browned, about 45 minutes. *Serves 6.*

## CORNMEAL CRISPS

⅞ cup cornmeal
1 cup stock, cold
2½ tablespoons oil
¼ teaspoon salt

Blend cornmeal and stock in saucepan until smooth. Bring gradually to boil and remove from heat. Blend in oil and salt and pour mixture into large, shallow oiled baking pans to depth of only ¼ inch. Bake at 325° F. for 25 to 30 minutes. Cool slightly and cut into squares. *Serves 6.*

# Soy Breads

HINTS:
In bread baking, soy flour may be combined with any whole grain flour. As, however, it contains no gluten, it is most successful combined with those whole grains which do.
Sift soy flour before measuring.
Baked products containing soy flour

brown readily. To avoid burning, reduce oven heat by 25 degrees when substituting soy for other flours.

## KNEADED SOY-WHOLEWHEAT BREAD

2 cakes or 2 tablespoons dried yeast
3 cups milk, scalded, cooled to lukewarm
1 tablespoon honey
1½ tablespoons salt
½ cup nutritional yeast
2 tablespoons molasses
5⅓ cups wholewheat flour, sifted
1⅓ cups soy flour, sifted

Soften cake or dried yeast in 1 cup milk with honey. Let stand for 10 minutes. Add rest of milk, salt, nutritional yeast and molasses. Blend. Stir in half the flours and beat until smooth. Beat in remaining flour. Cover. Set in warm place for about 1½ hours to rise. Turn onto lightly floured board. Knead for 5 minutes, adding only enough flour to handle dough. Shape into 2 loaves and put into 2 oiled bread pans. Let rise again in warm place for 30 minutes. Bake at 375° F. for about 40 minutes.

## NO-KNEAD SOY-WHOLEWHEAT BREAD

2 cakes or 2 tablespoons dried yeast
1 quart stock, lukewarm
1½ tablespoons salt
½ cup molasses
½ cup nutritional yeast
½ cup milk powder
1½ cups soy flour, sifted
6 to 7 cups wholewheat flour, sifted

Soften cake or dried yeast in 1 cup stock with salt and molasses. Stir. Let rise for 10 minutes. Add remain-

[Recipe continued on next page]

[Recipe continued from previous page]

ing stock, nutritional yeast, milk powder, soy flour and only enough wholewheat flour to make soft dough. Beat until well blended. Cover. Set in warm place and let rise until double in bulk. Spoon dough into 2 oiled bread pans. Smooth top with spoon dipped into cold water. Let rise again for 30 minutes. Bake at 350° F., 45 to 50 minutes.

## SOY SPOON BREAD

1 cup soy flour
3 cups milk, cold
2 tablespoons oil
1 teaspoon salt
1/4 cup nutritional yeast
3 eggs, separated

Beat soy flour into 1 cup cold milk in saucepan. Blend in remaining ingredients except eggs. Heat gradually, stirring constantly, and when mixture is hot, cook for 5 minutes more. Remove from heat. When cool, mix in egg yolks and then fold in stiffly beaten egg whites. Turn into oiled casserole. Bake uncovered at 375° F. for 30 minutes. *Serves 6.*

## Specialty Breads

HINTS:
Lima-bean flour as well as soybean flour can be combined successfully with other flours in making breads. Substitute 1 cup of soybean flour for each 4 cups of wholewheat flour, and 1 cup of lima-bean flour for each 5 cups of wholewheat flour.
To vary a white-flour recipe, substitute the following quantities for each cup of white flour re-

placed: 7/8 cup rice flour; 3/4 cup buckwheat flour; 13/8 cups barley flour; 3/4 cup potato flour.

## BARLEY BREAD

1 cake or 1 tablespoon dried yeast
2 cups stock, lukewarm
4 cups wholewheat flour
1/4 cup oil
2 tablespoons honey
1 teaspoon salt
1/2 cup nutritional yeast
4 cups barley flour

Soften cake or dried yeast in stock. Blend in wholewheat flour. Set in warm place to rise. Add other ingredients and blend. Knead for 10 minutes. Oil dough, put into bowl and cover. Let rise again in warm place. Punch down. Shape into 2 loaves and place each in an oiled bread pan. Bake at 350° F., 35 to 40 minutes.

## NUT-RAISIN BREAD

1 cake or 1 tablespoon dried yeast
2 cups potato water, lukewarm
1/2 cup honey
1 cup wheat germ
7 cups wholewheat flour (about)
1/2 cup oil
1 egg
1 teaspoon salt
1 teaspoon cinnamon, ground
1/2 cup nutritional yeast
1 cup raisins, seedless
1 cup nuts, ground

Soften cake or dried yeast in potato water. Add honey, wheat germ and 2 cups wholewheat flour. Blend well. Cover and set in warm place. Let rise for 20 minutes. Add rest of ingredients, using enough flour to make stiff dough. Blend well. Oil dough, place in bowl and cover. Let

rise again and punch down. Shape
into 2 loaves and place in oiled
bread pans. Let rise once more in
warm place. Bake at 350° F. for 1
hour.

## HERBED BREAD

2 cakes or 2 tablespoons dried yeast
2 cups milk, scalded, cooled to lukewarm
3 tablespoons honey
1 tablespoon salt
2 eggs, beaten
3 tablespoons oil
½ cup nutritional yeast
½ cup mixed herbs, minced
1 tablespoon celery seeds, ground
1 tablespoon caraway seeds, ground
1 tablespoon dill seeds, ground
7 to 8 cups wholewheat flour

Soften cake or dried yeast in 1 cup
milk with honey and salt. Set in
warm place. Let rise for 15 minutes.
Add enough flour to make dough
easy to handle, along with remaining ingredients. Turn dough onto
lightly floured board. Let rest for
15 minutes; knead until smooth and
elastic. Oil, place in bowl, cover and
let rise until double in bulk. Punch
down. Shape into 2 loaves, and
place in oiled bread pans. Cover.
Let rise until again double in bulk.
Bake at 400° F. for 40 minutes.
Brush top with garlic butter, if desired, when bread is removed from
oven.

## CHEESE BREAD

2 cakes or 2 tablespoons dried yeast
2 cups milk, scalded, cooled to lukewarm
2 tablespoons honey
2 tablespoons salt
½ cup nutritional yeast
½ pound hard cheese, grated

¼ cup soy flour
5 cups wholewheat flour

Soften yeast in 1 cup milk, with
honey and salt. Stir. Let rise for
10 minutes. Add remaining milk
and other ingredients. Blend. Turn
dough onto lightly floured board.
Knead, adding more flour if necessary, until dough is smooth and elastic. Oil. Place in bowl, cover, set
in warm place to rise until double
in bulk. Shape into 2 loaves and
put into oiled bread pans. Let rise
in warm place until again double
in bulk. Bake at 375° F. for about
45 minutes.

## POTATO BREAD

1 cake or 1 tablespoon dried yeast
1 cup potato water, lukewarm
1 tablespoon salt
½ cup nutritional yeast
½ cup milk powder
4 cups potatoes, cooked, puréed (or
sweet potatoes, squash, pumpkin,
peas or beans)
¼ cup oil
8 cups rye flour (approximately)

Soften cake or dried yeast in potato
water. Let stand for 10 minutes.
Add enough rye flour to form stiff
dough, and then add other ingredients. Set in warm place. Let rise
until nearly double in bulk. Turn
into 2 oiled bread pans. Set in warm
place and let rise again. Bake at
350° F. for 50 to 60 minutes.

# Yeast Rolls

HINTS:
Many recipes for bread doughs may
also be used for rolls. Rolls usually are baked at higher tempera-
[Recipe continued on next page]

[Recipe continued from previous page]

tures than bread, and baking time is reduced.

An egg added to roll dough improves color and flavor. When adding an egg, reduce the amount of oil in the recipe by 1 tablespoon.

Puréed potatoes may replace from ⅓ to ½ of the flour in roll and biscuit recipes.

## WHOLEWHEAT ROLLS

1 cake or 1 tablespoon dried yeast
1⅓ cups milk, lukewarm
½ cup honey
½ cup oil
2 teaspoons salt
¼ cup nutritional yeast
3 eggs, beaten
4 cups wholewheat flour (approximately)

Soften cake or dried yeast in ⅓ cup milk with honey. Stir. Let stand for 10 minutes. Add remaining milk, 3½ cups of flour, and other ingredients. Blend. Cover and let rise in warm place until double in bulk. Punch down. Add enough of remaining flour to make dough stiff enough to handle. Knead. Shape into rolls and place on oiled cooky sheets. Brush with oil. Set in warm place to rise until again double in bulk. Bake at 350° F. for about 15 minutes. *Makes about 2 dozen rolls.*

## WHOLEWHEAT CLOVERLEAF ROLLS

1 cake or 1 tablespoon dried yeast
2 cups milk, scalded, cooled to lukewarm
5 tablespoons honey
6 tablespoons oil
1 tablespoon salt
¼ cup nutritional yeast

¼ cup milk powder
5 cups wholewheat flour (approximately)

Soften yeast in 1 cup of milk with honey. Stir. Let stand for 10 minutes. Add remaining milk, only 3 cups of flour and other ingredients. Beat until smooth. Gradually blend in enough of remaining flour to form soft dough. Knead on lightly floured board until smooth and satiny. Oil, place in bowl and cover. Set in warm place. Let rise until double in bulk. Punch down. Knead. Shape into small balls, ½ inch in diameter. Place 3 balls in each well of oiled muffin pans. Brush with oil. Cover and let rise in warm place again until double in bulk. Bake at 400° F. for 15 to 20 minutes. *Makes about 30 rolls.*

## WHOLEWHEAT BUTTERHORNS

1 cake or 1 tablespoon dried yeast
1¼ cups milk, lukewarm
¼ cup oil
¼ cup honey
1¼ teaspoons salt
¼ cup nutritional yeast
3 eggs, beaten
6 cups wholewheat flour (approximately)

Soften cake or dried yeast in milk. Add honey, oil, salt, nutritional yeast and eggs. Beat thoroughly. Slowly beat in as much flour as necessary to give dough good consistency. Knead until elastic. Oil, place in bowl and cover. Let rise in warm place until double in bulk. Punch down. Let rise again and punch down. Divide dough in half. Shape into 2 round balls and roll each ball on board into circle 12 inches in diameter. Cut each circle into 8 pie-shaped wedges. Roll up each piece, working from outer edge inward. Press down pointed end. Place on oiled cooky sheets and brush with oil. Set in warm place. When again double in bulk, bake at 400° F. for 15 to 18 minutes. *Makes 16 large horns.*

## WHOLEWHEAT PARKER HOUSE ROLLS

1 cake or 1 tablespoon dried yeast
¼ cup milk, lukewarm
1 tablespoon honey
1½ teaspoons salt
¼ cup nutritional yeast
¼ cup soy flour
3½ cups wholewheat flour (about)
2 tablespoons oil

Soften cake or dried yeast in milk with honey. Stir. Let stand 10 minutes. Add salt, nutritional yeast, soy flour, 2 cups wholewheat flour and oil. Beat until bubbles rise to surface. Add enough wholewheat flour to make soft dough which fairly cleans bread-bowl sides. Turn onto floured bread board. Let dough rest for 10 minutes. Knead until smooth and elastic. Oil. Place dough in bowl, cover, set in warm place to rise until double in bulk. Punch down, again let rest for 10 minutes. Shape into rolls and arrange on oiled cooky sheets. Brush with oil. Let rise until double in bulk. Bake at 425° F., 10 to 15 minutes. *Makes about 2 dozen rolls.*

## WHOLEWHEAT ENGLISH MUFFINS

1 cake or 1 tablespoon dried yeast
2 cups milk, scalded, cooled to lukewarm
4 tablespoons oil

2 tablespoons honey
1 tablespoon salt
5½ to 6 cups wholewheat flour,
 sifted

Soften yeast in 1 cup milk. Let stand for 10 minutes. Add remaining ingredients, using enough flour to form a soft dough. Knead on lightly floured board until smooth and elastic. Place in an oiled bowl. Cover. Let rise in warm place 1 to 1½ hours, until double in bulk. Punch down. Toss on board sprinkled with cornmeal. Roll dough to ¼-inch thickness. Cut with 3-inch round cooky cutter. Let rounds rest on board, cover with damp cloth and allow to rise for ½ hour, until again double in bulk. Arrange on moderately hot griddle, cornmeal side down first, and bake for 15 minutes on each side. *Makes about 20 muffins.*

## POTATO ROLLS

1 cake or 1 tablespoon dried yeast
¼ cup milk, scalded, cooled to lukewarm
1 tablespoon honey
2 tablespoons oil
½ teaspoon salt
3 tablespoons nutritional yeast
¼ cup potatoes, cooked, puréed
1 egg, beaten
¼ cup soy flour
½ cup wholewheat flour

Soften cake or dried yeast in milk with honey. Let stand for 10 minutes. Add all other ingredients. Blend well. Toss on lightly floured board. Shape into rolls. Arrange on oiled cooky sheets, cover with damp cloth and let rise in warm place until double in bulk. Bake at 400° F. about 10 to 15 minutes. *Makes 2 dozen rolls.*

## CORNMEAL-OATMEAL ROLLS

1 cake or 1 tablespoon dried yeast
1¼ cups milk, scalded, cooled to
    lukewarm
¼ cup honey
¼ cup oil
1 egg, beaten
1 teaspoon salt
¼ cup nutritional yeast
1 cup cornmeal
½ cup oatmeal
3 cups wholewheat flour

Soften cake or dried yeast in ¼ cup
milk with honey. Stir. Let stand for
10 minutes. Blend in all other ingredients. Knead for 5 minutes. Oil
dough. Place in bowl, cover, set in
warm place to rise until double in
bulk. Punch down. Shape into small
rolls. Place on oiled cooky sheets
and let rise until again double in
bulk. Bake at 375° for 15 minutes,
then at 400° F. about 10 minutes
longer. *Makes 2 dozen rolls.*

# Biscuits

### BASIC RAISED BISCUIT

½ cake or ½ tablespoon dried yeast
1⅛ cups stock, lukewarm
¼ cup honey
1 tablespoon oil
¼ teaspoon salt
2 tablespoons nutritional yeast
3 cups wholewheat flour, or any
    combination of whole grains

Soften cake or dried yeast in ⅛ cup
stock with honey, oil and salt. Let
rise for 10 minutes. Add rest of
stock and all other ingredients and
blend thoroughly. Oil dough. Place
in bowl and cover. Let rise for 1
hour in warm place. Knead dough
on floured board until spongy. Cut
into biscuits. Arrange on oiled

cooky sheets. Let rise for 10 minutes
more. Bake at 350° F. for 25 minutes. *Makes about 30 biscuits.*

## UNRAISED WHOLEWHEAT-OATMEAL BISCUITS

1¾ cups wholewheat flour
½ cup oatmeal
1 egg, beaten
3 tablespoons oil
3 tablespoons honey
⅛ teaspoon salt
2 tablespoons nutritional yeast
    milk

Mix flours in bowl, make a well and
put in rest of ingredients, with
enough milk to mix. Blend all
thoroughly. Roll thin on lightly
floured board. Cut into biscuits and
arrange on oiled cooky sheets. Brush
with milk and prick surface with
tines of fork. Bake at 375° F. until
light brown, about 20 minutes.
*Makes about 2 dozen biscuits.*

## UNRAISED SOY BISCUITS

¼ cup soy flour
¼ cup rice flour
1 cup wholewheat flour
¼ cup wheat germ
½ teaspoon salt
2 tablespoons nutritional yeast
¼ cup milk powder
2 tablespoons poppy seeds, whole
3 tablespoons oil
½ cup milk (approximately)

Blend all ingredients, using enough
milk to make soft dough. Roll out
to ½-inch thickness on lightly
floured board. Cut into biscuits.
Place on oiled cooky sheets. Bake
at 425° F. for 10 to 15 minutes.
*Makes about 2 dozen biscuits.*

## GARNISHES FOR BREADS, ROLLS AND BISCUITS

sesame seeds, whole
sunflower seeds, whole
poppy seeds, whole
caraway seeds, whole
dill seeds, whole
celery seeds, whole
cumin seeds, whole
wheat germ
grated cheese
grated nuts, mixed with egg yolk
sautéed onions
egg yolk, thinned with cold water
herbed butter
garlic butter
butter mixed with honey
butter mixed with honey and cinnamon

LEFTOVER BREAD AND BREAD CRUMBS

Toast bread cubes. Dip in garlic butter, toss in salad, or use as a garnish for soup.

Slice bread very thin. Bake in low oven until thoroughly dried out. Cool and store in tight container. Serve with spreads.

Cut thin slices of very stale bread into cubes. Toast. Cool and store in tight container. Use as croutons for soups and salads.

Dry leftover bread crumbs, if still soft, and store in tight container. Use in loaves, stuffings, casseroles, patties, porridge, bread dough.

# 19

# QUICK BREADS

## Muffins

HINTS:

Muffins made without baking powder or baking soda will not be as light and airy as traditional muffins, but they will still be tasty.

Reserve bran that is sifted out of wholewheat flour used for muffins and add to bread dough or porridge.

Muffins can be made successfully with a higher proportion of soy flour to whole-grain flour than can be added to yeast breads or rolls. Try a homemade muffin-mix flour of 1 part wholewheat, ½ part rye flour, ½ part cornmeal and ¼ part soy flour.

To fill muffins, place spoonful of muffin batter in oiled well of muffin pan or oiled custard cup. Arrange piece of fruit or cube of cheese in center. Cover with another spoonful of batter.

For flourless batter base for muffins, see under Pastries.

Oil muffin pans with soy lecithin spread for easy removal of muffins.

SUGGESTED ADDITIONS TO MUFFINS:
wheat germ
sesame seeds
ground nuts
ground Roasted Soybeans
raisins
dried fruit, chopped
fresh fruit, diced
grated cheese
soy flour
bran
bone meal
soy grits
fruit rind, grated, Powdered or Honeyed
Coconut Shreds
berries
sunflower seeds or meal
yoghurt
nutritional yeast
potato water
leftover bread dough
leftover porridge
unsweetened fruit juices
milk powder
soy milk
carob powder
cake or cooky crumbs
whole-grain bread crumbs

flavoring seeds such as poppy, anise, fennel, ginger, coriander, cumin

flavoring spices, ground, such as nutmeg, ginger, clove, mace, allspice, cinnamon, cardamom

## WHOLEWHEAT MUFFINS
(in blender)

1½ cups wholewheat flour
1 teaspoon salt
1 tablespoon nutritional yeast
2 tablespoons soy flour
1 cup milk
2 eggs
2 tablespoons oil
4 tablespoons molasses
½ cup seedless raisins

Sift flour, salt, yeast and soy flour together into a bowl. Place remaining ingredients in blender. Blend until raisins are chopped fine. Combine mixtures and blend lightly by hand. Batter will not be smooth. Drop by spoonfuls into oiled muffin pans. Bake at 375° F., about 20 minutes, until muffins are crisp and brown. *Makes 18 muffins.*

## WHEAT GERM MUFFINS

2 eggs, separated
1 teaspoon salt
1 teaspoon honey
½ cup oil
3 tablespoons sunflower meal
1½ cups milk
1½ cups wholewheat flour
2 tablespoons soy flour
1 cup wheat germ
1 tablespoon nutritional yeast

Beat egg yolks until thick. Add salt, honey and oil. Stir in sunflower meal, milk, flours, wheat germ and yeast. Blend thoroughly. Fold in stiffly beaten egg whites. Bake in *hot,* well-oiled muffin pans at 350°

F. for about 40 minutes. *Makes 18 muffins.*

## WHOLE-GRAIN YEAST MUFFINS

⅓ cake or 1 teaspoon dried yeast
⅛ cup lukewarm potato water
1 egg, beaten
3 tablespoons oil
1 tablespoon nutritional yeast
3 tablespoons honey
¼ teaspoon salt
¼ cup lukewarm milk
1 cup whole-grain flour or any combination of whole-grain flours

Start preparation the night before. Soften cake or dried yeast in potato water. Add egg, oil, nutritional yeast, honey, salt and milk. Beat. Let mixture set for 10 minutes, until bubbly. Gradually blend in flour. Knead until smooth and elastic. Place in oiled bowl. Cover. Set in warm place overnight. Next morning, punch down. Divide dough into 12 pieces and put into muffin pans. Allow to rise 10 minutes. Bake at 350° F. for 25 minutes. *Makes 12 muffins.*

## CORN-WHOLEWHEAT MUFFINS

1 cake or 1 tablespoon dried yeast
¼ cup lukewarm potato water
2 cups milk, scalded, cooled to lukewarm
3 tablespoons molasses
¼ cup soy grits
2 tablespoons nutritional yeast
2 eggs, beaten
½ teaspoon salt
2 cups cornmeal
2 cups wholewheat flour
2 tablespoons soy flour

Soften yeast in potato water. Add milk, molasses, soy grits, yeast, eggs and salt, and blend thoroughly. Gradually stir in all flours. Half fill oiled muffin pans with mixture. Let

[Recipe continued on next page]

[Recipe continued from previous page]

rise in warm place 10 to 15 minutes. Bake at 400° F. until delicately browned, 20 to 25 minutes. *Makes 18 muffins.*

LEFTOVER MUFFINS

May be reheated to freshen or, if very stale, crumble, dry thoroughly and add to cake and cooky crumbs.

# Gems

HINTS:

Gems can be made with any whole-grain flour. Batter should be thicker than muffin batter.

Bake in heavy "gem" pans, preheated to hissing hot and well oiled.

### WHOLEWHEAT GEMS

3 eggs, separated
2 cups milk
2 tablespoons nutritional yeast
2 cups wholewheat flour (about)
2 tablespoons soy flour
3 tablespoons honey

Beat egg yolks until thick. Add milk alternately with dry ingredients, using enough flour to make thick batter. Add honey. Fold in stiffly beaten egg whites. Turn into well-oiled, *hot* gem pan. Bake at 400° F. for 20 to 25 minutes. *Makes 12 gems.*

### WHOLEWHEAT-BUTTERMILK GEMS

2 cups buttermilk *
½ cup honey
2 tablespoons nutritional yeast
⅛ teaspoon salt
3 cups wholewheat flour
3 tablespoons soy flour

Combine buttermilk, honey, yeast and salt. Stir in flours. Blend thoroughly. Turn into well-oiled, *hot* gem pan. Bake at 400° F. for 20 to 25 minutes. *Makes 12 gems.*

### WHOLEWHEAT-DATE GEMS

½ cup honey
½ cup oil
2 eggs, beaten
½ teaspoon salt
2 teaspoons nutritional yeast
1 cup milk
2 cups wholewheat flour
2 tablespoons soy flour
1 tablespoon Powdered Fruit Rind
1½ cups dates, pitted and chopped
¼ cup nuts, ground
¼ cup Roasted Soybeans, ground

Blend honey, oil and eggs. Add salt, yeast and milk. Stir in flours and other ingredients. Turn into well-oiled, *hot* gem pans. Fill ⅔ full. Bake at 350° F. for 30 to 40 minutes. *Makes 18 gems.*

LEFTOVER GEMS

Reheat to serve. If gems are very stale, crumble, dry thoroughly and add to cake and cooky crumbs.

# Popovers

HINTS:

Popovers are lighter than muffins and gems; lightness is achieved by a liberal use of eggs, beating air into mixture, and high oven heat.

Popover batter is thin. It is usually made with equal quantities of liquid and flour.

Bake in popover or muffin pans, hissing hot and well oiled.

When baking popovers, do not open oven until end of baking time.

## WHOLEWHEAT POPOVERS

3 eggs, beaten
¾ teaspoon salt
1 teaspoon oil
1¼ cups milk
1 cup wholewheat flour, sifted (bran may be used in bread dough or porridge)

Blend eggs, salt, oil and milk. Stir in flour. Place small amount of extra oil in each well-oiled popover pan. Heat pan in oven. When pan is *hot,* stir batter once more so flour will be well distributed, pour into cups and fill ⅔ full. Return to oven immediately. Bake at 450° F. for 30 minutes, then at 350° F. for 15 minutes longer. *Makes 12 popovers.*

## SOY-GLUTEN POPOVERS

2 eggs, beaten
¾ cup milk
¼ teaspoon salt
1 tablespoon nutritional yeast
¾ cup soy flour
¼ cup gluten flour

Blend eggs and milk. Sift rest of ingredients together and stir into liquid mixture. Blend thoroughly. Turn into well-oiled *hot* popover pan. Bake at 450° F. for 30 minutes. *Makes 12 popovers.*

## RYE POPOVERS

2 eggs, beaten
1 cup milk
1 tablespoon oil
¼ teaspoon salt
1 cup rye flour, sifted

Blend eggs, milk, oil and salt. Stir in flour. Beat until smooth. Turn into well-oiled *hot* popover pan. Bake at 500° F. for 10 minutes, then at 350° F. for 20 minutes longer. *Makes 12 popovers.*

## CORNMEAL POPOVERS

1¼ cups cornmeal
2 cups milk, hot
1 tablespoon oil
½ teaspoon salt
3 eggs, beaten

Scald cornmeal with milk. Add oil and salt. Cool to lukewarm. Add eggs. Beat. Turn into well-oiled *hot* popover pan. Bake at 450° F., 25 to 30 minutes. *Makes 12 popovers.*

LEFTOVER POPOVERS
Split popovers open. Fill hollow center with fruit, custard or ice cream.

# Puffs

## BOHEMIAN PUFFS

1 cake or 1 tablespoon dried yeast
3 tablespoons lukewarm potato water
2 tablespoons honey
3 eggs, separated
3 tablespoons oil
1½ cups lukewarm milk
½ teaspoon salt
2 tablespoons nutritional yeast
2 cups wholewheat flour
2 tablespoons soy flour

Soften cake or dried yeast in potato water with honey. Let mixture rest until bubbly. Blend egg yolks with milk. Combine with yeast mixture. Sift remaining ingredients together. Stir into liquid mixture and blend thoroughly. Fold in stiffly beaten egg whites. Turn into oiled bowl. Cover. Put bowl in a pan of hot water and set in warm place to rise for 40 minutes. Heat well-oiled muffin pans.

[Recipe continued on next page]

[Recipe continued from previous page]
Pour small amount of additional oil into each muffin well, and then 2 tablespoons of batter. Bake at 400° F. for 15 to 20 minutes. *Makes 24 puffs.*

## GERMAN PUFFS

4 eggs, separated
2 cups milk
5 tablespoons wholewheat flour
1 teaspoon salt

Beat egg yolks until thick and lemon-colored. Add milk and flour alternately, beating constantly to keep smooth. Add salt to egg whites and beat stiff. Fold egg whites into batter. Turn into well-oiled hot muffin pan. Bake at 450° F. for 30 minutes. *Makes 12 puffs.*

## BACON-BARLEY PUFFS (flourless)

6 slices bacon, halved, uncooked
2 cups whole barley, cooked
1 egg, beaten
1 tablespoon nutritional yeast
¼ teaspoon basil
1 tablespoon parsley, minced

Line oiled muffin cups with half-slices of bacon. Combine remaining ingredients. Fill pans ⅔ full of mixture. Bake at 400° F. for 20 minutes. *Makes 12 puffs.*

LEFTOVER PUFFS
Split plain puffs in half. Fill with fruit, custard or ice cream.

# Pancakes

HINTS:
When making pancakes, a higher proportion of soy flour can be added to whole-grain flour than when making yeast breads or rolls. A good homemade pancake-mix flour consists of 1 part wholewheat, ½ part rye flour, ½ part cornmeal and ¼ part soy flour.

For suggested additions to pancake batter, see listing under Muffins, p. 186.

If a soapstone griddle is used, no additional oil nor butter is necessary.

Pancakes should be turned only once.

## WHOLEWHEAT PANCAKES (in blender)

3 eggs
1½ cups milk
½ teaspoon salt
1 tablespoon oil
1 cup wholewheat flour
1 tablespoon soy flour

Blend eggs, milk, salt and oil. Sift flours together into bowl. Pour liquid mixture over flour. Blend all until smooth. Batter should be thin. Pour batter onto hot, unoiled soapstone griddle or into heated, oiled pan. Brown lightly on both sides. This unsweetened pancake may also be served with a filling of meat, fish, cheese, vegetable or egg. For sweet pancakes, add to batter 3 tablespoons honey, 1 teaspoon orange rind and ¼ teaspoon cinnamon. *Serves 4-6.*

## WHOLEWHEAT PANCAKES (with yeast)

1 cake or 1 tablespoon dried yeast
1½ cups lukewarm milk
2 tablespoons honey
2 tablespoons oil
1 egg, beaten

½ teaspoon salt
1¼ cups wholewheat flour
¼ cup wheat germ

Soften yeast in ¼ cup of milk with honey. Let set until bubbly. Combine rest of milk with oil, egg and salt. Add to yeast mixture. Stir in flour and wheat germ. Blend until smooth. Pour batter onto hot, unoiled soapstone griddle or into heated, oiled pan. Brown lightly on both sides. *Serves 4-6.*

## OAT PANCAKES

1 cup oat flour or fine oatmeal
1 cup wholewheat flour
2 tablespoons soy flour
½ teaspoon salt
warm potato water
4 tablespoons oil
3 tablespoons honey

Sift flours. Add salt, oil, honey and enough potato water to make a dough easy to roll into balls. Roll into balls, and press flat. Arrange on oiled cooky sheet. Bake until brown on both sides, about 25 minutes in 350° oven. *Serves 4-6.*

## RYE-CORNMEAL PANCAKES

2 eggs, beaten
6 tablespoons molasses
1 cup milk
1 cup rye flour (about)
1 cup cornmeal
2 tablespoons nutritional yeast

Blend eggs, molasses and milk. Sift remaining ingredients and stir into liquid mixture. Add more rye flour, if necessary, to make batter stiff. Drop by spoonfuls onto hot, unoiled soapstone griddle or into heated, oiled pan. Brown lightly on both sides. *Serves 4-6.*

## RYE PANCAKES

3 eggs, beaten
⅓ cup molasses
1½ cups milk
3 cups rye flour
2 tablespoons nutritional yeast
1 teaspoon salt

Blend eggs, molasses and milk. Sift remaining ingredients and stir into liquid mixture. Drop spoonfuls onto hot, unoiled soapstone griddle or into heated, oiled pan. Brown lightly on both sides. *Serves 6.*

## BAKED JOURNEYCAKES

2 cups cornmeal
¾ teaspoon salt
3 cups potato water
1 tablespoon oil

Make paste of cornmeal, salt and ½ cup of potato water. Place rest of potato water in top of double boiler over direct heat. Bring to boil. Add oil and cornmeal paste. Continue to cook, stirring until smooth. Cover. Place over bottom of double boiler, to which hot water has been added. Cook gently for 15 minutes. Remove from heat, cool and shape into pancakes. Arrange on oiled cooky sheet. Bake at 450° F. for about 25 minutes, until brown on both sides. *Serves 6.*

## RAISED BUCKWHEAT PANCAKES

⅓ cake or 1 teaspoon dried yeast
1 pint lukewarm potato water
1 tablespoon molasses
½ teaspoon salt
1⅓ cups buckwheat flour
½ cup wholewheat flour

Start preparation the night before pancakes are to be served. Soften

[Recipe continued on next page]

[Recipe continued from previous page]

yeast in ¼ cup of potato water with half of molasses. Let set until bubbly. Add rest of potato water, salt and flours. Beat. Batter should be thin. Pour batter into large pitcher, cover and set in warm place overnight. In the morning, add remaining molasses. Stir batter thoroughly. Pour onto hot, unoiled soapstone griddle, or into heated, oiled pan. Brown lightly on both sides. *Serves 4-6.*

## ALL-SOY PANCAKES

2 cups milk
4 eggs, separated
1 teaspoon salt
1½ cups soy flour, sifted (about)

Blend milk, egg yolks and salt. Stir in flour. Beat well. Fold in stiffly beaten egg whites. Drop by spoonfuls onto hot, unoiled soapstone griddle or into heated, oiled pan. Brown lightly on both sides. *Serves 4-6.*

## SOUR DOUGH PANCAKES

1 cake or 1 tablespoon dried yeast
2 cups lukewarm potato water
1½ cups buckwheat flour
½ cup wholewheat flour
2 tablespoons soy flour
2 eggs, beaten
¾ teaspoon salt
3 tablespoons nutritional yeast
1 tablespoon molasses
1 cup sour dough (from last batch)
  (See Sour Dough Starter)

Start preparations the night before these are to be served. Soften yeast in ½ cup potato water. Let rest until bubbly. Add remaining potato water. Stir in all flours. Beat. Turn batter into large pitcher. Cover and let stand in warm place overnight. Next morning, remove 1 cup of batter as sour-dough starter for next batch and to the rest add eggs, salt, yeast, molasses and sour dough from last batch. Blend well. Pour onto hot, unoiled soapstone griddle or into heated, oiled pan. Brown lightly on both sides. *Serves 6.*

## CHEWY MEAL CAKES

1 cup millet, raw
1 cup cracked wheat, raw
1 cup sunflower seeds, hulled
1 cup nuts

Soak millet and cracked wheat overnight in 2 cups water or stock. Grind all ingredients to make coarse batter. Form cakes and spread on dry griddle. Heat until cakes are brown on both sides but still **raw** inside. *Serves 6.*

VARIATION:
Add dried fruits to mixture before blending.

## SCOTTISH BARLEY MEAL SCONES

2 cups milk
3 tablespoons oil
1 teaspoon salt
3 cups barley meal (about)

Combine milk, oil and salt in saucepan. Gradually bring to boil. Remove from heat. Stir in enough barley meal to make thick dough. Allow dough to stand for 5 minutes. Then roll it out to ¼-inch thickness. Cut into rounds. Brown on each side on hot, unoiled soapstone griddle or in heated, oiled pan. *Serves 6.*

# Filled Pancakes

## PANCAKES FILLED WITH COTTAGE CHEESE

BATTER:

1½ pints yoghurt *
2 eggs, beaten
½ cup oil
1 teaspoon salt
2 tablespoons nutritional yeast
3 cups wholewheat flour, sifted
    (about)

Blend yoghurt, eggs, oil and salt. Stir in yeast and flour. Blend thoroughly. Pour batter onto hot, unoiled soapstone griddle or into heated, oiled pan. Brown lightly on both sides. Fill each pancake with the following:

FILLING:

2 cups dry cottage cheese *
1 egg
½ cup wheat germ
3 tablespoons poppy seeds

Blend all ingredients together.
    Place filling on top of each pancake, fold pancake over filling, forming triangles. Pinch edges firmly. Arrange in shallow oiled baking dish. Bake until brown at 350° F., about 30 minutes. *Serves 6.*

## PANCAKES FILLED WITH FRUIT

To make batter, use recipe for Wholewheat Pancakes (in blender). Sweeten or leave plain, as desired. Fill with any one of the following or make your own combination:
    diced raw apples, walnuts, cinnamon and raisins
    fresh strawberries or other berries in season
    sliced fresh peaches and sesame seeds

sliced fresh pears, grated lemon rind and nutmeg
Place spoonful of filling in center of pancake. Roll up and serve.

OTHER PANCAKE RECIPES

See: Baked Potato Pancakes; Sweet Potato Pancakes; Calf's Brain Pancakes; Baked Sweetbread and Pancake Casserole; Baked German Puffed Pancakes; Cottage Cheese Pancakes; Tangy Cottage Cheese Filled Pancakes.

LEFTOVER PANCAKES

Unsweetened pancakes: Fill with fish, meat, cheese, egg or poultry spread and reheat; or cut into thin strips and use as soup garnishes.
Sweetened pancakes: Fill with fruits, nuts, cottage cheese, soy cheese, custard, etc. May be served cold.

# Waffles

HINTS:

Waffles may be raised successfully by using yeast in batter.
Wheat germ is a good addition to waffle batter. Add ⅓ cup of wheat germ to each cup of dry ingredients in recipe, and increase liquid by ¼ cup. For other additions to waffle batter, see suggestions under Muffins.

## WHOLEWHEAT WAFFLES

1 cake or 1 tablespoon dried yeast
1 cup lukewarm milk
4 eggs, beaten
2 tablespoons oil
¼ teaspoon salt
2 cups wholewheat flour, sifted

Soften yeast in milk. Combine eggs with oil and salt, and then with

[Recipe continued on next page]

[Recipe continued from previous page]
yeast mixture. Stir in flour and blend well. Cover bowl. Let rise in warm place for 1 to 1½ hours. Bake in hot, oiled waffle iron.

This unsweetened waffle may be used as base for meat, fish, fowl, cheese, egg or vegetable dishes. Sweeten, if desired, by adding ¼ cup of honey to batter, and use as base for fruit, pudding, ice cream. *Makes 8 waffles.*

## MILLET WAFFLES

1 cake or 1 tablespoon dried yeast
1 cup lukewarm potato water
½ cup millet flour
1 teaspoon honey
1 tablespoon oil
1 egg, beaten
⅛ teaspoon salt
2 cups whole-grain flour (wheat, rye, cornmeal, oatmeal, buckwheat, in any combination)

Soften yeast in ½ cup potato water. Boil the remaining half cup and pour over millet. Add honey and cool to lukewarm. Combine with yeast mixture and allow to rise until bubbly. Add remaining ingredients. Bake in hot, oiled waffle iron. *Makes 6 waffles.*

## MILLET-OAT WAFFLES
(in blender)

1 cake or 1 tablespoon dried yeast
¼ cup lukewarm potato water
½ cup milk
4 eggs
2 teaspoons honey
3 tablespoons oil
½ teaspoon salt
½ cup whole oats
⅓ cup wholewheat flour
¼ cup wheat germ
¼ cup millet

Soften yeast in potato water. Combine milk, eggs, honey, oil, salt and oats in blender and blend until smooth. Add remaining ingredients to blender and blend once again. Stir into yeast mixture and bake in hot, oiled waffle iron. *Makes 6 waffles.*

## CORNMEAL WAFFLES

1 cake or 1 tablespoon dried yeast
2 cups lukewarm sour milk *
3 tablespoons molasses
3 eggs, separated
2 tablespoons nutritional yeast
1 teaspoon salt
3 tablespoons oil
1 cup wheat germ
1¼ cups cornmeal
2 tablespoons soy flour

Soften yeast in milk. Blend in remaining ingredients, except egg whites. Cover bowl. Keep in warm place for 2 hours or longer, stirring batter down each time it doubles in bulk. Fold in stiffly beaten egg whites. Bake in hot, oiled waffle iron. *Makes 6 waffles.*

## WHEAT GERM WAFFLES

1 cake or 1 tablespoon dried yeast
2 cups warm sour milk*
2 tablespoons molasses
1 teaspoon salt
2 tablespoons nutritional yeast
⅓ cup oil
3 eggs, separated
2½ cups wheat germ

Soften cake or dried yeast in milk. Add molasses, salt, yeast, oil and egg yolks. Stir in wheat germ. Blend. Cover bowl. Let rise in warm place for 2 hours, stirring down batter each time it doubles in bulk. Fold in stiffly beaten egg whites. Bake in hot, oiled waffle iron. *Makes 6 waffles.*

## OATMEAL WAFFLES

1 cake or 1 tablespoon dried yeast
2 cups lukewarm milk
1 tablespoon honey
3 tablespoons oil
⅛ teaspoon salt
2 cups oatmeal

Soften yeast in ½ cup milk. Let rise until bubbly. Add remaining ingredients. Blend well. Cover bowl and set in warm place to rise for 1 to 1½ hours. Bake in a hot, oiled waffle iron. *Makes 6 waffles.*

## SOY WAFFLES

1 cake or 1 tablespoon dried yeast
1 cup lukewarm milk
¼ cup soy flour
¾ cup whole-grain flour (wheat, corn, rye, buckwheat, oatmeal, in any combination)
3 tablespoons nutritional yeast
1 tablespoon honey
1 tablespoon oil
1 teaspoon salt

Soften cake or dried yeast in milk. Add remaining ingredients. Blend. Cover bowl. Set in warm place for 1½ hours. Bake in hot, oiled waffle iron. *Makes 6 waffles.*

LEFTOVER WAFFLES
Dry waffles slowly in oven. Cut into wedges. Use as toast (Melba-type) for spreads. Or, if unsweetened, cut into croutons for soup garnishes.

GARNISHES FOR PANCAKES AND WAFFLES:
honey, plain or spiced with cinnamon, nutmeg, allspice, mace, clove or ground ginger
honey, fruit juice and sesame seeds
honey, fruit juice and grated orange rind
honey and Powdered Fruit Rind
molasses, plain or spiced with any of above-mentioned spices
applesauce or other puréed fruits
Nut Butter
yoghurt
soy cheese
cottage cheese
grated cheese

# Quick Bread Spreads

## ORANGE-HONEY SPREAD

¼ cup honey
¾ cup unsweetened fruit juice
4 tablespoons oil

Blend all ingredients. Serve over waffles or pancakes. *Makes 1 cup.*

## MOLASSES SPREAD

1 cup molasses
2 tablespoons oil
2 tablespoons nutritional yeast
juice of 2 lemons

Heat molasses. Blend in rest of ingredients. Serve warm, over waffles or pancakes. *Makes 1 cup.*

See also: Spreads, Dessert Sauces.

# 20

# DESSERTS

## Fruits and Fruit Puddings, Dessert Omelets, Soufflés

### FRUIT JUMBLE (uncooked)

½ pound dried apricots
½ pound dates, pitted
¼ pound prunes, pitted
½ pound figs
¼ pound raisins, seedless
1½ cups prune juice, unsweetened
½ cup lemon juice and rind, grated
yoghurt *

Cut fruit in small pieces. Soak overnight in fruit juices with rind. Top with yoghurt.

### FRUIT COMPOTE (uncooked)

Soak dried apples, apricots, nectarines, currants and raisins overnight in sweet cider. Top with sesame seeds.

### DANISH WINTER COMPOTE

½ cup prunes, pitted
½ cup dried apricots
¼ cup seedless raisins
¼ cup sweet cider

2 ripe bananas, quartered
1 tablespoon honey
½ cup unsweetened orange juice
2 tablespoons Powdered Fruit Rind

Soak prunes, apricots and raisins overnight in cider. Put into oiled casserole and arrange bananas over mixture. Drizzle with honey, pour orange juice over, and top with rind. Cover. Bake at 350° F. for 30 minutes. Serve hot. *Serves 6.*

### FRUIT PUDDING

¼ cup rye flour
½ teaspoon salt
2½ cups boiling sweet cider
1 cup berries or other fruit, fresh or dried, chopped
¼ cup honey
1 teaspoon oil
2 teaspoons lemon rind, grated
2 teaspoons orange rind, grated
¼ teaspoon nutmeg, ground

Sift flour and salt into cider in saucepan. Cook over gentle heat, stirring constantly, until mixture thickens. Add fruit. Cook 1 minute longer. Remove from heat and blend in rest of ingredients. Turn into individual serving dishes. Serve hot or cold. *Serves 6.*

## FESTIVE FRUIT PLATTER
(uncooked)

4 bananas, halved, then cut into strips
½ cup wheat germ
2 grapefruits, in segments
3 oranges, in segments
½ cup yoghurt *
1 tablespoon Powdered Fruit Rind
1 cup berries in season
½ cup Coconut Shreds

Roll banana strips in wheat germ. Dip grapefruit and orange segments in yoghurt and garnish with rind. Mix berries with coconut shreds. Arrange each variety separately on large, flat platter. *Serves 6.*

## WHOLEWHEAT-FRUIT SLICES

DOUGH:

4 tablespoons honey
4 tablespoons oil
½ cup wholewheat flour
rind of ½ lemon, grated
1 tablespoon soy flour
cold milk to mix

Blend honey and oil. Stir in rest of ingredients, using enough milk to make stiff batter. Chill. Divide dough in half. Roll into two very thin sheets. Arrange one at bottom of shallow, oiled pan. Dust with flour. Spread with filling (see below). Cover with remaining layer. Brush with milk. Bake at 375° F. for 30 minutes. Let cool and cut into slices to serve. *Serves 6.*

FILLING:

1 pint apple slices with skins, stewed and drained
½ cup currants or other berries
1 teaspoon cinnamon, ground
¼ cup wheat germ

Mix all ingredients and spread over bottom layer of dough.

## BAKED FRUIT ROLY

4 tablespoons oil
4 tablespoons honey
1½ cups wholewheat flour
rind of ½ lemon, grated
cold milk to mix
2 cups mixed dried fruits, chopped

Blend oil and honey. Stir in flour, rind and enough milk to form smooth dough. Chill. Roll out thin on lightly floured board. Cover with fruit. Roll up like a jelly roll, then shape into a ring. Place on oiled cooky sheet. Brush with milk. Bake at 375° F. for about 40 minutes. Serve hot or cold. *Serves 6.*

## BASIC FRUIT SOUFFLÉ

1 cup fruit, cut fine, or puréed (berries, peaches, apples, apricots, pineapple, prunes, bananas, pears)
small amount of honey (depending on choice of fruit)
¼ cup unsweetened fruit juice (orange, grape, grapefruit, cranberry, sweet cider)
4 egg whites, beaten stiff but not dry
⅛ teaspoon salt
1 teaspoon orange or lemon rind, grated

Mix fruit with honey and fruit juice. Add salt and rind. Fold egg whites gently into fruit mixture. Turn into 1-quart oiled casserole. Bake, uncovered, at 375° F. for 25 to 30 minutes, until puffed and light brown. Do not open oven door until end of baking time. *Serves 4-6.*

## RAW APPLESAUCE (in blender)

Wash, quarter and core juicy apples, leaving skins on. Put in blender, a few pieces of apple at a time, with small amount of sweet cider. Stop

[Recipe continued on next page]

[Recipe continued from previous page]

motor frequently to scrape down sides of container and to add more pieces of apple. Other fruits, such as bananas, pears, etc., may be combined with apple if desired. To keep color and flavor, raw applesauce should be prepared immediately before serving. It can also be added to batters for cake, muffins, yeast bread, steamed breads, puddings and gingerbread, and cookies, to enhance their flavor and give them a moist, rich texture.

### APPLE FOAM (uncooked)

3 tart apples, with skins, shredded
1 teaspoon Powdered Fruit Rind
3 egg whites, beaten stiff
3 tablespoons honey

Mix apple shreds with rind. Blend egg whites and honey. Fold egg-white mixture into shredded apple. Pile mixture into sherbet glasses. Chill. Garnish with fresh berries or other fruit, or sprig of mint. *Serves 6.*

### APPLE OMELET

6 eggs, beaten
⅓ cup milk
1 tablespoon honey
3 tablespoons oil
¼ teaspoon salt
½ teaspoon cinnamon, ground
½ teaspoon Powdered Fruit Rind
1 cup unsweetened applesauce

Blend all ingredients except applesauce. Cook omelet. Spread applesauce over top. Roll. *Serves 6.*

### HONEYED BAKED APPLE

Wash baking apples and core, but leave part of core in bottom of apple to act as plug. Fill cavity with walnuts or chopped dried fruits. Brush skins with oil. Drizzle honey over skins. Dust with ground allspice. Bake at 350° F. for 30 minutes.

VARIATIONS:
Use molasses or unsweetened grape juice instead of honey.

### BAKED APPLE SLICES

4 large apples with skins, sliced
juice and rind of 1 lemon
3 tablespoons honey
4 tablespoons sesame seeds
¼ teaspoon cinnamon, ground
2 tablespoons oil

Arrange half the apple slices in oiled casserole. Sprinkle with half of lemon juice and rind, honey, seeds and oil. Repeat with remaining ingredients. Bake uncovered at 350° F. for 30 minutes. Serve hot or cold, topped with yoghurt. *Serves 4-6.*

### DANISH APPLE-NUT PUDDING

6 large apples with skins, sliced
⅓ cup honey
1 teaspoon lemon rind, grated
½ cup sweet cider
⅛ teaspoon salt
¼ cup seedless raisins

Simmer all ingredients together gently until apples are tender. Turn half of mixture into oiled casserole. Cover with half the filling made by blending all ingredients below:

2 cups whole-grain bread crumbs
½ cup soy grits, soaked in
½ cup sweet cider
¼ cup sesame seeds
3 tablespoons honey

3 tablespoons oil
½ cup walnuts, chopped
½ cup Soybeans, Roasted, chopped

Make another layer with rest of apple mixture and rest of crumb mixture. Bake at 350° F. for 1 hour. Serve hot or cold, topped with yoghurt. *Serves 6.*

## APPLE CRISP

6 large apples with skins, sliced
¾ cup wholewheat flour
¼ teaspoon nutmeg, ground
¼ teaspoon allspice, ground
1 tablespoon nutritional yeast
5 tablespoons honey
4 tablespoons oil
¼ cup soy grits, soaked in
¼ cup sweet cider
½ cup nuts, ground

Arrange half the apple slices in oiled casserole. Combine flour, spices, yeast, honey and oil to make a crumbly mixture. Add soaked soy grits and nuts. Strew half the mixture over apples. Make another layer of remaining apples and cover with remaining crumb mixture. Bake at 350° F., about 30 minutes. Serve hot or cold, topped with yoghurt. *Serves 6.*

## FIG-APPLE CRISP

20 figs, dried
4 large apples with skins, sliced
½ cup wheat germ
4 tablespoons honey
4 tablespoons oil
½ cup nuts, chopped

Steam figs for 5 minutes in vegetable steamer. Reserve liquid for fruit compotes. Clip stems and cut figs into small pieces. Arrange figs and apples in oiled casserole. Combine remaining ingredients. Sprin-

kle mixture over fruit. Bake at 350° F. for about 30 minutes. Serve hot or cold, topped with yoghurt. *Serves 6.*

## HONEYED BAKED PEARS
## (or peaches)

12 pear halves with skins
¼ cup lemon juice
¼ cup honey
1 teaspoon ginger, ground
2 tablespoons oil
12 whole cloves

Arrange pears in shallow, oiled casserole. Stick one clove into each piece of fruit. Blend lemon juice, honey, ginger and oil together. Pour over fruit. Bake at 350° F. for about 15 minutes. Fill each hollow with a tablespoon of cottage or soy cheese. Serve hot or cold. *Serves 6.*

## BAKED RHUBARB
## (with natural sweeteners)

1½ pounds rhubarb, cut in 1-inch pieces
boiling water to cover
1½ cups raisins
⅓ cup pineapple juice, unsweetened
1 cup fresh strawberries
¼ teaspoon nutmeg, ground

Pour boiling water over rhubarb. Let stand 10 minutes, then drain. This reduces objectionable oxalic acid. Put rhubarb into oiled casserole. Add raisins and pineapple juice. Cover and bake at 350° F. for about 25 minutes. To serve, garnish with strawberries and dust with nutmeg. *Serves 6.*

VARIATIONS:
Substitute dates or figs for raisins.
Substitute unsweetened grape juice for pineapple juice.

## BASIC BERRY PUDDING

¼ cup whole-grain flour (rye, cornmeal, oatmeal, or wheat)
1 quart berries
1 quart hot milk
1½ cups whole-grain bread crumbs
4 tablespoons honey
¼ teaspoon salt
¼ cup soy grits, soaked in
¼ cup additional milk

Sprinkle flour over berries. Let
stand for 30 minutes. Pour hot milk
over bread crumbs. Add rest of ingredients. Combine with berry mixture. Turn into oiled casserole.
Bake at 350° F. for about 45 minutes. Serve hot or cold, topped with
yoghurt. *Serves 6-8.*

## RHUBARB BROWN BETTY

3 cups rhubarb, cut; scalded as in
above recipe
2 cups whole-grain cake crumbs
½ cup honey
¼ cup unsweetened pineapple juice
½ teaspoon ginger, ground
3 tablespoons oil
1 cup yoghurt *

Arrange rhubarb in bottom of oiled
casserole. Sprinkle with crumbs.
Blend honey, pineapple juice and
ginger and drizzle over the top.
Bake at 325° F. for 30 to 40 minutes. Serve hot or cold, topped with
yoghurt. *Serves 6.*

## STRAWBERRY OMELET
## (or other berries)

1 quart fresh strawberries
2 tablespoons unsweetened fruit
juice
rind of ½ orange, grated
6 eggs, beaten
¼ cup yoghurt *
3 tablespoons oil

⅛ teaspoon salt
¼ teaspoon anise seeds, crushed

Mix with fruit juice and rind 2
dozen large, perfect strawberries
and reserve for garnish. Mash remaining berries. Blend all the rest
of the ingredients together and
make an omelet. Spread top with
mashed berries. Roll up. Garnish
with reserved whole strawberries
and juice. *Serves 6.*

## DATE PUDDING (or fig)

2 eggs, beaten
1 cup milk
1 teaspoon fennel seeds, crushed
2 cups dates, pitted, cut fine
½ cup Coconut Shreds
1 tablespoon Powdered Fruit Rind

Blend all ingredients. Turn into
oiled casserole. Bake in 325° F. oven
until set. Serve hot or cold, topped
with yoghurt. *Serves 6.*

## BAKED PRUNE WHIP

1½ cups prunes, pitted and puréed
1 tablespoon lemon juice
¼ teaspoon cumin seeds, crushed
4 egg whites, beaten stiff
⅛ teaspoon salt
4 tablespoons honey

Blend prunes and lemon juice. Add
seeds. Add salt to egg whites and
gradually blend in honey. Fold egg-
white mixture into prune mixture.
Turn into oiled 1½-quart casserole
and set in shallow pan of hot water.
Bake at 350° F. for 45 to 55 minutes.
Serve hot or cold. *Serves 6.*

## RAISIN-GINGER PUDDING
## (steamed or baked)

½ cup whole-grain cake crumbs
1 pint milk, scalded

¼ cup soy grits, soaked in
¼ cup cold milk
4 tablespoons honey
4 tablespoons oil
3 eggs, beaten
1 teaspoon ginger, ground
1 teaspoon Powdered Fruit Rind
1 cup raisins

Stir cake crumbs into milk, add soaked soy grits, honey and oil. Cool to lukewarm. Add eggs, flavorings and raisins. For steaming, turn into oiled pudding mold, cover and steam about 1½ hours. Or turn into oiled casserole and bake, covered, at 325° F., about 1½ hours. *Serves 6.*

### CHESTNUT PUDDING (flourless)

1 pound chestnuts, shelled and
    blanched
1 cup milk
4 tablespoons honey
2 tablespoons carob powder

Simmer chestnuts in milk until soft. Purée. Blend with honey and carob powder. Chill and serve. *Serves 6.*

### CHESTNUT SOUFFLÉ (flourless)

1 pound chestnuts, shelled and
    blanched
1 cup milk
4 tablespoons honey
4 tablespoons oil
6 eggs, separated
2 tablespoons unsweetened grape
    juice
¼ teaspoon coriander seeds, crushed

Simmer chestnuts in milk until soft. Purée. Blend with honey and oil. Cool to lukewarm. Add egg yolks, grape juice and seeds. Fold in stiffly beaten egg whites. Turn into oiled casserole. Bake at 375° F. for 40 minutes. *Serves 6.*

# Custard Desserts

HINTS:

Many custard recipes may also be used for making fillings for pies.

Custards may be prepared in large casseroles or individual custard cups. Reduce baking time for individual custards.

Soy milk may be substituted for cow's milk in custard recipes below.

## COCONUT CUSTARD

1 quart hot milk
1 cup Coconut Shreds
1 cup whole-grain bread crumbs
2 tablespoons oil
2 eggs, slightly beaten
3 tablespoons honey
⅛ teaspoon salt
1 teaspoon Powdered Fruit Rind

Pour milk over coconut and bread crumbs. Soak for 1 hour. Add rest of ingredients. Turn into oiled custard cups. Bake at 350° F. until custard is firm and brown, about 1 hour. Serve hot or cold. *Serves 6.*

## HONEY CUSTARD

¼ cup honey
3 eggs, slightly beaten
¼ teaspoon salt
2 cups milk, scalded, cooled to lukewarm
1 teaspoon soy flour
⅛ teaspoon nutmeg, ground

Blend all ingredients except nutmeg. Turn into oiled custard cups. Dust tops with nutmeg. Set cups in pan of hot water. Bake at 350° F. until custard is firm, about 45 minutes. Serve hot or cold. To serve cold, unmold and surround with fresh berries (or other fruit). *Serves 6.*

**[Recipe continued on next page]**

[Recipe continued from previous page]

VARIATIONS:

Put 2 tablespoons of pitted, finely chopped dates at bottom of each custard cup before pouring custard mixture over.

Glaze custard by sprinkling a small amount of raw sugar on top as soon as it is firm. Set custard cups 5 to 6 inches from broiler heat and broil for 1 minute.

## STEAMED COLONIAL CUSTARD

3 eggs, beaten
¼ cup molasses
¼ teaspoon salt
1 teaspoon pure vanilla extract
1 teaspoon soy flour
2 cups milk, scalded

Blend eggs, molasses, salt, vanilla and soy flour. Stir into hot milk. Turn into oiled custard cups. Cover each cup with brown or waxed paper and tie securely with string. Place cups in hot water, which should reach halfway up sides of cups. Cover pan tightly. Steam gently about 15 minutes or until knife comes out clean. Do not allow water around cups to boil, or custard may curdle. *Serves 6.*

This custard may also be baked. In that case, leave custard cups uncovered, set in pan of hot water and bake in 300° F. oven for 40 to 50 minutes.

## HONEY-PEANUT BUTTER CUSTARD (in blender)

2 cups milk
½ cup peanut butter *
2 tablespoons nutritional yeast
⅓ cup honey
2 eggs
½ teaspoon salt

Blend all ingredients until smooth. Turn into oiled custard cups. Set cups in pan of hot water. Bake at 350° F. for about 30 minutes. Serve hot or cold. *Serves 6.*

## SWEET POTATO CUSTARD

3 cups sweet potatoes, raw, grated
3 eggs, beaten
2½ cups milk, scalded
3 tablespoons soy flour
¼ teaspoon salt
2 tablespoons nutritional yeast
4 tablespoons molasses
2 teaspoons allspice, ground

Mix sweet potatoes and eggs. Slowly stir in milk. Add rest of ingredients. Turn into oiled custard cups. Set cups in pan of hot water. Bake at 325° F. for about 1 hour. Serve hot or cold. Top with soy cheese. *Serves 6.*

## CARROT CUSTARD

2 cups carrots, cooked, puréed
2 cups milk
4 eggs, beaten
1 tablespoon nutritional yeast
4 tablespoons honey
⅛ teaspoon salt
¼ teaspoon cardamom seeds, crushed
1 tablespoon soy flour

Blend all ingredients. Turn into oiled custard cups. Set cups in pan of hot water. Bake at 325° F. for about 50 minutes. Dust with ground nutmeg and serve hot or cold. *Serves 6.*

## SQUASH OR PUMPKIN CUSTARD (in blender)

3 cups squash or pumpkin, cooked, puréed

2 eggs
4 tablespoons honey
½ cup yoghurt*
2 tablespoons lemon juice
¼ teaspoon ginger, ground
¼ teaspoon cinnamon, ground
¼ teaspoon nutmeg, ground
4 tablespoons soy flour
2 tablespoons nutritional yeast

Blend all ingredients until smooth. Turn into oiled custard cups and set in pan of hot water. Bake at 350° F. for about 30 minutes. Serve hot or cold, topped with yoghurt. *Serves 6.*

# Dairy Desserts

## EGG FROTH (ZABAGLIONE)

6 egg yolks
4 tablespoons honey
3 tablespoons sweet cider
⅛ teaspoon cinnamon, ground

Put egg yolks in top of double boiler and beat vigorously with rotary beater. Gradually add honey, then cider, continuing to beat. Place over bottom of double boiler, to which hot water has been added, and cook over gentle heat, beating constantly, until mixture is frothy and consistency of thick cream. Dust with cinnamon and serve hot or cold. *Serves 6.*

## CLABBERED MILK DESSERT

Let fresh milk sour at room temperature. Carefully drain off whey. Turn into cups. When curd forms custard-like consistency and is firm, chill. Unmold and serve with fresh berries or other fruits, or top with ground nuts, ground Roasted Soybeans, sesame seeds or wheat germ.

## BUTTERMILK SHERBET

4 tablespoons honey
¾ cup fruit, unsweetened, puréed
1½ cups buttermilk*
1 tablespoon lemon juice
rind of 1 lemon, grated
2 egg whites, beaten stiff

Blend honey and fruit purée. Add buttermilk, lemon juice and rind. Freeze in refrigerator tray until firm. Turn into bowl. Beat well and fold in egg white. Freeze once again and serve. *Serves 6.*

## COEUR À LA CRÈME

½ pound (1 cup) cream cheese*
½ cup yoghurt*

Blend ingredients until smooth. Pack into mold (heart-shaped *coeur à la crème* mold is traditional). Chill at least 2 hours. Unmold. Garnish with berries or other fresh fruit. *Serves 6.*

## MOLDED COTTAGE CHEESE DESSERT (PASKHA)

¾ pound dry cottage cheese*
½ cup yoghurt*
½ cup butter, softened
1 cup nuts, ground
½ cup dried fruits, chopped
¼ cup Honeyed Fruit Rind
½ cup raisins, chopped
1 tablespoon Powdered Fruit Rind

Blend all ingredients. Line mold with muslin. Fill with mixture and place weight on top to press down. Let stand overnight. Next morning, unmold. *Serves 6-8.*

VARIATION:
When mixing ingredients, add 2 beaten eggs.

## COTTAGE CHEESE DESSERT

2 cups dry cottage cheese *
1 egg yolk
¼ cup raisins
3 tablespoons honey
¼ teaspoon cinnamon, ground
1 tablespoon orange rind, grated

Blend all ingredients. Chill. Pile in sherbet glasses and top with sesame seeds, grated nuts, grated Roasted Soybeans or fresh fruit. Or serve as spread on whole grain crackers. *Serves 6.*

## SOY CHEESE SHERBET

soy cheese *
honey
dash of pure vanilla extract
pinch of nutmeg, ground

Mash cheese until soft and fluffy. Sweeten to taste with honey. Flavor with vanilla as desired. Pile into sherbet glasses. Chill. Dust with nutmeg before serving.

VARIATION:

Add grated nuts or grated Roasted Soybeans.

## HOMEMADE YOGHURT
(thick Bulgarian style)

GENERAL INSTRUCTIONS:
Yoghurt can be prepared successfully at home, with or without special equipment. A dairy thermometer that registers lukewarm temperatures (100° F. to 120° F.) is desirable but not indispensable. A simple test for lukewarm temperature can be made by sprinkling liquid on the wrist. An electric incubator is also convenient but not absolutely essential. Any pot with a tight lid deep enough to hold the yoghurt bottles, will be satisfactory provided that temperature is checked frequently and maintained at lukewarm.

Length of incubation time should also be carefully checked.

Yoghurt can be prepared from any clean, fresh milk (cow, goat, soy, etc.), raw, pasteurized or homogenized. Reconstituted skim milk may also be used.

Obtain a batch of Bulgarian yoghurt culture (see Sources of Supply for Natural Foods). Use the original yoghurt culture only once, for the first batch. Thereafter, save a part of each batch for the next one. Continue this practice for one month, making fresh batches at least twice a week. Renew the original culture at the end of the month; after that, the potency of the culture is weakened. Although it may still be capable of souring and coagulating milk, it will not produce an effective and balanced yoghurt.

Incubation time will vary. This depends largely on temperature at which culture is maintained, but also on the weather (hot weather may increase incubation time), and the kind of milk and heating equipment used. It will require more time to incubate batches of yoghurt made from the original Bulgarian yoghurt culture (from 2½ to 10 hours) than successive batches (2 to 3 hours). If whey forms on top of yoghurt, it has been over-incubated. Stir whey back into curd and reduce incubation time for subsequent batches.

Keep cultures refrigerated until needed. Fresh yoghurt made at least twice weekly keeps from 3 to 5 days when refrigerated.

Tartness or mildness can be controlled. Long incubation produces tart, tangy yoghurt. Quick refrigeration—as soon as the yoghurt begins to thicken slightly—produces a milder product.

Thickness can also be controlled. If thick yoghurt is desired, add a full tablespoon of skimmed-milk powder to each quart of milk before bringing the milk to a boil. Let the milk simmer about 15 minutes, which will evaporate part of the moisture and result in a thicker yoghurt.

*Method No. 1* (for first batch, using an electric incubator):

Plug electric incubator into socket. The knob at the bottom of the incubator has been set at the correct incubating temperature (105° F. to 115° F.) and should not be reset. Pour a quart of fresh milk into a pot. Be sure all materials and utensils you will use are scrupulously clean. Bring to a boil or near boil. Cool to lukewarm (105° F. to 115° F.). Test with a dairy thermometer or sprinkle milk on wrist—it should feel warm to the skin, but not hot. When milk is lukewarm, pour entire contents of a bottle of Bulgarian yoghurt culture into the milk. Mix well with a wooden spoon. Pour the milk into prewarmed glasses, cups or jars. Place containers in incubator. Cover. Leave undisturbed for about 2 hours. Remove cover. Gently tilt glasses to observe whether or not the yoghurt has started to thicken. It should be about the consistency of heavy cream: it should still cohere when container is tilted slightly. When it has reached this point, remove containers from incubator. Refrigerate. (If yoghurt is still liquid, keep containers in incubator a while longer and check again.) Yoghurt will continue to thicken as it cools in refrigerator. Chill for several hours before serving.

*Method No. 1* (for subsequent batches, using an electric incubator):

Set aside in the refrigerator a small portion of the yoghurt from the first batch. Within 3 to 5 days, prepare another batch, using this reserved culture as a starter. Use 2 tablespoons of culture for each quart of milk. Up to seven pints of yoghurt may be prepared at one time in the incubator. Proceed as for first batch. Renew culture after one month.

*Method No. 2* (for first batch, without special equipment):

Select a heavy, deep pot with a lid, which will hold the yoghurt jars.

Pour a pint of fresh milk into a pot. (Be sure all materials and utensils you will use are scrupulously clean.) Bring to a near or actual boil. Cool to lukewarm (105° F. to 115° F.). Test with a dairy thermometer or by sprinkling milk on wrist. It should feel warm to the skin, but not hot. Pour entire contents of a bottle of Bulgarian yoghurt culture into the milk. Mix well with a wooden spoon. Pour the milk into prewarmed glasses, cups or jars, and put them in the pot. Pour lukewarm water into the pot, till it reaches necks of containers. Cover pot. Wrap a heavy towel around pot to conserve heat. Check temperature of the water from time to time. When the water cools, add hot water to maintain lukewarm

[Recipe continued on next page]

[Recipe continued from previous page]
temperature. This must be done carefully, without disturbing the yoghurt containers. Let yoghurt thicken as in Method No. 1 for first batch. Remove from pot, refrigerate to chill. Serve.

*Note that the proportion of milk to culture has been reduced in Method No. 2 (for first batch).*

Method No. 2 (for subsequent batches, without special equipment):

Proceed as with Method No. 1. for subsequent batches. The quantity of yoghurt that can be made at any one time will be determined by the size of the pot.

## YOGHURT DESSERT

When heating milk for preparation of yoghurt, 3 to 6 tablespoons of honey may be stirred in. Or, just after the culture has been stirred into the milk, add 5 to 6 tablespoons of pure fruit syrup or preserve, or carob powder. Incubate as usual and chill before serving.

## YOGHURT SHERBET

1 pint yoghurt
2 cups fresh fruit, cut fine

Turn yoghurt into refrigerator tray. Freeze to soft mush. Remove from refrigerator, turn into bowl. Beat well. Blend with fruit. Freeze again to soft mush, beat and return to refrigerator. When frozen to firm consistency, pile into sherbet glasses. *Serves 6.*

VARIATIONS:

Substitute 2 cups dates, pitted and chopped, for fresh fruit.
Add ½ cup ground nuts.

## KEFIR CHEESE

Prepare Kefir Beverage. Warm kefir to 110° F. Drain off whey. The remaining curd is a soft spreading cheese. This may be varied in flavor by adding grated Roquefort, bleu, or any other strongly flavored cheese.

# Grain Desserts

## BAKED WHOLEWHEAT BERRY PUDDING (or rye berry)

3 eggs, beaten
3 cups milk
1 cup raisins
2 cups cooked wholewheat berries
4 tablespoons honey
1 tablespoon orange rind, grated
⅛ teaspoon salt
⅛ teaspoon mace, ground

Mix all ingredients. Turn into oiled casserole. Bake at 325° F., about 1 hour. Serve hot or cold, topped with fresh fruit. *Serves 6.*

## CRACKED WHEAT STEAMED PUDDING (or cracked rye)

1 quart milk
1½ cups cracked wheat cereal
½ teaspoon salt
4 tablespoons honey
¼ teaspoon nutmeg, ground
½ cup raisins, dates or figs, chopped

Pour milk into top of double boiler over direct heat. Bring to boil. Lower heat. Stir in cereal and blend until smooth. Add rest of ingredients. Place over bottom of double boiler, to which hot water has been added. Cook, covered, over low heat, until cereal is thick and has absorbed all liquid. Serve hot, topped with yoghurt. *Serves 6.*

## WHOLEWHEAT STEAMED PUDDING (or rye)

2 cups wholewheat flour
½ cup wheat germ
¼ teaspoon salt
1 cup milk
⅓ cup honey
1 cup raisins, berries or apples, chopped

Blend all ingredients in top of double boiler. Cover and cook over hot water for 2 hours. Serve hot, topped with yoghurt. *Serves 6.*

## BULGUR RAISIN PUDDING

¼ cup bulgur
2 cups milk
¼ teaspoon salt
½ cup raisins
1 tablespoon Powdered Fruit Rind
2 eggs, separated
4 tablespoons honey
¼ teaspoon nutmeg, ground

Mix bulgur, milk and salt in top of double boiler. Cover. Cook for 1 hour over hot water, stirring occasionally. After removing from heat, stir in raisins and rind, and cool to lukewarm. Stir a small quantity of the bulgur mixture into beaten egg yolks. When blended, stir egg yolks into bulgur. Add honey and nutmeg. Fold in stiffly beaten egg whites. Turn into oiled casserole and set in a pan of hot water. Bake at 325° F., about 1 hour. *Serves 4-6.*

## SPROUTED WHEAT BALLS

1 cup Sprouted Wheat
½ cup cream cheese*

1 cup nuts, ground
1 cup raisins

Blend all ingredients. Shape into balls. Roll in desired covering (see Confection Balls, Covering for).

## BAKED INDIAN PUDDING

1 quart milk
⅓ cup cornmeal
2 tablespoons soy flour
⅓ cup sweet cider
½ teaspoon salt
½ teaspoon cinnamon, ground
½ teaspoon ginger, ground
½ cup molasses
3 tablespoons nutritional yeast
½ cup dried fruit, chopped (optional)

Scald milk in top of double boiler over direct heat. Make paste of cornmeal and soy flour in cider. Blend with milk, cover and cook over hot water for 20 minutes. Add rest of ingredients. Remove from heat. Turn into oiled casserole. Bake at 325° F. for 2 hours or until set. Serve hot, topped with yoghurt. *Serves 6.*

## CORNMEAL PUDDING

1 pint milk, scalded
4 tablespoons cornmeal
2 eggs, beaten
6 tablespoons honey
1 pint cold milk
⅛ teaspoon salt
1 tablespoon soy flour
⅛ teaspoon nutmeg, ground

Blend hot milk with cornmeal. Blend rest of ingredients, except nutmeg. Combine two mixtures and turn into oiled custard cups. Dust tops with nutmeg. Bake at 350° F. until set, about 30 minutes. Serve hot with fresh fruit. *Serves 6.*

## CORNMEAL PUFFS

1 pint milk
⅓ cup cornmeal
1 tablespoon soy flour
4 eggs, beaten
¼ teaspoon salt
2 tablespoons honey

Cook milk and cornmeal together for 15 minutes. Blend in soy flour. Cool to lukewarm. Add eggs and salt. Turn into oiled custard cups. Bake at 375° F. for about 20 minutes. Add 1 teaspoon honey to each cup and put under broiler for 1 minute. Serve hot. *Serves 6.*

## OATMEAL PUDDING

3 cups milk
¾ cup oatmeal
1 teaspoon salt
6 tablespoons honey
1 teaspoon cinnamon, ground
1½ cups apples with skins, grated

Heat milk in top of double boiler over direct heat. Slowly stir in oatmeal. Blend well. Add rest of ingredients. Cover and continue cooking over bottom of double boiler, to which hot water has been added. Stir occasionally. Cook until all liquid is absorbed and pudding is thick. *Serves 6.*

## MILLET PUDDING

2 cups milk
¼ cup millet
2 eggs, beaten
4 tablespoons molasses
1 tablespoon nutritional yeast
2 tablespoons soy flour
1 tablespoon Powdered Fruit Rind
¼ cup sesame seeds

Heat 1½ cups milk in top of double boiler, directly over heat. Blend rest of milk with millet. Add millet mixture to hot milk. Cook for 45 minutes, covered, over bottom of double boiler, to which hot water has been added. Stir occasionally. Remove from heat. When lukewarm, add remaining ingredients. Cook 5 minutes longer. Serve hot or cold, topped with fresh fruit. *Serves 6.*

## RICE PUDDING

2 cups cooked brown rice
3 cups milk
⅓ cup honey
1 apple with skin, grated
1 tablespoon soy flour
3 eggs, beaten
1 cup raisins
½ cup nuts coarsely ground
½ teaspoon cinnamon, ground
1 teaspoon Powdered Fruit Rind

Blend all ingredients. Turn into oiled custard cups. Bake at 350° F. until set, about 30 minutes. Serve hot or cold, topped with yoghurt. *Serves 6-8.*

## STEAMED FLUFFY RICE PUDDING

½ cup raisins
2 cups milk, scalded
2 eggs, separated
¼ teaspoon salt
⅓ cup honey
1¼ cups brown rice, cooked
¼ teaspoon cinnamon, ground
⅛ teaspoon nutmeg, ground

Add raisins to hot milk. Let stand 15 minutes. Beat egg yolks, salt and honey. Slowly combine beaten eggs with milk and raisins. Add rest of ingredients except egg whites. Turn all into top of double boiler. Cook over hot water until thickened. Remove from heat. When cool, fold in stiffly beaten egg whites. Chill. Serve cold, topped with fruit. *Serves 6.*

## BAKED RICE RING

3 cups cooked brown rice
1 cup milk
rind of 1 lemon, grated
⅛ teaspoon salt
⅓ cup honey
3 eggs, beaten
3 eggs, separated

Blend all ingredients, except whites of 3 separated eggs. Beat these stiff and fold into mixture. Turn into oiled ring mold. Bake at 350° F. until well set, about 30 minutes. Unmold on large platter. Garnish with fruit. *Serves 6-8.*

## MOLDED RICE PUDDING

1 envelope or 1 tablespoon
   unflavored gelatin
1 pint unsweetened fruit juice
4 tablespoons honey
⅛ teaspoon salt
1 cup brown rice, cooked
¾ cup fruit
½ cup yoghurt *

Soften gelatin in ½ cup fruit juice. Heat rest of juice. Dissolve gelatin mixture. Add honey and salt. Chill mixture until it begins to thicken. Blend in rest of ingredients. Turn into mold. Chill until firm. Unmold to serve. *Serves 6.*

## BARLEY-APPLE PUDDING

4 apples with skins, sliced
2 cups barley, cooked
⅓ cup unsweetened orange juice
1 tablespoon oil
4 tablespoons honey
½ teaspoon nutmeg, ground
½ teaspoon cinnamon, ground
1 tablespoon Powdered Orange
   Rind

Arrange apple slices at bottom of oiled casserole. Blend remaining ingredients together and turn mixture over apple slices. Bake at 350° F. for 30 minutes. *Serves 6.*

LEFTOVER PUDDING OR CUSTARD
Use as topping over plain cake or fresh fruit.

# Gelatin Desserts

HINTS:
Agar-agar is a natural food with jellying properties. It will set within ½ hour after preparation. It may be reboiled without losing its jellying power. For thickening, use 1 rounded teaspoonful of agar-agar powder (softened in 1 tablespoon of cold liquid) to each cup of boiling liquid. After softening in cold liquid, boil for 1 minute in hot liquid. Dishes prepared with agar-agar are not as clear as those made with ordinary gelatin.
Unflavored gelatin comes in envelopes, each containing 1 tablespoon of powdered gelatin. Soften 1 envelope of gelatin in ⅛ to ¼ cup of cold liquid. Dissolve in additional hot liquid to total of 1 pint. Any fruit juice may be used as a base, with the exception of *fresh* pineapple. Raw pineapple juice contains an enzyme which prevents gelatin from jelling. Fresh pineapple juice must be scalded before combining with gelatin.
Tea cups, sherbet glasses and custard cups make good individual molds. For large platter arrangements use shallow china bowls, glass ovenware or special molds. Rinse the mold with cold water before filling with gelatin mixture. To unmold individual por-

[Recipe continued on next page]

[Recipe continued from previous page]

tions, simply run thin blade around inside of mold and tip out contents. To unmold large containers, set in basin of warm water for a few seconds. Run a spatula around edge of mold. Cover with platter and invert.

To whip gelatin desserts, use rotary beater. Wait until mixture has cooled and thickened slightly, before whipping. Chill again. Remember that whipping doubles the bulk.

Many gelatin desserts can also be used as fillings for pies.

## BASIC FRUIT GELATIN

1 envelope or 1 tablespoon
    unflavored gelatin
½ cup cold fruit juice
1½ cups hot fruit juice
pinch of salt
¼ cup honey (may be omitted if naturally sweet fruit juices are used: fig, prune, pineapple, orange, grape, etc.)

Soften gelatin in cold juice. Add hot juice, honey and salt. Stir until dissolved. Fresh fruit slices may be added, if desired. Mold and chill until firm. Unmold to serve. *Serves 4-6.*

## BASIC FRUIT WHIP

Use same ingredients as above. Chill until consistency is slightly thicker than that of unbeaten egg whites. Turn into bowl. Beat with rotary beater until light and fluffy, and double in volume. Mold or pile into sherbet glasses. Chill again until firm. Top with fresh fruit. *Serves 6.*

## FRUIT YOGHURT WHIP

1 envelope or 1 tablespoon
    unflavored gelatin
¼ cup cold fruit juice
1½ cups fresh fruit, hot, puréed
1 tablespoon honey
1 tablespoon lemon juice
pinch of salt
1½ cups yoghurt *

Soften gelatin in cold juice. Add hot purée, honey, lemon juice and salt. Chill until slightly thick. Beat with rotary beater until light and fluffy. Fold in yoghurt. Mold. Chill again until firm. Top with fresh fruit. *Serves 6.*

## BERRY WHIP

2 tablespoons honey
1 cup fresh berries
2 eggs, separated
2 cups fruit juice
1 envelope or 1 tablespoon
    unflavored gelatin

Add honey to berries. Let stand for 1 hour. Beat egg yolks with 1½ cups fruit juice in top of double boiler. Cook gently over hot water, stirring constantly, until mixture is just thick enough to coat spoon. Soften gelatin in remaining ½ cup fruit juice. Pour egg mixture over gelatin. Chill until it begins to set. Beat with rotary beater until light and fluffy. Fold in berry mixture and stiffly beaten egg whites. Mold and chill again. Unmold to serve. *Serves 6.*

## ORANGE-MILK SHERBET

1 envelope or 1 tablespoon
    unflavored gelatin
2 cups unsweetened orange juice
¾ cup milk powder
⅛ teaspoon salt
⅛ teaspoon nutmeg, ground

Soften gelatin in ½ cup orange juice. Sprinkle milk powder on top. Let stand for 5 minutes. Then beat with rotary beater to blend. Heat rest of juice. Add salt and nutmeg and combine with gelatin mixture. Mold. Chill. When slightly thickened, beat with rotary beater until light and fluffy. Chill again. Unmold to serve. *Serves 6.*

## CRUSTED HONEY-ALMOND CREAM

1 envelope or 1 tablespoon
  unflavored gelatin
2 cups milk
2 eggs, separated
⅛ teaspoon salt
4 tablespoons honey
¼ teaspoon pure almond extract
1½ cups wheat germ
¼ cup almonds, slivered
1 tablespoon oil

Soften gelatin in ½ cup cold milk. Combine remaining milk with egg yolks and salt in top of double boiler and cook gently over hot water until mixture thickens just enough to coat spoon. Remove from heat. Add gelatin mixture and chill until it begins to set. Beat egg whites stiff. Blend in honey and flavoring. Fold into gelatin-yolk mixture. Turn into shallow pan, 8 inches x 8 inches, which has been rinsed in cold water. Mix wheat germ, almonds and oil and sprinkle over top. Chill until firm. Cut into squares to serve. *Makes 9 squares.*

## BLANCMANGE

1 envelope or 1 tablespoon
  unflavored gelatin
2 cups milk
4 tablespoons honey
¼ teaspoon pure vanilla extract

⅛ teaspoon salt
½ teaspoon carob powder
¼ cup sesame seeds

Soften gelatin in ½ cup cold milk. Heat rest of milk and in it dissolve gelatin mixture. Add honey, vanilla and salt. Chill until firm. Unmold. Garnish with carob powder and sesame seeds. *Serves 4-6.*

## SPANISH CREAM

1 envelope or 1 tablespoon
  unflavored gelatin
2 cups milk
2 eggs, separated
4 tablespoons honey
1 teaspoon pure vanilla extract
⅛ teaspoon salt
Soybeans, Roasted, ground

Soften gelatin in ½ cup cold milk. Beat egg yolks with honey in top of double boiler. When smooth, add remaining milk. Cook gently over hot water until mixture is just thick enough to coat spoon. Remove from heat and combine with gelatin mixture. When cool, add vanilla and salt. Fold in stiffly beaten egg whites. Turn into mold. Chill until firm. Unmold. Garnish with soybeans. *Serves 4-6.*

## APRICOT-BAVARIAN CREAM
(in blender)

1 envelope or 1 tablespoon
  unflavored gelatin
¼ cup fruit juice
1 egg, separated
4 tablespoons honey
1 cup soaked dried apricots
1 cup stock from soaked dried apricots
1 teaspoon lemon juice
1 tablespoon Powdered Fruit Rind
¾ cup yoghurt *

[Recipe continued on next page]

[Recipe continued from previous page]

Soften gelatin in fruit juice. Combine in blender egg yolk, honey, apricots, stock, lemon juice and Fruit Rind, and blend until smooth. Turn mixture into saucepan. Bring to boil. Remove from heat and add gelatin. Chill until it begins to set; then fold in stiffly beaten egg white and yoghurt. Mold and chill again. Unmold to serve. *Serves 6.*

## Sherbets and Mousses

The following sherbets and mousses are especially suitable for preparation in a blender.

### CRANBERRY SHERBET

1 pound cranberries
4 cups sweet apple cider
½ cup honey
1 sprig mint

Simmer cranberries in cider. Cool. Blend all ingredients until smooth. Turn into ice tray of refrigerator and freeze until mushy. Beat thoroughly. Finish freezing. *Serves 6.*

### STRAWBERRY MOUSSE

1 pint heavy cream
1 pint strawberries, hulled and washed
¼ cup honey
1 sprig mint

Whip cream in blender until stiff. Turn into bowl. Reserve 6 large, perfect strawberries as garnish. Blend remaining strawberries, honey and mint until smooth. Fold gently into the whipped cream. Freeze, without stirring, in ice tray of refrigerator. Serve topped with whole strawberries. *Serves 6.*

### AVOCADO SHERBET

pulp of 1 large avocado, or
  2 small ones
⅓ cup lemon juice
4 tablespoons honey
rind of 1 lemon
1 cup milk
½ cup milk powder
⅛ teaspoon salt

Blend all ingredients until smooth. Turn into ice tray of refrigerator. Stir twice while freezing. Garnish with fruit to serve. *Serves 6.*

### COTTAGE CHEESE SHERBET

1½ cups cottage cheese *
1 tablespoon lemon juice
1 teaspoon Powdered Fruit Rind
4 tablespoons honey
1½ cups yoghurt *
⅛ teaspoon each nutmeg and
  cinnamon, ground

Blend all ingredients together in blender until smooth. Turn into ice tray of refrigerator. Stir twice while freezing. Garnish with fruit. *Serves 6.*

### DATE MOUSSE

1½ cups heavy cream
4 tablespoons honey
1½ cups dates, pitted
1½ cups sweet cider
4 egg yolks
¼ teaspoon salt

Whip cream and honey in blender until stiff. Turn into bowl. Blend rest of ingredients until smooth, then cook gently in top of double boiler, over hot water, stirring frequently, until mixture is just thick enough to coat spoon. Remove from heat. When cool, fold in cream and honey mixture. Freeze in ice tray of refrigerator. *Serves 6.*

# Ice Cream

HINTS:

Although homemade ice cream made in an old-fashioned freezer is, in general, superior in texture and flavor to that made in a refrigerator, most people prefer the latter for convenience' sake. To help in achieving smooth texture and good flavor when making refrigerator ice cream, freeze at lowest temperature on dial and in most cases beat at least twice during freezing process.

## HONEY ICE CREAM (uncooked)

2 eggs, separated
½ cup honey
2 cups heavy cream, whipped
1 teaspoon pure vanilla extract

Beat yolks until thick. Add honey gradually. Blend in cream and vanilla. Freeze until almost firm. Place in chilled bowl. Add stiffly beaten egg whites and beat all until smooth. Return to ice tray of refrigerator. Freeze again until firm. *Serves 6.*

## HONEY ICE CREAM (cooked)

2 cups milk
¾ cup honey
¼ teaspoon salt
2 eggs, beaten
1 cup heavy cream, whipped
1 teaspoon Powdered Fruit Rind

Scald milk in top of double boiler over direct heat. Remove from heat, add honey and salt and cool to lukewarm. Gradually add eggs. Cook over hot water, stirring constantly, until mixture thickens slightly. Cool. Fold in cream and rind and turn into refrigerator tray. Freeze until firm. *Serves 6.*

## HONEY ICE CREAM
## (with gelatin)

1 envelope or 1 tablespoon
    unflavored gelatin
3 cups light cream
⅓ cup honey
¼ teaspoon salt
1 teaspoon anise seeds, crushed

Soften gelatin in ½ cup cream. Place rest of cream and other ingredients in top of double boiler. Heat over hot water until cream is scalded. Remove from heat and combine with gelatin mixture. Chill. When slightly thickened, beat with rotary beater until light. Freeze in ice-cube tray of refrigerator. *Serves 6.*

## FRUIT ICE CREAM

1 envelope or 1 tablespoon
    unflavored gelatin
½ cup sweet cider
2 eggs, separated
½ cup honey
⅛ teaspoon salt
1 teaspoon Powdered Fruit Rind
1 teaspoon pure vanilla extract
2 cups fruit, cut small
2 cups cream
⅓ cup milk powder

Soften gelatin in ¼ cup sweet cider. Heat remaining cider and in it dissolve gelatin mixture. Cool to lukewarm. Add all ingredients except egg whites and milk powder. Freeze until firm in ice trays of refrigerator. Turn into bowl, sprinkle with milk powder and beat until smooth and

[Recipe continued on next page]

[Recipe continued from previous page]
fluffy. Fold in stiffly beaten egg whites. Freeze again. *Serves 6-8*

## NUT ICE CREAM

¾ cup honey
4 eggs, separated
1 teaspoon pure vanilla extract
2 cups heavy cream, whipped
1 cup nuts, ground

Beat honey, egg yolks and vanilla until mixture is very creamy. Stir in cream and nuts. Fold in stiffly beaten egg whites. Freeze in ice tray of refrigerator, beating twice during process. *Serves 6.*

## BERRY ICE CREAM (in blender)

¾ cup heavy cream
3 cups fresh berries
3 tablespoons honey
½ cup fruit juice
juice of 1 lemon
1 sprig mint

Whip cream in blender. Turn into bowl. Blend rest of ingredients until smooth and fold into cream. Freeze in ice trays of refrigerator until firm, beating twice while freezing. *Serves 6.*

## LEMON ICE CREAM (in blender)

¾ cup heavy cream
juice and rind of 2 lemons
½ cup milk powder
1 cup milk
4 tablespoons honey
⅛ teaspoon salt
1 teaspoon Powdered Fruit Rind

Whip cream in blender. Turn into bowl. Blend all other ingredients until smooth and fold into cream. Freeze until firm in ice tray of refrig-

erator. Beat twice while freezing. *Serves 6.*

VARIATIONS:
Substitute 1 banana or ½ cup fresh pineapple or peaches for lemon juice.
Substitute 1 cup yoghurt for 1 cup liquid milk.

## FRENCH VANILLA ICE CREAM

4 egg yolks
½ cup honey
⅛ teaspoon salt
2 teaspoons pure vanilla extract
1 pint heavy cream, whipped

Beat egg yolks slightly. Add honey, salt and vanilla; fold in cream. Turn into ice trays of refrigerator. When mixture freezes ¼ inch around edges of tray, beat. Repeat this partial freezing and beating several times. Let freeze and serve. *Serves 6.*

## DATE ICE CREAM (in blender)

1½ cups dates, pitted
1 cup water
1 cup heavy cream
⅛ teaspoon mace, ground

Quarter dates. Put in blender. Add water and blend until smooth. Add cream and mace and blend again. Pour into 6 custard cups and freeze. *Serves 6.*

## TAFFY ICE CREAM

2 eggs, beaten
⅓ cup molasses
2 cups light cream
2 tablespoons nutritional yeast
⅛ teaspoon salt
1 teaspoon pure vanilla extract
¼ cup nuts, ground
¼ cup Soybeans, Roasted, ground

Blend all ingredients thoroughly. Turn into ice trays of refrigerator. Freeze until firm. Beat twice while freezing. *Serves 6.*

DESSERT TOPPINGS:
nuts, whole or ground
Roasted Soybeans, whole or ground
wheat germ
sesame seeds
sunflower seeds
poppy seeds
anise seeds
fennel seeds
ginger seeds
coriander seeds
cumin seeds
yoghurt
cottage cheese
soy cheese
Coconut Shreds
dried fruits, chopped fine
fresh fruits, whole or sliced
fresh berries
Powdered Fruit Rind
Honeyed Fruit Rind
carob powder
cake or cooky crumbs
dusting of ground spices such as nut-
    meg, ginger, clove, mace, allspice,
    cinnamon, cardamom, etc.
leaves of mint, angelica, etc.
honey
molasses

# Dessert Sauces

## ALMOND SAUCE (in blender)

2 cups almonds
1 tablespoon orange rind
1/3 cup honey

2 tablespoons oil
2 cups wheat germ
1/4 cup sweet cider

Grind almonds in blender. Add rest of ingredients. Blend until smooth. Serve on puddings or ice cream.

## RAW RHUBARB SAUCE (in blender)

1 cup raw rhubarb, cut into pieces
1 cup unsweetened pineapple juice
1/2 cup fresh strawberries

Blend all ingredients until smooth. Serve over pudding or ice cream.

## LOW CALORIE SAUCE

1/2 cup water
1 tablespoon lemon juice
1 tablespoon pure vanilla extract
1/2 cup milk powder
3 tablespoons honey

Blend water, lemon juice and vanilla in large mixing bowl. Beat with rotary beater. Gradually sprinkle milk powder into mixture, beating constantly, until mixture thickens. This will take time. Add honey a little at a time. Continue beating until mixture is stiff enough to stand in peaks.

## NUT CREAM (in blender)

1 cup Nut Butter
1/2 cup milk

Blend ingredients until well mixed. Use as a sauce over pudding or cereal, or as a base for soup.

# 21

# CAKES

Cakes made without baking powder or baking soda will not be as light and airy as traditional cakes. When adapting conventional recipes, the absence of these leavenings may be compensated for, however, by using yeast or extra egg whites. Beat whites stiff and fold into batter just before baking. Turn into *warm* baking dish and bake in preheated oven.

Cakes baked with honey will stay fresh for several days or longer. When substituting honey for refined sweeteners in adjusting recipes, use ¼ cup less of other liquid to each cup of honey. As honey caramelizes quickly, use lower oven temperature than with other sweeteners, to insure thorough baking inside as well as browning outside.

Oil cake pans with soy lecithin spread for easy removal of cakes.

Sift bran out of wholewheat flour used for cakes and reserve for porridge or bread baking.

## SIMPLE FRUIT-NUT CAKE (unbaked)

1 pound dates, pitted
1 pound figs
1 pound walnuts, shelled
1 pound Coconut Shreds
1 pound seedless raisins

Grind all ingredients and mix thoroughly. Press firmly into loaf pan. Chill. After 4 hours, turn onto platter. Slice thin to serve. *Makes 1 5-pound loaf.*

## FRUIT-WHEAT GERM CAKE (unbaked)

1½ cups whole grain bread crumbs
1 cup dates, pitted
¾ cup sweet cider
1 cup wheat germ
½ cup Soybeans, Roasted, ground
1 cup mixed dried fruits (figs, apricots, apples, nectarines, prunes)
1 cup seedless raisins
1 cup nuts
¼ cup honey

Grind all ingredients. Mix thoroughly. Press firmly into loaf pan. Chill for 2 days. Unmold. Slice thin to serve. *Makes 1 large loaf.*

## MEXICAN FRUIT CAKE (unbaked)

½ pound dates, pitted
½ pound figs
½ pound raisins
½ pound dried currants

1 cup sesame seeds
Coconut Shreds from 1 coconut
½ pound almonds
½ pound pignolias (pine nuts)
½ pound sunflower seeds or meal
½ cup unsweetened grape juice
(about)

Grind all ingredients. Mix thoroughly. Press firmly into loaf pan. Pour small amount of grape juice over cake. Set away for a few days, or even weeks, adding more grape juice from time to time. Chill. Slice thin to serve. *Makes 1 5- to 6-pound loaf.*

## AMERICAN FRUIT CAKE (unbaked)

1 cup unsweetened grape juice
1 cup unsweetened blackberry juice
⅛ teaspoon nutmeg, ground
4 whole cloves or ¼ teaspoon ground clove
1 teaspoon allspice, ground
1 stick cinnamon or ½ teaspoon ground cinnamon
2 cups oatmeal, raw
½ pound sunflower seeds, hulled
1½ cups whole grain bread crumbs
¾ cup honey
4 tablespoons oil
1½ pounds seedless raisins
½ pound dried currants (soaked overnight and drained)
½ cup figs, chopped
¾ pound pecans, ground

Combine fruit juices and spices. Let stand overnight so that juice will absorb flavor of spices. Remove cloves and stick cinnamon. Stir in oatmeal and bread crumbs. Blend thoroughly. Let stand overnight. Combine honey and oil. Add to fruit-juice mixture. By hand, work in rest of fruits, nuts and seeds. Blend thoroughly. Line loaf pan with heavy waxed paper, brush with oil and pack mixture down, a little

at a time. Decorate top with additional nuts and sunflower seeds. Cover with paper brushed with oil. Chill for several weeks or longer. Several days before cutting, wrap cake in cloth soaked in grape juice. *Makes 1 large loaf.*

## ENGLISH FRUIT CAKE (unbaked)

2 cups oatmeal, raw
2 cups cracked wheat, raw
2 cups unsweetened grape juice
2 pounds seedless raisins, chopped fine
2 pounds seeded raisins, chopped fine
2 pounds dates, pitted and chopped fine
2 pounds walnuts, chopped coarsely
rind of 3 oranges, grated
rind of 3 lemons, grated
1 cup honey
6 tablespoons oil
1 tablespoon each cinnamon, nutmeg, allspice, ground
½ teaspoon cloves, ground

Mix together oatmeal, wheat and grape juice. Let stand overnight. Add rest of ingredients. Blend thoroughly by hand. Line loaf pans with heavy waxed paper, brush with oil. Pack mixture down, a little at a time. Put heavy weight on top and let stand at least 24 hours. Slice thin to serve. *Makes 2 loaves.*

## BAKED FRUIT CAKE

2 cakes or 2 tablespoons dried yeast
½ cup lukewarm sweet cider
½ cup oil
¾ cup honey
1 cup hot applesauce, unsweetened
2 cups wholewheat flour
1 tablespoon soy flour
½ cup nuts, coarsely chopped
½ cup Honeyed Fruit Rind
4 tablespoons Powdered Fruit Rind
½ teaspoon coriander seeds, crushed

[Recipe continued on next page]

[Recipe continued from previous page]

Soften yeast in cider. Blend honey and oil; combine with powdered fruit rind, seeds and hot applesauce. Cool to lukewarm. Add yeast mixture, flours, nuts and honeyed fruit rind. Beat well to get air into batter. Turn into oiled tube pan. Set in warm place to rise until very light. Bake at 350° F. for about 1 hour. Allow cake to ripen for one day before cutting.

## BAKED ENGLISH FRUIT CAKE

1 cup honey
1 cup oil
8 eggs, separated
2 cups wholewheat flour
1 teaspoon each, ground: cinnamon, allspice, nutmeg
½ teaspoon each, ground: clove, mace, ginger
¼ cup unsweetened grape juice
1 pound raisins, seedless
1 pound currants, dried
rind of 3 oranges, grated
rind of 3 lemons, grated
½ pound dates, pitted and cut
1 cup nuts, coarsely chopped
1 cup Soybeans, Roasted, chopped

Blend honey, oil and egg yolks. Sift 1½ cups flour and spices. Combine with honey, oil and yolks, and add grape juice. Mix remaining ½ cup flour with raisins, currants and dates. Add to batter. Stir in rind, nuts and soybeans. Mix thoroughly. Fold in stiffly beaten egg whites. Turn into oiled and floured loaf pans, filling only ⅔ full. Place oiled wax paper over tops; secure with string. Put large pan of hot water on lowest rack of oven. Set cake on rack above and bake at 300° F., about 3 hours. When thoroughly baked, cake should burst open. *Makes 2 cakes, 3 to 3½ pounds each.*

## BOHEMIAN BRAIDED RING

1 cake or 1 tablespoon dried yeast
½ cup lukewarm sweet cider
1 cup milk, scalded
½ cup honey
¼ cup oil
4½ cups wholewheat or rye flour
2 eggs, beaten
rind of 1 lemon, grated
¼ teaspoon mace, ground
1 teaspoon salt
½ cup seedless raisins
½ cup nuts, chopped

Soften yeast in cider. Combine milk, honey and oil, cool to lukewarm and add to yeast mixture. Beat in half the flour and eggs. Add rest of ingredients and remaining flour. Knead until smooth. Turn into oiled bowl. Cover. Set in warm place to rise. When double in bulk, divide dough in half, and divide each half into 3 pieces. Shape each piece into long roll. Oil 2 cooky sheets and put 3 rolls on each. Braid each 3-roll section and shape each braid into a ring. Cover. Let rise until light. Brush with oil, chopped nuts, ground Roasted Soybeans or sesame seeds. Bake at 350° F. for 25 to 30 minutes. *Makes 2 rings.*

## SCANDINAVIAN HOLIDAY LOAVES (JULE KAGA)

2 cakes or 2 tablespoons dried yeast
¼ cup lukewarm sweet cider
½ cup honey
½ cup oil
1½ teaspoons salt
1 cup milk, scalded
5½ cups wholewheat or rye flour, sifted
2 eggs, beaten
rind of 2 oranges, grated
rind of 2 lemons, grated
¼ cup dried currants

6 cardamom seeds, crushed fine
½ cup nuts, chopped

Soften yeast in cider. Add honey, oil and salt to milk. When lukewarm, beat in 2 cups of flour. Add yeast mixture and eggs. Stir in rest of ingredients and remaining flour. Knead until smooth. Turn into oiled bowl, cover and set in warm place to rise until double in bulk. Divide dough in half. Shape each half into loaf and put into oiled 8½-inch × 4½-inch pans. Set in warm place. Let rise until nearly double in bulk. Bake at 375° F. for 35 to 40 minutes. *Makes 2 loaves.*

## GERMAN HOLIDAY LOAVES (HUTZELBROT)

2 cakes or 2 tablespoons dried yeast
1 pint lukewarm sweet cider
7 cups rye flour (about)
4 cups wholewheat flour
½ teaspoon salt
¾ cup unsweetened prune juice
¾ cup pear nectar or purée
1 pound seedless raisins
1 pound dried currants
1 cup dates, pitted and chopped
rind of 3 oranges, grated
rind of 3 lemons, grated
1 cup almonds, split
2 tablespoons cinnamon, ground
1 teaspoon each, ground: clove,
    allspice
½ cup grape juice, unsweetened

Soften yeast in cider. Add 4 cups rye flour and 2 cups wholewheat flour and salt. Mix well or knead. Let mixture rise in warm place for about 4 hours. Add prune juice and pear nectar or purée. Meanwhile, soak fruits, rind, nuts and spices in grape juice. Add them to mixture. Stir in enough of remaining flours to make stiff dough. Knead. Shape into 4 or 5 round or oval loaves

(about 2 pounds each), and place on oiled, floured cooky sheets. Set in warm place to rise. When loaves are ⅓ larger than original size, brush with egg yolk diluted in cold water and bake at 350° F. about 1 hour and 20 minutes. This cake will improve with age and will keep for a long time.

## MIXED GRAIN FRUIT CAKE

3 cakes or 3 tablespoons dried yeast
½ cup lukewarm sweet cider
½ cup honey
½ cup oil
3 eggs
1 cup cold sweet cider
1 cup buckwheat flour
¼ cup wholewheat flour
1¾ cups rye flour
1 teaspoon salt
1 cup prunes, pitted and cut
1 cup dried apricots, cut
1 cup raisins, figs or dates, cut
½ teaspoon anise seeds, crushed
½ cup sesame seeds
½ cup sunflower seeds, hulled

Soften yeast in cider. Blend honey and oil. Add eggs to honey-oil mixture, one at a time. Combine with softened yeast and cold cider. Stir in flours and salt. Mix fruits and seeds and blend thoroughly with batter. Turn into oiled 8½-inch × 8½-inch pan. Set in warm place. When slightly risen, bake at 350° F., about 1 hour. *Makes 1 square cake.*

## DATE RING

whole-grain bread dough from
    favorite recipe for bread
    or rolls
dates, pitted and chopped

For each date ring prepare enough dough for medium-sized loaf. Roll dough into rectangle, ½-inch thick.

[Recipe continued on next page]

[Recipe continued from previous page]

Cover with dates. Roll up like jelly roll. Shape into ring on oiled cooky sheet. With sharp knife or pair of kitchen scissors, cut at intervals, halfway through ring, starting from outside edge. Spread out slightly. Set in warm place to rise. Bake at 375° F. for 20 to 25 minutes. Brush with honeyed butter and sprinkle with chopped nuts or seeds to serve.

## BANANA BREAD

½ cake or 1 teaspoon dried yeast
⅛ cup lukewarm sweet cider
2 tablespoons honey
2 tablespoons oil
2 eggs, beaten
1¾ cups mixed whole-grain flours
    (rye, buckwheat, corn, oatmeal,
    wheat)
¼ teaspoon salt
¼ teaspoon fennel seeds, crushed
½ cup bananas, mashed

Soften yeast in cider. Mix honey, oil and eggs. Add to yeast mixture. Stir in flours, salt and seeds. Set in warm place for ½ hour to rise. Blend in bananas. Turn into oiled loaf pan. Let rise for 10 minutes more. Bake at 325° F., about 40 minutes.

## APPLESAUCE CAKE

½ cake or 1 teaspoon dried yeast
⅛ cup lukewarm sweet cider
¼ cup honey
¼ cup oil
1 egg, beaten
1 cup unsweetened applesauce
2 cups mixed whole-grain flours
    (see preceding recipe)
¼ teaspoon salt
1 cup dates, pitted and chopped
1 cup nuts, chopped
1 teaspoon each, ground: cinnamon,
    allspice, nutmeg

Soften yeast in cider. Mix honey, oil, egg and applesauce and combine with softened yeast. Stir in flour and salt. Add rest of ingredients. Blend thoroughly. Turn into oiled loaf pan. Set in warm place to rise for 30 minutes. Bake at 350° F. for 45 to 55 minutes.

## GERMAN APPLE CAKE

⅛ cup milk, scalded, cooled to
    lukewarm
1 cake or 1 tablespoon dried yeast
3 tablespoons honey
3 tablespoons oil
½ teaspoon salt
3 eggs, beaten
rind of 1 lemon, grated
1 teaspoon cinnamon, ground
2 cups wholewheat flour
6 large cooking apples with skins,
    sliced thin

Soften yeast in milk. Add honey, oil and salt. Allow to stand until bubbly. Add eggs, rind and cinnamon. Stir in flour. Knead well. Put into oiled bowl. Cover. Set in warm place for 3 hours to rise. Turn onto floured board. Knead again and roll out very thin. Spread on oiled cooky sheet. Brush with oil. Arrange rows of apples over dough. Let stand in warm place for 30 minutes. Bake at 400° F. for 30 minutes. To serve, cut into squares and, if you like, put dab of yoghurt or sour cream on each square. Serve hot or cold. *Serves 8.*

## APRICOT BREAD

½ cake or 1 teaspoon dried yeast
⅛ cup lukewarm water in which
    apricots have been soaked
⅓ cup honey
2 tablespoons oil
¼ teaspoon salt

2 eggs, beaten
1¾ cups mixed whole-grain flours
(rye, buckwheat, corn, oatmeal,
wheat)
½ cup dried apricots, soaked and
cut
¼ cup sunflower seeds, hulled
¼ teaspoon coriander seeds, crushed

Soften yeast in water. Blend honey, oil, salt and eggs. Combine with yeast mixture and stir in flours. Add apricots and seeds. Mix thoroughly. Turn into oil loaf pan. Let rise slightly in warm place. Bake at 325° F. for about 40 minutes. *Makes 1 loaf.*

## FRUIT TORTEN (MUERBE TEIG)

BASIC DOUGH:

1 tablespoon honey
¼ cup oil
1 egg yolk, raw
1 cup wholewheat flour
rind of 1 lemon, grated
milk (if necessary)

Blend honey, oil and egg yolk. Stir in flour and rind. Add a small amount of milk, if necessary, to make stiff dough. Pat dough to a depth of ¼ inch in unoiled pan. Chill. Spread with one of fruit fillings below:

## BASIC FILLING
(for Muerbe Teig)

1 pound dried apricots, prunes, nectarines, apples or peaches, or a combination of these. Soak overnight, drain, pit, if necessary, and cut into pieces, reserving juice for compote or fruit drinks. Or use proportionate amount of fresh berries or other fruit, cutting up, if necessary, and reserving juice. After fruit has been spread over chilled dough, top with custard:

## BASIC CUSTARD
(for Muerbe Teig)

2 eggs
3 tablespoons honey
1 teaspoon pure vanilla extract
2 tablespoons rich milk

Blend all ingredients and pour over fruit. Bake Muerbe Teig at 375° F. for 20 minutes, then at 300° for 20 to 30 minutes or until custard is set. Serve hot or cold, adding a dab of yoghurt or sour cream to each portion, if desired. *Serves 8.*

VARIATIONS:

Add one of the following to Muerbe Teig dough: hard-cooked, sieved egg yolks; grated nuts; sesame seeds; sunflower meal; ground spices.
Substitute orange rind for lemon rind.
Replace part of flour with wheat germ.

## DATE TORTE (in blender)

1 cup nuts
1 cup unsweetened prune juice
4 tablespoons honey
1 tablespoon oil
2 eggs
1 cup dates, pitted
1 cup mixed whole-grain flours
(rye, buckwheat, corn,
oatmeal, wheat)

Grind nuts in blender. Set aside in a bowl. Put juice, honey, oil, eggs and dates into blender. When smooth, add to nuts. Stir in flours. Turn into pan lined with oiled wax paper. Bake at 300° F. for about 45 minutes. When cool, cut into squares. If desired, serve with a dab of yoghurt or sour cream on each square. *Makes 9 squares.*

## CHESTNUT TORTE (flourless)

1 pound chestnuts, shelled,
    blanched, steamed
½ cup honey
½ cup oil
1 egg, beaten, and 2 egg whites
1 teaspoon pure vanilla extract
½ teaspoon cardamom seeds,
    crushed
¼ teaspoon salt

Purée chestnuts. Add honey and oil.
Let cool to lukewarm. Add whole
egg, flavorings and salt. Beat until
smooth. Fold in stiffly beaten egg
whites. Turn into oiled 9-inch cake
pan. Bake at 325° F. for 1 hour.

## DATE LOAF

1½ cups cider, hot
1 cup dates, pitted and chopped
½ cup honey
1 tablespoon oil
1 egg, beaten
1¾ cups wholewheat flour
½ cup soy flour
2 tablespoons nutritional yeast
½ teaspoon salt
1 cup Soybeans, Roasted, ground

Pour cider over dates. Let stand for
30 minutes. Add remaining ingredients. Turn into oiled loaf pan. Bake
at 350° F. about 30 minutes.

## DATE-NUT LOAF

1 cup wholewheat flour
½ cup powdered milk
½ teaspoon salt
1 pound dates, pitted and chopped
½ cup honey
½ cup oil
4 eggs, separated
1 teaspoon pure vanilla extract
3 tablespoons Powdered Fruit Rind
1 pound nuts, coarsely chopped

Sift flour, milk powder and salt.
Sprinkle over dates. Mix until dates

are well coated. Blend honey, oil,
egg yolks and flavorings, and combine with date mixture. Add nuts.
Fold in stiffly beaten egg whites.
Turn into oiled and floured loaf
pan. Bake at 350° F. for 1 hour.

## APPLE-NUT LOAF

1 cake or 1 tablespoon dried yeast
¼ cup sweet cider, lukewarm
½ cup honey
¼ cup oil
2 eggs, beaten
½ teaspoon salt
1 teaspoon pure vanilla extract
1 tablespoon orange rind, grated
2 cups wholewheat flour
1 cup raw apples with skins, grated
½ cup nuts, coarsely chopped

Soften yeast in cider. Blend honey,
oil, eggs, salt and flavorings. Combine with yeast mixture. Stir in rest
of ingredients. Turn into oiled loaf
pan. Set in warm place to rise for
30 minutes. Bake at 350° F., about
40 minutes.

## NUT CAKE (flourless)

10 eggs, separated
1 cup raw sugar
¾ pound nuts, ground fine
1 teaspoon pure vanilla extract

Beat egg yolks with sugar until light
and creamy. Add nuts and vanilla.
Fold in stiffly beaten egg whites.
Turn into well-oiled tube pan or
2 8-inch layer-cake pans. Bake at
325° F., 1 hour in tube pan, 40 to
45 minutes in regular pans. *Makes
1 large tube cake or 2 layers.*

## WALNUT CAKE

5 eggs, separated
¾ cup honey
1 cup walnuts, ground fine

¼ cup fine whole-grain
  bread crumbs
3 tablespoons wheat germ
pinch of clove and mace, ground
rind of 1 lemon, grated

Beat egg yolks with honey. Add rest
of ingredients. Fold in stiffly beaten
egg whites. Turn into well-oiled loaf
pan. Bake at 300° F., about 1½
hours.

## BRAZIL NUT CAKE (in blender)

2 cups Brazil nuts
6 eggs, separated
⅓ cup honey
¼ teaspoon salt

Grind nuts in blender, a few at
a time. Put into bowl. Blend egg
yolks, honey and salt and combine
with nuts. Beat egg whites with rotary beater until stiff. Fold into mixture. Turn into 3 well-oiled 8-inch
layer-cake pans lined with oiled wax
paper. Bake at 350° F. for about 35
minutes. When cool, spread yoghurt
or crushed fruit between layers and
put together into 3-layer cake.
*Makes 3 thin layers.*

## COTTAGE CHEESE CAKE

2 cups whole-grain bread crumbs
3 tablespoons wheat germ
4 tablespoons honey
4 tablespoons oil
4 eggs, beaten
⅛ teaspoon salt
1 teaspoon cinnamon
1½ tablespoons lemon juice
1½ teaspoons lemon rind, grated
1 cup top milk
1½ pounds cottage cheese *
4 tablespoons wholewheat flour

Mix bread crumbs and wheat germ
with oil and 2 tablespoons honey.
Spread half this mixture on bottoms

and sides of 9-inch spring-form pan.
Beat eggs, salt and cinnamon with
remaining 2 tablespoons honey.
Add rest of ingredients. Beat thoroughly and strain through sieve.
Turn into lined pan. Sprinkle remaining crumb mixture on top.
Bake at 350° F. until center of cake
is firm, about 1 hour. Turn off heat,
open oven door and let cake stand
in oven about 1 hour, or until cool.
*Serves 12.*

## TANGY CHEESE CAKE

DOUGH:

2 cups wholewheat flour
4 egg yolks
¼ cup oil
4 tablespoons honey

Make well in center of flour. Pour
in egg yolks, oil and honey. Gradually work into ingredients in center
until smooth paste results. Roll out
and line 8-inch cake pan with
dough.

FILLING:

½ cup honey
¼ cup oil
2 eggs, separated
1 teaspoon nutmeg, ground
1½ teaspoons lemon rind, grated
3 tablespoons lemon juice
1 pound cottage cheese,* sieved
9 ounces cream cheese *
4 tablespoons cheddar cheese,
  grated

Blend honey, oil and egg yolks. Add
flavorings and cheeses. Fold in stiffly
beaten egg whites. Turn into pastry-
lined pan. Bake in medium oven
until golden brown on top. Turn
off heat, open oven door and let
cake stand in oven about 1 hour, or
until cool. Invert to serve. *Serves 12.*

## COTTAGE CHEESE-YOGHURT CAKE (in blender)

crumb shell from favorite recipe
  (see under Pie Shell)
1 cup yoghurt *
3 eggs, separated
1 teaspoon pure vanilla extract
1 tablespoon lemon juice
rind of 1 lemon
⅓ cup honey
¼ teaspoon salt
¼ cup wholewheat flour
1 pound cottage cheese *

Pat crumb shell mixture in bottom of 9-inch spring-form or round cake pan at least 3 inches deep. Place yoghurt, egg yolks and rest of ingredients in blender. Blend until smooth. Beat egg whites until stiff with rotary beater. Fold egg whites into mixture. Turn mixture into 9-inch crumb shell. Bake until center of cake is firm. Run knife around edge of pan to loosen cake from sides. Cool completely before removing from pan.

## REFRIGERATED CHEESE CAKE

crumb shell from favorite recipe
  (see under Pie Shell)
2 envelopes or 2 tablespoons
  unflavored gelatin
½ cup cold unsweetened
  fruit juice
2 eggs, separated
½ cup honey
½ cup milk
1 teaspoon salt
1 pound cottage cheese,* sieved
1 lemon, juice and grated rind
1 teaspoon pure vanilla extract
1 cup yoghurt *

Pat ⅔ of crumb-shell mixture into spring-form pan, lining bottom and sides. Soften gelatin in fruit juice. Blend egg yolks, honey, milk and salt in top of double boiler. Heat

over hot water until mixture thickens. Stir in gelatin mixture. When dissolved, remove from heat. Cool and add cottage cheese, lemon, vanilla and yoghurt. Fold in stiffly beaten egg whites. Turn mixture into 9-inch crumb shell. Sprinkle remaining crumb-shell mixture over top. Chill until firm. Unmold.

## PUMPKIN CAKE

¾ cup molasses
⅓ cup oil
½ cup yoghurt,* sour cream * or
  sour milk *
3 eggs, beaten
⅔ cup cooked pumpkin, puréed
1¾ cup wholewheat flour
¼ teaspoon salt
½ teaspoon each, ground: nutmeg
  and cinnamon
¼ teaspoon each, ground: mace,
  clove, allspice
1 teaspoon ginger, ground
3 tablespoons nutritional yeast

Blend all ingredients. Turn into oiled 8- x 12-inch pan. Bake at 350° F. for 45 to 50 minutes. Cool. Cut into squares to serve. *Makes 12 squares.*

## SQUASH CAKE

1 cake or 1 tablespoon dried yeast
¼ cup sweet cider, lukewarm
1 cup summer squash, raw,
  grated fine
½ cup molasses
½ cup oil
1 egg, beaten
⅓ cup buttermilk *
1 cup cornmeal
1 cup wholewheat flour
1 tablespoon mixed spices, ground
  (nutmeg, cinnamon, clove,
  mace, allspice, ginger)
3 tablespoons nutritional yeast
¼ cup seedless raisins

Soften cake or dried yeast in cider. Blend squash, molasses, oil, egg and buttermilk. Blend with yeast mixture. Stir in rest of ingredients. Turn into oiled 8- x 12-inch pan. Set in warm place for 20 minutes to rise slightly. Bake at 350° F. for 30 to 40 minutes. Cut into squares to serve. *Makes 12 squares.*

## FRUIT-FILLED WHOLEWHEAT RING

DOUGH:

1 cake or 1 tablespoon dried yeast
1 cup milk, scalded, cooled to
  lukewarm
¼ cup honey
3 tablespoons oil
½ teaspoon salt
½ teaspoon cardamom seeds,
  crushed
2 eggs, beaten
3½ cups wholewheat flour

Soften yeast in milk. Blend honey, oil, salt, seeds and eggs. Combine with yeast mixture and stir in flour. Knead lightly. Turn into oiled bowl. Cover. Set in warm place to rise for 2 hours. Roll out into oblong shape ¼ inch thick. Brush with oil. Cover with filling below:

FILLING:

½ cup dates, pitted and chopped
½ cup seedless raisins
½ cup wheat germ
rind of 1 orange, grated
rind of 1 lemon, grated
¾ cup fresh fruit, mashed

Mix all ingredients together. After spreading filling over dough, roll up as for jelly roll. Shape into a circle on oiled cooky sheet. Make cuts on top of ring to expose filling. Cover and set in warm place to rise again for 1 hour. Brush with oil.

Bake at 375° F. for about 30 minutes.

## SWEDISH RING

2 cakes or 2 tablespoons dried yeast
¼ cup sweet cider, lukewarm
⅓ cup honey
⅓ cup oil
2 eggs, beaten
1 cup milk, scalded, cooled to
  lukewarm
4½ cups wholewheat flour
1 teaspoon cardamom seeds,
  crushed

Soften yeast in cider. Blend honey, oil, eggs and milk and combine with yeast mixture. Stir in flour and cardamom. Turn out on board and knead until smooth. Form into ball. Put in oiled bowl, cover and set in warm place to rise until double in bulk. Roll into rectangular sheet ½ inch thick. Brush with oil and drizzle with honey. Sprinkle with cinnamon, if desired. Roll up dough as for jelly roll. Arrange in ring shape on oiled cooky sheet. Cut slits at 1-inch intervals with sharp knife or kitchen scissors. Set in warm place to rise for 1 hour. Bake at 375° F. for 25 to 30 minutes. *Makes 1 ring.*

## WHOLEWHEAT SPONGE CAKE

4 eggs, separated
2 teaspoons lemon juice
1 teaspoon Powdered Fruit Rind
1 cup raw sugar
1 scant cup wholewheat flour,
  sifted 3 times

Beat egg yolks until lemon-colored. Add lemon juice, rind, sugar and sifted flour. (Reserve sifted-out bran for porridge or bread baking.) Fold in stiffly beaten egg whites. Turn into oiled cake pan. Bake at 300° F. for about 30 minutes.

## WHOLEWHEAT POUND CAKE

1½ cups honey
1½ cups oil
¼ teaspoon salt
6 eggs, separated
6 tablespoons orange rind, grated
¾ cup unsweetened orange juice
2 cups wholewheat flour
¼ teaspoon mace, ground

Blend honey, oil, salt and egg yolks, one at a time. Beat until very well mixed. Stir in rest of ingredients except egg white. Beat these stiff and turn into oiled loaf pan. Bake at 300° F. until cake springs back when touched gently in center, about 1 hour.

## WHEAT GERM CAKE LOAF

1 cake or 1 tablespoon dried yeast
1 cup sweet cider, lukewarm
1 tablespoon honey
1 teaspoon salt
2 eggs, beaten
1 tablespoon oil
⅓ cup soy flour
⅓ cup rice polishings
2 cups bran siftings (saved from sifting wholewheat flour)
3 cups wheat germ
1½ cups unsweetened orange juice (about)
1 tablespoon nutritional yeast

Soften cake or dried yeast in cider. Add honey and salt. Let mixture stand for 20 minutes. Then add rest of ingredients, adding only enough orange juice to make stiff batter. Turn into oiled loaf pan lined with wax paper. Let rise in warm place for 1 hour. Bake at 325° for 1 hour and 20 minutes.

## PEANUT BUTTER LOAF

1 cake or 1 tablespoon dried yeast
¼ cup lukewarm milk
1 teaspoon salt
½ cup honey
1 cup cold milk
½ cup peanut butter *
2 cups wholewheat flour
2 tablespoons nutritional yeast

Soften cake or dried yeast in luke-warm milk. Blend honey, salt and cold milk. Stir in peanut butter and blend. This is most easily done in blender. Add yeast mixture, flour and nutritional yeast and beat until smooth. Turn into 3- x 7-inch loaf pan. Bake at 350° F. for about 1 hour. Cut and serve the following day.

## RYE BREAD TORTE

6 eggs, separated
¾ cup honey
1 cup whole-rye bread crumbs
¾ cup walnuts, ground
¼ teaspoon cinnamon, ground
½ cup cooked potatoes, riced
¼ cup unsweetened fruit juice
½ cup fresh strawberries or other fresh berries or fruit

Beat egg yolks with honey. Add all ingredients except fruit. Blend thoroughly. Fold in stiffly beaten egg whites. Turn into oiled 9-inch spring-form pan. Bake at 350° F. for 1 hour. Cool. To serve, garnish with strawberries or other fruit. *Serves 12.*

## POTATO FLOUR SPONGE CAKE

4 eggs, separated
1 cup honey
2 tablespoons lemon juice
⅛ teaspoon salt
¼ teaspoon anise seeds, crushed
1 scant cup potato flour

Beat egg yolks until thick. Blend honey into yolks. Add lemon juice, salt and seeds. Alternately fold in potato flour and stiffly beaten egg whites. Turn into oiled 9-inch pan. Bake at 325° F. for 20 minutes, raise heat to 350° F. and continue baking 15 to 20 minutes longer.

## OATMEAL CAKE

1 cake or 1 tablespoon dried yeast
1/4 cup sweet cider, lukewarm
1/2 cup honey
1/2 cup oil
4 eggs, beaten
3 1/2 cups oatmeal
1 teaspoon salt
1 tablespoon nutritional yeast
1 1/2 teaspoons cinnamon, ground
1 teaspoon nutmeg, ground
1 teaspoon pure vanilla extract
1/4 cup nuts, coarsely ground
1/4 cup Soybeans, Roasted, ground
1/2 cup seedless raisins

Soften cake or dried yeast in cider. Blend honey, oil and eggs. Add yeast mixture. Stir in oatmeal, nutritional yeast and flavorings. Add nuts, Soybeans and raisins. Turn into oiled loaf pan. Set in warm place to rise for 30 minutes. Bake at 350° F. for about 45 minutes.

## BOSTON BROWN BREAD

1 cake or 1 tablespoon dried yeast
1/8 cup sweet cider, lukewarm
1 cup cornmeal
1 cup rye flour
1 cup wholewheat flour
1 teaspoon salt
2 tablespoons nutritional yeast
2/3 cup molasses
1 pint yoghurt,* buttermilk * or
    sour milk *
1 cup seedless raisins (optional)

Soften cake or dried yeast in cider. Sift all dry ingredients together. Blend with molasses and yoghurt. Add yeast mixture and raisins. Beat

thoroughly. Turn into oiled 2-quart mold. Cover. Let rise for 20 minutes. Steam gently for 3 hours.

## Small Cakes

### WHOLEWHEAT CUPCAKES

1 cake or 1 tablespoon dried yeast
1 1/4 cups milk, scalded, cooled to
    lukewarm
1/4 cup honey
1/3 cup oil
2 eggs, beaten
1/2 teaspoon cinnamon, ground
1/2 teaspoon anise seeds, crushed
1/2 teaspoon salt
3 1/4 cups wholewheat flour
1/4 cup soy flour
1/4 cup nuts, chopped

Soften yeast in 1/4 cup milk. Blend rest of milk with honey, oil, eggs, seasonings and salt. Stir in flours. Add yeast mixture and nuts. Turn into oiled bowl. Cover. Let rise in warm place for 2 hours. Punch down dough. Drop by tablespoonfuls into oiled custard cups. Fill cups halfway. Let rise until double in bulk. Bake at 375° F. about 25 minutes. *Makes 24 cupcakes.*

### WHOLEWHEAT BUNS

1 cake or 1 tablespoon dried yeast
1 cup milk, scalded, cooled to
    lukewarm
3 tablespoons honey
4 tablespoons oil
1 egg yolk
1 teaspoon salt
1 teaspoon cinnamon, ground
2 1/2 cups wholewheat flour
1/2 cup raisins, soaked, drained and
    dusted with flour
1/4 cup sunflower seeds or meal

Soften yeast in milk. Add honey, oil, egg yolk and salt. Sift flour and cin-

[Recipe continued on next page]

[Recipe continued from previous page]
namon together and stir in. Turn into oiled bowl. Cover. Let rise in warm place until double in bulk. Knead, adding raisins and sunflower seeds. Shape into small, round balls and place close together in shallow, oiled pan. Set in warm place to rise again. Bake at 400° F. for about 30 minutes. Brush with diluted honey or molasses and return to oven briefly to glaze. *Makes 24 small buns.*

## MOLASSES CUP CAKES

1 cake or 1 tablespoon dried yeast
⅞ cup sweet cider, lukewarm
⅔ cup molasses
2 cups wholewheat flour
⅓ cup oil
rind of 1 lemon, grated
1 tablespoon nutritional yeast
1 egg, beaten

Soften cake or dried yeast in cider. Add 1 tablespoon molasses and 1 cup flour. Let yeast mixture stand until bubbly. Add remaining molasses, flour and other ingredients. Beat thoroughly. Turn batter into oiled custard cups, filling them halfway. Place cups in cold oven. Turn heat to 150° F. and let batter rise. Remove cups from oven, raise temperature to 350° F. and return them to oven to bake about 20 minutes. *Make 12 cupcakes.*

For flourless batter base for cupcakes see under Piecrust.

## OATMEAL SHORTBREAD

3½ cups oatmeal
¼ cup wholewheat flour
⅓ cup honey
⅓ cup oil
½ teaspoon salt
1 teaspoon pure vanilla extract

Mix all ingredients together to make stiff dough. Oil and flour a 9- x 13-inch pan. Press dough firmly into pan. Bake at 325° F. until light brown, about 30 minutes. Cool for 10 minutes, then cut into squares. *Makes 12 squares.*

## OATMEAL FRUIT SQUARES

⅔ cup honey
½ cup oil
1½ cups oatmeal
1 cup wholewheat flour
½ cup wheat germ
3 tablespoons soy flour
⅛ teaspoon salt
2 cups fruit, cut into small pieces

Blend honey and oil. Add flours, wheat germ and salt. Press half of mixture firmly into oiled 7- x 11-inch pan. Spread top with fruit. Cover with remaining mixture. Bake at 400° F. for about 25 minutes. When cool, cut into squares. *Makes 15 small squares.*

## RYE-OATMEAL SQUARES

4 tablespoons honey
⅓ cup oil
2 eggs, beaten
½ teaspoon salt
½ cup rye flour
½ cup oatmeal
1 tablespoon Powdered Fruit Rind
1 cup nuts, coarsely ground

Blend all ingredients together. Turn into oiled 9- x 9-inch pan. Bake at 350° F. for 30 to 35 minutes. Cool and cut into squares. *Makes 16 squares.*

## WHOLEWHEAT-CAROB BROWNIES

½ cup honey
½ cup oil
½ cup carob powder

2 eggs, beaten
2 cups wholewheat flour
¼ teaspoon salt
½ cup Soybeans, Roasted, ground
1 teaspoon pure vanilla extract

Blend honey, oil and carob powder. Gradually add eggs. Stir in flour and salt. Add soybeans and vanilla. Turn into oiled 8- x 8-inch pan. Bake at 350° F. for about 30 minutes. Cool and cut into squares. *Makes 16 squares.*

## NUT SQUARES

1 egg, separated
⅓ cup honey
3 tablespoons wholewheat flour, sifted
⅛ teaspoon salt
½ cup nuts, chopped
¼ cup sesame seeds

Beat egg yolk until thick. Blend in honey. Combine with flour, salt, nuts and seeds. Fold in stiffly beaten egg white. Turn into oiled square pan. Bake at 350° F. for 20 to 25 minutes, until light brown. Cool. Cut into squares. *Makes 9 squares.*

## NUT STICKS

⅓ cup oil
1 cup wholewheat flour (for crust)
¼ cup wheat germ (for crust)
½ cup honey
2 eggs, beaten
4 tablespoons wholewheat flour (for batter)
4 tablespoons wheat germ (for batter)
¼ teaspoon salt
1 cup nuts, coarsely ground
¼ cup sunflower seeds, hulled

Mix oil, 1 cup flour and ¼ cup wheat germ. Pat this crumb mixture into bottom of oiled 8- x 12-inch pan. Blend rest of ingredients to-

gether for batter. Pour over crust. Bake at 325° F. for about 25 minutes. Cool and cut into long sticks. *Makes 24 sticks.*

## ALMOND SQUARES

⅓ cup honey
⅓ cup oil
½ cup wholewheat flour
½ cup soy flour
½ cup wheat germ
1 tablespoon nutritional yeast
2 eggs, beaten
½ cup almonds, ground
1 cup Coconut Shreds
½ cup dried fruit, chopped

Blend honey and oil. Stir in flours, wheat germ and yeast. Pat mixture into bottom of oiled 8- x 12-inch pan. Bake in 350° F. oven for 10 minutes. Remove from oven and let cool. Beat eggs, almonds, coconut shreds and fruit together. Pour mixture over baked crust, return to oven and bake at 350° F. another 25 minutes. Cut into squares when cool. *Makes 12 squares.*

## FILLED FRUIT BARS
### (Dates or Figs)

DOUGH:

½ cup honey
½ cup oil
1½ cups mixed whole-grain flours (rye, buckwheat, corn, wheat)
1¼ cups oatmeal
½ teaspoon salt
1 egg, beaten

Combine honey and oil. Add rest of ingredients. Mix until batter has a crumblike texture. Spread half the batter in oiled rectangular pan. Cover with filling below.

FILLING:

1½ cups dates or figs, pitted, chopped

[Recipe continued on next page]

[Recipe continued from previous page]

⅔ cup unsweetened prune juice
¼ cup honey
2 tablespoons lemon juice
rind of 1 lemon, grated

Combine all ingredients in saucepan. Cook gently until thick. Cool.
After fruit filling is spread over dough, cover with remaining dough. Bake at 400° F. for 20 to 25 minutes. When cool, cut into bars. *Makes 24 bars.*

LEFTOVER CAKE AND CAKE CRUMBS
Crumble stale cake and use crumbs as topping for fresh fruit or puddings. Use also as base for crumb pastry shells.
Cake crumbs may be thoroughly dried by heating slowly in low oven. Store in tightly capped container. Cake crumbs and cooky crumbs can be combined and stored together.
See also Rhubarb Brown Betty; Raisin-Ginger Pudding.

# Cake Fillings

Most cake fillings can be prepared easily in a blender.

## RAISIN FILLING

1½ cups seedless raisins
¾ cup sweet cider
¼ cup molasses
2 tablespoons wholewheat flour
1 tablespoon nutritional yeast
½ teaspoon cinnamon, ground
⅛ teaspoon cloves, ground
1 tablespoon oil
½ teaspoon lemon rind

Blend all ingredients together in blender until smooth. Good with yeast cakes. *Makes about 2¾ cups (enough to fill 2 cakes).*

## ALMOND FILLING

2 cups almonds (or other nuts)
½ cup unsweetened orange juice
½ cup honey

Blend all ingredients to a smooth paste in blender. Store in covered jar in refrigerator until used. Good with yeast cakes. *Makes about 3 cups (enough to fill 2 cakes).*

## DATE FILLING

¾ cup dates, pitted and chopped
⅓ cup wholewheat flour
1 tablespoon soy flour
¾ cup yoghurt *
1 egg
½ cup honey

Combine all ingredients in top of double boiler. Cook gently over hot water until thick. Cool. Use as filling for layer or yeast cakes. *Makes about 2¾ cups (enough to fill 2 cakes).*

## FIG FILLING

2 cups figs, ground
½ cup honey
2 tablespoons unsweetened prune juice
1 tablespoon lemon juice
1 tablespoon orange juice

Combine all ingredients in a saucepan. Cook for 15 minutes, stirring constantly. Cool. Use as filling in yeast cakes. *Makes about 2½ cups (enough for 2 cakes).*

LEFTOVER FILLING
Use as cooky garnishes or pudding topping. Blend with sandwich

spreads where sweet spread is desired. Add to muffin batter, pastry tarts or hollowed center of baked apples.

# Cake Frostings

### HONEY FROSTING (uncooked)

1 egg white
⅛ teaspoon salt
½ cup warm honey
½ teaspoon pure almond extract

Beat egg white with rotary beater. Add salt. Continue to beat. Pour honey in thin stream over egg-white mixture, then add flavoring, continuing to beat meanwhile until thick and fluffy. *Will cover one 9-inch layer.*

### HONEY MERINGUE (uncooked)

1 egg white
½ cup honey

Beat egg white with rotary beater until it begins to froth. Add honey gradually, beating until meringue stands high in peaks. This will take 5 to 10 minutes. Use to top cakes or puddings.

VARIATIONS:
Flavor meringue with 1 teaspoon Powdered Fruit Rind.
Tint meringue with 1 teaspoon unsweetened grape or cranberry juice.

### HONEY SAUCE

⅔ cup honey
½ cup oil
2 tablespoons wholewheat flour
2 eggs, beaten
½ cup lemon juice
1 cup yoghurt *

Blend honey, oil, flour and eggs in top of double boiler. Cook gently over hot water, stirring frequently, until thickened. Remove from heat. Add lemon juice. Cool. Fold in yoghurt. Serve over plain cake or pudding.

### HONEY HARD SAUCE (uncooked)

⅓ cup butter, softened
¾ cup honey
1 teaspoon lemon juice

Cream butter. Beat in honey gradually. Add lemon juice. Chill. Serve over plain cake or pudding.

### BOILED HONEY FROSTING

1½ cups honey
⅛ teaspoon salt
2 egg whites, beaten stiff

Add salt to honey and cook to 238° F. or until honey will spin thread or make soft ball when dropped into cold water. Pour hot honey in thin stream over egg whites, beating meanwhile with rotary beater until all honey has been added and frosting stands in peaks. Spread over cake.

### TINTED CREAM CHEESE FROSTING

Blend cream cheese with small amount of unsweetened grape juice or cranberry juice. Frost plain cake or cupcakes.

### TINTED COCONUT SHRED FROSTING

1 cup Coconut Shreds
3 tablespoons unsweetened grape or cranberry juice
Boiled Honey Frosting (see above)

[Recipe continued on next page]

[Recipe continued from previous page]

Tint Coconut Shreds in juice. Frost cake or cupcakes with Boiled Honey Frosting and top with tinted shreds. *Will frost 1 cake.*

# Frostings Prepared in Blender

The next six frostings are made by combining all ingredients in blender and blending until smooth.

## HONEY-APRICOT FROSTING

1 recipe Boiled Honey Frosting
⅔ cup dried apricots
¼ teaspoon pure almond extract
¼ teaspoon pure lemon extract

*Will frost 1 cake.*

## RAISIN-YOGHURT FROSTING

¼ cup yoghurt *
¼ cup unsweetened orange juice
rind of 1 orange
1 teaspoon lemon juice
¾ cup honey
½ cup seedless raisins

*Will frost 1 loaf cake.*

## BANANA FROSTING

2 bananas, well ripened
1 teaspoon lemon juice
2 tablespoons oil
½ teaspoon pure vanilla extract
¼ teaspoon salt
¾ cup honey

*Will frost 2 9-inch layers.*

## LEMON-ORANGE FROSTING

2 tablespoons unsweetened orange juice
rind of 1 orange
rind of 1 lemon
2 tablespoons lemon juice
3 tablespoons oil
1 egg yolk
⅛ teaspoon salt
⅔ cup honey

*Will frost 1 cake.*

## CAROB FROSTING

⅓ cup carob powder
⅔ cup milk powder
2 tablespoons oil
¼ cup honey
4 tablespoons top milk
1 teaspoon pure vanilla extract

*Will frost 1 cake.*

## PEANUT BUTTER FROSTING

¼ cup peanut butter *
2 tablespoons oil
⅓ cup honey
¼ cup warm milk

*Will frost 2 8-inch layers.*

GARNISHES FOR FROSTINGS:
Soybeans, Roasted ground
nuts, whole or ground
wheat germ
seeds (sunflower, poppy, anise, fennel, ginger, coriander, cumin)
ground spices (nutmeg, ginger, clove, mace, allspice, sesame, cinnamon, cardamom)
fresh berries
fresh cherries
Coconut Shreds
dried fruits, chopped fine

Powdered Fruit Rind
Honeyed Fruit Rind
carob powder
cake or cooky crumbs
angelica leaves
mint leaves

LEFTOVER FROSTING
Use to garnish cookies; to top puddings or ice cream; in pastry tarts. Blend with sandwich spreads or beverages, where sweet taste is desired.

# 22
## COOKIES

Milk powder may be added in great quantity to cooky batters. In some recipes up to 10 times more milk may be used in dry form than in liquid. Since cookies containing large quantities of milk powder brown more quickly than those made with liquid milk, they generally require lower baking temperatures.

When using soy flour in cookies, substitute 2 tablespoons of soy flour for 2 tablespoons of whole-grain flour in each cupful of flour. Soy grits may be substituted for all, or part, of nuts in recipes.

Bake on cooky sheets or inverted baking pans. Oil sheets or pans lightly when baking cookies that are low in oil, or those that contain molasses or a large quantity of milk. Soy lecithin spread is good for oiling cooky sheets.

When baking drop cookies, space 2 inches apart in pan. Between batches, scrape pans clean with spatula or wipe with paper towel. Test for doneness by touching lightly with finger—if no print remains, cookies are done. Remove with spatula and place on cooling rack. Let cool in single layers.

Soft cookies will keep moist and fresh in a tightly covered container. Add a piece of apple or orange to help keep them moist. Rolled and refrigerator cookies will remain crisp if stored in a loosely covered container. To preserve individual flavor, store one variety only to a container.

Cookies can be made successfully without baking powder.

FLAVORINGS FOR COOKIES:
crushed seeds (fennel, ginger, cardamom, poppy, cumin, coriander, etc.)
ground spices (ginger, mace, cinnamon, allspice, clove, nutmeg, etc.)
pure extract of vanilla

### RAW FRUIT-CAROB COOKIES

2 cups dates, pitted
1 cup seedless raisins
carob powder

Grind dates and raisins together. Add as much carob powder as mixture will hold. When dough is stiff enough, roll out and cut into wafers. Expose to sunshine for several hours to dry slightly. *Makes 2 dozen cookies.*

## FRUIT COOKIES
(apple, pineapple or peach)

¼ cup honey
½ cup oil
1 egg, beaten
¾ cup fruit, drained (thick, un-
    sweetened applesauce, fresh
    pineapple or unsweetened
    stewed peaches, cut fine)
½ teaspoon cinnamon, ground
½ teaspoon salt
2½ cups wholewheat flour (about)
1 cup oatmeal
1 cup seedless raisins, chopped or
    whole

Blend honey and oil. Add egg and
fruit. Mix well. Sift together dry
ingredients. Stir into fruit mixture.
Add raisins. Dough should be of
drop consistency. If too thick, add
more fruit; if too thin, add more
flour. Drop by teaspoonfuls onto
lightly oiled cooky sheet. Bake at
400° F. until light brown in color,
15 to 20 minutes. *Makes 4 dozen
2-inch cookies.*

## LEMON COOKIES (or orange)

½ cup honey
½ cup oil
3 tablespoons orange rind, grated
3 tablespoons lemon rind, grated
1 tablespoon lemon juice (or
    orange juice)
1 egg, beaten, and 1 egg white
2½ cups wholewheat flour (about)
½ cup wheat germ
¼ cup nuts, ground, or Soybeans,
    Roasted and ground

Blend honey and oil. Combine with
rinds and fruit juice. Beat in whole
egg. Add remaining ingredients, except egg white and nuts. Batter
should be stiff. If not, add more
flour. Roll out and cut into rounds
or any desired shape. Brush tops

with egg white and sprinkle with
nuts or soybeans. Arrange on oiled
cooky sheet. Bake at 350° F. until
light brown, about 10 minutes.
*Makes 4 dozen cookies.*

## DATE-COCONUT COOKIES

½ cup honey
½ cup oil
2 cups wholewheat flour (about)
2 cups oatmeal
⅔ cup sweet cider
1 teaspoon pure vanilla extract
½ teaspoon salt
½ cup nuts, ground
1 cup dates, pitted and chopped
½ cup Coconut Shreds

Blend honey and oil. Add flours and
rest of ingredients. Drop by teaspoonfuls onto lightly oiled cooky
sheet. Bake at 350° F. for 10 to 15
minutes. *Makes 4 dozen cookies.*

## BANANA-OATMEAL COOKIES
(in blender)

½ cup nuts
½ cup honey
½ cup oil
1 egg
2 large bananas
1¾ cups oatmeal
1½ cups wholewheat flour (about)
1 teaspoon salt
¼ teaspoon nutmeg, ground
¾ teaspoon cinnamon, ground

Grind nuts in blender. Turn into
bowl. Blend honey, oil, egg and
bananas. Add to nuts and mix thoroughly. Combine with rest of ingredients to make a stiff batter. If too
thick, add unsweetened fruit juice;
if too thin, more flour. Drop by teaspoonfuls onto lightly oiled cooky
sheet. Bake at 400° F., about 15 minutes. *Makes 4 dozen cookies.*

## COCONUT-OATMEAL COOKIES

3 eggs
½ cup honey
2 tablespoons oil
¾ teaspoon pure vanilla extract
1 cup Coconut Shreds
2 cups oatmeal flour

Beat eggs. Add remaining ingredients. Blend thoroughly. Drop by half-teaspoonfuls onto oiled cooky sheet. Bake at 350° F., about 8 minutes. *Makes 4 dozen cookies.*

## MOLASSES COOKIES

½ cup oil
⅓ cup honey
1 egg
½ cup molasses
¼ cup milk
1 cup wholewheat flour
½ cup powdered milk
½ cup wheat germ
½ teaspoon salt
½ teaspoon cinnamon, ground
½ teaspoon ginger, ground
1 teaspoon Powdered Orange Rind
3 tablespoons sesame seeds

Blend all ingredients. Drop by half-teaspoonfuls onto oiled cooky sheet. Bake at 350° F., about 12 minutes. *Makes 4 dozen cookies.*

## GOLDEN COOKIES

½ cup molasses
⅓ cup oil
1 cup sweet potatoes (or carrots, pumpkin or squash), cooked, mashed
2 eggs, beaten
1 cup wholewheat flour (about)
½ cup wheat germ
2 tablespoons nutritional yeast
1 cup milk powder
1 teaspoon salt
¼ teaspoon each, ground: cinnamon, nutmeg, mace, allspice, ginger

Blend molasses and oil. Add rest of ingredients. Batter should be stiff. If too thick, add unsweetened fruit juice; if too thin, more flour. Drop by teaspoonfuls onto lightly oiled cooky sheet. Bake at 350° F. until lightly browned, about 15 minutes. *Makes 4 dozen cookies.*

VARIATIONS:
Add to batter ½ cup pitted prunes, chopped; or ½ cup raisins; or 2 teaspoons grated orange or lemon rind.
Substitute ¼ cup oatmeal for ½ cup wheat germ.

## CARROT-MOLASSES COOKIES

½ cup molasses
2 tablespoons oil
1 cup grated raw carrots or
½ cup cooked, mashed carrots
1½ cups wholewheat flour (about)
½ cup soy flour
2 tablespoons nutritional yeast
½ teaspoon cinnamon, ground
½ teaspoon nutmeg, ground
1 cup nuts, coarsely broken
1 cup dates, pitted and chopped
2 tablespoons nutritional yeast

Blend molasses and oil. Add rest of ingredients to make stiff batter. If too thick, add unsweetened fruit juice; if too thin, more flour. Drop by teaspoonfuls onto lightly oiled cooky sheet. Bake at 350° F., about 15 minutes. *Makes 4 dozen cookies.*

## WHOLEWHEAT-OATMEAL COOKIES

½ cup honey
½ cup oil
2 eggs, beaten
1 teaspoon pure vanilla extract
1 cup oatmeal
1 cup wholewheat flour (about)

½ teaspoon salt
½ cup Soybeans, Roasted, ground

Blend honey and oil. Beat in eggs and vanilla; stir in flours, salt and soybeans. Batter should be stiff. If too thick, add milk; if too thin, more flour. Roll in waxed paper and refrigerate for a few hours. Slice thin. Place on lightly oiled cooky sheet. Bake at 375° F. until lightly browned, 10 to 15 minutes. *Makes 4 dozen cookies.*

## WHOLEWHEAT COOKIES

½ cup honey
½ cup oil
2 eggs, beaten
½ teaspoon pure vanilla extract
2 cups wholewheat flour (about)
½ cup nuts, chopped

Blend honey and oil. Beat in eggs. Add vanilla, flour and nuts and blend well. Batter should be stiff. If too thick, add unsweetened fruit juice; if too thin, more flour. Drop by teaspoonfuls onto lightly oiled cooky sheet. Flatten cookies with bottom of glass dipped each time in cold water. Bake at 375° F. for 10 to 12 minutes. *Makes 4 dozen cookies.*

## RYE-HONEY COOKIES

2 cups honey
1 cup rye flour (about)
1 cup wholewheat flour
¼ teaspoon cloves, ground
1 teaspoon ginger, ground
1 tablespoon unsweetened fruit
    juice (about)
½ teaspoon anise seeds, crushed

Heat honey to boil. Sift flours into warm skillet over low heat, stirring constantly so flours will not brown. Add spices. Mix quickly. Quickly stir part of flour into hot honey. Add rest of flour and other ingredients to honey mixture. Stir with wooden spoon. Beat until dough comes off spoon easily. Shape into long roll and chill. Cut in slices ½-inch thick. Place on oiled and floured cooky sheet. Bake at 325° F. until light brown, about 30 minutes. Cookies should be quite dry. *Makes 4 dozen cookies.*

## OATMEAL COOKIES

⅓ cup honey
1 tablespoon oil
2 eggs, beaten
1 tablespoon Powdered Fruit Rind
½ teaspoon salt
1½ cups oatmeal (about)

Blend honey, oil and eggs; stir in rest of ingredients. Dough should be stiff. If too thick, add milk; if too thin, more oatmeal. Drop by teaspoonfuls onto lightly oiled cooky sheet. Bake at 400° F. until golden brown, for 8 to 10 minutes. *Makes 3 dozen cookies.*

VARIATIONS:
Add ½ cup of one of the following to batter: Coconut Shreds, chopped dates, raisins or figs; chopped nuts; Roasted, ground Soybeans.
Substitute ½ cup cornmeal for ½ cup oatmeal.

## OATMEAL SQUARES

4 tablespoons honey
4 tablespoons oil
2 eggs, beaten
1 cup oatmeal (about)
1 cup wholewheat flour
¼ teaspoon cinnamon, ground
¼ teaspoon allspice, ground
rind of 1 lemon, grated

[Recipe continued on next page]

[Recipe continued from previous page]

Blend honey, oil and eggs. Stir in flours, spices, rind. Dough should be quite stiff. If too thick, add milk; if too thin, more oatmeal. Pat about ½-inch thick into oiled pan. Bake at 375° F. for about 20 minutes. When cool, cut into squares. *Makes 9 squares.*

## RICE FLOUR COOKIES

1 cup rice flour
½ cup oil
4 tablespoons honey
¼ teaspoon pure vanilla extract
1 egg, slightly beaten
1 cup nuts, ground

Blend all ingredients thoroughly. Chill for several hours or overnight. Roll into balls the size of walnuts. Arrange on well-oiled cooky sheet. Press flat with bottom of glass. Bake at 350° F., about 12 minutes. *Makes 2 dozen cookies.*

## SOY COOKIES

¾ cup honey
½ cup oil
¼ teaspoon salt
½ teaspoon cardamom, crushed
2 eggs
3 tablespoons soy flour
1½ cups Soybeans, Roasted, ground

Blend honey and oil. Add salt and cardamom. Blend in eggs, 1 at a time. Stir in flour and soybeans. Drop by teaspoonfuls onto oiled cooky sheet, 2 inches apart. Bake at 300° F. until golden brown, about 10 minutes. *Makes 2 dozen cookies.*

## FLOURLESS SOY COOKIES

2 eggs
1 cup raw sugar

½ teaspoon anise seeds, crushed
3 cups Soybeans, Roasted, ground
½ teaspoon salt

Beat eggs. Add sugar, anise seeds, soybeans and salt. Dough should be stiff. Drop by teaspoonfuls onto oiled cooky sheet 2 inches apart. Pat to ¼-inch thickness by pressing with bottom of glass wet each time in cold water. Bake at 350° F. until brown, about 10 minutes. *Makes 4 dozen cookies.*

## SOY-WHOLEWHEAT COOKIES

½ cup honey
½ cup oil
3 eggs, beaten
1 teaspoon salt
2 tablespoons nutritional yeast
1 teaspoon coriander seeds, crushed
1 cup soy flour
1½ cups wholewheat flour (about)
½ cup nuts, chopped

Blend honey and oil. Add eggs, salt, yeast and seeds. Beat well. Stir in flours and nuts. Dough should be stiff. If too thick, add milk; if too thin, add more wholewheat flour. Drop by teaspoonfuls onto lightly oiled cooky sheet. Press cookies down with tines of fork and make crisscross design. Bake at 350° F., about 15 minutes. *Makes 4 dozen cookies.*

## YOGHURT COOKIES
### (or sour cream)

⅓ cup honey
3 tablespoons oil
⅓ cup yoghurt* or sour cream* (about)
1 teaspoon pure vanilla extract
2 eggs, beaten
1¼ cups wholewheat flour (about)
½ cup seedless raisins

Blend honey and oil. Mix in vanilla, eggs and half the yoghurt. When well blended, stir in rest of yoghurt and flour. Dough should be stiff. If too thick, add more yoghurt; if too thin, more flour. Using half the batter, drop by half-teaspoonfuls onto lightly oiled cooky sheet. Place a few raisins on top of each cooky. Drop remaining batter by half-teaspoonfuls on top of cookies, so that raisins are enclosed in batter. Bake at 400° F., about 8 to 10 minutes. These cookies will be soft rather than crisp. *Makes 2 dozen cookies.*

## CREAM CHEESE COOKIES

¼ cup honey
⅓ cup oil
½ cup cream cheese*
1 cup wholewheat flour (about)
¼ teaspoon salt
3 tablespoons poppy seeds

Blend honey, oil and cream cheese. Stir in flour, salt and seeds. Dough should be stiff. If too thick, add milk; if too thin, more flour. Shape into long rolls. Wrap in wax paper. Chill. Cut into thin slices. Place on oiled cooky sheets. Bake at 400° F. for 5 to 8 minutes. *Makes 2 dozen cookies.*

## SESAME COOKIES

½ cup honey
½ cup oil
2 eggs, beaten
¼ teaspoon salt
1 cup sesame seeds
1 teaspoon cumin seeds, crushed
rind of 1 orange, grated
1½ cups wholewheat flour (about)

Blend honey and oil. Add eggs, salt, seeds and rind. Stir in flour. Dough should be stiff. If too thick, add unsweetened fruit juice; if too thin, more flour. Drop by teaspoonfuls onto oiled cooky sheet. Bake at 375° F., about 8 minutes. *Makes 4 dozen cookies.*

## SESAME-OATMEAL CRISPS

½ cup honey
½ cup oil
1 egg, beaten
2 tablespoons milk
1¼ cups oatmeal
1¼ cups wholewheat flour (about)
1 teaspoon cinnamon, ground
¼ teaspoon salt
¾ cup sesame seeds
½ cup seedless raisins, chopped

Blend honey, oil and egg. Stir in milk, flours, cinnamon, salt, seeds and raisins. Blend well. Dough should be stiff. If too thick, add more milk; if too thin, more flour. Drop by teaspoonfuls onto oiled cooky sheet. Flatten with the bottom of a glass dipped in cold water each time. Bake at 375° F., about 10 minutes. *Makes 4 dozen crisps.*

## PECAN COOKIES

½ cup honey
½ cup oil
2 eggs, beaten
¼ cup milk
½ teaspoon salt
½ teaspoon fennel, crushed
2 cups wholewheat flour (about)
¾ cup pecans (or other nuts), ground
¾ cup seedless raisins, chopped

Blend honey, oil and eggs. Add milk, salt and fennel. Stir in flour, nuts and raisins. Dough should be stiff. If too thick, add more milk; if too thin, more flour. Drop by teaspoonfuls onto oiled cooky sheet. Bake at 350° F. for about 15 minutes. *Makes 4 dozen cookies.*

## COCONUT-NUT COOKIES

½ cup honey
2 eggs, separated
1 cup Coconut Shreds
1 cup dates, pitted and cut
2 cups nuts, ground
½ cup wheat germ
additional Coconut Shreds for
   rolling

Blend honey and egg yolks. Add coconut shreds, dates, nuts and wheat germ. Blend thoroughly. Fold in stiffly beaten egg whites. Dough should be stiff. If too thick, add milk; if too thin, add more wheat germ. Roll into balls and coat with coconut shreds. Flatten each cooky and arrange on oiled cooky sheet. Bake at 325° F. until lightly browned, 15 to 20 minutes. Do not remove from cooky sheet until completely cool. *Makes 3 dozen cookies.*

## NUT COOKIES

2 eggs, separated
½ cup honey
1 cup nuts, ground
6 tablespoons wholewheat flour
   (about)
¼ teaspoon salt
¼ teaspoon ginger, ground

Beat egg yolks until thick. Add honey gradually. Blend in nuts, flour, salt and ginger. Fold in stiffly beaten egg whites. Dough should be stiff. If too thick, add unsweetened fruit juice; if too thin, more flour. Drop by teaspoonfuls onto oiled cooky sheet. Bake at 350° F., about 10 minutes. *Makes 1 dozen cookies.*

## FILBERT COOKIES (flourless)

3 cups filberts (or other nuts),
   ground
2 eggs

½ cup honey
¼ teaspoon salt
½ teaspoon pure vanilla extract

Blend all ingredients. Chill for 3 hours. Roll into small balls, the size of hickory nuts. Arrange on oiled cooky sheet. Bake at 325° F. for about 15 minutes. *Makes 4 dozen cookies.*

## ALMOND COOKIES

¼ cup honey
½ cup oil
1 egg, beaten
1 teaspoon pure almond extract
rind of 1 lemon, grated
½ teaspoon cinnamon, ground
½ teaspoon nutmeg, ground
¼ teaspoon allspice, ground
2 cups wholewheat flour (about)
¾ cup almonds (or other nuts),
   ground

Blend honey, oil and egg. Add extract, rind and spices. Stir in flour and almonds. Dough should be stiff. If too thick, add milk; if too thin, more flour. Shape into long rolls. Wrap in wax paper and chill for 4 hours or overnight. Slice thin. Arrange on oiled cooky sheet. Bake at 350° F. for 5 to 8 minutes. When done, cookies should be light brown. *Makes 8 dozen 2-inch cookies.*

## PEANUT BUTTER DANDIES
(uncooked)

½ cup honey
½ cup peanut butter *
2 tablespoons nutritional yeast
¾ cup milk powder
¾ cup wheat germ

Blend all ingredients together. Chill. Shape into balls the size of walnuts. If desired, roll each ball in additional wheat germ, Coconut Shreds, ground nuts or Roasted, ground Soybeans. *Makes 2 dozen balls.*

## CHRISTMAS SPICE COOKIES

1 cup molasses
½ cup oil
¾ teaspoon ginger, ground
¾ teaspoon cinnamon, ground
¼ teaspoon clove, ground
¼ teaspoon nutmeg, ground
¼ teaspoon allspice, ground
¼ teaspoon mace, ground
1 cup milk powder
3 tablespoons nutritional yeast
4½ cups wholewheat flour (about)

Blend molasses and oil. Add rest of ingredients, using hands to mix this stiff dough. Chill. Roll dough very thin. Cut into fancy shapes on well-floured board. Arrange on oiled cooky sheet. Bake at 375° F. for 6 to 8 minutes. These cookies should be made from 2 months to 2 weeks before Christmas to allow time for them to "ripen." *Makes 5 dozen cookies.*

VARIATION:
Add Honeyed or Powdered Fruit Rind.

## VANILLA COOKIES

⅓ cup honey
½ cup oil
1 egg, beaten
1 teaspoon pure vanilla extract
¾ cup wholewheat flour (about)

Blend oil, honey, egg and vanilla. Stir in flour. Dough should be stiff. If too thick, add unsweetened fruit juice; if too thin, more flour. Drop by teaspoonfuls, two inches apart, onto oiled baking sheet. Bake at 375° F., about 15 minutes, until edges of cookies are brown. *Makes 3 dozen cookies.*

## SPRINGERLE

2 eggs
½ cup honey
2 cups wholewheat flour
1 tablespoon anise seeds, crushed

Beat eggs until light. Gradually add honey. Blend thoroughly. Add flour and anise seeds. Use hands to mix until dough is stiff and smooth. Roll out to ¼-inch thickness. Press springerle form over dough to impress patterns. Cut into squares. Arrange squares close together on un-oiled cooky sheets. Allow to remain on sheets 8 hours or overnight. Then bake at 325° F. for about 10 minutes, or until light brown. *Makes 5 dozen cookies.*

## BUTTER COOKIES

1 cup butter, softened
½ cup honey
2 egg yolks, hard-cooked
2 egg yolks, raw
3½ cups wholewheat flour (about)
juice and rind of ½ lemon
¼ teaspoon salt
¼ teaspoon cardamom, crushed

Blend all ingredients together. Dough should be stiff. If too thick, add more lemon juice; if too thin, more flour. Chill. Roll out on floured board. Cut into fancy shapes and arrange on unoiled cooky sheet. Bake at 375° F. for about 10 minutes. *Makes 5 dozen cookies.*

## EGGLESS COOKIES

½ cup honey
½ cup oil
2 cups wholewheat flour (about)
½ teaspoon cinnamon, ground
¼ teaspoon allspice, ground
¼ teaspoon nutmeg, ground

[Recipe continued on next page]

[Recipe continued from previous page]

Blend honey and oil and heat for 1 minute. When cool, add rest of ingredients, which have been sifted together several times. Dough should be stiff. If too thick, add unsweetened fruit juice; if too thin, more flour. Chill. Roll out to 1/4-inch thickness. Cut with cooky cutter. Arrange on oiled cooky sheet. Bake at 350° F. for 12 to 15 minutes. *Makes 4 dozen cookies.*

## TEETHING COOKIES FOR BABIES

2 tablespoons honey
2 tablespoons molasses
2 tablespoons oil
1 egg yolk, beaten
1 teaspoon pure vanilla extract
1/4 teaspoon salt
1 tablespoon soy flour
1 scant cup wholewheat flour (about)
1 tablespoon wheat germ

Blend honey, molasses, oil and egg yolk. Stir in vanilla, salt, flours, and wheat germ. Dough should be stiff. If too thick, add milk; if too thin, more flour. Roll dough to 1/4-inch thickness. Cut into rectangular pieces 1 × 1 1/2 inches. Place on unoiled cooky sheet. Bake at 350° F. until lightly browned, 15 to 20 minutes. *Makes 4 dozen 2-inch cookies.*

VARIATION:
Milk powder may be added to this dough.

LEFTOVER COOKIES
Grind into crumbs and store like cake crumbs. Moist crumbs should be dried in a slow oven before storing. Use as topping for puddings and fruits, or in preparing unbaked pastry shells.

# 23
# PASTRIES

## Piecrusts

HINTS:

Piecrusts are in general easier to handle if they are chilled before rolling out, or rolled between sheets of wax paper or on pastry cloth.

Potato water can be used as liquid in piecrusts.

To vary piecrusts and pie shells, add one or more of the following:

wheat germ
sunflower meal
sesame seeds
bone meal
ground nuts
milk powder
rice polishings
crushed seeds, such as fennel, ginger, cardamom, poppy, cumin, coriander
soy flour
ground, Roasted Soybeans
nutritional yeast
cake or cracker crumbs
dried fruit, ground fine
Powdered Fruit Rind
grated cheese
ground spices (especially for fruit pies) such as ginger, mace, cinnamon, allspice, clove, nutmeg

## WHOLEWHEAT PIECRUST No. 1

1½ cups wholewheat flour
½ teaspoon salt
½ cup oil
3 tablespoons ice water

Sift together flour and salt. Blend in oil. Add water. Mix thoroughly until it forms a ball of dough. Divide in half. Roll out each half ⅛ inch thick on floured board. Bake at 425° F. for 15 to 20 minutes. Cool. Fill. *Makes 2 9-inch piecrusts.*

## WHOLEWHEAT PIECRUST No. 2

½ cup boiling water
1 cup oil
2 cups wholewheat flour
¾ teaspoon salt

Pour boiling water over oil. Blend. Sift flour and salt. Stir into liquid. Mix thoroughly. Chill for 30 minutes. Divide and roll out on pastry cloth. Follow favorite recipe for filling and baking. *Makes 2 9-inch crusts.*

## WHOLEWHEAT-SOY PIECRUST

2 cups wholewheat flour
½ cup soy flour
¾ teaspoon salt

[Recipe continued on next page]

[Recipe continued from previous page]

6 tablespoons oil
2½ tablespoons ice water (about)

Sift flours and salt. Stir in oil. Add enough water to make stiff dough. Roll on floured board. Follow favorite recipe for filling and baking. *Makes 2 9-inch crusts.*

VARIATION:
Rye flour may be substituted for wholewheat.

## YEAST PIECRUST

½ cake or 1 teaspoon dried yeast
⅛ cup lukewarm water
1 egg, beaten
1½ tablespoons oil
⅓ cup milk
¾ teaspoon salt
1½ cups wholewheat flour

Soften yeast in water. Blend egg, oil, milk and salt. Heat to lukewarm. Combine with yeast. Stir in flour and mix well. Turn into oiled bowl. Cover. Set in warm place to rise for 45 minutes. Turn onto floured board. Knead gently. Divide dough in half. Roll thin. Follow favorite recipe for filling and baking. *Makes 2 9-inch crusts.*

## YEAST PIECRUST WITH POTATOES

⅓ cup lukewarm potato water
½ cake or 1 teaspoon dried yeast
4 tablespoons honey
⅓ cup potatoes, cooked, mashed
½ cup oil
1 egg, beaten
¾ teaspoon salt
1 cup wholewheat flour (about)

Soften yeast in potato water. Add honey and potatoes; let rise for 1 hour. Blend in oil, eggs and salt. Add enough flour to make stiff dough. Knead well. Turn into oiled bowl. Cover. Set in warm place until doubled in bulk. Punch down. Roll out in two circles, each about ½ inch thick. Fit dough into two oiled pie pans. Cover with fruit. Set in warm place. Let rise. Bake at 350° F. for 30 to 35 minutes. *Makes 2 9-inch crusts.*

## RYE-RICE PIECRUST

¾ cup rye flour
¾ cup rice flour
½ teaspoon salt
½ cup oil
4 tablespoons ice water (about)

Sift flours and salt. Stir in oil. Add enough water to make firm dough. Roll out. Follow favorite recipe for filling and baking. *Makes 2 9-inch crusts.*

VARIATION:
Rice polishings may be substituted for part of rice flour.

## NUT PIECRUST

1¾ cups wholewheat flour
½ teaspoon salt
½ cup ground nuts
⅓ cup oil
1 tablespoon honey
¼ cup ice water (about)

Sift flour and salt. Mix with nuts. Stir in oil and honey. Blend. Add enough water to make stiff dough. Roll. Fill and bake at 350° F. for 30 to 35 minutes. *Makes 2 9-inch crusts.*

## CREAM CHEESE PIECRUST
(or cottage cheese)

¼ pound cream cheese *
1 cup oil
1 cup wholewheat flour (about)

Blend cream or cottage cheese and oil. Stir in enough flour to make firm dough. Chill. Roll. This dough may be used for pies, or cut into squares or triangles and filled with fruit (drained of juice) or meat, fish, cheese or egg spreads. Bake at 350° F. for 30 to 35 minutes. *Makes 1 9-inch piecrust.*

## CHEDDAR CHEESE PIECRUST

Prepare desired piecrust. After dough has been rolled out, sprinkle with ½ cup grated cheese. Roll up like double jelly roll, starting at opposite sides and rolling toward center. Fold ends to meet at center. Fold in half again. By now, pastry is folded into small square. Roll out once more. Cheese should now be evenly distributed throughout crust. This crust is especially good as top crust over apple pie.

## SOY-CHEESE PIECRUST

1 cup soy flour
1 teaspoon salt
1 tablespoon nutritional yeast
2 egg yolks, beaten
3 tablespoons milk
5 tablespoons cheese, grated

Sift flour, salt and yeast. Blend egg yolks with milk. Gradually add liquids to sifted ingredients. Work in cheese. When blended thoroughly, chill. Roll dough thin. Follow favorite recipe for filling and baking. *Makes 1 9-inch piecrust.*

## FLOURLESS BATTER BASE

3 eggs, separated
1 cup powdered milk
4 tablespoons milk

Beat egg yolks. Stir in powdered milk. Gradually add liquid milk,

continuing to beat. Fold in stiffly beaten egg whites. Mix with rotary beater until smooth (this takes a long time). This batter may be used for pastries, and to top meat, fowl, fish and vegetable casseroles.

VARIATION:
Sweeten dough with 2 tablespoons honey and use for fruit tarts, muffins, cup cakes.

# Pie Shells

## WHEAT GERM PIE SHELL (unbaked)

½ cup wheat germ
¾ cup wholewheat cracker or cake crumbs
⅓ cup oil
1 tablespoon honey

Blend all ingredients. Press into 9-inch pie pan. Chill and fill.

## WHOLEWHEAT-RAISIN PIE SHELL

1½ cups wholewheat flour
½ cup raisins, chopped fine
3 tablespoons oil
pinch of allspice, ground

Blend all ingredients. Press into 9-inch pie pan. Chill and fill. Bake.

## RYE PIE SHELL

2 cups rye flour
½ teaspoon salt
1 tablespoon poppy seeds
½ cup oil
small amount ice water

Sift flour and salt. Add seeds. Stir in oil. Add enough water to make firm dough. Press into 9-inch pie pan. Chill and fill. Bake.

## ZWIEBACK PIE SHELL (unbaked)

1 cup Zwieback crumbs
⅓ cup oil
¼ teaspoon lemon juice
pinch of nutmeg, ground

Blend all ingredients. Press into 9-inch pie pan. Chill and fill.

## CAKE CRUMB PIE SHELL (unbaked)

1½ cups cake and cooky crumbs, or wholewheat breadcrumbs, sweetened with
1 tablespoon honey
½ cup oil

Blend ingredients. Press into 9-inch pie pan. Chill and fill.

## CORNMEAL PIE SHELL

½ cup cornmeal
¾ cup cake and cooky crumbs
⅓ cup oil

Blend all ingredients. Press into 9-inch pie pan. Chill and fill. Bake.

## NUT-CRUMB PIE SHELL (unbaked)

½ cup nuts, ground
½ cup cake and cooky crumbs
⅓ cup oil

Blend all ingredients. Press into 9-inch pie pan. Chill and fill.

## BRAZIL NUT PIE SHELL (unbaked)

1½ cups Brazil nuts, ground
1 tablespoon oil
1 tablespoon honey
pinch of mace, ground

Blend all ingredients. Press into 9-inch pie pan. Chill and fill.

VARIATION:
Pecans, walnuts or almonds may be substituted for Brazil nuts.

## COCONUT PIE SHELL (unbaked)

1 cup Coconut Shreds
½ cup wheat germ
1 tablespoon honey
1 tablespoon oil

Blend all ingredients. Press into 9-inch pie pan. Chill and fill.

## TOASTED SOYBEAN PIE SHELL

½ cup oil
1 tablespoon hot water
2 tablespoons buttermilk *
1½ tablespoons honey
1¼ cups wholewheat flour
½ teaspoon salt
⅓ cup Soybeans, Roasted, ground

Mix oil, water, buttermilk and honey. Sift flour and salt together over these. Blend into a dough. Roll out 2 circles. Line pie pans. Press ground soybeans into pastry. Prick shells with fork. Bake at 450° F. for 10 to 15 minutes. Cool and fill. *Makes 2 9-inch shells.*

## MUERBE TEIG PIE SHELL

½ cup oil
1 cup wholewheat flour
1 egg yolk, hard-cooked, sieved
1 tablespoon honey
½ teaspoon salt
rind of 1 lemon, grated

Blend all ingredients. Press into 9-inch pie pan. Chill. Bake at 350° F. for 15 minutes or until golden brown. Cool. Fill. *Makes 1 9-inch pie shell or 6 tarts.*

LEFTOVER PASTRY DOUGH
After trimming edges of pies, re-work leftover pieces of dough.

Roll out and cut into squares, circles or triangles. Bake. When cool, top with preserves. Or fill unbaked dough with drained fruit, meat, fish, fowl, egg or cheese spreads and then bake.

# Pie Fillings

HINTS:

Many pie fillings can be served as puddings, without piecrust.

Place drip pan under fruit and berry pies while baking to prevent juices from spilling into oven.

## RAW FRUIT FILLING

Mix mashed bananas with grated apples or other fruits in season. Turn into pie shell. Top with grated nuts or yoghurt.

## FRUIT FILLING FOR DEEP DISH PIE

1 cup cranberries
½ cup raisins
2 apples with skins, cored, quartered
½ cup walnuts

Grind all ingredients together. Turn into deep oven dish lined with pie shell. Bake with meringue or serve with topping of yoghurt.

## FILLING FOR DEEP DISH APPLE PIE

Wash, core and quarter 2 to 3 pounds apples. Leave skins on. Cut into thin slices. Put into oiled deep baking dish. Add few tablespoons of raisins. Drizzle 4 tablespoons honey and 2 teaspoons lemon juice over fruit. Sprinkle with cinnamon

or allspice. Cover with favorite pastry dough. Prick crust to allow steam to escape. Bake at 400° F. for about 40 minutes.

VARIATIONS:

Mix apple slices with sesame seeds, chopped nuts, soy grits, peaches or berries.

## BERRY FILLING

3 cups berries
4 tablespoons honey
1 egg, beaten
1 teaspoon soy flour
½ teaspoon cinnamon, ground
1 tablespoon oil

Blend all ingredients. Turn into pie pan lined with unbaked piecrust. Cover with crisscross strips of pastry dough. Bake at 450° F. for 10 minutes, then at 350° F. for 30 minutes.

## MOLASSES-PRUNE FILLING

2 cups prunes, soaked, pitted, chopped
¼ cup prune juice
½ cup molasses
2 tablespoons nutritional yeast
3 eggs, separated
1 tablespoon lemon juice
1 tablespoon lemon rind, grated
¼ cup oil
pinch of clove, ground

Mix prunes, juice, molasses (reserving 1 tablespoon), yeast, egg yolks, lemon juice, rind, oil and clove. Turn into pie pan lined with unbaked piecrust. Bake at 450° F. for 10 minutes, then at 350° F. for 30 minutes. Cool. Beat egg whites stiff, add reserved tablespoon molasses and beat again. Spread over filling. Place under broiler until meringue is light brown.

## FLUFFY PRUNE FILLING
### (in blender)

1 pound prunes, soaked, pitted
¼ cup unsweetened orange juice
1 teaspoon lemon juice
1 cup nuts
3 tablespoons honey
¼ teaspoon salt
2 egg whites, beaten stiff

Blend prunes, juices and nuts in blender. Stir honey and salt into beaten egg whites and fold into prune mixture. Turn into pie pan lined with unbaked piecrust. Bake at 325° F. for 30 minutes. When cool, top with yoghurt.

## FIG FILLING (in blender)

1 cup figs, dried
1 cup yoghurt *
2 eggs, separated
½ teaspoon cinnamon, ground
½ teaspoon ginger, ground
1 tablespoon honey

Steam figs 5 minutes in vegetable steamer. Reserve liquid for fruit compote. Clip stems off figs. Quarter figs and put into blender. Add yoghurt, egg yolks and spices. Blend until smooth. Turn contents into pie pan lined with unbaked piecrust. Bake in 400° F. oven for about 35 minutes. Remove from oven and cover with meringue made by beating egg whites stiff and blending with honey. Return pie to oven and bake at 325° F. about 15 minutes longer.

## DATE CHIFFON FILLING

1 envelope or 1 tablespoon
    unflavored gelatin
¼ cup sweet cider
1¼ cups milk
2 eggs, separated

⅛ teaspoon salt
1 tablespoon nutritional yeast
¼ teaspoon nutmeg, ground
1 tablespoon Powdered Fruit Rind
1 cup dates, pitted, cut fine
2 tablespoons honey
½ cup heavy cream, whipped

Soften gelatin in cider. Blend milk, egg yolk, salt, yeast and nutmeg in top of double boiler. Cook gently over hot water, stirring constantly, until mixture thickens. Remove from heat and add softened gelatin. Chill. When almost set, stir in rind and dates. Beat egg whites stiff and blend with honey. Fold whipped cream and egg whites into date mixture. Turn into baked, cooled piecrust. Chill until firm.

## STRAWBERRY CHIFFON FILLING

1 envelope or 1 tablespoon
    unflavored gelatin
¼ cup unsweetened orange juice
½ cup sweet cider, hot
1 sprig mint, minced
1 cup fresh strawberries or other
    fruit, sliced or crushed
pinch of salt
1 tablespoon lemon juice
1 cup cream, whipped

Soften gelatin in orange juice. Add hot cider and mint. Stir until dissolved. Cool. When mixture begins to thicken, beat with rotary beater until frothy. Mix fruit with salt and lemon juice and fold, with whipped cream, into gelatin mixture. Turn into baked piecrust. Chill.

## ORANGE-COCONUT FILLING

1 envelope or 1 tablespoon
    unflavored gelatin
½ cup unsweetened orange juice
1 cup milk, hot
rind of 1 orange, grated

rind of 1 lemon, grated
2 tablespoons lemon juice
pinch of salt
dash of cinnamon, ground
2 eggs, separated
4 tablespoons honey
⅓ cup Coconut Shreds

Soften gelatin in orange juice. Add hot milk. Stir until dissolved. Add rinds, lemon juice, salt and cinnamon. When lukewarm, stir in egg yolks. Cool gelatin mixture and when it is thickened slightly, beat with rotary beater until frothy. Fold in egg whites, which have been beaten stiff and blended with honey. Turn into baked piecrust. Sprinkle top with coconut shreds. Chill until firm.

## FROZEN LEMON FILLING

1 envelope or 1 tablespoon
   unflavored gelatin
⅓ cup unsweetened grapefruit
   juice
1 sprig mint, minced
4 eggs, separated
juice and rind of 1 lemon
4 tablespoons honey

Soften gelatin in cold fruit juice in top of double boiler. Then heat over hot water until dissolved. Add mint. When cool, add egg yolks, lemon juice and rind. Blend thoroughly. Chill until thick, then beat with rotary beater. Beat egg whites stiff and blend in honey. Fold egg white and honey into gelatin mixture. Turn into baked piecrust or pie shell. Freeze until firm.

## CARROT-CHIFFON FILLING

1 envelope or 1 tablespoon
   unflavored gelatin
¼ cup milk, cold
½ cup milk, hot

1½ cups carrots, cooked, sieved
¼ teaspoon salt
½ teaspoon ginger, ground
½ teaspoon cinnamon, ground
1 tablespoon nutritional yeast
2 eggs, separated
2 tablespoons honey

Soften gelatin in cold milk. Dissolve in hot milk in top of double boiler. Add carrots, salt, spices and yeast. Cook over hot water until thick. Remove from heat. When lukewarm, beat in egg yolks. Cool. When mixture begins to set, beat with rotary beater. Beat egg whites stiff and blend in honey. Fold egg-white mixture into gelatin. Turn into baked piecrust or pie shell. Chill until firm.

## PUMPKIN CHIFFON FILLING
### (or squash or sweet potato)

1 envelope or 1 tablespoon
   unflavored gelatin
¼ cup sweet cider
½ cup milk, hot
1¼ cups pumpkin, cooked, puréed
3 tablespoons molasses
½ teaspoon ginger, ground
1 teaspoon cinnamon, ground
½ teaspoon nutmeg, ground
¼ teaspoon salt
2 tablespoons nutritional yeast
3 eggs, separated

Soften gelatin in cider. Dissolve in hot milk in top of double boiler. Add pumpkin, molasses, spices, salt and yeast. Cook over hot water until thick. Remove from heat. Cool to lukewarm. Beat in egg yolks. Cool. When mixture begins to set, beat with rotary beater. Fold egg whites, which have been beaten stiff, into gelatin mixture. Turn into baked piecrust or pie shell. Chill until firm.

## SWEET POTATO FILLING
## (or squash or pumpkin)

1½ cups cooked sweet potatoes;
  puréed
⅓ cup honey
½ teaspoon salt
¼ teaspoon allspice, ground
1 tablespoon nutritional yeast
2 eggs, beaten
1 tablespoon lemon juice
1 cup top milk
10 whole pecans

Mix all ingredients except nuts. Turn into pie pan lined with piecrust. Bake at 450° F. for 15 minutes; lower oven to 325° F. and bake for an additional 30 minutes. When cool, decorate top with pecans. Chill until firm.

## CHESTNUT FILLING (flourless)

1½ cups chestnut meal (see
  directions below)
¼ teaspoon salt
2 tablespoons oil
1½ cups water
2 tablespoons raisins, chopped
2 tablespoons pignolias, ground
¼ teaspoon rosemary

To make meal: Shell chestnuts, simmer for 20 minutes or until soft, and put through sieve.
  Mix with remaining ingredients. Pat into piecrust in 9-inch pie plate. Bake at 375° F. for 45 minutes, until top is crisp and piecrust done. This may also be baked and served without crust.

## SPICED SOYBEAN PIE

¾ cup cooked soybean pulp (dried
  soybeans that have been boiled
  and puréed)
¾ cup milk
½ cup honey
¼ teaspoon salt

4 tablespoons wholewheat flour
3 tablespoons nutritional yeast
¼ teaspoon ginger, ground
¼ teaspoon cinnamon, ground
pinch of mace, nutmeg, allspice,
  ground
1 tablespoon Powdered Fruit Rind
1 egg, beaten
1 tablespoon oil

Blend all ingredients except egg and oil in top of double boiler. Cook over hot water until mixture thickens. Remove from heat. Cool to lukewarm. Blend egg and oil together and stir into soybean mixture. Turn into piecrust and bake at 350° F. for 30 minutes, or until center is firm.

## YOGHURT FILLING
## (or sour cream)

2 eggs, separated
1 cup yoghurt * (or sour cream *)
½ cup honey
1 cup raisins, chopped
½ teaspoon cinnamon, ground
½ teaspoon nutmeg, ground

Beat egg yolks. Blend with yoghurt. Add honey, raisins and spices. Fold in stiffly beaten egg whites. Turn into unbaked piecrust and cover with top crust. Bake at 450° F. for 10 minutes, lower oven to 300° F. and bake for an additional 30 minutes.

VARIATION:
Add 1 cup puréed fruit (prunes, applesauce, peach or apricot pulp) to yoghurt mixture.

## YOGHURT-CREAM CHEESE FILLING

1 cup yoghurt *
½ pound cream cheese *

1 tablespoon honey
3 tablespoons Powdered Fruit Rind
½ cup fresh pineapple, cubed
garnish (see below)

Blend yoghurt, cheese, honey and Rind. Add pineapple. Turn into baked piecrust or pie shell. Chill. To serve, garnish with wheat germ, grated nuts, Roasted Soybeans or sesame seeds.

## COTTAGE CHEESE FILLING

1 pint cottage cheese *
4 tablespoons honey
2 tablespoons soy flour
¼ teaspoon salt
2 eggs, separated
¼ cup milk
½ teaspoon lemon rind, grated
3 tablespoons lemon juice

Blend cottage cheese with half the honey. Add flour, salt, egg yolks, milk, lemon rind and juice. Beat egg whites stiff and blend with remaining honey. Fold egg white mixture into cottage cheese mixture. Turn into unbaked piecrust. Bake at 400° F. for 15 minutes, then at 325° F. for 45 minutes more.

## REFRIGERATED COTTAGE CHEESE FILLING

1 envelope or 1 tablespoon
    unflavored gelatin
¼ cup sweet cider
1 egg, separated
3 tablespoons honey
¼ cup milk
¼ teaspoon salt
½ teaspoon anise seeds, crushed
1 cup cottage cheese *
1 tablespoon lemon juice
½ teaspoon lemon rind, grated
½ cup cream, whipped

Soften gelatin in cider. Beat egg yolk in top of double boiler until thick and lemony in color. Add honey, milk, salt and seeds. Blend well. Cook over hot water, stirring frequently, until thickened to consistency of custard. Remove from heat. Dissolve softened gelatin in custard. Add cheese, lemon juice and rind. Cool. When mixture begins to set, fold in whipped cream and stiffly beaten egg white. Turn into baked piecrust, or unbaked-type pastry shell. Chill.

## BASIC CUSTARD FILLING

3 eggs
3 cups milk
¼ teaspoon salt
3 tablespoons honey

Blend all ingredients. Turn into unbaked piecrust. Dust with nutmeg or mace. Bake at 375° F. for 40 minutes.

VARIATIONS:
Add to mixture 1 cup of any of the following: pitted dates, raisins, soaked, pitted prunes, figs, Coconut Shreds.
Sprinkle top of custard with sesame seeds, ground nuts, wheat germ, Roasted, ground Soybeans, cake crumbs, etc.

LEFTOVER FILLINGS
Use leftover fillings in tarts or puffs; over muffins, waffles, or griddlecakes; as topping for fruit desserts.

## Tarts

HINTS:
Many pie fillings can be used for tarts as well; for additional ideas see Pie Fillings section above.

[Continued on next page]

[Continued from previous page]

Tarts can be baked in muffin pans or custard cups.

For additional pastry recipes see Piecrust and Pie Shell sections, pp. 243-47.

## TART PASTRY

2 cups wholewheat flour
¼ teaspoon salt
½ cup oil
1 cup cottage cheese *
3 tablespoons honey

Sift flour and salt. Add oil, honey and cheese. Blend with pastry blender or two knives. If cheese is very dry, add few drops of ice water. Roll into ball and chill. Roll out thin on lightly floured board. Cut into 4-inch squares. Put heaping teaspoon of filling in center. Moisten edges and press together, forming a triangle, to enclose filling. Press fork tines along edges and pierce centers with fork. Brush tops with egg yolk diluted with cold water. Chill for 10 minutes, then bake at 450° F. for 15 minutes. *Makes 18 tarts.*

## OLD-FASHIONED TART FILLING

1¼ cups prunes or dates, soaked, pitted, chopped
¼ cup walnuts, coarsely chopped
¼ cup unsweetened orange juice
3 tablespoons Powdered Fruit Rind
favorite pastry

Combine fruit, nuts and juice. Sprinkle with Rind. Roll pastry ⅛ inch thick. Cut into rounds 3½ inches in diameter, 3½-inch squares, or triangles with base of 3½ inches. Put 1 teaspoon of filling on each. Fold over. Moisten edges and press together. Bake at 450° F. for 15 minutes. *Makes 18 tarts.*

## APPLE TART FILLING

4 large cooking apples
¼ teaspoon cinnamon, ground
¼ teaspoon nutmeg, ground
¼ teaspoon allspice, ground
2 tablespoons nutritional yeast
1 tablespoon oil

Core apples, leaving skins on. Slice thin. Cut again into small pieces. Mix with spices, yeast and oil. Fill Tart Pastry (above).

## BANBURY TART FILLING

1 cup raisins, chopped
¼ cup honey
4 tablespoons soy grits
1 egg, beaten
1 tablespoon oil
½ teaspoon salt
1 tablespoon lemon juice

Blend all ingredients. Roll Tart Pastry (recipe above) thin. Cut into 3-inch squares. Place teaspoon of Banbury filling in center of each square. Moisten edges and press together, folding into triangle. Press fork tines along edges. Prick center with fork. Bake at 450° F. for 15 minutes. *Makes 12 tarts.*

## WHOLEWHEAT-FRUIT TART FILLING

½ cup raisins, chopped
½ cup dried currants
¼ cup figs, cut fine
2 tablespoons water
2 teaspoons wholewheat flour
1 tablespoon oil
½ cup nuts, chopped
½ cup unsweetened orange juice

Cook fruits and water together over low heat for 20 minutes. Blend in flour and cook 10 minutes longer.

Remove from heat. Stir in oil, nuts and orange juice. When cool, spoon into tarts made from favorite pastry and bake at 450° F. for 15 minutes. *Makes 18 tarts.*

## COVENTRY TART FILLING

½ pound cottage cheese*
4 tablespoons honey
4 tablespoons oil
2 egg yolks
½ teaspoon salt
¼ teaspoon nutmeg, ground
2 tablespoons Powdered Fruit Rind
1 tablespoon unsweetened orange
   juice

Blend all ingredients. Beat until of creamy consistency. Line individual tart molds, muffin pans or custard cups with Tart Pastry (recipe above). Prick pastry. Fill with cheese mixture. Bake at 450° F. for 10 minutes, then lower heat to 325° F. and continue baking until golden brown and firm. *Makes 12 tarts.*

## RUSSIAN CHEESE TARTS

1 pound cottage cheese,* drained,
   rubbed through sieve
2 eggs
4 tablespoons honey
1 tablespoon yoghurt* or sour
   cream*
¼ cup raisins

1 teaspoon cardamom seeds,
   crushed
¼ teaspoon salt

Combine all ingredients. Place teaspoon of mixture in center of 3-inch rounds of favorite pastry dough rolled thin. Pinch edges to flute border, but keep top open so that filling shows. Bake at 375° F. for 20 to 25 minutes or until pastry browns. *Makes 24 tarts.*

## WHOLEWHEAT PUFFS

½ cup oil
1 cup boiling water
1 cup wholewheat flour
4 eggs

Blend oil and boiling water in top of double boiler. Stir in flour. Beat vigorously. Cook over hot water, stirring constantly, until mixture is thick, smooth, and no longer sticks to side of saucepan. Remove from heat. Cool to lukewarm. Break eggs into mixture, one at a time, beating thoroughly after each addition. Drop by tablespoonfuls on oiled baking sheet. Allow 1½-inch space between puffs. Bake at 400° F. for about 30 minutes. When completely cool, cut slit in side of each puff. Fill with fruit, ice cream, custard, leftover pudding, yoghurt, etc. *Makes 10 puffs.*

# 24

# CONFECTIONS

Soy grits may be substituted for all, or part, of nuts in recipes.
To prepare Coconut Shreds, open a fresh coconut. Reserve juice for dessert recipes requiring liquid. Cut coconut meats into 1-inch cubes. Shred, a few at a time, in a blender or food grinder. Do not sweeten. Store in a container with a tightly-fitting cover, such as a glass jar. Refrigerate. They will keep for several days.
To prepare Powdered Fruit Rind (orange, lemon, grapefruit) select only rinds which are neither artificially colored, waxed, gassed, fumigated, nor sprayed with insecticides or mold retarders. Wash and dry fruit. Cut thin shavings of rind. Place on cooky sheet in warm place to dry. When thoroughly dry, pulverize in blender. Put through sieve, and return pieces remaining in sieve to blender to pulverize further. Store in tightly covered jar. Keeps indefinitely. Use in breads, muffins, waffles, griddle cakes, frostings, desserts, toppings, cookies, beverages, confections, spreads.

SUGGESTED COVERINGS FOR
CONFECTION BALLS:
ground nuts
sesame seeds
sunflower seeds or meal
Roasted Soybeans, whole or ground
Powdered Fruit Rind (see above)
wheat germ
Coconut Shreds (see above)
soy grits
carob powder

## HONEYED FRUIT RIND

orange, lemon or grapefruit rind
water
salt
honey

Select rinds as suggested in *Hints* section, above. Cut into strips. Cover with water to which 1 teaspoon of salt has been added for each cup of rind. Boil for 30 minutes. Drain. Cover with fresh water. Boil again until peel is tender. Drain. Add honey to cover (approximately ¾ cup of honey for each cup of rind). Simmer slowly until peel is clear. This will take about 45 minutes. Spread out on wax paper. Let stand for 2 or 3 days. It will then be ready for use in fruit-nut breads, muffins, cakes, desserts, toppings, cookies and confections; or rolled in one of the coverings suggested above, serve as a confection.

## STUFFED PRUNES (uncooked)

1 pound prunes, soaked, pitted
1 cup sunflower seeds, hulled

Fill prune cavities with sunflower seeds.

## SESAME-FRUIT BALLS (uncooked)

½ pound dates, pitted
⅓ cup seedless raisins
½ pound dried apricots
¼ cup sesame seeds

Grind fruit. Mix. Shape into small balls. Roll in sesame seeds or any desired covering. *Makes 2 dozen balls.*

## FRUIT ROLLS (uncooked)

1 cup figs
1 cup dates, pitted
1 cup seedless raisins
1½ cups nuts, chopped
2 tablespoons lemon juice
½ cup Powdered Fruit Rind

Grind fruit. Mix with nuts, lemon juice and rind. Shape into small rolls. *Makes 2 dozen rolls.*

## DATE-PECAN ROLL

1 cup milk
1½ cups honey
1 cup dates, pitted, chopped
½ cup dried apricots, chopped
½ cup pecans, chopped
¼ cup soy grits

Bring milk to boil. Blend in honey. Add dates and apricots. Continue to cook gently until mixture forms soft firm ball when dropped into cold water. Remove from heat. When cool, add nuts and soy grits. Beat mixture until stiff. Turn out on wet cloth. Roll into one long roll. Let stand until firm enough to slice.

## DATE-COCONUT-CAROB BALLS (uncooked)

1 pound dates, pitted, chopped
½ cup Coconut Shreds
2 tablespoons warm water
6 tablespoons carob powder
1 tablespoon Powdered Fruit Rind

Mix all ingredients together. Shape into balls. Roll in covering (see p. 254). *Makes 2 dozen balls.*

## FRUIT-NUT STICKS

2 cups nuts
1 cup dates or prunes, pitted, or dried apricots
2 eggs, beaten
1 cup honey

Grind nuts and fruit. Blend with eggs and honey. Shape into sticks. Place on lightly oiled cooky sheet. Bake at 375° F. for about 10 minutes. *Makes 2 dozen sticks.*

## WATERMELON POPSICLES (in blender, uncooked)

watermelon cubes, without rind or seeds
1 sprig mint

Blend watermelon with mint in blender. Pour into popsicle molds. Freeze. This may also be served as a dessert sherbet.

## BANANA POPSICLES (uncooked)

Peel and cut banana crosswise in half. Roll in any desired covering (see p. 254). Mount on sticks. Freeze.

## FRUIT LOLLIPOPS (uncooked)

½-pound mixture seedless raisins
    and dates, pitted
½ pound dried apricots
1 cup Brazil nuts
1 cup wheat germ
¼ teaspoon salt
½ cup honey

Grind fruits and nuts. Add wheat germ, salt and honey. Mix thoroughly. Shape into balls. Roll in any desired covering. Insert a wooden skewer or toothpick in each ball. *Makes 4 dozen lollipops.*

## PEANUT BUTTER BALLS (uncooked)

½ cup peanut butter *
½ cup honey
¾ cup milk powder
½ cup wheat germ
¼ cup soy grits
1 tablespoon Powdered Fruit Rind
1 tablespoon nutritional yeast

Mix all ingredients together. Shape into balls. Roll in covering (see p. 254). *Makes 2 dozen balls.*

## PEANUT BUTTER SQUARES (uncooked)

½ cup peanut butter *
2 cups Coconut Shreds
4 tablespoons lemon juice
1 tablespoon nutritional yeast

Mix all ingredients together. Pat into oiled square pan. Chill. Cut into squares. Wrap in wax paper. *Makes 16 squares.*

## COLLEGE CONFECTION (uncooked)

½ cup peanut butter *
1 cup powdered milk
½ cup molasses or honey
1 tablespoon nutritional yeast
½ cup raisins
½ cup Soybeans, Roasted, ground

Mix all ingredients together. Knead until consistency of pie dough. Pat out on waxed paper. Chill. Cut into pieces.

## BIG SEVEN CONFECTION (uncooked)

½ cup honey
½ cup peanut butter *
¼ cup wheat germ
¼ cup soy grits
½ cup sunflower seeds, hulled
½ cup sesame seeds, toasted
½ cup carob powder
1 teaspoon Powdered Fruit Rind

Mix all ingredients together. Form into small balls. Roll in desired covering (see p. 254). *Makes 2 dozen balls.*

## NUT BALLS

2 cups wholewheat flour
3 tablespoons soy flour
¼ teaspoon salt
4 tablespoons honey
1 cup oil
3 tablespoons Powdered Fruit Rind
2 cups nuts, ground

Sift flours and salt. Blend in honey, oil and rind. Add nuts and mix well. Shape into ½-inch balls. Place on lightly oiled cooky sheet. Bake at 350° F. about 30 minutes. Cover balls with brown paper while baking to prevent overbrowning. When cool, roll in desired covering (see p. 254). *Makes 3 dozen balls.*

## ALMOND CONFECTIONS

4 tablespoons honey
1 cup oil
2 cups wholewheat flour
3 tablespoons soy flour
¾ cup almonds, toasted, ground
½ teaspoon pure almond extract
1 teaspoon lemon rind, grated
pinch of salt

Blend honey and oil. Sift flours together. Stir into honey-oil mixture. Add rest of ingredients and blend thoroughly. Shape into balls. Place on lightly oiled cooky sheet. Bake at 400° F. about 15 minutes. Roll in covering while still hot. *Makes 3 dozen balls.*

## SUNFLOWER MACAROONS

1⅓ cups honey
1 cup sunflower seeds, hulled
3½ cups Coconut Shreds
½ teaspoon anise seeds, crushed
6 egg whites, beaten stiff

Blend honey, sunflower seeds, coconut shreds and anise. Fold in egg whites. If too loose, bind with more coconut. Drop by teaspoonfuls on lightly oiled cooky sheet. Bake at 300° F. about 30 minutes. *Makes 4 dozen.*

VARIATION:
Add ½ cup carob powder to mixture.

## WHOLEWHEAT MACAROONS

1 cup Coconut Shreds
¾ cup honey
3 egg whites
3 tablespoons wholewheat flour
1 teaspoon soy flour
½ teaspoon cardamom seeds, crushed

Blend all ingredients in saucepan. Cook gently until mixture thickens. Half-fill oiled muffin pans with batter. Bake at 325° F. about 30 minutes or until brown. *Makes 1 dozen macaroons.*

## OATMEAL MACAROONS

4 egg whites, beaten stiff
½ cup honey
2 cups oatmeal
1 cup Coconut Shreds
1 teaspoon salt
½ teaspoon fennel seeds, crushed
1 tablespoon oil

Add honey to egg whites. Blend. Gradually stir in rest of ingredients. Drop by teaspoonfuls on lightly oiled cooky sheet. Bake at 325° F. for about 20 minutes. *Makes 1½ dozen macaroons.*

## CREAM CHEESE BONBONS

1 cup cream cheese *
pinch of salt
2 tablespoons honey
¼ cup nuts, chopped
½ cup Coconut Shreds

Mix all ingredients together. Shape into balls. Chill. *Makes 2 dozen bonbons.*

## SESAME CONFECTION
(uncooked)

1 cup sesame seeds
⅓ cup honey
soy flour

Blend seeds and honey. Add enough flour to stiffen. Pat into oiled pan. Chill. After a few days mixture will dry out and harden. Cut into squares. *Makes 9 squares.*

## SESAME BALLS

⅓ cup light cream
⅔ cup honey
⅓ cup molasses
1 tablespoon oil
¼ cup soy grits
1 cup sesame seeds, toasted

Place cream, honey, molasses and oil in a saucepan. Blend. Heat until mixture forms soft ball when dropped into cold water. Remove from heat. Add soy grits and seeds. Beat until thick. Drop by teaspoonfuls on lightly oiled platter. Chill. When cool, roll into balls. Keep cold until ready to serve. *Makes 2 dozen balls.*

## WHOLEWHEAT-OATMEAL CHEWS

2 cups wholewheat flour
1 cup oatmeal flour
½ cup soy flour
½ teaspoon salt
1 cup Coconut Shreds
½ cup honey
½ cup molasses
1 cup oil
¼ cup Powdered Fruit Rind
2 tablespoons nutritional yeast

Sift flours and salt. Add all other ingredients. Blend well. Drop by teaspoonfuls on oiled cooky sheet. Bake at 350° F. for 10 minutes or until brown. *Makes 4 dozen chews.*

## HONEY-COCONUT SQUARES

1 envelope or 1 tablespoon
  unflavored gelatin
¼ cup coconut juice
1 cup honey
¾ pound Coconut Shreds

Soften gelatin in coconut juice. Warm honey. Add gelatin mixture.

Beat until very light and fluffy. This will take 10 minutes with an electric beater or 20 minutes by hand. Turn mixture into oiled pan. Let stand for 2 days. Spread coconut over bottom of large pan. Cover with gelatin mixture. Cut into squares with a knife dipped in cold water. Roll squares in additional coconut. *Makes 20 squares.*

## HONEY-SOYBEAN SQUARES

1 envelope or 1 tablespoon
  unflavored gelatin
¼ cup unsweetened fruit juice
1 cup honey
½ cup Soybeans, Roasted, ground

Soften gelatin in fruit juice. Heat honey. Stir in gelatin mixture until dissolved. Cool. When it begins to set, beat until light and fluffy. Chill 24 to 48 hours. Cut into squares. Roll in soybeans. *Makes 9 squares.*

## COCONUT DROPS

1½ cups Coconut Shreds
6 tablespoons honey
1 egg white, beaten stiff
pinch of cinnamon, ground

Cook coconut and honey together in top of double boiler for 10 to 15 minutes. When coconut is transparent, fold in egg white. Continue to cook, stirring occasionally, for 10 to 15 minutes longer, or until mixture is sticky. Add cinnamon. Drop by teaspoonfuls on lightly oiled cooky sheet. Bake at 325° F. about 20 minutes. When done, remove from sheet at once. *Makes 2½ dozen drops.*

## CAROB-HONEY SQUARES

1 envelope or 1 tablespoon
  unflavored gelatin
¼ cup unsweetened fruit juice
1 cup honey
3 tablespoons oil
½ cup carob powder

Soften gelatin in fruit juice. Heat honey. Stir in gelatin mixture until dissolved. Add oil and carob powder. Beat vigorously until fluffy. Turn into oiled square pan. Chill. Cut into squares. *Makes 9 squares.*

# 25
# RELISHES

FOR THE RELISH TRAY:
Sprouts
carrot curls or sticks
radish roses
raw turnip sticks
green pepper rings
celery sticks
herbed cottage cheese
wedges of cheese
onion rings
stuffed eggs
avocado slices
tomato wedges
Roasted Soybeans
nuts
Coconut Shreds
roasted chick peas
ripe olives
soy cheese

For additional suggestions, see under Spreads; Eggs.

## RAW APPLE RELISH

3 tart apples
1 green pepper
1 sweet red pepper
1 onion
2 stalks celery and tops
3 tablespoons honey
3 tablespoons lemon juice
lemon rind

Grind all ingredients together.
Serve with cold meat, fowl, or fish.
*Makes 1 pint.*

## RAW RADISH RELISH

2 dozen radishes, sliced thin
3 scallions and tops, sliced thin
1 clove garlic, minced
3 tablespoons oil
3 tablespoons cider vinegar*
¼ cup sesame seeds, toasted

Marinate radishes, scallions and garlic in oil and vinegar for 10 minutes. Add seeds. Chill. *Makes 1½
pints.*

## RAW CRANBERRY RELISH

2 cups cranberries
½ cup sweet cider
4 tablespoons honey
¼ teaspoon allspice, ground
pinch of clove, ground

Grind all ingredients together.
*Makes 1½ pints.*

VARIATIONS:
Add: 1 apple with skin, quartered
      and cored.
   1 cup fresh diced pineapple.

½ cup diced celery or cucumber.

½ cup chopped raisins.

½ cup chopped nuts.

## COOKED CRANBERRY-APPLE RELISH

1 pound cranberries
1 cup sweet cider
2 tart apples with skins, sliced
1 cup honey
lemon rind, grated
pinch of mace, ground

Simmer gently cranberries, cider and apples until fruit is soft. Add honey, rind and mace. Simmer for 5 minutes. Cool. Serve with meat, fowl or fish. *Makes 2 pints.*

## RAW CRANBERRY-BEET RELISH

1 cup cranberries
1 cup raw beets
3 tablespoons honey
pinch of nutmeg, ground

Grind all ingredients together. Serve with meat, fowl or fish. *Makes 1 pint.*

## ONION RINGS IN BEET JUICE

2 cups onions
beet juice to cover
2 tablespoons tarragon vinegar *
1 bay leaf

Slice onions into thin rings. Separate rings. Marinate for a few hours in juice, vinegar and bay leaf. These tinted rings make attractive garnishes.

## MINTED ONION RINGS

½ cup mint vinegar *
1 tablespoon honey

¾ cup fresh mint, minced
1 cup onions

Simmer vinegar, honey and mint for 10 minutes. Slice onions into thin rings. Separate rings. Marinate. Chill. *Makes 1½ cups.*

## TOMATO RELISH

1 pound onions, diced
1 bunch celery and tops, diced
1 quart tomatoes, sliced
1 tablespoon honey
juice and rind of 2 lemons
2 bay leaves
¼ teaspoon sweet basil
1 teaspoon salt

Simmer all ingredients together until vegetables are tender and flavors are blended. Remove bay leaves. Chill. If desired, preserve by pouring into hot sterilized jars. *Makes 3 pints.*

## HOMEMADE SAUERKRAUT
### (in quart canning jars)

Remove outer leaves from firm, mature heads of cabbage. Wash and drain. Cut into quarters. Remove cores and shred. Allow 2 pounds of shredded cabbage for each quart canning jar. Sprinkle 4 tablespoons salt over each 2 pounds of cabbage. Mix thoroughly by hand. Pack mixture into jars. Press down firmly with wooden spoon or tamper. Brine will form over cabbage. Cover packed cabbage with pad of clean white cheesecloth. Fit two thin, flexible wooden strips crosswise into neck of each jar so that they press down on cabbage. Set jars in shallow pan or on folded newspaper, as brine may overflow during fermentation. Leave lids loose. After about 10 days, if jars have been kept at a

[Recipe continued on next page]

[Recipe continued from previous page]
fairly constant temperature of 70° F., brine level will drop rather suddenly. This means that fermentation is about over. Remove cheesecloth and wooden strips. Fill jars to within 1 inch of top with 2½ per cent brine (1 ounce salt to 1 quart water). If kraut is to be used soon, simply close jars and keep cool. If kraut is to be kept longer than a few weeks, preserve in a boiling water bath. To do this, press cabbage down firmly with spoon to release gas bubbles. Fill jars with brine and cover but do not seal. Put in kettle with water to cover tops of jars. Bring to boil and continue boiling for 30 minutes. Seal and store.

When serving sauerkraut, flavor with one of the following: dill seeds, caraway seeds, celery seeds or ground juniper berries.

### RAW INDIAN CHUTNEY

2½ pounds fresh coconut, shredded
½ teaspoon salt
½ teaspoon lemon juice and grated rind
2½ pounds tomatoes, cut fine
2 onions, cut fine
pinch of nutmeg, ground

Mix all ingredients thoroughly. Serve with rice dishes. *Serves 6.*

### HONEY CHUTNEY (in blender)

2 quarts sour apples with skins
2 green peppers
3 onions
¾ pound raisins, seedless
1 tablespoon celery seeds
½ teaspoon salt
1 cup honey
juice and rind of 2 lemons
1½ cups cider vinegar (see below)
¾ cup unsweetened orange juice

Blend apples, peppers, onions and raisins in blender. Turn into saucepan. Add remaining ingredients. Bring to slow boil. Reduce heat and simmer gently until thick. Pack into hot sterilized jars. *Makes 6-8 pints.*

## Vinegars

### HOMEMADE CIDER VINEGAR

*Method No. 1* (with electric juicer):
Select sound, tart apples. Wash and cut into small pieces, retaining skins, cores and stems. Make a mush of the apples in an electric juicer. Strain through muslin bag. Pour juice into clean, dark glass jugs. Cover tops of jugs with several thicknesses of cheesecloth, held in place with string or rubber bands. Place in cool, dark place for about 6 months. Strain, bottle and cork.

*Method No. 2* (with potato ricer):
Select, wash and slice apples as in Method No. 1, but instead of using an electric juicer, hand press in a potato ricer lined with cloth. Proceed as above.

*Method No. 3* (from sweet cider):
Allow sweet cider to stand in a warm place in an open jug for a few weeks. It will gradually turn to vinegar.

*Method No. 4* (from apple wastes):
Put peelings, cores and bruised apples in a wide-mouthed jar or crock. Cover with cold water. Keep covered in a warm place. Add fresh peelings, cores and bruised apples from time to time. The "mother"

that forms on top will gradually thicken. This is a starter for more vinegar. When the vinegar tastes sufficiently strong, strain, bottle and cork. Save the "mother" as a starter for the next batch.

*Method No. 5* (to hasten the process):

Add "mother" to sweet cider. When it has turned the sweet cider to vinegar which tastes sufficiently strong, remove the "mother." Strain, bottle and cork.

## HOMEMADE HERB VINEGAR

Wash and strip leaves from stems of herbs (basil, tarragon, mint and dill are all good). Spread leaves on cooky sheets lined with wax paper and put in very low oven until leaves begin to curl; or dry small bunches of herbs in a warm, clean attic, away from sunlight.

Measure 1 closely packed cupful of herbs for each pint of cider vinegar. Place herbs and vinegar in clear glass jugs. Cover. Let jugs stand for two weeks in a sunny window. Shake bottles once or twice each day. When the flavor tastes sufficiently strong, strain, bottle and cork.

The following may also be added to herb vinegars: finely chopped fresh chives; finely chopped celery leaves; cloves of garlic (remove these after 24 hours).

## HOMEMADE HONEY VINEGAR

Add "mother" to homemade mead (for mead recipes, see under Mead).

## HOMEMADE WINE VINEGARS

Add "mother" to homemade berry, fruit or vegetable wines.

## Pickles

### APPLE PICKLES

8-10 cups quartered apples with skins
2 cups honey
1 cup mint vinegar *
2 inches stick cinnamon
6 whole cloves

Combine honey, vinegar and spices. Heat to boiling. Cook 2 to 3 cups apples at a time in liquid, handling them gently. When transparent, lift out and place in bowl. Continue until all apples are cooked. Remove spices. Pour remaining liquid over apples. Chill. Or preserve, if desired, by pouring into hot sterilized jars. Serve with meat, fish or fowl. *Makes 3 quarts.*

### PICKLED RIND
### (for 20 cups of rind)

rind of watermelon, unripe cantaloupe, summer or winter squash, ripe cucumber—or vegetables such as green beans, carrots, turnips, etc.
5 cups honey
2 cups cider vinegar *
½ teaspoon cloves, ground
1 teaspoon cinnamon, ground
¼ teaspoon allspice, ground

Thinly shave off outer rind of cantaloupe. This is not necessary for other fruits or vegetables. Cut rind into 1-inch cubes. Parboil until rind can be pierced with fork but still retains crispness. Blend honey, vinegar and spices and bring to boil. Pour over rind. Let stand overnight. Next morning, drain off liquid, reheat and pour back over rind. Let stand overnight a second time. Next morning, repeat draining and reheating process, and

[Recipe continued on next page]

[Recipe continued from previous page]
again let stand overnight. On the third morning, heat rind and liquid together. Pour into hot, sterilized jars and seal. *Makes 5 quarts.*

## THOUSAND ISLAND PICKLES

1 quart cucumbers, sliced thin
1 onion, sliced thin
1/4 cup salt
3 pints water
1 pint cider vinegar *
1 cup honey
1 tablespoon mustard seeds
1 green pepper, diced
1 sweet red pepper, diced
1 cup celery and tops, chopped
1 tablespoon celery seeds

Cover cucumbers, onion and salt with water. Let stand 2 hours. Drain. Heat vinegar, honey and mustard seeds to boiling point. Add vegetables and celery seeds. Simmer gently for 30 minutes. Pour into hot sterilized jars. Seal. Green tomatoes or cauliflower may also be added. *Makes 8-10 pints.*

## PICKLED AMERICAN JERUSALEM ARTICHOKES

2 1/2 cups Jerusalem artichokes, chopped
1 cup green pepper, diced
1 cup sweet red pepper, diced
1 cup onion, sliced
1/2 clove garlic, minced
1 cup cider vinegar *
1 teaspoon dill seeds
2 1/2 teaspoons salt
3 tablespoons honey

Put artichokes, peppers, onion and garlic in bowl. Marinate with vinegar for 15 minutes. Turn into saucepan, bring to boil and simmer gently about 45 minutes or until thickened, stirring frequently.

Add salt and honey. Simmer an additional 5 minutes. Pour to overflowing into hot sterilized jars. *Makes 2 pints.*

## DILL PICKLES

small cucumbers
ice water
salt
sprigs of dill
dill vinegar *

Let cucumbers soak in ice water 24 hours with 1 1/2 cups salt to each gallon of water. In morning, alternating cucumbers and dill, pack into hot sterilized 2-quart canning jars. Finish with dill on top. Make brine solution with 4 quarts vinegar to each quart water and 1/2 cup salt. Boil brine for 5 minutes. Cool. Pour to overflowing over pickles. Seal. They will be ready to eat in a few weeks.

## RAW PICKLED BLUEBERRIES

2 tablespoons molasses
2 cups cider vinegar *
1/3 cup honey
1 teaspoon salt
1/4 teaspoon nutmeg, ground
1 pint blueberries

Mix molasses, vinegar, honey, salt and nutmeg. Pour over blueberries. Let stand for several days, until enough juice has been drawn out to cover berries. Pour into sterilized jars. Seal. *Makes 2 1/2 pints.*

## PICKLED MUSHROOMS

2 cups small mushrooms, whole
1 teaspoon salt
1 bay leaf
1 clove garlic, minced

tarragon vinegar *
1 stalk fennel

Sprinkle mushrooms with salt. Add
bay leaf and garlic. Heat enough
vinegar, with fennel, to cover mushrooms. When vinegar simmers, add
mushroom mixture. Cook for 5
minutes. Pour into hot sterilized
jars. Seal. *Makes 1 pint.*

LEFTOVER PICKLING JUICE
Blend with spreads or with salad
dressings, instead of lemon juice
or vinegar.

## Preserves

### PLUM BUTTER

greengage or damson plums, puréed
honey
allspice, ground
nutmeg, ground

To each cup of plum pulp add ½
cup honey. Add small amounts of
spices. Cook slowly until thick and
clear. Pour into hot sterilized jars.
Seal.

### HONEY-APPLE BUTTER

2 quarts tart cooking apples with
    skins
1 teaspoon cinnamon, ground
⅛ teaspoon allspice, ground
½ teaspoon mace, ground
2 cups honey
½ lemon, juice and grated rind
2 cups mint vinegar *

Core and slice apples. Put with
all other ingredients into large kettle. Cook slowly for several hours,
stirring frequently, until thick. Pour
into hot sterilized jars. Seal. *Makes
6 pints.*

### CARROT-RHUBARB JAM

3 cups carrots, grated
6 cups rhubarb, diced
3 oranges, juice and grated rind
1 cup honey
½ teaspoon salt
¼ teaspoon nutmeg, ground

Pour boiling water over rhubarb.
Let stand for 10 minutes. Drain.
This reduces objectionable oxalic
acid. Mix all ingredients and let
stand overnight. Next morning,
bring to slow boil. Cook only until
rhubarb is transparent and mixture
thickened. Pour into hot sterilized
jars. Seal. *Makes 2½ pints.*

### RAW FRUIT CONSERVE

2 cups fresh currants
2 cups rose hips
2 cups dates
1 teaspoon dried mint

Grind all ingredients together. Mix
well. Press into small jars with tight
covers. Fill jars to top. Coat with
paraffin. Cap. Will keep well. *Makes
6 small jars.*

VARIATION:
Rhubarb and strawberries also may
    be conserved this way.

### BEET-LEMON CONSERVE

2 lemons, sliced thin
1 pint sweet cider
1 pound beets, cooked, grated
⅓ cup honey
1 teaspoon ginger, ground
¼ teaspoon cinnamon, ground
½ cup hazelnuts, toasted

Simmer together lemon slices and
cider for 15 minutes. Add honey and
beets. Bring to slow boil. Simmer

[Recipe continued on next page]

[Recipe continued from previous page]
for 20 minutes. Add spices and nuts. Simmer 15 minutes longer. Pour into hot, sterilized jars. Seal. *Makes 2 pints.*

## HONEY-PEACH JAM

¾ teaspoon allspice, ground
3 teaspoons stick cinnamon
1½ teaspoons whole cloves
3 pounds peaches, puréed
2 cups honey
3 tablespoons lemon juice
¾ cups unsweetened orange juice

Put spices in cheesecloth bag. Cook all ingredients together slowly until mixture thickens. Remove spices. Pour jam into hot sterilized jars. Seal with paraffin and cover. *Makes 3 pints.*

## MOCK MARMALADE

2 cups dried apricots
boiling water to cover
2 tablespoons honey
1 tablespoon Powdered Orange
   Rind

Cover apricots with boiling water. Let stand overnight. Drain, reserving juice for compote, etc. Mince apricots. Add remaining ingredients. Pack into hot sterilized jars. Cover. Keep at least 2 weeks before using. *Makes 1 pint.*

## HOMEMADE PECTIN

Pectin, or apple jelly stock, may be made and preserved for use in making combination jellies or blending with other fruits in season when fresh apples are not available. This jelly stock may also be used with fruits which lack pectin and therefore do not jell readily, such as strawberries, pears, peaches, cherries, blueberries, elderberries, mulberries, raspberries.

Wash apples. Cut into thin slices. Add 1 pint water for each pound of fruit used. Boil slowly in covered kettle for 15 minutes. Strain off free-running juice through 1 thickness of cheesecloth. Return pulp to kettle. Add same amount of water again. Cook slowly for 15 minutes. Let stand 10 minutes longer. Strain again through 1 thickness of cheesecloth. Squeeze out all juice. Combine two juices: there should be about 1 quart for each pound of apples used. This stock may be used immediately for blending with other fruit juices to make jelly, or it may be preserved for later use.

To preserve: Heat stock to boiling point. Pour immediately into hot sterilized pint or quart canning jars. Seal. Invert jars to cool.

"Apple thinnings," the small, immature green apples sold early in the summer, are rich in acid and pectin. These will make good jelly stock. The jelly made from these apples, however, will not be as clear and transparent as that from fully mature apples.

## HONEY JELLY

2½ cups honey
½ cup water
1 pint homemade pectin (see above)

Mix honey and water in large kettle. Bring to quick boil. Add pectin, stirring constantly. Again bring to full, rolling boil. Lower heat and simmer gently until mixture thickens. Pour into hot sterilized glasses. Seal with paraffin and cap glasses. *Makes about 4 8-ounce glassfuls.*

## LEMON-HONEY JELLY

2½ cups honey
¾ cup lemon juice
½ cup homemade pectin (see p. 266)
few lemon geranium leaves (optional)

Place all ingredients in large kettle. Bring to quick boil, then simmer gently until mixture thickens. Remove leaves. Pour into hot sterilized glasses. Seal with paraffin and cap glasses. *Makes 5 6-ounce glassfuls.*

HINTS FOR USING HONEY IN CANNING AND PRESERVING:

All-honey syrup is somewhat darker than sugar syrup. Canning and preserving syrups made with honey tend to darken peaches and pears. However, honey intensifies the original fruit flavor. In using honey for canning and preserving, observe two precautions:

1. Because honey has a tendency to foam when heated, use a large kettle for cooking, so that contents do not boil over.
2. As honey is part water, cook the fruit slightly longer than with other syrup to obtain desired consistency.

Proportions for honey syrups in preserving fruits and berries: 2 cups of honey to 3¾ cups of water.

# INDEX

## ABOUT THE AUTHOR

*Beatrice Trum Hunter, a native New Yorker, now lives on 150 acres of woodlands, meadows and beaver pond in the foothills of New Hampshire's White Mountains. Formerly a teacher of visually handicapped children in New York City and New Jersey schools, she now owns and operates, with her husband, John Frank Hunter, a small guesthouse. In addition to doing all the cooking, she prepares all grains for cereal, bread and muffins in her own stone-grinding mill. She also writes a monthly column,* The Book Hunter, *which appears in* Herald of Health *and contributes articles and book reviews to* Organic Gardening & Farming, Natural Food & Farming, Land Fellowship *(Canadian),* Journal of the Soil Association *(England) and other publications in the fields of food, gardening and nutrition. She has lectured throughout the country on these topics and is well known throughout New England for her demonstrations of whole-grain bread baking. She is a past vice-president of the American Academy of Applied Nutrition, and an honorary member of the Board, Federation of Homemakers. Her third book, an exhaustive investigation of food adulteration, is scheduled for publication in the near future.*

*Mrs. Hunter holds a B.A. from Brooklyn College and a Master's degree from Columbia University. She has also done graduate work at State Teachers College, Buffalo, New York, at Harvard University and elsewhere.*

Printed in the United States
By Bookmasters